Ruth Prawer Jhabvala

SILENCE, EXILE AND CUNNING

Silence, Exile and Cunning

THE FICTION OF RUTH PRAWER JHABVALA

SECOND EDITION

Yasmine Gooneratne

Sangam Books

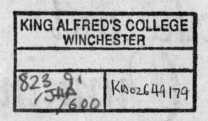
SILENCE, EXILE AND CUNNING

SANGAM BOOKS LIMITED
57 London Fruit Exchange
Brushfield Street
London E1 6EP, UK

By arrangement with
Orient Longman Limited
3-6-272 Himayatnagar
Hyderabad 500 029

© Orient Longman Limited 1983

First Published 1983
Revised Edition 1991

ISBN 0 86311 144 0

Published by
Sangam Books Limited
3-5-820 Hyderguda
Hyderabad 500 029 (A.P.)

Typeset by
Scribe Consultants
B4/30 Safdarjung Enclave
New Delhi 110 029

Printed in India at
Nu Tech Photolithographers
10/1 & 2-B Jhilmil Industrial Area
Shahdara, Delhi 110 032

For Brendon

Foreword

The author whose work in fiction and the film is the subject of this book is very much of the twentieth century. All Ruth Prawer Jhabvala's novels and short stories have been published within the last thirty-five years, the films for which she has written screenplays have all been released within the last thirty, and her personal history of displacement and a triple exile makes her seem very representative of our own times: a period of history that will no doubt be typified in future ages (if our world survives to write its own history) by the figure of the wanderer and the refugee.

The India Ruth Jhabvala entered in 1951 was the post-Independence urban world of Delhi which she seems to have set herself, from the very first, to draw as accurately as possible in her fiction. *Amrita* (1955) and *The Nature of Passion* (1956) reflect her joy in her surroundings; and in subsequent novels, even when that early delight begins to evaporate, her gaze remains steady and her picture precise. By depicting in her work (in a characteristically ironic mode) certain social and cultural changes that have occurred in India over a quarter of a century, Ruth Jhabvala has run the risk of being regarded as a writer of dismissive satire and of fictional journalism. It is not, perhaps, sufficiently recognized how often and how consistently she is the object of her own ironic analysis. This is not to say that critics in India and outside have failed to appreciate the quality and seriousness of her art. But that art, deceptively simple on first acquaintance, withholds its riches from the casual or prejudiced reader. There exists at present a division of critical opinion on the validity of her picture of India which I have tried to represent fairly both in my bibliography and in extensive quotation. It would give me the deepest satisfaction to have played some small part, by the writing of this book, in resolving that division.

The present study of Ruth Prawer Jhabvala's work is based on thirty-three years' acquaintance with her work in fiction and for the cinema; some of these years having been spent exploring her novels and short stories in the company of colleagues and English Literature students at Macquarie University — where, incidentally, *A Backward Place* and *Like Birds Like Fishes* were being taught as texts two years before the award of the Booker Prize in 1975 to *Heat and Dust* brought its author world-wide attention. And it no doubt expresses not only my admiration for Ruth Jhabvala's work, but my conviction (intensified in recent years, as India has gradually become as much a metaphor as a real place in her fiction) that she is one of the writers of our day destined for permanent fame in literature.

First published in 1983 and reprinted in 1990, *Silence, Exile and Cunning* builds on research published in the following journals: *World Literature Written in English, New Literature Review,* the *Journal of Indian Writing in English, Ariel,CRNNE Reviews Journal* and *Kunapipi.* Some of the ideas it explores were first presented in papers given at the University of the South Pacific in 1980, and the University of Western Australia in 1982. I would like to express my gratitude in this connection to the Editors of these respective journals, to the Association for Commonwealth Literature and Language Studies, and to the Centre for Studies in Australian Literature.

Among many debts, the following are most gratefully acknowledged: to Haydn Moore Williams, whose pioneering studies of Ruth Prawer Jhabvala's fiction have considerably encouraged my own; to Ramlal Agarwal, Fritz Blackwell, Margaret Gooneratne, Andrew Pike, Osyth Leeston, Philip Levine, Janet Powers Gemmill and Diana Roberts, who helped collect scattered materials; to James Ivory and to Peter Ansin of Merchant Ivory Productions, for their kindness in making available to me the screenplays of certain films as well as the stills that appear as illustrations in this book; to Mark MacLeod and Theo Van Leeuwen, whose enthusiasm and expertness in the area of film have helped to shape Chapter XI; to Peggy and Peter Nightingale, and to members of the Macquarie Centre for the study of Post-Colonial Literature and Language, who have contributed so much over the years to my own appreciation and understanding of certain novels and films; to the late Herbert (Pip) Piper, who first proposed the establishment of Asian Writing in English as a course at Macquarie, to my students in the University who responded to it with intelligence and pleasure, and to Di Yerbury and Colin Yallop, whose support has done so much to help the New Literatures in English flourish at Macquarie.

Finally, my very special thanks to Brendon Gooneratne, to Deirdre MacPherson, to Pam Peters, and to Sujit Mukherjee, whose reading of my manuscript yielded practical advice and constructive suggestions; and to Ruth Prawer Jhabvala and C.S.H. Jhabvala for their friendship, and for the frankness and good humour with which they answered my questions.

Macquarie University   YASMINE GOONERATNE
May 1990

CONTENTS

Foreword/*vii*

I Introductory/*1*
II To Whom She Will or, Amrita/*34*
III The Nature of Passion/*76*
IV Esmond in India/*94*
V The Householder/*123*
VI Get Ready for Battle/*150*
VII A Backward Place/*166*
VIII A New Dominion or, Travellers/*195*
IX Heat and Dust/*224*
X The Short Stories/*250*
XI Writing for Film/*278*
XII Immersion into America/*321*
Bibliography/*337*
Index/*349*

"The classic definition for me of the writer's life is that laid down by James Joyce: 'Silence, exile and cunning'. This I interpret for myself to mean that I must keep my mouth shut, stay aloof from the world around me and carry on my business like a thief in the night, pillaging what I need and hoarding it in the secret recesses of my imagination to make of it what I can".

RUTH PRAWER JHABVALA
The Illustrated Weekly of India (1971)

CHAPTER

I

Introductory

Ruth Prawer Jhabvala was born on 7 May 1927 in the German city of Cologne, the younger child and only daughter of a Polish/Jewish lawyer named Marcus Prawer and his wife, Leonora Cohn Prawer. The children made their first contact with the English language during their school days in Germany, but when Ruth Prawer wrote her first stories they were in German. When the family emigrated to England in 1939, the 12-year-old child rapidly made the transition to a new language. 'I was practically born a displaced person, and all any of us ever wanted was a travel document and a residential permit. One just didn't care as long as one was allowed to live

somewhere.'[1] The experiences of losing in the Nazi holocaust
'my father's entire family, part of my mother's family, most of
the children I first went to school with, and most of my parents'
family friends — in fact, our entire social and family circle'[2],
and of living as 'displaced persons' in Britain, she transmutes
into the ironic comedy of "A Birthday in London", a story
published in her first collection of short fiction, *Like Birds, Like
Fishes* (1962). This piece of writing, isolated amongst a group
of stories set in India as its characters are isolated in an alien
environment, is Ruth Jhabvala's only published attempt to
recreate her life as an expatriate in Britain.

1939-1951: Student and Apprentice

Ruth Prawer's experience of growing up in Britain included the
taking of a degree in English at the University of London and
the writing of an M.A. thesis on "The Short Story in England,
1700-1750". It is possible that 'the time she spent in the
Reading Room at the British Museum overwhelms all other
memories'[3], but she continued to write fiction, which 'came as
naturally as breathing. I've always had cupboards stuffed full
with unfinished novels, plays, stories. I wrote through my school
years and college years and then when I came to India I went
on writing'.[4]

The theme of loneliness and isolation that runs through "A
Birthday Party" was to remain untouched until, six years after
her departure from Britain, Ruth Jhabvala wrote her first novel
of expatriation, *Esmond in India* (1957). Since then it has been
a theme to which in moods

> when, sick for home,
> She stood in tears amid the alien corn

this second Ruth has constantly returned, tirelessly exploring
the sensibility of the Western expatriate in India. It is a theme
that, given her personal history of displacement, naturally
transforms India into a fictional land of the spirit in which her
protagonists try to feel at home and only rarely succeed. It has
overflowed from her fiction into her work for the cinema, and
the scripts she has written for two films, ROSELAND (1977) and
THE EUROPEANS (1979), explore the theme of expatriation and

alienation in American settings.

1951-1960: Marriage and a Family

In 1951 Ruth Prawer left Britain for India as the 24-year-old wife of Cyrus Jhabvala, a young Parsi architect. She has said, looking back, that 'as a writer I consider myself exceedingly fortunate to have come here when I did and the way I did'[5] Her descriptions of this first encounter with India suggest that writing and living blended for her into an intense joy of discovery:

> It came about instinctively. I was enraptured. I felt I understood India so well. I loved everything.[6]

The first stage of Ruth Jhabvala's experience of India, invariably described by her in terms of 'excitement', 'rapture' and 'love', included the birth of the Jhabvalas' three daughters and the publication of four novels, *To Whom She Will* (1955), *The Nature of Passion* (1956), *Esmond in India* (1957) and *The Householder* (1960). It lasted nine years, during which time she never left India, but entered with increasing delight into the experiences it held out to her.[7]

Although she had entered a family of Indian Parsis who themselves possess a history of expatriation from Persia that is many centuries old, and live somewhat fastidiously apart from their Hindu or Muslim compatriots, the large extended family of her husband's Punjabi business partner provided Ruth Jhabvala with an opportunity, extended over many years, to observe Indian — and particularly Hindu — life at close quarters, on a footing of casual acceptance and intimacy. The fruits of this experience are to be seen in the lively recreations of Hindu family life in her first two novels, and in the awareness (expressed in Ruth Jhabvala's fiction as a whole) of the importance of food and of the rituals of its preparation and consumption in the lives of Indian families. While hardly conventional, her presentation of directions for preparing a variety of Indian dishes at the back of her first novel is of a piece with this awareness. The first glimpse we have from her pen of an Indian family at home is in *To Whom She Will*, as Pandit Ram Bahadur Saxena's family sits down in his ornate

dining room to an elaborate Indian meal served by well-trained
servants; a scene which is later contrasted with others in which
the head of a poor Punjabi refugee family eats his evening meal
in the courtyard of a jointly-occupied and owned house while
being served by his mother, and the artistic Vazir Dayal Mathur
lavishes time and creative effort on a luncheon that a greater
artist might have devoted to the composition of a poem. There
is a significant difference between the delicious meals lovingly
prepared for her spiritual teacher by an ex-princess still inspired
(if somewhat fitfully) by India's artistic heritage, and the
revolting mess or rice and lentils hastily and ignorantly thrown
together by a guru's three Western disciples (A New Dominion).
An Indian widow binds her grown sons to her by indulging their
greed ("The Aliens"); a young school-teacher awakens to his
wife's attractiveness as she kneads the dough for her light,
delicious parathas (The Householder); a housewife forgets her
frustrations and disappointments in preparing pickles for her
absent son (Esmond in India). The contrasts of texture and
temperature so important in Indian food appear to have
suggested, and certainly harmonise with, some of the contrasts
effected among Ruth Jhabvala's characters. Food is the only
'weakness' of that strong man, Mr Gupta, in A Backward Place;
a meal he consumes during an evening out with his Hungarian
mistress satisfies him so much that, forgetting her presence,
he longs for his wife's expert massage afterwards to turn
satisfaction into exquisite pleasure. Hari Sahni (of To Whom She
Will) has a sentimental heart — and a healthy appetite.
Summoned by his beloved to a romantic nocturnal interview,
he complains that he has not yet had his dinner.

Ruth Jhabvala consistently bases the conflicts that arise
between Indians and Westerners in her novels upon the
complexities of culture, history and psychology, avoiding the
simpler, more obvious issue of colour. Her Indian characters,
as seen by Western eyes, range from the comic to the beautiful;
her Westerners, as seen by Indian eyes, range from the sexually
titillating to the grotesque. By using descriptive terms that are
non-associative in terms of colour, she keeps her subject clear
of the superficial, the boring, and —a trap into which many
Third World writers fall — the merely racist or sensational. Once
they have crossed the initial barrier set up by what is unfamiliar
or foreign, her characters respond to one another as individuals.

Those who are unable or reluctant to do so reveal their immaturity, or the falseness of their claims to liberalism or spirituality. Prem (*The Householder*), Gopi (*A New Dominion*), Nalini ("A Course of English Studies"), Clarissa (*A Backward Place*), Bockelman ("The Man with the Dog") and the swami in "An Experience of India" are characters on both sides of the cultural 'fence' who, when angry, uncertain or excited, comically reveal cultural prejudices that betray their immaturity, insularity, and the superficiality of their vaunted sophistication or spiritual poise. The prejudices that distorted human relationships in India's colonial past and are reflected in E.M. Forster's *A Passage to India* and the lesser novels that emerged from that past are dwarfed, in Ruth Jhabvala's picture of the new India, by a theme that I find equally impressive and, personally, more moving in its tragic implications for our world and our times. There begins to emerge as early as in her second novel, *The Nature of Passion*, an impression of India as a mysterious presence, half medieval, half modern, intensely spiritual, immensely old, and scarred by an inescapable poverty, that looks ironically down through its storied centuries upon the unheroic antics of the present breed of 'gazetted Government officers', business tycoons, artistic scroungers and shallow socialites who multiply in her new 'society'.

As time and experience revealed how much there is and always will be to learn about India, Ruth Jhabvala's lens shifts from the comic incongruities of Indian life to focus more and more searchingly on those who pretend that such knowledge is easily acquired or inherited by birth. Her portraits of 'experts' on India include a number of Indian characters such as Har Dayal (*Esmond in India*) and Pandit Ram Bahadur Saxena (*To Whom She Will*) who present a picture of India to their youthful relations and Western friends that is severely limited by the narrowness of their own views and experience. Gopi (*A New Dominion*) is possibly Ruth Jhabvala's most satiric study of an ignorant Indian who sets himself up as an authority on India's cultural traditions, deeming himself better qualified by his 'Indian-ness' to penetrate to essential truths than any Western seekers after knowledge, however intelligent they may be or earnest. These sketches acquire a deeper ironic shading (and an occasional element of self-satire) when they begin to include Westerners who seek to interpret India to the Indians,

characters such as Professor Hoch (*To Whom she Will*), Esmond
Stillwood (*Esmond in India*) and the Western experts on yoga
whom Prem encounters with wondering perplexity at a party
in *The Householder*.

1960-1975: Challenge and Struggle

In 1960 Ruth Jhabvala paid Britain a brief visit and found, on
her return to India, that her attitude to India had altered. Some
of the sources of her discontent (together, perhaps, with some
relief in the idea that writing about social problems justifies
the self-absorption and self-indulgence that creative writing
involves) are to be found in her fourth novel, *Get Ready For
Battle* (1962): the only one among the eight she has published
to centre almost exclusively upon India's extreme poverty, and
upon the exploitation of the poor and helpless by the corrupt,
the wealthy and the hypocritical. Ruth Jhabvala had taken up
the subject of corruption in business and political life before,
in *The Nature of Passion*; but in that novel the dishonesty of
an Indian tycoon had appeared forthright, even endearing, in
comparison with the pretentious social climbing of his selfish
children, and had been continuously qualified by a sympathetic
evocation of his peasant background and of his sentimental
love of a wayward daughter. There are no such moderating
factors in *Get Ready For Battle* in which, as Haydn Moore
Williams has noted, the moral values put forward propose a
straightforward conflict between the 'Babbittry' represented by
big business and the spiritual values embodied in the novel's
'Yogi' figure, the high-principled Sarla Devi:

> The tragedy of modern India as depicted in Jhabvala's novels
> is the total failure of communication between the Babbitt
> and the Yogi.[8]

Ruth Jhabvala's disillusionment with the India that she had
begun by 'loving' so passionately found additional expression
between 1960 and 1975 in three collections of short stories:
Like Birds, Like Fishes (1962), *An Experience of India* (1966)
and *A Stronger Climate* (1968). The second of these is prefaced
by an essay titled "Myself in India" in which Ruth Jhabvala

provides a description, based on her own experience and her observation of Westerners in India, of a cycle of intense emotional variations to which she sees all sensitive Westerners who spend any appreciable time in India as being inevitably, inescapably, bound:

> There is a cycle that Europeans — by Europeans I mean all Westerners, including Americans — tend to pass through. It goes like this: first stage, tremendous enthusiasm —everything Indian is marvellous; second stage, everything Indian not so marvellous; third stage, everything Indian abominable. For some people it ends there, for others the cycle renews itself and goes on. I have been through it so many times that now I think of myself as strapped to a wheel that goes round and round and sometimes I'm up and sometimes I'm down. When I meet other Europeans, I can usually tell after a few moments conversation at what stage of the cycle they happen to be.[9]

These feelings are mirrored in the yearning for Europe that overtakes her Western characters in the three novels published during this period: *A Backward Place* (1965), *A New Dominion* (1972) and *Heat and Dust* (1975). After a few successful trial-runs [notably in the story "The Aliens", in cameo portraits undertaken in her early novels of Western visitors and residents such as Professor Hoch (*To Whom She Will*), two European musicians (*To Whom She Will* and *The Nature of Passion*), and Hans Loeuwe (*The Householder*), and in an attempt at a full-length study in *Esmond in India*], Ruth Jhabvala applies her theory to the characterisations of Westerners in India that are a feature of *A Backward Place*. Etta, Judy, Clarissa and the Hochstadts are poised at different points on a turning wheel of emotional experience, and their respective fates result as much from their being Westerners in India as from individual temperament or social and cultural background. In short stories written since, Ruth Jhabvala focuses upon one or more stages of the 'cycle': "An Indian Citizen", "Miss Sahib", or "The Englishwoman" are examples. For her novel *A New Dominion*, she selects a time-span identical with the period of time it takes her two Western characters, Raymond and Lee, to experience the intense effects of a full turn of the wheel of torture and disillusionment. Raymond plans, as Esmond did before him,

to leave India; for Lee the fascination of India reasserts itself.
In *Heat and Dust* the experiences of an English woman in the
India of 1923 are recreated and analysed, after a pause of fifty
years, by another of extraordinary courage for whom the cycle
'renews itself' and is poised to make another revolution. These
studies are penetrating analyses of states of mind, some of
which are personally familiar to Ruth Jhabvala whose essay
"Myself in India" refers to the indescribable sense of '*oppression*'
she has felt on occasion during her years there, and who has
noted of her Western characters that they 'of course include
myself'.[10]

Just when India appeared to have failed the novelist as a
source of spiritual and emotional sustenance, a new challenge
directed her energies to another 'battle', this time of an artistic
kind. She was invited to write the screenplays for a series of
films directed by James Ivory in association with Ismail
Merchant, beginning with a cinematic version of her own novel,
The Householder, which was issued in 1963. The creative
association inaugurated in 1960 has survived during the
twenty-eight years that have followed, and has generated
fourteen remarkable films: THE HOUSEHOLDER (1963),
SHAKESPEAREWALLAH (1965), THE GURU (1969), BOMBAY TALKIE
(1970), AUTOBIOGRAPHY OF A PRINCESS (1975), ROSELAND (1977),
HULLABALOO OVER GEORGIE AND BONNIE'S PICTURES (1978), THE
EUROPEANS (1979), JANE AUSTEN IN MANHATTAN (1980), QUARTET
(1981), HEAT AND DUST (1981), THE BOSTONIANS (1984), A ROOM
WITH A VIEW (1987), AND MAURICE (1988). Since 1960
RuthJhabvala has divided her time between writing fiction and
writing for the cinema, and the chapter titled "Writing for Film"
in this book undertakes an examination of her screenplay
writing in its effects upon her development as a novelist and
short-story writer.

The recurrence of similar characters and subjects in the film-
scripts and fiction she worked on alternately or concurrently
during this period indicates the nature and intensity of Ruth
Jhabvala's preoccupations as a woman and an artist in these
crucial years. It will be found, for example, that the figure of
a Western woman seeking self-fulfilment in India is explored
successively (one might almost say obsessively) in the
characters of the American novelist Lucia Lane in BOMBAY
TALKIE, the narrator of "An Experience of India", Jenny in

THE GURU, and the triple studies of Lee, Margaret and Evie in *A New Dominion*. It is taken up again, with greater ironic complexity than before, in the characterisation of the narrator of *Heat and Dust*. Similarly, the swami or 'guru' figure who appeared in a favourable light in the early novels, *The Householder* and *Get Ready For Battle*, is handled again with less and less respect in BOMBAY TALKIE, "An Experience of India", "A Spiritual Call", THE GURU and *A New Dominion*. These studies of spiritual seekers and swamis are, although recurrent, never merely repetitive; when viewed separately and together they seem to distil the essence of Ruth Jhabvala's own early enthusiasm for, and subsequent disillusionment with, India. Other themes that appear to dominate the writing of this period include the exploitation of one individual by another, or the domination of one culture by another; the analysis of a sensitive personality trapped in a hostile environment; the integrity of the creative artist; and — a theme stemming, perhaps, from Ruth Jhabvala's personal history of displacement and expatriation — the helplessness of the socially disadvantaged.

1975: *The Unhoused Writer*

After spending twenty-four years — 'most of my adult life' —in India, Ruth Jhabvala took up residence in New York in 1975. Interviewed in London soon after receiving the Booker Prize for *Heat and Dust* that year, she said:

> I'd like to live much more in the West, going back to India sometimes but not as much as before. Having assimilated all this Indian experience I don't want to forget it or cast it off; what I want to do is to take it out again as a Westerner, enriched by what I have learnt there ... I can't throw away the past twenty-four years, nor do I want to. What I'd really like to do is record the journey back. I don't know if it's possible. It's also a matter of age. I was twenty-four when I went to India, I'm now forty-eight and one is not so flexible. But it's not as if I'm going to a new place; I am going back West, so it might work out. I don't know, we'll just have to see.[11]

Her published work after 1975 has included numerous short

stories, some of which are reprinted in the collection *How I Became a Holy Mother* (1976), and focus on the experiences of lonely, ageing, exploited and unhappy women at every level on the Indian social scale. They are written with an insight and skill that indicate how much Ruth Jhabvala's world has opened out since 1960:

> I got around quite a lot in later years, mainly through the films we made — I saw quite different levels of society from the one I (officially) lived in.[12]

Many of the characters in these stories are Indian, a few are Westerners. One story, "Bombay", is a compassionate and searching study of the in-bred, conservative Parsi community of which her marriage made her — in some degree, and for a time at least — a part; it is a subject that she has never touched before in all her years of writing. Another, "The Englishwoman", is the story of a Westerner who prepares after many years in India to return to England:

> She is eloping, leaving everything behind her — husband, children, grandchildren, thirty years of married life. Her heart is light and so is her luggage.[13]

There seems to echo here a new freedom and lightness of spirit carried over from the last words of "An Experience of India" and *Heat and Dust*, a suggestion that nothing is resolved or decided except the decision to keep moving, 'travelling', and no doubt — like the narrator of *Heat and Dust* — 'climbing' too, in increasingly strenuous, deliberately unencumbered striving towards greater self-knowledge and hidden heights of artistic achievement. In a perceptive essay on Ruth Jhabvala's fiction, Meenakshi Mukherjee has noted:

> Prawer Jhabvala is an extreme case of the outsider in the Commonwealth context. Her situation is far too unique to offer a model, but it certainly warns the writers who are outside a literary tradition that in order to exploit their situation they must peregrinate and remain 'unhoused', and not get caught in their own self-created grooves.[14]

In chapters X and XII, I have looked with particular attention at the fiction she has published after 1975, following her decision to take up residence in the United States. To rightly assess the wisdom of that decision, readers will undoubtedly seek the evidence in her 'American' novels *In Search of Love and Beauty* (1983) and *Three Continents* (1987). On that evidence — and especially on that of the first — it certainly seems that Ruth Jhabvala has found the way to make her 'true triumphs happen, as they have in the case of V.S. Naipaul, by reaching and remaining in a free state'.[15]

In New York as in Delhi, Ruth Jhabvala writes in complete isolation. Her habit of living like a recluse while resident in Delhi had raised doubts in some critical minds (chiefly Indian) as to the authenticity of her picture of India, doubts of which she seems to have been well aware:

> People say: 'She lives like this, how can she know about India'? Well, a novelist doesn't have to go out like a journalist. You meet one person and he can split into twenty people. There's no shortage of people for me.[16]

As many authors of both East and West have done before her, it appears that Ruth Jhabvala splits up certain modern phenomena that interest her deeply into various aspects that she embodies in the settings and characters of her fiction, contriving by this means not only to study the whole[17], but to explore with admirable objectivity her own identity in its relation to India. Her approach to writing in and about India could well be explained in terms of the Indian concept of *avatar*, the manifestation of the divine personality, according to which Vishnu and other deities manifest themselves in various forms across time and space while mankind, worshipping them in one form or another, finds paths opening to the divine nature as a whole.

In "Myself in India" Ruth Jhabvala predicted wryly that her struggle to retain her individuality and 'survive' in India was quite likely to end only with her death:

> Of course, this can't go on indefinitely and in the end I'm bound to lose — if only at the point where my ashes are immersed in the Ganges to the accompaniment of Vedic hymns, and then who will say that I have not truly merged with India?[18]

Despite her claim to write as a Westerner mainly for Western readers[19], the stages of her literary career fit with unexpected

neatness the several phases into which Indian philosophical
tradition divides the human life-span, an interesting fact in the
light of which I have set out the plan of this biographical note.
It is a fact which strengthens the impression conveyed by her
deliberate choice after 1975 of an unencumbered way of life
that, on an artistic level, in some ways parallels
vanaprastha[20], that she has become more Indian than she
suspects, or her critics are willing to admit.

In 1978 Ruth Jhabvala was awarded the Neil Gunn
International Fellowship, and in 1984 the British Film Institute
and the Museum of Modern Art, New York, jointly published
a book devoted to the Merchant-Ivory-Jhabvala films. In
February 1984 she received the liberal and (as she stated in
a note to *Three Continents*) 'liberating' support for her writing
of a MacArthur Foundation Fellowship. In December of the
same year she was awarded the Fellowship of her former
London University college, Queen Mary College, and London
University's honorary degree of Doctor of Literature.

*   *   *   *

As an account of her literary career makes evident, the major
and minor concerns that interweave in Ruth Jhabvala's novels
arise from personal or observed experience. It is, no doubt,
tempting to speculate on the extent to which her fiction reflects
her personal life. But her characters are so closely interwoven
with the interest of a particular work that speculation of this
kind becomes quickly irrelevant: her story, "A Birthday in
London", indicates how thoroughly the trauma of persecution
and expatriation has been transmuted into comic art. Although
in her first novel, *To Whom She Will*, Ruth Jhabvala notes that
'all characters are entirely fictitious', there is no need to insist
on the point in later works. 'Like most novelists, I mix up a
number of people I know (or have witnessed) in order to arrive
at one character'[21] Since she admits that she includes herself
among her Western characters, the contempt and revulsion
displayed by such characters as Esmond Stillwood and Etta
towards India are sometimes seen by her critics as reflecting
her permanent point of view.[22] It is not often kept in mind that
by the same token, such characters as Judy (*A Backward Place*)
and Olivia Rivers (*Heat and Dust*) almost certainly reflect

something of Ruth Jhabvala's own commitment, through bonds of personal affection, to India. In Esmond, Raymond (*A New Dominion*), Major Minnies (*Heat and Dust*) and others could be traced some of the approaches she has made herself, through the exploration and enjoyment of Indian art, music and literature, to a better understanding of the country of her adoption.

Far more rewarding than such speculation is the evaluation of the degree to which her personal life has enriched and extended the techniques of her art. In a sense, everything she has written springs from the fact that her marriage to a young Indian architect brought her to India in 1951 and kept her there for twenty-four years. The architectural validity of Delhi in her earliest fiction comes, surely, straight out of being 'Mrs. Jhabvala': the awareness not only of how buildings look, but of the materials used in their construction, the care or neglect to which they have been subjected, and the ways in which they show forth the history and the personalities of their various inhabitants. These are ways of regarding a city with its houses and buildings that Ruth Jhabvala applies to the literary task of observing a society and interpreting the thoughts and inner lives of its members. Pandit Ram Bahadur Saxena of *To Whom She Will* lives in the tallest and most respectable house in a street of 'tall yellow houses, heavy with respectability' (p.7). In contrast with this symbol of remote, almost obsolete gentility, in which time seems to have stood still, are the uncomfortably intimate households of the Anands and the Sahnis, the trunks which form the main items of furniture in the latter being quiet reminders of the family's refugee background. In contrast with both these is the *nouveau riche* dwelling of Hari's elder sister Prema, a house situated 'in a road of privately built ... fairly large houses, detached from one another and incorporating all the favourite whims of the owners' (p.18). Spared, by reason of her European origins, the complicated inhibitions bred in some Commonwealth or Third World writers by their colonial inheritance, she does not share V.S. Naipaul's reluctance to do 'a simple thing like mentioning the name of a Port of Spain street'.[23] Nor is she, like R.K. Narayan, forced to invent her own 'Malgudi'. Delhi's streets, squares, quarters and colonies are all named in her early fiction, and so accurately located that the favourite haunts of her characters and the settings

of some memorable scenes in her fiction could be marked upon
a map of the city: Chandni Chowk, down which Etta walks as
if it were the Champs Elysees; the coffee houses in which Bal,
Hari Sahni, Viddi and numerous other young men philosophise
about life and discuss their prospects; Delhi University, on the
staff of which institution Krishna Sen Gupta, the aspiring young
lecturer of "The Award", and the father of the narrator of "My
First Marriage" are all employed; the modern hotels owned by
Guppy and his like and patronised by Asha and her friends,
the tennis club of which Nimmi, Rajen Mathur , Pheroze
Bhatliwala, and Indira and Amrit (from *Esmond in India*) are
all regular playing members; the shopping centre Radha loves
to visit and to which Madhuri takes Indira shopping for a
wedding-present, in one section of which no doubt stands the
replacement for the doll Raj Kumar breaks in "A Loss of Faith";
and Janpath, where Shakuntala shops for shoes, and Esmond
dreams of England. To these could be added the Government
offices where Jaykar's son and Prem's friend Raj work at their
files, and the rows of uniform houses to which they return at
the end of each day; the obscure colleges, in one of which Prem
struggles manfully with his fate, while Gopi seeks only for a
means of escape; and the business offices in New Delhi and
the old part of the city, where Lalaji sits uneasily at the centre
of a web of corruption and intrigue.

Forming patterns of their own within this general view of
Delhi but still consonant with its urban reality are the houses
in different quarters of the city that are shared with other
dwellers by the Sahnis and Anands in *To Whom She Will*, Judy
and Bal in *A Backward Place*, and Ram Nath and Lakshmi in
Esmond in India; or inhabited in splendid privacy by the
Saxenas, the Mathurs, Hari Dayal and Madhuri, Rao Sahib and
Sunita, the Kapurs and the Kauls. There are, too, the modest
boarding houses in which Sudhir Bannerjee and Hari Mathur
(of film BOMBAY TALKIE) find rooms they can afford to rent, and
the smart little flats in which Esmond, Etta and other
sophisticates try to recreate the Europe they have left behind.
The characters of Ruth Jhabvala's early novels are, in a sense,
near-contemporaries. Some of them, like the Saxenas of *To
Whom She Will* and Gulab's parents in *Esmond in India*, have
lived in Delhi for many years, others — like the Bengali
intellectuals Krishna and Sudhir, and the provincial school-

teacher, Prem — are comparative newcomers. Some, like Shanti
in *A Backward Place*, have never ventured far from Delhi, some
(like Guppy in the same novel) are continually on the move while
others, like Etta, seem to be trapped there for life. A network
of fictional relationships is built up so convincingly in the early
novels that the reader can, with a very slight stretch of the
imagination, extend that network from one novel to another.
The Mathur family with whom Nimmi is on friendly terms in
The Nature of Passion could quite conceivably be related by
marriage to Amrita's aunt Tarla Mathur in *To Whom She Will*,
and include a young relative for whom Indira selects a wedding
present in *Esmond in India*. Mrs Bhatnagar, the social service
queen of *Get Ready for Battle*, could well be Shakuntala's future
mother-in-law in *Esmond in India* .... The ramifications are
almost endless, and the minute detail in which — if he were
so inclined — the reader of Ruth Jhabvala's fiction could trace
them indicates the fidelity with which she set herself when first
writing about India to draw characters and situations that were
part of the solid, observable world she knew at first hand.

That world being subject to change, Ruth Jhabvala's 'Delhi'
necessarily reflects social and cultural developments over a
period of twenty-four years that need not affect an invented
community such as Narayan's 'Malgudi' (or, for that matter,
Jane Austen's tranquil Highbury or Mansfield Park), which can
remain essentially the same whatever changes may take place
in the metropolis. Indian society, which in the past was as
rigidly stratified as any in feudal Europe, has undergone
profound social changes in the last quarter-century; Delhi, as
the Indian capital, is necessarily in the forefront of such change,
and is frequently its source. In the days immediately following
the withdrawal of the British Raj, when traditional Indian
courtesies were beginning to be revived and respected, the
dividing line in society could be drawn on the point of manners
and behaviour; in keeping with the thinking of other youthful
liberals of her time, Amrita in *To Whom She Will* turns away
from the vaunted 'breeding and fortune' of her Westernized
family to seek identification with 'Indian-ness', with simple, true
and unostentatious people. The decline in the status of English
and the rise of a powerful business class are two agents of social
change in India that Ruth Jhabvala examines in *The Nature
of Passion*; although Nimmi may admire 'England-returned'

Pheroze Bhatliwala's sophistication, and Kanta may plan to
educate her children beyond all point of contact with their
grandfather's world, it is with Lalaji (crude and mannerless
though Nimmi and Kanta think him) that real power lies. In
"The Biography", a visitor finds that a new political model
—canny but brash, loud and unrefined — has replaced the old-
style English-educated Indian statesman. Money having become
the source of influence and power by the 1960s, the Guptas
and Gulzari Lals dominate society, subtly supported by an
ambitious and corruptible administrative service. The English-
educated upper-class romantic, Nalini, described with
amusement in the story "A Course in English Studies", can
be easily imagined developing into the type of the new woman
described with loathing in "Myself in India", who ostentatiously
(and unconvincingly) identifies with Indian tradition. When
standards shift and ideals seem to change into their opposites,
the individual must discover grace and meaning where he can.
In Ruth Jhabvala's novels such discoveries are constantly made,
although, significantly, they are made less often and with
increasing ambiguity when the novels are encountered in the
chronological order of their publication. Hope begins to seem
to lie much more in individual qualities of character than in
the conscious mouthing of this or that 'tradition'; the characters
of true worth in her fiction, despite many weaknesses and
failings, are the inconspicuous and unsung, but gallant,
nonconformists: Krishna Sen Gupta in *To Whom She Will*,
Sudhir Bannerjee in *A Backward Place*, Narayan in *Esmond
in India*, Sarla Devi in *Get Ready For Battle*, Raymond in *A New
Dominion*, the narrator, 'Ms. Rivers', in *Heat and Dust*, and
Natasha of *In Search of Love and Beauty*.

In turning to examine the techniques that make fiction out
of real life in Ruth Jhabvala's writing, the reader is frequently
reminded that she is not only an analyst of life in India but
a student of the European masters of the novel and the short
story. Literary parody and literary allusion are sources of
constant delight in her work, and are used for the most serious
as well as for straightforwardly comic purposes. In *A Backward
Place*, Dr Hochstadt quotes Forster when expounding his views
on the 'rhythm' of Indian life; unfortunately, while Forster
conveys a universally significant experience in *A Passage to
India*, Hochstadt only demonstrates his inability to grasp actual

experience, or appreciate (except as a theoretician) the difficulties Judy and Etta experience in coming to terms with India. The fact that Dev Prakash writes Yeatsian verse in "The Award" not only shows how derivative and dated is his passion for India, but indirectly reveals his creator's awareness of the danger to art of the nostalgia created by exile in the soul of the creative artist. Ruth Jhabvala's literary models are by no means exclusively European: Jaykar (*A Backward Place*) writes deeply-felt speeches in the style of pre-independence patriotic floridity; there is an amusing parody of 'social problem' plays and commercial film-decor in *The Nature of Passion*; the real-life tragedies of Anjana and Sultana, ageing film-actresses in "Suffering Women", fall into the familiar patterns provided by popular films; and in perhaps the most detailed and sustained effort of this kind, Ruth Jhabvala structures her satire of the Bombay film industry, BOMBAY TALKIE, on the cliches of the commercial Indian film.

Her early satiric studies of middle- and upper-class Indian society prompted the comparison of her work by readers and critics to Jane Austen's sunnier novels. Reviewers tended to write of her as an Indian Jane Austen:

> If you have never read a novel by her, start now. She is as astringent as Jane Austen[24]

is a typical comment. In 1974 an interviewer discussed with Ruth Jhabvala the question of literary influences on her writing:

RA: You have been frequently compared to Jane Austen. Have you consciously modelled your writing after her?

RPJ: I haven't *consciously* modelled myself on anyone. Unconsciously (or does one say subconsciously?) more or less on every writer I have loved and admired. Any writer who had deeply thrilled me — and there have been many, many — has as it were entered into me; and so has influenced me. ... The reason I used to be compared to (Jane Austen) is because my earlier books dealt with the same sort of society as hers did — i.e., the leisured middle classes, mostly concerned with eating and marrying. Also perhaps my way of looking at things may have been somewhat similar to hers —a sort of ironic detachment? May be. Anyway, that was

in my earlier books. In my later ones I've been mostly
compared to Russian writers. Chekhov, for example.
Again I feel not because of any similarity between us
— how could there be! I wish it were so, even by a
thousandth of a fraction — but because one deals with
similar societies. Present-day India does seem to have
a lot in common, socially and economically, with
nineteenth century Russia.[25]

Most comparisons of Ruth Jhabvala's work with that of other
authors have indeed concerned themselves chiefly with
similarities between the societies described: post-Independence
India on the one hand, and Regency England or pre-
Revolutionary Russia on the other. Her own thoughts on
likenesses that might go very much deeper are tentatively
offered in connection with Jane Austen — 'a sort of ironic
detachment? May be' — and modestly withdrawn even as the
possibility is mentioned in the case of Chekhov. And yet, as
she has admitted elsewhere, she has never ceased to study the
art of fiction, with a special interest in the European writers
of the late eighteenth and early nineteenth centuries.[26] In fact,
even her earliest novels resemble Jane Austen's not only in their
settings and social backgrounds, but in theme. Acid satirical
portraits of Indian snobs, social workers and literary lions are
woven into plots concerning the amusing errors made by
youthful, misguided, but ultimately maturing or contented
lovers that inevitably recall *Pride and Prejudice* and *Emma*. The
similarity goes beyond even these externals to the language of
these early works; a habit of ironic undercutting within a
sentence frequently brings Jane Austen to mind, as in the
following description of an Indian party in *Get Ready for Battle*:

> These being modern times, many people had brought their
> wives, *who sat in a semi-circle at one end of the room and
> sipped pineapple juice.* (p. 8; italics added)

Haydn Moore Williams, in one of the earliest serious studies
of Ruth Jhabvala's fiction, refers to Jane Austen as her 'literary
ancestor', noting the dependence of both authors on an 'acute
observation of contemporary life' for their material, the
predominance of satire and irony in their work, and the self-
imposed limitations in regard to setting and social class that

both display.[27]

The influence of Jane Austen, Fanny Burney and other English writers of the eighteenth century on Ruth Jhabvala's writing is most clearly visible in *To Whom She Will* and *The Nature of Passion*, the two novels she wrote when she was still a newcomer to India and her approach to it inevitably shaped by her literary studies in Britain. *To Whom She Will* resembles *Pride and Prejudice*, both in directing a good deal of satire at marriage in middle-class society and in being a novel about growing up. The superior 'wisdom' of the young lovers' elders is shown to be quite often dubiously motivated, and although the activities of these elders are vigorously directed towards the ending of their 'unsuitable' love-affair, it is really brought to an end by the gradual emergence of hitherto unrecognized attitudes and feelings in the lovers themselves. Subtly influenced by their own emotional and physical maturing, the young people grow, in effect, out of sentimentality into sense, out of romantic dreams into real life. Conflicts occur (as in *Northanger Abbey*) between sense and sensibility on the one hand, and between literature and sentimental trash on the other. In fact, romantic sentimentality is generally a warning signal in Ruth Jhabvala's novels, as it is in Jane Austen's: it is to be met with again and again in such flawed characters as Viddi in *The Nature of Passion*, Asha and Gopi in *A New Dominion*, and Major Minnies in *Heat and Dust*, all of whom display a taste for verse 'squashy' with too much moonlight, too many roses and nightingales.

Ruth Jhabvala's development of the characters of Krishna and Amrita, and of their relationship with each other, has much in common with Jane Austen's treatment of her more sensitive heroes and heroines. Krishna, whom Amrita makes her confidant and go-between in her love-affair with Hari, spends a good part of the novel in the anguished frame of mind to which Edward Ferrars's engagement to Lucy Steele and Edmund Bertram's admiration of Mary Crawford reduce Elinor Dashwood and Fanny Price in *Sense and Sensibility* and *Mansfield Park* respectively. Both Krishna and Amrita are accused of heartlessness by her mother, Radha — 'None of you young people has any feelings!' (p. 161). Yet their reticence masks more genuine feeling than is possessed by any of the other characters in the story, and their sensibility is far greater than the shallow, sentimental emotion of such advocates of 'feeling' as Radha and Hari; contrasts that recall those between Catherine Morland and Isabella Thorpe in *Northanger Abbey*, Elizabeth Bennet and her mother in *Pride and Prejudice*, and Elinor Dashwood and Lucy Steele in *Sense and Sensibility*. A delicacy, emerging as a concern for others and for moral principle even at the cost of personal pain or loss, is common to Amrita and Krishna, making the gradual flowering of their relationship (amid much that is either crudely or elegantly mercenary) something to wonder at and to value. Readers of *To Whom She Will* who know their Austen can hardly avoid seeing the three Saxena sisters, Amrita's mother and aunts, as Indian avatars of indolent, selfish and kindly Lady Bertram (Mira), restless Mrs Norris (Tarla) and slovenly, impecunious Mrs Price (Radha) in *Mansfield Park*. Tarla's Delhi mansion, inhabited by people of wealth and leisure who achieve little communication with one another, bears an affinity to Sir Thomas Bertram's residence. Radha's grand invasion of the Sahni household, undertaken in order to put a stop to Amrita's romance with Hari, resembles Lady Catherine de Bourgh's call on Elizabeth Bennet (with the same intention) in *Pride and Prejudice*. Amrita, fragile in appearance yet morally firm, has a good deal in common with such Austen heroines as Fanny Price and Anne Elliot. Such resemblances, like the imposition of a comic dramatic structure on the events of real life, strike the reader of *To Whom She Will* as imported elements. In writing her first novel, Ruth Jhabvala seems to have been experimenting with styles and modes, fitting what she found in India in the 1950s into moulds that were familiar to her, the balanced, patterned structures of English eighteenth century drama and fiction.

To Whom She Will is 'an uneasy blending of two worlds'[28], not only of the conservative and the modern in a changing society, but of materials and methods drawn from the West and the Orient. The blending of different elements is 'uneasy' because, despite all the youthful author's efforts, the seams show on a literary level, the textures do not quite match, and the threads interweave imperfectly. This 'uneasiness' is best seen in Ruth Jhabvala's contrasting pictures of the Saxena and Mathur households on the one hand, and the Sahni and Anand households on the other. The drawing-room comedy, mainly

verbal, of the former does not only represent (as it is intended
to do) another kind of Indian life from that represented by the
vigorous slapstick that obtains among the Sahnis and Anands,
but is composed in a different literary mode. That mode is
imported, and it does not quite succeed in blending with what
is 'indigenous' in the novel, Ruth Jhabvala's vivid evocation,
in a series of detailed and sympathetic studies, of Punjabi family
life as lived by the Sahnis, the Anands and their innumerable
relatives.

In describing the Punjabi family clans, Ruth Jhabvala
emphasizes their vigour, resourcefulness, energy and health,
drawing her material from her observations of the 'large Punjabi
family' of her husband's Hindu partner[29]. The delight in detail
and in every aspect of a rich subject that emerges in her
descriptions of Indian family life in both *To Whom She Will* and
The Nature of Passion is part of the 'rapture' with which, at
the age of twenty-four, she first encountered India:

> As soon as I got here, I began writing about India .... It came
> about instinctively. I was enraptured. I felt I understood India
> so well. I loved everything. The first nine years I never left
> India ....
>
> Perhaps I loved it then because of my being Jewish. The
> Indian family life, the humour was closer to the Jewish world
> I knew than the Anglo-Saxon world.[30]

It is significant that when drawing the stiflingly conservative
Saxenas Ruth Jhabvala turned for her models to the 'Anglo-
Saxon world' of eighteenth century fiction and satiric comedy
that had been the subject of her academic study; when
confronted with the rich material yielded by her observation
of Punjabi family life she turned 'instinctively' to the Jewish
springs of her own nature.

Recent criticism makes little reference to eighteenth century
literary influences on Ruth Jhabvala's writing. No doubt one
reason for this is that by moving so clearly beyond satire in
her most recent fiction, she has ceased to present marriage
debates that instantly recall *Pride and Prejudice*, or character-
portraits (such as those of Kanta and Viddi in *The Nature of
Passion*) that bring Jane Austen's Fanny Dashwood or Fanny
Burney's young Mr Branghton of *Evelina* to mind. Another
reason might be that her fiction, though retaining comic

elements, is no longer light-hearted, and appears to concern itself more with self-analysis and a dissection of the psychological condition of various characters than with social criticism. The influence of the eighteenth century in Ruth Jhabvala's work, which announces itself at first in such external similarities as those of setting, structure, plot and characterisation, goes much deeper than that, however,even in her earliest novels. Far from being dead or outmoded, it may be traced throughout her writing (including her latest work in the novel and for the cinema), and should be recognized for what it is: a source from which she continually draws strength in matters relating to both style and sensibility.

I have drawn attention to the literary influences that have helped to shape Ruth Jhabvala's writing, in chapters devoted to specific novels, and to her short stories and screen-plays. In doing this I would not care to give the impression that I regard her highly individual art as dependent in any weakly imitative way upon the literary attitudes and techniques this German-born authoress absorbed during the years of her graduate and postgraduate study in Britain, or from later reading. On the contrary, she is most 'Augustan' in the propriety and skill with which she selects material from eighteenth century and other sources, and shapes them to her artistic needs. She 'imitates', in fact, in the eighteenth century manner, recreating her models in terms and images of modern India in her earliest novels: concentrating on the human and essential truth to life of her selected originals, she places them in carefully observed Indian settings, and filters their speech through an artistically modified version of spoken Indian English idiom. In her later work, when a better knowledge of her Indian subject and of life itself gives her a wider range of alternatives upon which to draw for models, the literary sources of her inspiration become much less easy to identify in any specific way. They continue, however, to yield elements upon which she bases the moral standards that support her works of imaginative art. Her characters of worth in both *A New Dominion* and *Heat and Dust*, for example, observe standards of decency in their personal relationships with others that originate in such Augustan 'virtues' as elegance of mind and delicacy of behaviour. Both Raymond and the Nawab of Khatm possess the attribute of 'delicacy', a term used frequently in Fanny

Burney's descriptions of the exemplary Lord Orville in *Evelina*. Jane Austen links a similar delicacy with courtesy in such heroes as Henry Tilney, Mr Darcy, Mr Knightley, and Captain Wentworth. Gopi's selfishness causes Raymond acute pain of mind in *A New Dominion*, and Swamiji's callous exploitation of Lee calls forth his chivalry; the Nawab of *Heat and Dust* is a true aristocrat trapped in a world growing increasingly subservient to the influence of money. Subjected to stress and mental torture and the prospect of losing that for which they care most deeply, both display the sensitive appreciation of other people's feelings and needs, and the intense reluctance to cause pain or embarrassment to those worth caring for, that Fanny Burney and Jane Austen call 'delicacy'. The possession and use of a critical intelligence, the ability to feel sincerely for others, and the self-discipline that alone makes civilised social conduct possible are criteria of human quality that Ruth Jhabvala has never ceased to apply throughout her writing career, perhaps because they are or have become identical with her own.

Ruth Jhabvala first made her mark as a satirist with a sharp eye for hypocrisy and inconsistency. Her novels make consistent use of a character whose astringent habit of mind — critical of flaws in society and in himself — and carefully controlled behaviour denote a person of sensitivity. This character (Krishna Sen Gupta in *To Whom She Will*, Sudhir Bannerjee in *A Backward Place*, Ram Nath in *Esmond in India*, Raymond in *A New Dominion* and Natasha of *In Search of Love and Beauty* are examples) becomes in a sense, and at certain times, the author's representative in the novel's fictional world, establishing through his thoughts, actions, and the words he usually refrains from uttering, a standard by which the behaviour of other characters may be assessed. Ruth Jhabvala's targets are not specifically nor exclusively Indian faults, but human weaknesses that have been diagnosed and subjected to satiric dissection by writers as far apart in time and locality as Chaucer, Moliere, Alexander Pope, Voltaire, Jonathan Swift, Boccaccio, Shakespeare, de Maupassant, V.S. Naipaul, Anton Chekhov, and the unknown authors of the *Jataka Tales* and *The Book of Job*. They are, in fact, the classic targets of the satirist: selfishness, vanity and egotism that interpret the world incorrectly because they place the self at its centre; affectation and insensitivity; hypocrisy (or its milder form of self-deception) that manipulates others for selfish or immoral ends. These all draw authentic satiric fire. Although Ruth Jhabvala's narrative tone remains cool and studiedly polite, the positives provided by her *personae* leave the reader in little doubt as to the positions on her scale of moral values occupied by the shallow, sentimental Hari Sahni whose self-deceiving protests of undying love for Amrita while moving towards marriage with another young woman contrasts with Krishna's unobtrusive but genuine concern for her happiness; by Mrs Kaul, whose egotism produces plans for the 'Culture Dais' in *A Backward Place* that are taken seriously by everyone but Sudhir Bannerjee; by the weak, pretentious Har Dayal whose insincerities are exposed by contrast with Ram Nath's austerity and directness in *Esmond in India*; and by the hypocritical Swamiji in *A New Dominion*, whose well-developed proselytising techniques as they work on neurotic Western disciples are in strong contrast with Raymond's conscientious efforts to refrain from imposing his personal views on others.

The pretensions of Western 'experts' on Indian culture who complacently fit India to their theories are occasionally exposed by a satiric *persona*, but are most consistently satirized by being viewed against Ruth Jhabvala's evocation in her novels of the infinite mystery and variety of India. Her portrait of the Hochstadts in *A Backward Place* takes insensitivity as its target: the Hochstadts' experience of India and their knowledge of its culture have been limited by the very short time they have spent in India, by their way of life, and by their habits of mind which lead them to conclusions based on theory rather than on experience. These limitations do not, however, inhibit them in the least from believing that India has no surprises for them, an attitude that (although they are unaware of it) betrays the superficiality of their knowledge and the inadequacy of their understanding. It would not be possible for a satiric *persona* — even a Sudhir Bannerjee — to dent such solid complacency. Ruth Jhabvala's method of satiric exposure is to describe in the Hochstadts' own words, on the last pages of *A Backward Place*, a 'cultural occasion' they have attended. As they struggle earnestly to accommodate within their theories about Indian culture the comic incongruities they have just witnessed in a local production of *The Doll's House* in Hindi, she simultaneously makes fun of the occasion (which has been allowed by its organisers to become social rather than cultural in any genuine sense), and nonsense of their theories:

> Captain Lakshman, as Torvald Helmer, had delivered all his lines with his right hand raised in the air: which might, the Hochstadts didn't know, be an Indian dramatic convention, but they rather felt it made, as far as the present production was concerned, for a certain stiffness. (p. 254)

By going on to express, in a narrative style that blends imperceptibly with their characteristic mode of expression, the enthusiasm the Hochstadts feel for the cultural heights achieved by this travesty of Ibsen, Ruth Jhabvala exposes their lack of sense and judgment, and the superficiality of their 'contact with this fabled land'.

In such passages as this, the moral standard adopted by Ruth Jhabvala as a base from which to dispatch her satiric shafts is an awareness of India's complexity that she creates in her reader's mind more by implication and by unobtrusive symbolic suggestion than by any direct statement. In contrast with it, the Hochstadts' patronising theories ring unmistakably false. Here, too, Ruth Jhabvala reveals her stature as a satirist in her choice of a worthy target. For although her description of the Hochstadts is indescribably funny in the reading, indeed one of the most amusing passages in the work of a mistress of the comic art, it also isolates for satiric dissection a growth so malignant upon India that it needs to be excised for the health of society. The Hochstadts' theories, though well-meaning, represent false conclusions; the respect in which these visitors to India are held by Mrs Kaul and her like gives their false views a quite undeserved currency.

Despite her occasional use of traditional satiric techniques, readers of Ruth Jhabvala's later fiction find themselves led far more frequently towards sympathetic understanding of a morally confused character than they find themselves pitched into easy laughter or tempted into rage and annoyance. 'Of course it has everything to do with the way I look at things and people', Ruth Jhabvala said in 1974:

> Perhaps I do tend to see the ridiculous aspects first, both in situations and in characters. But I don't think I just sit

and laugh at them. Especially not in my later books. On the
contrary, I'm beginning to feel that what is ludicrous on the
surface may be tragic underneath. That's especially true in
India. All those Indian paradoxes and comical situations that
Western writers especially like to exploit and make fun of
... well, perhaps one laughs at first (I'm afraid I used to laugh
more than I should in my early books) — but afterwards you
see that it is not comic at all but quite the opposite. Then
one stops laughing: at which point perhaps one's writing
opens up?[31]

The cool detachment of her tone in *A Backward Place* as she
takes the Hochstadts apart for her reader's instruction and
pleasure, and the flexibility of a narrative style that can appear
to take on the colours of a character's voice and habits of
thought are features of Ruth Jhabvala's writing that develop
increasing subtlety with each published novel. It is not long
before the confident satire with which the Hochstadts are
exposed gives way — as her writing 'opens up' — to a kinder,
because ironic, view.

   Ruth Jhabvala's movement from the comparative simplicities
of satire towards the complexities of an ironic mode can be seen
from a literary point of view as a maturing process, and from
a personal one as a means of survival. The satiric mind, moved
by intense feeling to a hatred only thinly masked by a casual
tone and a polite manner, is only too apt (as her studies in
eighteenth century English literature cannot fail to remind her)
to turn destructively upon itself. The irony to which she
subjects the satiric *personae* of her novels and short stories
indicates that they are not only externalisations of her moral
viewpoint, but projections of her personal dilemma. The use
of irony becomes for her, as it is for many satirists and ironists,
a means of self-discipline and self-chastisement. The Nawab
of Khatm in *Heat and Dust*, who would be glad, like his heroic
ancestor, to visit a ferocious punishment on those who insult
and persecute him, develops a studied courtesy (akin to his
creator's best satiric manner) with which he masks his
contempt and hatred for the British political agents upon whose
goodwill his position depends. He does not, however, attempt
to develop an understanding of their difficulties, or sympathy
for their point of view. Inevitably, the time comes when his

nature can support the tension of this situation no longer, and a personality that once possessed the potential for true leadership dwindles into comic ineffectualness. Ruth Jhabvala prefers — at any rate, she chooses — the cooler regions of irony to the heat and dust of satiric indignation: a preference that is, perhaps, symbolically represented in *Heat and Dust* by Olivia's choosing to live with the Nawab in a mountain eyrie from which he periodically descends to battle with the enemies of his peace but which she, significantly, never leaves.

It is from frustration and tension comparable to that of the Nawab, possibly, that Ruth Jhabvala has developed her richly varied ironic style:

> I know I am the wrong type of person to live (in India). To stay and endure, one should have a mission and a cause, to be patient, cheerful, unselfish, strong. I am a central European with an English education and a deplorable tendency to constant self-analysis. I am irritable and have weak nerves.[32]

It is all here, though it is presented (with characteristic ironic dissimulation) as weaknesses: the cosmopolitan experience, the English academic training, the impulse to project facets of her own personality and experience in her characters and by this means to attempt to understand and control them, the extreme sensitivity, all of which contribute so much to Ruth Jhabvala's strength as a novelist. I have referred, in the chapter on *Heat and Dust*, to her use of irony as an instrument of social and self-analysis. By the time she wrote this novel it had become her characteristic authorial tool, shaped by her individual, indeed unique, experience as an 'outsider' in India. But its beginnings can be traced to sources very much like those to which D.W. Harding traces Jane Austen's irony in his essay 'Regulated Hatred': a way of life in dealing with which writing offered a means to increased self-comprehension and self-control.[33] As with Jane Austen, and Ruth Jhabvala's own Nawab of Khatm, it is wise to be especially on one's guard when her style is ostensibly at its most polite. The passions of resentment, anger, scorn and self-contempt hidden beneath her coolly detached tone and manner are likely to be intense.

Ruth Jhabvala's mature novels, far from being the cynical attacks upon India that some critics have taken them to be,

seem to be most properly viewed as artistic expressions of the
process of understanding life and of coming to terms with it.
As in real life, there are no 'answers' provided in either *A New
Dominion* or *Heat and Dust*, only ironic ambiguities that seem
to point in one direction at certain times, in another at others:
a feature that suggests Ruth Jhabvala is becoming increasingly
interested by the challenge of reflecting the hidden workings
and perplexities of real life in her fiction.

Her early novels imposed neatly balanced, intricately worked
out patterns upon life: indeed both *To Whom She Will* and *The
Nature of Passion* have plots that their author manipulates so
that they move with the grace and ease of stage comedy. In
these first novels, too, the narrator does a great deal of
explaining. The technical problems besetting the novelist who
writes about India in English are many. They include the
adoption or invention of an idiom that reflects the rhythms and
tones of Indian speech patterns without comic distortion,
together with a means of conveying to readers unfamiliar with
Indian society essential information they would be apt, through
unfamiliarity or ignorance, to miss. Certain very important
factors that profoundly affect social relationships in India (for
example, differences in caste or community), would only need
to be delicately implied for an Indian reader to grasp without
delay or difficulty the 'message' contained in a family- or place-
name, a phrase characteristic of a region or a social class, or
the significant misuse of some well-established and recognized
tradition. These subtleties must either be directly explained to
the Western reader (thereby possibly slowing down action,
rendering narrative unduly obtrusive, or robbing a conversation
of a good deal of the delicate nuance which is the very essence
of the social exchanges, comic and serious, through which Ruth
Jhabvala develops her picture of India), or very delicately worked
into the narrative. Part of Ruth Jhabvala's maturing as a writer
is her gradual development of various means by which
explication can be cut to a minimum. She conveys a good deal
indirectly, through the dialogue or the thoughts of characters,
as in the following presentation of a traditional point of view
through the thoughts of Prem, in *The Householder*:

> (Prem) frowned, for he did not like girls to be indelicate. They
> should be remote and soulful; like Goddesses they should
> be. (pp. 30-31).

In *A New Dominion*, what is unfamiliar to a Western reader is skilfully interwoven with the thoughts and experiences of Raymond, a newcomer to India, whose habit of writing detailed letters to his mother about every moment of his day, every shift of his thoughts and feelings, is part of his character; or with the changing emotions of Lee, an American spiritual seeker given to questioning intensely each experience that comes her way. By these means Ruth Jhabvala directs her reader's eye through what seems to be a view of India's external landscapes to a view of human nature in its hidden, secret depths. As Raymond and Lee travel from Delhi to Banaras and from Banaras to Maupur, Ruth Jhabvala's descriptions of landscapes and interiors take on symbolic dimensions that turn these characters into seekers after truth in the often terrifying kingdom of the human personality. India, at this level, is not so much a country as a metaphor, and her people — as represented by the Indian characters in *A New Dominion* —function at the level of myth and symbol. Raymond's travel in and out of India necessitates the drawing up of itineraries and the making of hotel bookings, just as Arjuna's battles in the *Mahabharata* involved the preparation of chariots and weapons. Raymond's quest, like Christian's in *The Pilgrim's Progress*, and quite as much as Arjuna's battle, is undertaken on behalf of a spiritual kingdom, and the subtle Swamiji is an antagonist as terrible as Apollyon or any many-headed demon.

Ruth Jhabvala's description of her own life in India in the essay "Myself in India" is frank, and deeply moving:

> So I am back again alone in my room with the blinds drawn and the airconditioner on. Sometimes, when I think of my life, it seems to have contracted to this one point and to be concentrated in this one room, and it is always a very hot, very long afternoon when the airconditioner has failed. I cannot describe the *oppression* of such afternoons. It is a physical oppression — heat pressing down on me and pressing in the walls and the ceiling and congealing together with time which has stood still and will never move again. And it is not only those two — heat and time — that are laying their weight on me but behind them, or held within them, there is something more which I can only describe as the whole of India. This is hyperbole, but I need hyperbole

> to express my feelings about those countless afternoons
> spent over what now seem to me countless years in a country
> for which I was not born.[34]

The vividness of the images she presses into her service
indicates the intensity of her Indian agony, and the strength
of her compulsion to work and re-work it in her fiction. Etta
in *A Backward Place*, Raymond in *A New Dominion*, Cyril Sahib
in the film AUTOBIOGRAPHY OF A PRINCESS, and Harry in *Heat
and Dust* are all, in part, expressions of this personal need.
But, as her own account and the record of her novels and
stories make clear, rapture, joy and love are also part of her
experience of India. Ruth Jhabvala externalises through fiction
every aspect, painful, puzzling, and exhilarating, of a complex
relationship with India. Major Minnies in *Heat and Dust* regards
India as:

> an opponent, even sometimes an enemy, to be guarded and
> if necessary fought against from without and, especially, from
> within; from within one's own being (p. 171).

Olivia Rivers, on the other hand, becomes one of those who
accept India as a lover:

> She followed him wherever he called her and did whatever
> he wanted. (p. 152).

Between these extremes there exist innumerable attitudes, and
Ruth Jhabvala explores a good many in her fiction, having
experienced them all at first or at second hand during her years
in India. Many of her Western characters (who include, one
must remember, 'myself') leave India, fleeing back to a setting
they can comprehend, which will not make too many demands
on them. But since, as she has noted, Ruth Jhabvala's India
includes intimations of both hell and heaven[35], the fugitive
from India's hell must also accept exile from India's 'heaven'.
And this is an end (to her stories, and presumably to her own
relationship with India) that seems to Ruth Jhabvala to be
neither 'very satisfying (n)or conclusive.'[36]

The chapter divisions adopted in this chronological study of
Ruth Jhabvala's writing permit concentration on various
aspects of her art while temporarily excluding others. But such
divisions by no means imply the existence of a similar

fragmentation in her fiction. On the contrary, her intention and her artistic method are so closely related, and their unity in turn so intricately interwoven with such other aspects of her writing as its timeliness and timelessness, its value as social documentation, and the sensitivity with which she interprets character and motive in relation to both individual temperament and cultural conditioning, that some such tool becomes indispensable. With its help we may, even if only temporarily, penetrate the wholeness of her created world, in order to look about us and discover our bearings. For it is a world essentially of the spirit that is glimpsed finally through the physically detailed fictional world of Ruth Jhabvala. Her characters travel in quest of a better knowledge of their own minds and hearts, although they journey through Indian or American landscapes, though 'Academies of Potential Development' and holy mountains are to be met with on the way, and though their Vanity Fair is recognizably the city of Delhi or New York.

Notes

1.   R. Agarwal, "An interview with Ruth Prawer Jhabvala", *Quest* 91 (1974), p. 36.
2.   Personal communication, 1978.
3.   A. Hamilton, "The Book of Ruth", *Guardian*, 30 November 1975. Writing of the author's smooth transition to English, Hamilton adds: 'Her brother, a crucial two years older, made no such radical rejection. Seriously engaged with the German classics, he persisted.' S.S. Prawer is now Professor of German Language and Literature at Oxford.
4.   R. Agarwal, op. cit., p. 33.
5.   Ibid., p. 36.
6.   "A novelist of India reflects two worlds", *New York Times*, Tuesday 17 July 1973; reprinted in the *National Times* of Australia of 7-12 January 1974 as "Rot and a deep sense of melancholy".
7.   See H.M. Williams, "R.K. Narayan and R. Prawer Jhabvala: Two interpreters of modern India", *Literature East and West* 16:4 (April 1975 for December 1972), p. 1142: Williams suggests that R.P. Jhabvala's 'consuming interest in the nature of the Indian joint family reflects perhaps her European origin ... Jhabvala, with her own personal history of exile and expatriation comes with great curiosity to such an immensely secure and complex institution and yet within which such tensions and rebellions can occur'.
8.   H.M. Williams, "The Yogi and the Babbitt: Themes and characters of

the new India in the novels of Ruth Prawer Jhabvala", *Twentieth Century Literature* 15:2 (July 1969), p. 89.

9. R.P. Jhabvala, "Myself in India", *An Experience of India* (John Murray, London: 1966) 1971 ed., p. 7.

10. R.P. Jhabvala, "Moonlight, jasmine and rickets", *New York Times*, 22 April 1975.

11. A. Rutherford and K.H. Peterson, "*Heat and Dust*: Ruth Prawer Jhabvala's experience of India", *World Literature Written in English* 15:2 (November 1976), p. 377.

12. Personal communication, 1978.

13. R.P. Jhabvala, "The Englishwoman", *How I Became a Holy Mother* (Harper and Row, New York: 1976) p. 22.

14. M. Mukherjee, "Inside the outsider", a paper read at the 4th Triennial ACLALS Conference held in Delhi in January 1977, p. 6.

15. Ibid.

16. "Rot and a deep sense of melancholy", op. cit.

17. 'That's how I get to know a place, through writing' — R.P. Jhabvala, quoted by John Pym, " 'Where could I meet other screenwriters?' A conversation with Ruth Prawer Jhabvala", *Sight and Sound* (1978).

18. R.P. Jhabvala, "Myself in India", op. cit., p. 20.

19. See R. Agarwal, op. cit.: To the question, 'Would you like to be considered an Indian writer?' Ruth Jhabvala replied: 'No, how could I be? I'm not, am I? There's no getting away from that fact. I write differently from Indian writers because my birth, background, ancestry, and traditions are different. If I must be considered anything, then let it be as one of those European writers who have written about India.' (p. 36) To the question, 'What, according to you, may be the reasons for your cold reception in India?', she replied: 'I don't feel particularly neglected here. I think Indians don't read much anyway, so I don't really expect them to read my novels' (p. 35).

20. *Vanaprastha*, retirement from the cares of the householder's existence and the dust of battle in order to lead a life of philosophic reflection. John Pym begins his article on R.P. Jhabvala's work for the Merchant-Ivory film THE EUROPEANS with the following description of her mode of life: 'Massachusetts, early October. The author Ruth Prawer Jhabvala occupies a bare, modern room in an anonymous modern hotel in Leominster. The room seems to contain only a typewriter, a few papers and a well-preserved copy of the Penguin edition of Henry James' novel *The Europeans*. She likes the hotel: it takes care of the domestic arrangements, not her forte, and the atmosphere is conducive to hard work.' (p. 15) Of her life in New York, Ruth Jhabvala notes: 'I have never actually met another screenwriter. Where could I? ... Henry James was only an inveterate diner-out when he was young, afterwards he couldn't stand it ... All he wanted to do was to get back home. I see that with other writers, too. After a time that's all they want to do ... I think it was all those years in India that really got me into it ... I was alone the whole day.' (pp. 16-18). John Pym, op. cit.

21. Personal communication, 1978.

22. A recent instance of this approach is C. Karnani's "Ruth Jhabvala's

backward place', a paper tabled at the 5th Triennial ACLALS Conference held in Fiji in January 1980; Karnani finds 'reason to suspect that Jhabvala treats India as a foreign exchange commodity' (p. 2), and goes on to state that Etta's behaviour indicates an identical attitude to India (p. 6). The comments made about India by two disillusioned young British travellers in *Heat and Dust* are treated by Karnani as proof that the novel itself 'is viciously prejudiced in its vision of the Indian scene' (p. 7). The views of the narrator of *Heat and Dust* on bus-travel in India are similarly read as evidence that the author's 'vision is one-sided and biased' (p. 8).

23. V.S. Naipaul, "Jasmine", *Times Literary Supplement*, 4 June 1964, reprinted in his *The Overcrowded Barracoon* (Deutsch,London: 1972), p. 25

24. An early review, quoted by R. Agarwal, "Outsider with unusual insight", *Times of India*, 25 March 1973.

25. R. Agarwal, op. cit., pp. 33-4.

26. See R.P. Jhabvala, "Myself in India", op. cit., p. 10.

27. H.M. Williams, "English writing in free India (1947-1967)", *Twentieth Century Literature* 16:1 (January 1970), pp. 8-11.

28. *Glasgow Herald* review of *To Whom She Will.*

29. See A. Rutherford and K.H. Petersen, op. cit, p. 375.
    Q: Could you say from where you have your experience of the Hindu world?
    A: A lot of it is due to the accident of my husband having a Hindu partner who has a large extended family. He considers us as part of his family, has adopted us as it were. They're a large Punjabi family and I've really learnt so much from them.

30. *New York Times* article of 1973 (see note 6 above).

31. R. Agarwal, op. cit., p. 34.

32. R.P. Jhabvala, "Myself in India", op. cit., p. 8.

33. D.W. Harding, "Regulated hatred: an aspect of the work of Jane Austen", *Scrutiny* VIII (1940) pp. 346-62, reprinted in W. Heath (ed.), *Discussions of Jane Austen* (D.C. Heath & Co., Boston, 1961), pp. 41-50.

34. R.P. Jhabvala, "Myself in India", op. cit., p. 16.

35. R.P. Jhabvala, "Moonlight, jasmine and rickets", op. cit.

36. Ibid.

CHAPTER

II

To whom she will OR Amrita

1955, 1956

... It was a novel about India, written by an English lady:
well-written too, Amrita could see that, all the proper
accoutrements of style and sensibility, but Amrita could not
understand why the lady had given Indian names to her
characters.[1]

Amrita, a young Indian graduate of intelligence and sensitivity,
is the heroine of Ruth Jhabvala's first novel.* In *Remember the*

---

*Published in Britain by Allen and Unwin in 1955 with the title *To whom
she will*, and in the United States by Norton the following year with the
title *Amrita*.

House, a novel published by the Indian author Santha Rama
Rau in the same year that *Amrita* appeared, the heroine arrives
at rather similar conclusions concerning English-language
fiction about India:

> The few novels about India that I had read seemed to concern
> a different kind of life, almost a different country from mine.
> It was like visiting a place that you have often heard
> described, of which you have a clear image, but when you
> see it you find that you were wrong ... the people ... aren't
> welcoming friends; they are hostile strangers, speaking a
> language you don't understand, making jokes behind your
> back, wondering when you will go. You know them and
> recognize them, but they are foreigners.[2]

Miss Rama Rau's heroine dismisses as unsatisfactory the
settings, the characters and the dialogue commonly found in
contemporary Indian fiction. The foreignness (pertaining
especially to character) that both authors complain of is
attributed by Ruth Jhabvala to the spirit in which such fiction
is generally written. Her use of the word 'accoutrements'
amusingly implies that the elements of 'style' and 'sensibility'
are assumed, 'put on' as equipment appropriate ('proper') to
one who attempts the literary passage to India. We may detect
here an indirect assertion that *Amrita* itself is a novel in which
the 'style' adopted and the 'sensibility' expressed are native and
natural to the author and her subject, neither borrowed nor
assumed.

Despite Ruth Jhabvala's conviction at the time of its
publication that she had reflected in it a true image of the
society she entered for the first time in 1951, *Amrita* could,
however, almost have been the novel she satirises. Its settings
and its plot (which hinges on the making of matches, of love
and by 'arrangement') are recognizably Indian, but its major
themes and the literary techniques the youthful author applies
to their expression appear to have been imported. She displays
considerable skill in blending her English cultural inheritance
with what she found around her in India, but in spite of her
obvious delight in the Indian scene and her efforts to capture
its spirit in her novel, India eludes her.

The plot of *Amrita* appears to endorse the wisdom of that
institution dear to oriental conservatism, the marriage
'arranged' by family elders between young people who lack the

experience or are denied the opportunity to choose partners for themselves. Amrita Chakravarty finds her Westernized upper-class relations uncongenial, and thinks herself in love with Hari Sahni, a poor young Punjabi who works at the New Delhi radio station where she is a part-time announcer. Their families scheme to prevent the marriage: Amrita's grandfather forbids it, her mother and her aunts begin to look about for a more acceptable suitor for her, and Hari's family wastes no time in negotiating a marriage settlement for him with the Anands, a family of their own community. Worn down at last by family pressure, Amrita and Hari settle for marriage with partners from socially suitable backgrounds. Since the title first selected for the novel emphasised the 'family matchmaking and stratagem' that constitute the plot[3], we could agree with Renee Winegarten's conclusion that in Ruth Jhabvala's earliest works, 'whatever the inner strains and stresses, the Indian family dominates, wrapping its members in a loving, protective cocoon'.[4]

The author's second choice of a title, however, places her heroine at the centre of the novel and underlines the fact that on a more important thematic level, *Amrita* is a story about maturing. Amrita, whose feeling for Hari is based on an idealized concept of the 'Indianness' she supposes him to represent, becomes gradually aware that of far greater importance to her happiness is the respect and companionship of Krishna Sen Gupta, the Bengali intellectual she eventually marries. (It is one of the novel's minor ironies that Krishna has already declared his love for Amrita and she has begun to love him by the time her mother begins to plan an 'arranged' marriage between the two young people.) The pliable Hari, for his part, abandons his sentimental attachment to Amrita as his senses become pleasurably overwhelmed by an attractive Punjabi girl of his family's selection. Haydn Moore Williams has pointed out that Ruth Jhabvala, 'like her literary ancestor, Jane Austen ... likes to develop plots in which romantic love is less than adequate'.[5] It is no accident that an early review described *Amrita* in terms that are strikingly applicable to *Pride and Prejudice*:

> *To Whom She Will* might be described as a social comedy .... The tale of family matchmaking and stratagem is told with a delightfully gentle irony[6]

for the light-hearted and amusing novel is, like Jane Austen's, 'a book that entertains supremely'[7].

Although Ruth Jhabvala extracts much comedy from the romantic excesses of her sentimental lovers, and ends the novel by resolving the conflict between youth and age in a manner satisfactory to all concerned, the picture she draws of the Indian family as 'a loving, protective concoon' is, to say the least, ambiguous. Krishna's parents withdraw from him, Amrita's mother scorns her brave attempts to earn her own living. Pandit Saxena plans to send Amrita to England as an 'assertion of his own importance, a justification of his reality' (p. 209); her quiet resolve to marry 'whom she will' has struck the old man deeply, penetrating 'right through the servants, the law books and notes, and lunch in the dining-room' (p. 212). Hari Sahni is 'booked' for Sushila Anand in the business-like way that a prize bull would be purchased for a stock-breeder's herd: money passes between the elders of the two families in the young people's presence, and it is only the youth and mutual physical attraction of Hari and Sushila that lend the transaction some slight gloss of beauty and charm.

The novel's lovers find happiness in their several ways in the teeth of family insensitivity to their deepest feelings. The reader knows that Amrita's decision to marry Krishna will cause no re-thinking, no restatement of established values in the Saxena household. Sunk in a lassitude from which nothing can awaken them, the older generation cannot appreciate their young relatives' need to think and act as individuals. Amrita's family feel

> their age. The heat clung to them, exhausted them .... Not a breath of wind stirred in the trees. A sickening scent of night-flowers rose from the bushes and spread itself like a pall. The summers of centuries seemed to be brooding over the old garden. (p. 73)

Ignorant and uncaring of the path Amrita's feelings have taken, her grandfather, mother and aunts will complacently view her final choice of a husband as a vindication of their own wisdom and experience.

Within this ambiguous but generally compassionate picture of youth and age in conflict, Ruth Jhabvala finds plenty of room for satiric vignettes of the 'new' India. Ram Bahadur Saxena

values what he calls his family's 'breeding and fortune' (p. 11),
and though he considers himself a man of liberal views his
treatment of his social inferiors marks him as a self-deceiving
snob. An atmosphere of decay hangs over the stately Saxena
residence, 'heavy with respectability ... taller and more
respectable than all the rest' (p. 9). The changes in Indian
society after Independence have isolated the old man: all that
he values has either disappeared (with his old associates and
friends, now dead or quietly ageing in retirement in Britain or
in Simla), or shrunk to very confined limits. As he grows older,
he experiences 'a curious sense of unreality' (p. 207), even of
insecurity: it is only in his own house, 'guarded by the servants
whose life had been his' that he feels safe, 'a man of importance'
(p. 208). Yet, despite the opulence of its furnishings, this house
betrays a moral and cultural emptiness. Its decorations consist
for the most part of souvenirs of Pandit Saxena's tours of
Europe; his daughters show little dignity or 'breeding' in their
conversation; and he himself stoops to using his superior
English education to humiliate young Hari.

It is quite credible that the idealistic Amrita should turn away
from this empty respectability to worship 'Indianness'. But it
is a sign of her immaturity (and part of the *Emma*-like comedy
of the novel) that her quest for 'Indianness' and the company
of simple, true and unostentatious people leads her to Hari's
elder sister Prema, in whom she will only discover the familiar
combination of wealth and ostentation, together with a new
kind of emptiness. Their newly acquired money give Prema and
her husband Suri superior status in their own community, so
that she amusingly tempers her cordiality to the Anands'
relations with 'a touch of condescension' (p. 230) and
confidently challenges the arrogance of the Saxenas:

> 'Do they think they are better than we are because they live
> in a big house and have been to England? I also live in a
> big house and if I wanted to I also could go to England. And
> we have a big car brought specially from America, and I have
> clothes fine enough for the finest lady in Delhi, one salwar-
> kamiz I have cost Rs 250, I do not know if the ladies in that
> family have such clothes. Why did you not tell him that?'
> (pp. 21-2)

Comic incongruities enrich Prema's tea-party for Amrita in

Chapter 9, their humour springing partly from a contrast in
intention between the two characters, partly from a conflict in
expectation. Prema wishes to impress 'Memsahib' Amrita with
her luxurious style of living; Amrita, for her part, hopes to find
in the home of Hari's sister the 'supreme simplicity' (p. 65) she
would like to identify herself with. While Prema talks of her
recent Simla holiday, her fondness for Delhi's most expensive
pastries, her imported car, her husband's impatience with old
things when new can be bought so easily, and her many
servants (pp. 66-9), her carefully assumed casualness is being
continually undercut by readers' awareness that her 'servants'
are merely untrained, possibly underpaid, and definitely badly
treated little boys (in contrast with the Saxenas' family
retainers, and Gian, the long-employed, expert old cook who
serves Amrita's mother). They are also in a position to compare
Prema's flowered divans, 'wildly patterned square of carpet', the
artificial flowers in her imitation fireplace, and the 'admirable
symmetry' with which all this is arranged (p. 65) with the far
wealthier and more pleasingly decorated home of Amrita's aunt,
Mrs Tarla Mathur. The party, from which so much had been
expected, leaves both young women dissatisfied: Prema
considers Amrita 'stupid' and devoid of true feeling (p. 70), while
Amrita is 'embarrassed; and also deeply disappointed' (p. 69).

Conflict is common in *Amrita* between sense and sensibility
on the one hand, and between good literature and sentimental
trash on the other. Hari can lose all sense of reality when
listening to Hindi film music, and dream meltingly sweet dreams
of Amrita within earshot of his younger sister's morning
sickness and his mother's grumbles regarding her son-in-law's
talent for producing children. The reader's first view of Prema
(who shares her brother's musical tastes) finds her weeping over
a sentimental story which she considers true to life's realities:

> 'Listen to this,' (Prema) said ... ' "for the heart is like a fruit
> which can only prosper in the warm sunshine of love; without
> love, the heart, like a fruit without the sun, must wither and
> die".' She looked up, her eyes shining with tears. 'Is it not
> beautiful? "The heart is like a fruit ... " Kaka, I tell you, this
> is *Truth*. I know, I have felt this truth in my own life'.
> Hari sighed. 'I too ...' he suggested. (pp. 20-21)

It is not surprising that both Prema and Hari are attracted by

the sensuous Sushila Anand, whose singing is 'so sad and full
of deep feeling that one could not help realising the sadness
of life in general and of one's own life in particular' (p. 110).
Amusingly, Prema (who thinks the sensitive Amrita stupid) finds
Sushila — also an enthusiastic reader of magazine stories
—'widely read' and possessed of 'a fine literary taste' (pp.
110-11). Yet, though Amrita is far more discriminating in
matters of literature and music than Hari, Prema or Sushila,
her thoughts of Hari (like his of her) are all romantic. She
glorifies his peasant simplicity, and hopes his family will not
despise her 'for having been bred to false, foreign ways' (p. 32).
Such ideas are proved to be mere romantic fantasies when the
reader has visited Prema's garish house and glimpsed the noisy,
graceless domesticity of Hari's household. Sentimentality is
refreshingly undercut in *Amrita* through constant comic
juxtaposition with everyday reality, as in the following
conversation between Hari and Krishna Sen Gupta on the
subject of Amrita:

> 'What does it matter,' Krishna cried, 'if I am angry or not!
> Who am I that you should trouble yourself about my feelings?
> It is Amrita's feelings you should be thinking about.'
> 'Oh I do, I do,' Hari said quickly, 'every moment of the day
> I think of her. She is the nightingale of my heart, the stars
> of my eyes, the juice of my liver, tell her that.'
> 'And that means you will go to England with her?'
> 'If only I could', he said. 'I would follow her to the ends
> of the earth.'
> 'It is only to England you need go'. (p. 143)

In its own way, *Amrita* is a debate on the subject of marriage.
Its end leaves unresolved the question of whether 'arranged'
or 'love' marriages are most conducive to happiness and
presents an alternative, a marriage to which the partners come
as intelligent and understanding adults. The strongest
advocates in the novel of the arranged marriage are Radha,
Amrita's widowed mother (whose experience of a 'love' marriage
has not been wholly satisfactory) and Prema, whose melancholy
at the failure of her own 'arranged' marriage does not inhibit
her from promoting a similar match for her younger brother
Hari. The delayed or voluntary marriage finds advocates, at least
in theory, in Pandit Saxena (who had himself married by

arrangement, and theoretically accepts the emancipation of women); his eldest daughter Tarla (a theoretician like her father, whose own unsuccessful marriage had been arranged by her aunts); and Tarla's husband, Vazir Dayal Mathur (victim of an arranged marriage, who likes doing what is unconventional and unexpected). The views put forward by these characters stem so clearly from self deceptions of various kinds and from personal concerns quite unconnected with Amrita's happiness that they cannot be taken seriously by the reader. It is not Amrita's attractive honesty of nature that is, in her mother's eyes, her chief qualification for marriage, but her beauty and her University degree (pp. 127-8).

The marriage-debate as conducted in the Sahni family camp is equally revealing of the various speakers' personal concerns. Mrs. Anand, who was betrothed at the age of eight and married (unhappily, it appears) at sixteen, protests with feelings that her daughter Sushila is too young to marry:

> Suri slapped the palm of his foot which he was holding under him: 'It is her youth we value'.
>   'The younger the wife, the better it is for the husband,' said Mr Anand, and would have giggled if his wife had not glanced at him; he scratched his thigh instead. (p. 103)

Although Tarla Mathur affects refinement with the assistance of chocolate cake, lemon tartlets and Limoges china, her 'showing' of her niece Amrita to a prospective mother-in-law is conducted with at least equal disregard for the happiness of the individual most concerned: Amrita is blandly credited by her aunts with interests, talents and accomplishments that she does not possess. The supreme irony on the question of marriage in *Amrita* is probably the moment (at the end of Chapter 25) when, after many hours of negotiation into which no thought of love or affection has entered, Hari's mother states that her son is so passionately in love with his future bride that he cannot wait a year, and will hardly wait a week for the marriage-day. Unblinkingly, she is able to say, 'Yes ... that is our reason'. (pp. 178-9)

The Anands and the Sahnis assess marriage propositions as they would assess fine stock animals — for strength, stamina, appearance and age. Theirs is the attitude, not so much of materialism or greed, as of a 'resourceful ... intensely practical people' (p. 45) who work hard for their living and their occasional success. Mrs Anand stares at Hari 'with undisguised penetration, weighing him up as he stood before her' (p. 51); Suri remarks of Sushila that she is 'strong and healthy .... She is what I call a beauty' (p. 72). The young people are passive in these arrangements; indeed, Hari has no inkling of his fate until the payment of twenty-one rupees seals the contract of betrothal:

> Mr Anand planted himself before Suri, and with an air of great importance put his hand in his pocket and brought out two ten-rupee notes and one one-rupee note. 'Well, Suri Sahib', he said, 'your boy is ours, we book him, here is our money,' and he counted it out, ten rupees, twenty rupees, twenty-one rupees, into Suri's hand. Suri held the money, 'He is booked,' he said and laughed .... Hari desperately pretended not to notice what was going on. (p. 148)

These arrangements contrast first with the romantic delicacy of Amrita's feelings for Hari, and then with the unspoken attachment between herself and Krishna that gradually replaces it. Pandit Saxena's theoretical 'liberalism' glosses over the fact that his daughters' marriages had been in fact arranged, though in a less frank and far more subtle manner than Hari's. Amrita is assessed by Lady Ram Prasad Khanna (pp. 154-7), though her ordeal takes place in Vazir Dayal Mathur's aesthetically appointed drawing-room and not (as does Hari's) in the Anands' crowded quarters over a tailor's shop. A moral difference between Amrita and Hari emerges in their varying responses to such 'assessment', for while Hari does not have the honesty or the strength of will to oppose what is being done to him, the more straightforward Amrita declares her plans to go to England, simultaneously putting off Lady Ram Prasad Khanna and ending the interview.

Side by side with these sharp satiric exposures of Indian forms of pride, pretentiousness, complacency and sentimentality, and of the attitudes to money and marriage that exist in Indian society, *Amrita* presents a compassionate study of Indian middle-class life. When the Sahnis visit the Anands on what turns out to be Hari's betrothal day, an important and intimate occasion is ruined by a neighbours' quarrel:

> Suddenly from the veranda two floors below came an uproar

of voices. Women shrilled and children howled and men boomed with anger. It was one of those family quarrels, sister-in-law against sister, wife against brother-in-law, grandmother against everybody, the tension of community living bursting into a sudden climax which had to rage itself out before it could sink back into the calm of everyday subdued resentment. (p. 14)

This is, and always will be, the background to Hari's life with Sushila. When they seek an intimate moment together near the parapet of her parents' roof garden, they are scrutinised by 'sharp smiling eyes watching ... from behind' (p. 147), and the only prospect before them is the homely sight of 'two men ... washing themselves in the dark by the pump' (pp. 146-7). Like thousands of other young couples, they will be 'joined together to the accompaniment of bands and gramophones while clattering crates of coca-cola' provide a 'sudden frenzy of canned joy' (p. 104). Film music and magazine romances will supply their married life with its only sure sources of beauty and 'feeling', and their happiest moments will be shadowed by the ugliness and noise of other people's resentments — as in the way the neighbours' battle touches off a double family quarrel between Mrs Anand and her mother-in-law, and between Prema and Suri, that makes poor Sushila cry. In a later novel, *The Householder*, the youthful Prem and Indu too will live this kind of life, snatches of beauty reaching them only very occasionally as they set up house among their middle-class neighbours and friends.

The novel's three principal characters, Hari, Amrita and Krishna, present a series of interesting contrasts. All of them on the threshold of maturity, they simultaneously reveal and reconcile individual traits and the influence of their traditional upbringing. Hari is a romantic youth, to whom Amrita is 'a goddess' of whom he likes to think himself quite unworthy (p. 31). Enmeshed far more deeply in the conventions and family life of his community than he is aware, Hari is at the same time 'a good son' (p. 18), the pride and joy of a mother who has brought him up to feel a proper regard for his sisters and his brother, and to enjoy very heartily the food she cooks for him with such loving care. Sociable, warmly appreciative of a pretty face and figure, and possessed of a healthy appetite, Hari is described by an amused, patronising friend as 'a true son

of India' (p. 56). His weaknesses — as well as his easy-going
charm — are well established in Chapter 13, when his
obtuseness irritates Amrita and his gregariousness hurts her.
Hari understands neither Amrita's feelings nor her need to
apologize later that same day for her irritable behaviour. The
whole incident bewilders him and his thoughts on the subject
are characteristic (and comic):

> Love should remain a feeling, something charming and
> romantic connected with flowers and moonlight and music
> in lotus-bowers. It should have nothing to do with things
> like being called for by strangers in the night, and being
> whisked away before one could have one's dinner, and being
> brought to strange houses to hear the object of one's love
> talking in riddles. That was so unsettling; and one could not
> love with the right feeling if one was unsettled. (p. 109)

Possessing neither Amrita's honesty nor her strength of will,
the weak and well-meaning Hari is caught between her love
for him and his family's determination to see him suitably
married. Wishing to please every one and offend nobody, he
eventually surrenders himself to 'fate'. The novel takes on the
atmosphere of farce as its action begins to hinge on the matter
of who will manage to get Hari to the altar first. When Krishna
interviews Hari in Chapter 18, a moral contrast becomes clear
between these two young men: there is a significant difference
between the poised calm of Krishna (who has been compelled
by his own active conscience to act as go-between for Amrita
and Hari) and Hari's guilty anxiety as he resorts to lies in order
to excuse his weakness.

The 'maturity' to which the novel's events bring Hari is neither
intellectual nor moral, but physical. His romantic dreams of
Amrita give way to visions of Sushila that are frankly sensual:

> He pictured to himself her smooth body, strong and brown
> and stark naked, bending in the shadowed light of the moon
> and her hair springing out like a black flame.
> (p. 147)

For Hari the present is everything, and the beckoning reality
of Sushila becomes gradually far more influential with him than
the vague ideal of Amrita. At the height of the betrothal
celebrations, Hari thinks of the vows of fidelity to Amrita he

has made through Krishna, and feels 'very uncomfortable' (p. 151); his conscience is active, but it can do little against family pressure to conform, his own growing bodily desire for Sushila Anand, and a long-cultivated habit of 'slurring over' unpleasant or uncomfortable things.

It is typical of Hari (and of his creator's approach to his character) that when he does make his decision, it should take the form of a popular film cliche, arise from selfishness masquerading as noble self-sacrifice, and be made in the most comic and unromantic of circumstances. The narrative blends imperceptibly with Hari's thoughts as they move from romantic attitudinizing to a frankly sexual intention:

> Was he to go to her and say, forgive me, I cannot go with you to England, next week I am to be married? He could imagine the scene — not as between himself and Amrita, but between two plump shadowy figures with garlands round their necks sitting in a jasmine-bower; his head was bowed, she stared dry-eyed into the distance; there was silence except for his heavy sighs; then she began to sing, very low and sad, a song of sorrow and separation.
>
> His eyes now were moist with tears, and he walked along chewing his pan and thinking of the inevitable, the fate-ordained ending of his great love. He framed the sentences — our souls are as one — the cruel world tears us asunder — and stepped out of the way of two pariah-dogs snuffling around the Muslim meatstall. He was to be sacrificed in marriage and the day that should have been full of enjoicing would be the unhappiest of his life, for he would think of nothing but Amrita, the lost .... But suddenly he visualised thick black lashes lowered over coy eyes, a surge of hair falling forward over a rounded cheek ... how thin Amrita was getting, it occurred to him, she looked so thin and weak always, not like a fresh young girl should look, not like —the strength of her, the youth of her, the bursting bud, the promise; next week, and weakness flowed into his thighs as he turned the corner by the huge poster advertising a cure for impotency, with a picture of the advertiser in rimless spectacles. (pp. 184-5)

It is entirely typical of Hari's infinite capacity for self-deception that he can see his decision to abandon Amrita for Sushila as

an act of self-sacrifice (p. 185). As the novel draws to its close,
Ruth Jhabvala removes him very firmly from the field of
individual action (and of seriousness) by involving him in
broadly comic scenes that emphasize his close ties with his
family. In one of these, Prema massages one leg of the prostrate
Hari (who imagines himself at the point of death) while Mrs
Anand massages the other. They carry on their personal battle
for supremacy quite literally over his 'dying' body, while he
prudently 'lay quite still', keeping 'his eyes shut and his body
rigid, letting anyone who cared stroke or massage him' (p. 246).

Amrita's other admirer, Krishna Sen Gupta, is repelled at the
start of his acquaintance with her by 'her complete mental
innocence, what he called her prudery,' her 'shy disregard of
his own sex' (p. 132). Her failure to see in him anything but
a brotherly presence in her mother's house rankles, though
he pretends not to care. When he begins to recognise her
prudery for what it really is, 'a natural, a very fitting, reticence'
(p. 133) in an intensely emotional personality, he appreciates
the strain to which she is being subjected by her unsatisfactory
relationship with Hari:

> He felt sorry for her. He knew very well, perhaps better than
> she did herself, what efforts it cost her not only to be thus
> having to take the initiative in the affair, but also in the first
> place to be loving Hari at all. He knew it was a constant
> struggle with her innate modesty, with all she believed and
> felt and had been taught to believe and feel. (p. 134)

Called a 'wicked girl' by her obtuse mother because of her
apparent waywardness, Amrita's carefully hidden inner turmoil
emerges in physical signs that are missed by Hari but perceived
by Krishna, who observes her every day and notes with concern
her weariness and the changes in her appearance (p. 162).

Like Hari, Krishna is partially a product of his upbringing:
in his case, the experience of being the only child of intellectual,
idealistic parents who had 'suffered long spells of imprisonment'
(p. 59) for their active membership of the Congress movement
in the years before Independence. He differs from every other
character in the novel by being unimpressed by Pandit Saxena,
aware of his father's contemptuous view of the old man as a
time-server who had attained a distinguished position only
because other men, of greater ability than he, had refused to

serve in the English courts of law (p. 137). Krishna's inherited
idealism leads him continually towards disenchantment with
the 'new' India, and towards an independent point of view.
When Hari tells him soulfully that he does not know how he
will be able to live without Amrita, Krishna's unspoken
assessment of this Romeo comes amusingly close to the truth:

> But Krishna knew how: Hari would come here to the coffee
> house in the mornings and in the evenings, drink coffee, talk
> with his friends, from time to time sigh deeply to show he
> had a sorrow, then expatiate upon sorrow in general, upon
> women, upon love, heave another sigh and then confide to
> whoever was nearest to him about Amrita, how he loved her
> and how her family had cruelly sent her away because of
> him. It would not be an altogether unpleasant life. (pp. 138-9)

Krishna is even more his creator's *persona* in *Amrita* than Henry
Tilney is Jane Austen's in *Northanger Abbey*, for not only do
his wit and good sense voice Ruth Jhabvala's own consistent
attitudes to pretentiousness and sentimentality, but as a young
Indian recently returned from study abroad he finds himself
locked in a conflict with his native land that mirrors her struggle
with India:

> He hated the uncomplaining poverty, the apathy he saw all
> round him, in the streets, the bazaars, on the steps of the
> temples. He hated the servants who took it for granted that
> he was the master, and that it was their life's duty to do
> his menial work for him. He hated the beggars and the
> insolence with which they made it clear that they belonged
> to this society, had every right to exist in it. He hated
> —perhaps most of all, because it hemmed him in all the time
> and threatened to engulf him — the complacency of his own
> class, the civil service mind, the stolid satisfaction with
> routine work, with salary and position for ever fixed, with
> yawning pleasures in once-English clubs. He hated the policy
> of intimidation on which the whole system seemed to rest
> — the instinctive subservience to superiors and instinctive
> bullying of social inferiors. He hated the frank immorality
> of business and the unashamed dishonesty of shopkeepers.
> He hated the women because they were ignorant and
> innocent and submissive. He hated the heat which

undermined and insulted his vigour. He hated — hated
everything .... (pp. 59-60)

On first returning from England, Krishna had sneered at the
melancholy of a good deal of Bengali verse: he found Bengali
lyrics 'facile and sentimental,' demonstrating only 'how shallow
and tinselled was the Indian soul that took delight in them'
(p. 63). Krishna's 'hate' for India gradually settles into
acceptance. Although surrender to melancholy (to which the
beauty of the Indian scene offers a perpetual invitation) is a
tendency which must, in Ruth Jhabvala's fictional world, be
countered with good sense by the characters of real worth in
her novels, Krishna finds that after four years in India Bengali
lyrics have regained their power to move him, 'and sometimes,
when he heard a good one, tears came into his eyes' (p. 63).
Scornful as he had been of his old friends' obvious contentment
(as good civil servants) to become 'a solid part of Indian society
(p. 252), Krishna's decision to ask Amrita to marry him is an
act of acceptance, not only of India, but of his own belonging
there (pp. 268-9).

The doubts and ambiguous uncertainties expressed by
Krishna in the brief and very important Chapter 37 are
repeated, much more powerfully stated yet still unresolved, in
Ruth Jhabvala's essay, "Myself in India". Acceptance is not easy
for Krishna; and ultimately it is not a rational line of argument
but a memory of Amrita 'walking towards him ... across the
moon-flooded lawn, enfolded in her sari, silver-lighted, sharply
shadowed' (p. 269) that brings him to it. There are suggestions
of weakness, of a mere giving-in, in Krishna's acceptance of
India that are impossible to overlook. We will recall them when,
after the satiric comedy of *The Nature of Passion* and the
affectionate humour of *The Householder*, disillusionment with
India casts its shadow over *Get Ready for Battle*, never
thereafter to leave Ruth Jhabvala's work in fiction. Within the
context of *Amrita*'s major theme, however, and gaining stature
and authority from the heroine's similar change of attitude,
Krishna's final resolution appears to indicate that he has
matured in mind and spirit to a point at which he can accept
the conditions of life in modern India without revolt, regret,
hypocrisy or slavishness.

Two satiric portraits of minor characters lend depth to

Krishna's change of attitude towards India. One of these is of a young Indian recently returned from study abroad who wishes to establish a magazine that will revitalise India's cultural world. Krishna meets him on a visit to Calcutta:

A young man, the son of a multi-millionaire government contractor, aged twenty-three and just back from America, with an American accent, a pink nylon shirt and a lot of ideas ... said he had been shocked on his return to India by the ignorance he found among the so-called intelligentsia; they were, he said, completely out of touch with modern ... Art and Literature. His magazine was intended to stir up this pool of intellectual stagnation. The educated, he said, tapping his signet ring, were going to be educated: they were going to be taught a thing or two about Modern Art and Literature. He had gathered about him a large and ever-growing group of young men — M.A. students, most of them, from modest homes — all very keen about Modern Art and Literature. They listened to him eagerly, admired his American accent, his advanced ideas and his father's money, and wished that their parents, too, could have sent them to a foreign University instead of only to the Calcutta colleges. (pp. 250-51)

The seemingly casual allusions to such signs of the would-be reformer's affluence as his accent, his ring, his shirt and his inherited wealth indicate the true worth of his 'criticism' of India; his is the pseudo-intellectual world of which Viddi longs to be a part in *The Nature of Passion*. Krishna's encounter with this young man enables him to glance back ironically at what he had been himself on his return to India. 'He laughed at himself ... and then thought only of going back to Delhi as soon as it was decently possible' (p. 251).

The second portrait Ruth Jhabvala provides as a foil for her characterization of Krishna is that of Professor Hoch, the first Westerner to appear in her fiction. 'A short rotund German with long grey hair and a little red beard', the Professor 'had lived in India for twenty-five years and prided himself on his Hindustani; though he had never yet realised that his German accent rendered it unintelligible' (p. 37). Professor Hoch is an expert on India's art and culture, 'a practised lecturer' (p. 40) and 'enthusiastic exponent of 5000 years of Cultural Heritage'

(p. 37), who is constantly 'called upon to show beautiful Culture to the Embassies' in Delhi (p. 39). Typical of his efforts on these occasions is the inspirational idea he produces for the Ladies' Council Garden Party Pageant:

> 'Our Pageant must show the beauty and simplicity of Indian village life ... We must show our women at the village well, the simple grace of their movements as they draw up the water or go about their household tasks, their unselfconscious dignity, the sublime rhythm of their gait'. (p. 39)

Professor Hoch's ideas are as beautiful and as remote from reality as Dr. Hochstadt's platitudes in *A Backward Place* will be. Ruth Jhabvala uses a gruff woman economist named Dr. Mukherji, a fellow-guest with the Professor at Tarla Mathur's luncheon party, to expose them for what they are. A dyed red beard provides an outward symbol of the falseness of the stance and the attitudes adopted by Hoch as interpreter of the Indian scene, a type of emphasis that Ruth Jhabvala discards in her later portraits of 'experts' on India: for example, Esmond Stillwood in *Esmond in India* and Dr. Hochstadt in *A Backward Place*. The activities of Hoch and the returned reformer interconnect and balance each other, lending validity to Krishna's point of view in a contrivance that gives early indication of Ruth Jhabvala's liking for a symmetrical structure: the reader learns that 'Professor Hoch of Delhi has consented to contribute a series of articles on The Influence of the Paris School on Modern Indian Painting' to the reformer's magazine (p. 251), and sees Krishna turn down his offer of a post as Assistant Editor before returning to Delhi.

While some traits possessed by Hari, Krishna and Amrita need to be seen as generally arising out of their 'traditional' upbringing, others — more personal and individual — plunge them in difficulties. Amrita's quietness is deceptive. It hides a resolution and strength of will that emerge in her firm resistance to her mother's duplicity and the tyranny of her grandfather. It hides deep and turbulent feelings: Prema is quite mistaken in deciding that 'this girl was not very interesting to talk to. She probably did not have any deep feelings' (p. 67). Unfailingly polite, Amrita avoids hurting Hari, feigns interest in Prema's servant-problems and thanks her uncle, Vazir Dayal

Mathur, for advice she knows to be selfishly given (p. 90). She
is, therefore, all the more impressive when she takes the
initiative and firmly, though with characteristic gentleness,
expresses her individual point of view. She courageously
opposes Pandit Saxena:

> 'May we take it as an indication,' her grandfather said, 'that
> he wishes to renounce all his pretensions to connection with
> our family?'
>
> Love and despair made Amrita bold, even before her
> grandfather.
>
> 'Perhaps, Grandfather,' she said, 'but I do not think it
> means he wishes to renounce *me*.' (p. 121)

When pressed by her mother to submit to the wishes of her
family, Amrita is silent ; but unlike Hari's in similar
circumstances, hers is not the silence of assent or of
prevarication:

> Amrita saw no point in any answer she could make : she
> knew they would listen to no words except words of
> submission. And she was not prepared to submit. (p. 122)

The plot furnishes a series of events and incidents — the
embattled family conferences on both sides, the mischievous
interference and unreliable withdrawal of Vazir Dayal Mathur,
the strategies employed by Radha and Prema —which function
as tests by which the strength of the love between Amrita and
Hari is tried. In both — though Amrita's courage and resolution
are shown to be far greater than her lover's — that strength
is found wanting, and Amrita and Hari retire with relief into
more promising relationships.

The gradual shift in the focus of Amrita's affections from Hari
to Krishna is delicately portrayed — so subtly, indeed, that it
has frequently been overlooked.[8] Amrita, in love with Hari but
still more with the idea of love, has become accustomed to
Krishna's company as a lodger in her mother's house, and does
not pause to examine the implications of her wish to be seen
by him 'when she was nicely dressed' (p. 152), or of her shame
at being seen by him at a restaurant in the company of Hari
and his friend Vaidya. The latter incident and the feelings of
annoyance and shame it provokes in Krishna and Amrita
respectively indicate — though not to them — that each places

an unusual value on the other's good opinion. Amrita becomes aware of Krishna's importance in her life only when she learns that he is planning to leave Delhi. This interview (pp. 163-4) delicately brings out the honesty of Amrita's nature. The news shocks her. She takes time to come to terms with the loss of her friend and confidant. She has not yet realised the true meaning of her concern — that she has been falling, without suspecting it, in love with Krishna.

When Amrita next meets Hari and misses in herself 'the usual sudden stab of love' at the sight of him (p. 172), she puts the change in her feelings down to physical strain and weariness. When Krishna leaves for Calcutta, Amrita misses him constantly and feels her need of him (p. 217). Her reticence in saying so contrasts amusingly with her mother's lack of it, for Radha acts like a neglected sweetheart: 'He could have sent a telegram, Radha sulked' (p. 217). Amrita begins to long for a letter from the absent Krishna (p. 234) and feels guilty at her discovery that the thought of Hari married to someone else causes her no pain (p. 234). She indulges fancies of Krishna's return to Delhi: 'She would look up and there he would be' (p. 263). She even hurries away from her last meeting with Hari so that she can meet the postman at half past two: 'She wanted to know quickly if there was a letter from Calcutta' (p. 272). During the whole of this last interview neither Amrita nor Hari can keep their thoughts focussed on the other. Amrita dismisses the thought of Hari with a casual shrug and 'almost ran to the bus-stop, she was in such a hurry to get home' (p. 275).

Amrita's characteristic reticence is matched by Krishna's, although, ironically, she believes she has been 'taught' by several years' acquaintance with him that 'he was not ... very good at hiding his feelings' (p. 61). This judgement is proved wrong when Krishna, falling in love with her, is forced by Amrita into the role of confidant and go-between in her love affair with Hari without her ever suspecting the nature of his feelings for her. Krishna's scrupulous sense of honour places him at a severe disadvantage in his interviews with the emotional Hari, for while the latter can openly show his distress at being persistently questioned and his actions subjected to the ruthless application of logic, Krishna's deeper disquiet cannot be displayed so freely. His true feelings are brilliantly captured by Ruth Jhabvala through the use of seemingly inconsequential detail:

'But how can I leave Delhi? My whole family is here, my mother, my sisters, my brothers, how can I leave them?'

'Why not?' ...

'My family will never let me go.'

'Then go without asking them,' Krishna said ...

'How can I go? My family —'

'But if you stay here, they will make you marry the other girl.'

Hari buried his head in his hands and moaned. 'Love,' he said; 'what does not the heart suffer for love.'

Krishna undid all the buttons of his shirt and fanned himself with the menu. It was intolerably hot. (pp. 140-42)

Amrita and Krishna have in common an ironic habit of speech and thought which furnishes a link between them of which they are themselves unconscious. They have also in common the fact that they do not use irony lightly: with both it is essentially a last resort, a mask for deep emotions (such as those of anger or disappointment), and shows itself invariably as politeness. In this they are comparable to the Nawab of Khatm in *Heat and Dust*, a man of noble birth and mind who is most studiously courteous when he has been most deeply offended or irritated. They direct their irony on occasion at Hari who, predictably, does not grasp the implications of what is being said. We have already seen Krishna resort to irony, irritated beyond bearing by Hari's sentimental insincerities (see page 28). Amrita uses irony to cover her anger when Hari disappoints her by his insensitivity:

'I will kill myself. I will pluck my own heart out.'

'Yes Hari,' she said. 'But you have to speak first with a man in the Pushtu section.'

'Yes,' he agreed sadly. 'Please tell me, Amrita, you are angry with me?'

She looked away from him. She was afraid that at any moment she might burst into tears.

'No,' she said very quietly, 'I am not angry with you ...'

'... But really you are not angry with me?'

She shook her head; she did not trust herself to speak.

'Then I am happy again,' he said, and broke into a pleased smile.

'Hurry,' she said, with an irony that was quite lost on him,
'or he will go away.' (p. 96)

In order to bring her lovers finally together, Ruth Jhabvala
interestingly uses an eighteenth century fictional device that
is true, at the same time, to Indian social realities: a letter that
solves all problems and clears up all uncertainties. Krishna
writes to Amrita from Calcutta, to tell her that he loves her.
The reader is not permitted to see the text of this letter but
left to surmise its nature from the intensity of the feeling he
has watched accumulating undisclosed during Krishna's last
weeks with Amrita, in Delhi, from Krishna's conviction that his
message would be more 'easily' conveyed in a letter than in an
actual meeting with Amrita, 'with her there before him, her
hands moving and the changes of expression on her face visible
to him' (p. 253), and from the effect that the letter has on Amrita
when she reads it in Delhi. Rapture makes her pace the lawn
with the letter in her hand and circle between hedge and
plantain tree, distressing her mother's cook by forgetting to eat
her dinner (p. 281). Such delicate reticence on the author's part
and her introduction at this emotional moment of a touch of
ironic comedy do full justice to the characters of the lovers,
both of whom are inclined to hide their feelings from the world
and often resort to irony as mask or shield. Such a subtle
adaptation of the epistle to her special needs in *Amrita* is one
among numerous instances of the way Ruth Jhabvala regards
(and successfully employs) literary modes and models drawn
from East and West as starting-points rather than as
boundaries for her own art.

Amrita displays many features that are reminiscent of stage
comedies of manners. A resemblance to the kind of farce in
which the denouement is all is touched off from the very start
by Ruth Jhabvala's introduction (omitted in the second edition)
of a 'cast' of characters in which only the social status or family
connections of each personality are mentioned. The important
functions of Krishna as Amrita's confidant are deliberately
masked by his creator, who describes him merely as a 'paying
guest' in Amrita's house and lists him among 'Other
Characters', all of them minor. This helps the reader keep the
characters' complicated social and familial relationships to one
another in clear focus throughout the action of the 'play',

without betraying its conclusion. In later novels, such as *A New Dominion*, a description of a cast of characters will, while still relating each individual to a specific social background, become not merely deceptive in the context of the novel as it unfolds (which is the case with Krishna in *Amrita*) but subtly ironic.

Ruth Jhabvala manipulates the plot to create awareness in the reader that certain incidents and conversations are occurring simultaneously. Chapter 24 begins: 'And while all this was going on ...' (p. 172); Chapter 37: 'Meanwhile Krishna was still lying in his room ...' (p. 268); Chapter 38: 'The day of the wedding was so near now ...' (p. 270). The three interconnected plots of the novel — Amrita's discovery that her love for Krishna is returned, Hari's joyful wedding with Sushila Anand, and the Saxenas' benevolent plans for Amrita's future — reach their happy conclusions on the evening of the very same day, as Radha (leaving Amrita at home where she receives, and glories in, Krishna's letter) sits tranquilly in her father's garden making plans with her sisters for Amrita's future happiness, and listens without knowing it to the wedding music that accompanies Hari on his ceremonial journey to become Sushila's bridegroom. The effect is one of continuous, integrated and lively action. The novel sweeps along, enlivened by vigorous dialogue and colourful, amusing incident, to its happy ending: the reader familiar with stage comedies from the pen of Goldsmith or Sheridan almost expects that the final page will furnish an epilogue 'spoken' by Krishna or Prema, expressing the author's wish to send her audience away amused and instructed, whatever their views on marriage might be.

Other features reminiscent of comic drama include the stressing of strong visual contrasts among certain characters who frequently appear together on the novel's 'stage': Tarla Mathur is 'thin and dried-up with her hair cut short and permanently waved into precise folds' (p. 12), while her sister Mira is 'very fat and very soft', indolent and good-humoured (p. 12). Idle, childless and wealthy, Prema is constantly contrasted with her younger sister Mohini who is burdened with domestic chores, insufficient means and a superfluity of children. Such a careful observation of the rules of the stage tends on occasion to make puppets of the novel's characters: Radha, for instance, is manipulated time and again to provide comic interludes, making a slovenly 'breakfast' out of a frying-pan on page 160 and deliberately overdressing for her visit to the Sahni family on page 165. She affects to scorn Tarla's modern ways (p. 13), but urges her own daughter to cut her beautiful hair short — 'it is very fashionable' (p. 26). Her lively exchanges with her father, sisters and brother-in-law provide some of the novel's most entertaining moments, but to gain these Ruth Jhabvala sacrifices verisimilitude and even credibility, by endowing Radha with a crudeness of speech and behaviour inconsistent with the dignity of the Saxena family of which she is a member.[9]

A particularly interesting aspect of *Amrita* is that while the characters of Radha and Prema are satirized in keeping with the active parts they play in the 'family matchmaking and stratagem' of its plot, as well as in the novel's exposure of sentimentality, both emerge as realistic, vigorous personalities in their own right. Despite certain inconsistencies in her characterization Radha retains her vitality because of other inconsistencies, stemming primarily from her confused relationship with her late husband and her ambivalent memory of him. Radha's marriage with Nirad Chakravarty had always been considered by her family 'as something of a calamity. But it was all so long ago that she had chosen to forget' (p. 36). Her view of herself and of her marriage is characteristically confused: frequently declaring her respect for her late husband's memory, dusting his photographs as a daily ritual and praising the cause of Indian independence to which he had given his strength and his substance, Radha still regards the atmosphere of her father's house as 'the air she had been born to breathe' (p. 9), and secretly resents the fact that her husband's patriotism has deprived her of diamond necklaces and motorcars comparable to those possessed by her sisters (p. 25). In this regard Radha may be seen as a preliminary sketch for the character of Lakshmi in *Esmond in India*, who shares a good many of Radha's life experiences as well as her capacity for envy, resentment and self-deception; like Radha's, Lakshmi's idea of what her husband might have achieved after Independence is quite mistaken.

Flowing directly out of Radha's experience of marriage outside her own community, and a result of her suppressed desire to be regarded as a part of her father's family rather than of her late husband's, are her spectacular show of disapproval at

Amrita's 'working girl' status, and her scornful dismissal of
Amrita's salary as 'those miserable few rupees' (p. 27); she does
not, we notice, actually prevent Amrita leaving for work at the
radio station. Similarly, Radha dislikes the connotations of the
word *lodger* which imply the existence of a business-like,
possibly even penny-pinching, landlady; she insists that
Krishna Sen Gupta's status in her house is that of a 'paying
guest' (p. 26). Radha furnishes her daughter, in fact, with a
daily reminder of the fate met by many young people of good
family who set themselves adrift in a convention-ridden society
by marrying into a class or community unconnected with their
own.

From the novel's first page, Radha is contrasted with her slim
pale, quiet daughter, and even though this first description is
limited to the two ladies' physical appearance as they drive in
a tonga to the Saxena residence, Radha's vigorous personality
speaks through its various elements: her thighs are 'large' and
'authoritative', and 'push' against her sari (normally one of the
world's most graceful — and restricting — garments). This is
clearly a formidable woman; and yet, as she meditates on the
immediate problem of finding a husband for Amrita, a softer
and more vulnerable side emerges:

> Feelings could come afterwards, after marriage; and with a
> little inward sigh she recalled that feelings before and after
> marriage were inclined to be very different. Not, as she always
> very hastily answered herself when such thoughts came up,
> that her own marriage ... had not been a happy one; but,
> nevertheless, it could not be denied that her feelings about
> (her husband) before marriage were very different from those
> that came after. And this always prompted the thought that
> supposing her parents had chosen for her instead of allowing
> her to have her own choice: supposing that they had chosen
> somebody of the same community and with the same social
> background as her own, someone who could have given her
> the kind of life to which she had been brought up; even if
> she had not at first been able to love the man they had
> chosen, would it not have been possible for her feelings to
> have changed after marriage and for love to have awakened,
> just as with Nirad it had — well not died then, but changed,
> yes love had changed —? (p. 214)

Such wistfulness links Radha, notwithstanding their outward differences, with Amrita. The inconsistencies in her character that result from her functions as matchmaker and satirical target dwindle into very minor flaws as Radha develops an impressively realistic vigour through the reader's perception of her psychological condition. Her wishful thinking, her self-deception, her delight in intrigue, and her vitality resist being pushed into rigid patterns and help to build an energetic personality that awakens the reader's sympathy, irritation ... and affection. It does not surprise us that Krishna in far off Calcutta, discovering his mother separated from him by time and the habit of years,

> found himself ... longing for Radha; for she at least would rush at one with all the responses and more that one might ask for; and if one did not ask, still she would rush; and however irritating her forthcomingness might be, it was at any rate, he felt now, more relaxing than his mother's attitude of complete withdrawal. (p. 253)

Prema is important in the scheme of the novel as a whole, for several reasons. First, her conscious and blatant materialism teaches Amrita that unwesternized 'Indianness' is by no means invariably synonymous with unostentatious simplicity: Amrita 'had not expected Hari's sister to be so ... *lavishly* dressed' (p. 66). Secondly, Prema's unsatisfactory marriage to Suri, a wealthy Punjabi businessman, stands as a permanent comment on marriage itself, contrasting now with Hari's romantic dreams of Amrita, now with his happy expectations of physical fulfilment with Sushila. Thirdly, it is Prema's strength of will that pulls Hari away from Amrita and pushes him towards Sushila, that forces the Anands against their wishes to advance the wedding day, finally ensures that the marriage takes place. Prema enters the novel as a self-indulgent eater of sweetmeats and reader of magazine romances. She leaves it having added to these traits a new sense of her personal power: she has subdued the older and much more experienced Mrs Anand in open confrontation, exercised her 'rights' as elder sister in a traditional family and found that they work and add to her own consequence, and developed (or is in the process of developing) a mature resignation to her husband's philandering.

Prema's materialism and insensitivity are evident in her

undisguised contempt for Amrita who, she says, 'came on the bus and ... told me herself they had only one servant' (p. 81). Her claims to know what life is all about — 'I know; I can read people's characters like I can read a book' (p. 71) — carry ironic overtones, for Prema reads only pulp magazines and romantic novels. (The well-meaning comment with which Amrita courteously deprecates her own lack of interest in Prema's preferred reading — 'I am afraid I have not many books' (p. 67) — merely increases Prema's contempt for her gentle guest.) Prema is the sad, neglected heroine of her own life until Hari's marriage gives her new interests and responsibilities. Her strong personality emerges in this new situation, and she prepares to play her proper role in life as eldest daughter and elder sister: 'But you need not worry yourself, Mataji,' she assures her fretful mother, 'as long as I live, Kaka will not marry this girl' (p. 81). Prema is the representative, in *Amrita*, of the traditional Indian extended family. 'The women I saw did not seem like slaves,' Radha tells Tarla after her visit to the Sahni household: 'we ourselves, I am ashamed to say, were powerless; yes powerless ... But you see, the boy's family had only to come and all was well. I think such a system is very good, and I am only sorry that it is lost among us' (p. 193). It is Prema who has provoked this praise, and personally demonstrated the strength of the system. Radha's view of the Sahni family provides amusing insight into her characteristic inclination to bend the truth into pleasing and flattering shapes. 'They are really very respectable people,' she assures Tarla, 'simple people of course, not our class, but really very respectable. They realise fully that a connection with our family would be quite out of the question; they are very well aware of their place in life' (p. 193). This could almost be Jane Austen's Emma Woodhouse talking of Mr Elton or of Robert Martin; and like Mr Elton, Prema would certainly have disputed (had she been able to hear it) such a concept of social 'respectability'. It would have startled Radha to learn that Prema thinks her lovely Amrita 'stupid' and plain, and that one meeting between the young women had been sufficient to provoke protective sisterly advice from her to Hari: 'Kaka ... this girl is not the girl for you.' (p. 70)

Ruth Jhabvala provides effective contrasts for Amrita, Radha and Prema in a number of satiric portraits of women. Tarla Mathur, the first of her studies of Indian committee-women,

finds 'rich compensation for an unsatisfactory husband' (p. 36)
in the power struggles for leadership and influence that appear
to be a feature (in Ruth Jhabvala's novels) of India's social
service organizations. Radha's personality gains vitality and
warmth when it is contrasted with Tarla's 'severe' speech (p. 12)
and habitual air of disdain. Tarla affects modernity and adopts
'liberated' views on education, marriage and working women,
but she is quite as class-conscious as Radha and their father:
'It is good for a girl to mix with other classes of society ... It
broadens the outlook' (p. 13) is a characteristic remark. Tarla's
closest associate is Lady Ram Prashad Khanna, a woman 'who
always, on all occasions and under all circumstances, made
a point of being charming' (p. 38). Dedicated, as the castlist
for *To Whom She Will* indicates, to 'social work', she uses Indian
culture as a means of self-aggrandizement, but her vague
allusions to 'our beautiful Culture', 'something very symbolical'
(p. 38) and the 'charming' Gupta and Moghul periods (p. 39)
show that she knows little about it. Her knowledge of what she
terms India's 'great History' has been gleaned from Professor
Hoch, the *Illustrated Weekly of India* and the *Sunday Statesman*
(p. 42). Timing her move for the moment before the Mathurs'
luncheon comes to an end, Lady Ram Prashad contrives to
enlist the tireless Tarla as her champion in getting herself
elected President of the Ladies' Committee for the Teaching of
Handicrafts, without ceasing to be charming and still 'seemingly
unconcerned' (p. 43) about the whole affair. We cannot wonder
that when Professor Hoch compliments her on her experience,
her influence and her diplomatic manner (p. 44), Lady Ram
Prashad modestly lowers her head but does not contradict him.
Tarla and her friend are fore-runners of the affluent social
workers in *Get Ready for Battle*, who are similarly subjected
to Ruth Jhabvala's satiric lash. Lady Ram Prashad will reappear
as Mrs Kaul, the organising spirit of the 'Culture Dais' in *A
Backward Place*, a far more subtle portrait than any of these,
and one in which irony replaces satire.

Mira, the youngest of Amrita's female relations, bears a strong
resemblance to Jane Austen's kindly but selfish character in
Mansfield Park, Lady Bertram. Mira is a creature of physical
instincts. She does not think deeply, and her 'opinion' on the
marriage question is characteristically uncomplicated and
conventional:

She herself, as far as she ever thought about it, was in perfect agreement with the principle of arranged marriages. She considered that it was the parents' duty to find suitable mates for their children; the young people, poor things, could not be expected to do it for themselves ... That was the way things were done; the way they had to be done. Just see what had happened to Radha, who had chosen her own husband and in consequence did not even possess a motor-car. (p. 215)

Her lack of logic, and the rhythm and phrasing characteristic of her speech are admirably captured in the last sentence. Mira's self-indulgence and slow wit contribute to the novel's entertainment. She adds nothing to its plot except that she does her best to prevent open hostility between her two sisters (pp. 13-14). She also contrasts in a limited way with Tarla's energetic activity and with Radha's shabbiness and perpetual economies. A family resemblance of a kind emerges in the selfishness that characterizes the Saxena family, manifesting itself in the various forms of the old man's tyranny, Radha's self-pity, Mira's greed and Tarla's preoccupation with her career as a social worker.

Selfishness, the chief target of Ruth Jhabvala's satire in *Amrita*, is also a rich source of comedy. Hari hopes 'he would not have to listen to (Prema's) sorrows: he had come to talk about his own' (p. 19); when Hari claims to have experienced the sorrows of love and invites his sister's sympathy, Prema is 'a trifle grudging' (p. 21). Every character in the novel (including Krishna and Amrita) is blinded to life's realities by a preoccupation with the self. Hari and Amrita admire in each other the qualities they believe wanting in themselves: he admires her Westernized background, she his simple 'Indianness'. While he tells her how much he loves her, she thinks 'about how much she loved him' (p. 30). When she tells him of her burning desire to submerge her despised Westernized ways in the 'Indianness' of his family, he takes refuge (from what he does not understand and fears to examine rationally) in murmuring romantic words of love (pp. 32-3). Without realizing it, each is lovingly exploiting the other.

Chapter 15 furnishes an admirable example of the way Ruth Jhabvala wrests comedy from selfishness without distorting the realism of her picture of Indian social arrangements. When the

Anands call formally on the Sahnis, everyone except Hari knows that a marriage is in the air, and that they must all work harmoniously to bring it about. (By a neat ironic touch there is a wedding being celebrated nearly, so that the marriage music provides an appropriate accompaniment to the negotiations.) The contribution each person present makes to that total harmony strikes, however, a separate note of selfishness. Prema's scornful remarks about the poverty of the family celebrating the wedding indirectly emphasise her own wealth and challenge Mrs Anand to provide Sushila with an appropriately large dowry and a magnificent wedding when she marries Hari. Mrs Anand, replying, scores a double hit: by showing that she has noted the differences in consequence between Prema and her younger sister Mohini she hints that Prema's wealth may be pretended; by stating that weddings are best celebrated simply, she prepares the ground for less expensive arrangements when Sushila is married. Hari's mother counters this with the seemingly innocent statement that a girl's wedding is her most precious memory, thus at once reminding Mrs Anand of her obligation to spend lavishly and indicating that *she* had done her duty by both daughters. Mrs Anand declares her intention to give Sushila an unforgettable wedding but, this major point having been lost to the Sahnis, she now turns to another front by angling for — and getting — the frankly masculine attention of Prema's husband, Suri. Prema, however, shows that she is capable of dealing with this new attack. Agreeing with her enemy, she adds that a wedding must be well celebrated, for 'the Lord knows what is to come after': an oblique swipe at her husband, misunderstanding which (and unconsciously increasing her childless elder sister's irritation) Mohini remarks that 'bearing children is also no joke'. The conversation has thus moved by stages from marriage to children, and the Anands have pledged themselves to marry Sushila well: from the main point of view, the visit has been an unqualified success. But the reader has been made aware of the private fears and resentments that haunt the individual members of this sociable group, and is able to forecast not only the wedding that is to take place, but the conflicts that will inevitably accompany it. The entire interview is presented on the level of the skilled manoeuvring that is a traditional part of marriage 'arrangements', and despite the hostility beginning to surface between Mrs Anand and Prema, the families have 'come as near to an understanding as they had meant to' (p. 105). It is one of Ruth Jhabvala's triumphs in this early novel that psychological and moral truths about individual character are clinically dissected in scene after scene without destroying social verisimilitude, or disturbing the comic equilibrium of the work as a whole.

Hari's deception of Amrita becomes yet another form of selfish manipulation in the novel: he feeds on her sympathy and her waning strength, while the limitations of his nature prevent his giving her any happiness in return beyond what she can manufacture for herself out of an accidental look or word (p. 173). The Anand grandmother's self-importance rests on the efficacy of her prayers and the holiness of her life: she considers that she has a direct line to God. Paying off a lifetime's grudge against her daughter-in-law (who has borne three girls only, and no son) she chooses a very public moment just before the wedding to prophesy that the young couple will never have a son because 'the proper rites and ceremonies have been neglected' (p. 228). There is something equally twisted and malevolent in Vazir Dayal Mathur's selfish 'generosity' to his niece Amrita, which arises

> out of a mixture of spite against her grandfather and a desire to show himself magnanimous and free-thinking. Vazir Dayal's thoughts were not on her but, as usual, on himself. (p. 90)

The deliberate attempts at destruction of the happiness of helpless young people by unscrupulous or self-deluding adults for entirely selfish motives is never wholly comic in *Amrita*. The older members of the Saxena, Sahni and Anand families are drawn with a corrosive irony quite different from the gentle humour that illumines the several self-deceptions of Amrita, Hari and Krishna.

One such elder is Vazir Dayal Mathur, Amrita's elegant and wealthy uncle, who is compared by Professor Hoch, expert on Indian culture, to the 'great Moghul Emperors' (p. 41). This flattering allusion pleases Mathur, who

> always thought of himself as having been born in the wrong age. He kept, in a special drawer in his dressing-room, a

costume of the Moghul period, a long coat of cloth of gold,
pale pink silk leggings, a turban studded with pearls. He even
had a pair of ear-rings. Sometimes he dressed himself up
in these things, sat on a carpet in front of his full-length
mirror and read Urdu poetry aloud to himself. (p. 41)

This is comic, but only on the surface. There is an unhealthy,
unnatural element in Mathur's attitudinising that he himself
points out in a characteristic moment of spiteful self-satire: 'I
am what you would call a decadent' (p. 73) he remarks to his
father-in-law, deliberately goading Pandit Saxena 'into a state
of chronic irritation' (p. 73). Tarla regards this modern avatar
of Shahjehan as 'an unsatisfactory husband' (p. 36), and finds
in social service and ladies' committees a focus for her energetic
'passion' (p. 36). Love has never warmed the Mathur household,
whose air-conditioned atmosphere is 'cool as the smell of ice-
cream' (p. 34) and whose chilly splendours are the expression
of Mathur's 'irresistible artistic instincts' (p. 35). He is useful
to his creator in occasionally puncturing Pandit Saxena's self-
importance:

> 'I have spoken to her once,' Pandit Ram Bahadur said. 'I
> have told her that she cannot marry this boy. She must
> regard that as final.'
> 'The word of God,' Vazir Dayal audibly murmured. (p. 75)

Some sympathy for Mathur is awakened in the reader on this
account, and because his whisky-drinking and general
'decadence' so clearly result from a useless life (that has not,
however, deprived his conversation of wit, nor steeped it in self-
pity). He impudently suggests that his father-in-law might
thank him for the lucky chance by which Tarla — unlike her
fertile sisters — does not 'also regale us with ... experiences
in pregnancy' (p. 74); he tells Amrita that her aunt's interest
in social work 'is her consolation for me' (p. 88). When, however,
he mischievously offers to pay Amrita's passage and Hari's to
Britain because 'it is my fancy' (p. 130), it becomes evident that
Mathur's delusions of Moghul grandeur are beginning to emerge
from the privacy of his dressing-room. In the light of day they
do not appear attractive. His wilful, if drunken, disruption of
Tarla's tea party for Lady Ram Prashad Khanna, like his
(fortunate) failure to keep his promise of financial assistance

to Amrita, is an outward sign of a progressive inward despair and deterioration. This detailed depiction of Vazir Dayal Mathur gives early promise of studies yet to come of personalities caught up in the process of decay: Esmond Stillwood in *Esmond in India*, Etta in *A Backward Place*, and the Nawab of Khatm in *Heat and Dust*.

Other interesting studies of minor characters exist in *Amrita*. One of these is Ruth Jhabvala's depiction of the Anands, a pair of which the wife — in contrast to her husband, 'a dried-up, rather dark little man' (p. 103) — is built on generous, even magnificent lines. His worship of Suri's business success contrasts with her frankly physical awareness of Suri as a man. The link that is established between Suri and Mrs Anand as the marriage negotiations progress, although limited by what is and is not possible within the conventions of Indian social and family life is an earnest of Ruth Jhabvala's ability to penetrate deeply into the life around her. Equally interesting is the portrait of Mohini, Hari's younger sister, a character both comic (in her fruitless efforts to discipline her wildly mischievous children) and pathetic (in her fate, which is, apparently, to be the family brood mare). Mohini represents the lowest level of sensibility in the novel: her mind cannot rise above the endless drudgery of childbearing and domesticity to which fate has bound her, and she has little to contribute to family discussions beyond silence and a giggle, or to family aspirations beyond her own resentment at Prema's better fortune.

In a different category from these comic, but essentially compassionate portraits is Ruth Jhabvala's brief caricature of Dr Mukherji a modern Indian intellectual and a 'brilliant economist' who shows her disregard for those less gifted than she is by being morose and unsociable (p. 38). Her function is to expose the full-blown pretensions of the other characters: thus, when Professor Hoch rhapsodises windily on the idyllic grace of Indian village women, Dr Mukherji adds a typical post-script — 'And also ... village women in labour, with the female scavenger standing by with a piece of glass to cut the naval cord' (p. 40). When Tarla describes the abolition of child marriage as 'the greatest step forward' in the advance of Indian womanhood, Dr Mukherji makes

her second contribution to conversation: 'Last week,' she
said, 'my sweeper's daughter was married. She is twelve.'
(p. 42)

A satiric tool, Dr Mukherji is herself subjected to irony: her
remarks appear to spring not so much from concern at the state
of the poor and uneducated folk of India, but from self-conceit.
Her comments reveal her knowledge of the India outside the
Mathurs' elegant drawing-room but her behaviour is as much
a selfish affectation as is her host's pose as a modern Mycaenas.
Although they have this attribute in common, however, each
feels, comically, only contempt for the other:

> Only Dr Mukherji grasped her cup fully in her fist and
> emptied it in two gulps, while Vazir Dayal squeamishly looked
> the other way. (p. 42)

Her portrait of Professor Hoch indicates that at this stage of
her writing career, Ruth Jhabvala regarded her European
characters from an Indian rather than from a Western
standpoint. Hoch's dyed beard appears grotesque to Amrita, his
attempts to converse in Hindustani are ridiculed, and Dr
Mukherji treats him with contempt. There are two other
portraits of Westerners in *Amrita*, both similarly caricatured.
One is of an American visitor to India, whom Hari and Amrita
observe as she sings Schubert songs for All-India Radio:

> She stood dead straight before the microphone; one hand
> was laid on her bosom, the other held a sensible leather
> handbag. Her calves bulged above a pair of court shoes ...
> (Hari) was surprised at the rigid stance of the American lady.
> She had not moved once since she had started singing; the
> hand on the bosom and the handbag seemed fixed for all
> time. Only her mouth opened and shut. (p. 91)

The other portrait consists only of two brief sentences, but it
is one that in later work will grow until it seems to fill the entire
canvas of a Jhabvala novel for it pictures an European artiste
stranded in India:

> The violinist was a middle-aged European; he was starred
> as Rudolf, the Well-known Artiste from Vienna. He had
> receding hair and prosaic spectacles; he played listlessly
> though with determination, as if he were adding up an

> unending column of figures. (p. 54)

The three-man band at the Cavalier Restaurant of which the violinist is a member is playing 'a potpourri of Westernised Indian tunes,' and the noisy gaiety of the music contrasts with his listlessness and determination. We shall remember him when, in Ruth Jhabvala's subsequent work, we encounter Dr Ernst in "An Indian Citizen"; Mr Boekelman in "The Man with a Dog"; Peggy in "The Aliens"; Esmond Stillwood in *Esmond in India*, and other Western characters in screenplays and fiction who are doggedly making the best of lives that have turned bitter after many years in India.

The Indian characters who make brief appearances in the novel are contributors, in the main, of local colour to Ruth Jhabvala's sketches of Indian life. The staid coolie who nearly loses his life on a Delhi street (p. 9), the cigarette boy 'dressed up in blue with red braidings and a little round hat' and the sweeper who 'crouched on the floor and surreptitiously swept the crumbs from under the tables' at the Cavalier, like the 'fat Sikh in a pink turban' who 'stuffed one cake after the other into his beard and stared at Amrita' (pp. 54-5) are merely there for the sake of authenticity. They do not contribute as much to *Amrita* as do similar figures to *The Nature of Passion*; numerous beggars, servants, hotel employees and others there comment, by their silent presence, on the greed and selfishness of the principal characters. The Sikh helps, however, to underline Amrita's innate modesty and reinforce the reader's conviction that Hari is not the man for her since he does not notice

> the offensive stares that afflicted her; he had been born into a society unused to disguising its interest for the sake of politeness, and considered staring at young women a perfectly natural reflex action. He did it himself without the slightest reticence. (p. 54)

Chapter 17 provides brief sketches of the Saxena servants whose existence 'like their master's, was a succession of long empty hours' (p. 118). The coachman, the butler, the cook, the gardener and the sweepers have all been in Pandit Saxena's service for years and regard his house as their refuge, their quiet lives jolted only by occasional visits by Radha to her father,

which give them something to think about and stir themselves
for. The panwala and the coffee-house doorman (p. 142) are
mere local colour and add nothing to the story. The two girls
who walk past Hari and Krishna 'in coloured kamiz and salwar,
with pigtails swinging down their backs' (p. 142), however, do:
for Hari

> looked them up and down turned to watch them from behind
> ... instinctively and at the same time as he pondered a reply
> to Krishna's question. (p. 142)

Since the 'question' concerns the all-important matter of
whether he will accompany Amrita to England or not, the little
incident brings out the fact that Hari's affection for Amrita is
little more than a pleasant habit of thought. Similarly, Ruth
Jhabvala's realistic descriptions of the Punjabi family clans as
they gather for Hari's wedding and cram the Anands' small
house from top to bottom imbue her picture of Indian middle-
class life with bustling energy:

> Relations, determined to be in on everything connected with
> the wedding, came and settled down, whole families of them
> ... The old women prayed, the young women cooked, the
> children screeched, the men sat on the floor talking of
> business and religion ... Without their presence well in
> advance of the actual days fixed for the ceremony, the whole
> spirit of festivity would have failed. (pp. 224-5)

At a name-giving ceremony, the singing of plaintive songs and
vigorous dancing capture and sustain the mood of such a
gathering (pp. 47-50). It is in this warmly sentimental
atmosphere, appropriately enough, that Hari hears Sushila
Anand sing and the image of Amrita begins to slip from his
heart.

There is nothing in *Amrita* of the symbolic weight carried by
climate and atmosphere in Ruth Jhabvala's later novels. Even
the summer heat acts on its characters merely as 'a pleasant
and irresistible soporific' (p. 15). The physical settings in which
they move, however, are rich in carefully observed and
suggestive detail. As Hari walks from his own home to his
sister's house, he passes a row of old houses whose

respectability had already degenerated. The houses oozed

brown wounds and bulged out of doors and windows with
children and washing and the jutting ends of furniture.
Banana-peels, tomato-skins and rotting bits of vegetable lay
squashed into the dust, sniffed by skinny pariah-dogs. On
a waste patch, tiny low huts made of mud and old planks
of wood had sprung up, stuffed with too many women and
too many children, old rags, newspapers, worn-out blankets
and discarded tins. Privately owned cows walked slowly up
and down the road or sat with spread haunches, flicking their
tails. A grey bullock, belonging to no one, grazed hopefully
among the huts. (p. 19)

Not once but twice in this passage Ruth Jhabvala places
children in the same category as 'old rags', 'washing', 'worn-
out blankets and discarded tins', thereby endowing these items,
human and inanimate, with a common superfluity and
dispensability. Houses 'ooze', 'bulge', and are 'stuffed' with
unwanted human material, while stray dogs and cattle make
what they can of the 'squashed' refuse that litters the road.
Responsibility and civic consciousness, like the grey bullock,
apparently belong to no one, and old civilization has
'degenerated' into poverty and squalor. The only new growth
to be seen is the weed-like proliferation of squatters' huts and
shanties, which detract further from the declining dignity of
the older houses and stamp the entire area with the character
of a slum.

While a shortage of money creates oozing 'wounds' in the old
houses of the street, too much money seems to have equally
unhealthy effects on the architecture of a neighbouring area
in which Prema and Suri live, producing erupting 'rashes' of
grotesque fancy and pillars 'like snakes' (p. 19). On Prema's
living-room walls, facing each other, are large coloured full-
length photographs of herself and her husband, 'dressed up
in (their) best clothes' (p. 65). To the horrors of this tasteless
exhibition of newly acquired wealth, Prema herself is happily
insensible:

Prema gazed round with satisfaction. Everything, she saw,
looked new and expensive. She herself looked new and
expensive ... (p. 65)

Contrasting with these pictures of sickening squalor and sickly

wealth is the impression of dark, even musty Victorian opulence
created by the Saxena's luxurious residence. 'Heavy',
'oppressive' and 'massive' are among the words Ruth Jhabvala
uses to describe its atmosphere and furnishings; souvenirs of
European travel, some of them broken, complete the picture
of obsolete grandeur (pp. 12-15). Vazir Dayal Mathur's house
is different again: here wealth is deployed in such a way as
to recreate, where possible, the lost splendours of Moghul glory
(p. 35).

Within these various settings, life follows patterns that
contribute their distinctive qualities to the variety and
complexity of the Indian scene. At the Saxena residence, a
family lunch proceeds smoothly,noiselessly, servants waiting
on the diners at the richly appointed table. As Hari 'shovel(s)
up his food,' his mother urges him on lovingly: 'Eat, son, eat'
(p. 16). Equally strikingly and amusingly contrasted are the
rituals of afternoon tea in the households of Tarla and Prema:

> Two bearers glided to and fro over the Persian carpet, bending
> over the guests with a caressing air to offer them, from trays,
> cheese pakoras and cucumber sandwiches and triangles of
> buttered toast; while Tarla sat enthroned at a table in the
> middle of the room efficiently pouring tea into Limoges cups,
> by her knee a three-tier cake-stand with doilies bearing
> French pastries and lemon tartlets and a magnificent
> chocolate layer-cake. (p. 152)

Prema tries vainly to achieve a similar effect with the aid of
sweet-meats from Ragho Mull's, uncouth servants, and brand-
new silver spoons. (p. 68)

Careful structural balancing is evident throughout *Amrita*,
Chapter 1 (devoted to the orderly splendour of lunch in Pandit
Saxena's household) is immediately followed by a chapter in
which Hari Sahni dines Indian-style in a noisy courtyard on
a typically chaotic evening at home. Chapter 20, in which Hari
is 'booked' by Mr Anand for Sushila, is followed by Chapter 21
in which Tarla arranges for Amrita to be looked over by Lady
Ram Prashad Khanna. The conflicting plans of their families
and friends bring Hari and Amrita to Delhi railway station at
the same moment, he to greet a relation who is arriving to
attend his wedding, she to say goodbye to Krishna as he leaves
for Calcutta. The final chapter, 39, links all the novel's

characters together in final accord. Happiness all round: it is
Ruth Jhabvala's first novel, and never again will she write one
so lighthearted. Her attractive, high-principled heroine finds the
lover who understands her best and loves her most deeply, the
rejected (and rejecting) Hari finds joy in his arranged marriage,
Pandit Saxena renews his belief in his own importance, and
Radha looks forward with pleasure to bringing about the match
that has just, unknown to her, arranged itself through mutual
esteem and affection. No one (except possibly the Anand
grandmother) could be distressed at the way events have turned
out, and supporters of early, delayed, arranged and voluntary
marriages alike would find here something to justify their point
of view.

Despite the attention paid to the novel's structure, a certain
immaturity is evident in the occasional obtrusiveness of the
author's point of view. Although the visit to her grandfather's
house with which the novel opens is clearly meant to be seen
through Amrita's eyes, her distinctive point of view is only
fitfully maintained. We are told that Pandit Ram Bahadur

> sat at the head of the table and dominated his family; which
> was all that was left to him to dominate. (p. 14)

This is not Amrita's view, but that of the author/narrator. As
Hari lies dreaming of Amrita,

> a few houses away, the inevitable wedding was being
> celebrated; familiar and sentimental songs came wailing
> unendingly through a loudspeaker. (p. 17)

The songs are 'familiar' to Hari, but 'sentimental' only to the
narrator; similarly, the wedding is 'inevitable' and the songs
an 'unending wail' to the narrator, not — most emphatically
— to Hari, who enjoys social occasions, and the singing that
is a part of them. There is, in addition, a comic incongruity
in the narrative description of Mohini, pregnant with her fourth
child, occasionally sticking her head out of the cowshed to scold
her quarrelling children and threaten 'to tear them to pieces'
(p. 16), that is surely much more Jhabvala than Hari.

This weakness is compensated for in some degree by Ruth
Jhabvala's ability to enter at other times into the most intimate
understanding of her Indian characters. Her handling of Punjabi
invective is far more skilful, in my view, than (for example) Mulk

Raj Anand's in his novel, *Coolie*, where a good deal is sacrificed
in pursuit of realism. In one of *Amrita's* family scenes,

> Mohini shouted from the next room that she would peel every
> shred of skin from the children's bodies if they did not keep
> quiet. 'With my own nails!' she cried. (p. 80)

Since even as she screams, Mohini is engaged in preparing
butter-milk for these very children, the startlingly unnatural
sentiments expressed ('Tonight I tear your tongues out!' Mohini
shouted after them) are instantly placed: the reader
understands that Mohini is merely venting her feelings, perhaps
even shouting from habit. No violence is intended, and no real
violence is offered. The Punjabi wedding that closes the book
is vividly evoked through the senses of Hari, the shy and
bewildered bridegroom. His actions become mechanical, he
registers sights and sounds without being fully aware of their
import. His characteristically emotional nature — and his
fatalism — speak through every line:

> ... He walked and walked in a circle, never looking up, the
> fire so hot and people pressing round and the pandit
> chanting again, he just walked, losing count, so that he did
> not know how many times he had already been round,
> prepared if they wanted him to walk thus for ever. His cheeks
> became wet, then his neck, right inside the collar, but it took
> him some time to realise that he was crying. He went on
> walking, aware only of the heat of the fire and the wetness
> of tears, though he could hear women sobbing and one
> cracked old voice shouting that the dupatta was tied in the
> wrong way ... He had led her round the fire seven times and
> now she was his, and though he still could not see her,
> hardly even thought of her, he was suddenly so happy, he
> felt he had never been so happy in all his life. (p. 283)

The agonising self-consciousness experienced by the average
Indian citizen in the presence of a member of the Westernised
Indian elite that Eunice de Souza describes as still present in
the India of the 1970s[10] is captured most skilfully by Ruth
Jhabvala in Chapter 2, as Hari recalls his humiliating interview
with Amrita's grandfather:

'The old man looking over his steel spectacles, his precise

voice, the large imposing desk — how it had all flustered him; and, as always when he was ill at ease, his English had deserted him. Usually he spoke English quite fluently, but under such circumstances he could somehow only speak in broken and incorrect sentences. And the old man waiting for him while he groped round for, and could not find, the English word, waiting with such exaggerated, such sardonic patience — Hari shuddered and quickly slurred over the memory. (p. 21)

Pandit Ram Bahadur is using the English language in the way it was frequently used in colonial times, as a means of separating the educated and affluent from those less fortunate. Hari is made to feel most acutely the contempt with which this punctiliously courteous patrician almost certainly regards him, as a poor, young, ill-educated and unsophisticated refugee. The scene is a good example, though an early one, of Ruth Jhabvala's ability 'to project ... the social pressures which produce (her) characters, the motivating forces and value systems that drive them to be what they are'.[11]

In comparison with the economy and precision of Ruth Jhabvala's later works, *Amrita* is over-long, and unnecessarily wordy. Here too, if nowhere else, can evidence be found that English was not her native language. Discordant notes are struck in the early chapters which, being part of the narrative, cannot be always attributed to experiments in the use of Indian-English idiom, of which there are many successful examples in the novel.[12] Side by side with these uncertainties are examples of Ruth Jhabvala's early use of metaphorical language and of the rhythms and phrasing of Indian speech that give promise of the pleasures to come. 'The city lay gaunt and parched in a shroud of white heat,' runs the opening description of Tarla Mathur's magnificent reception,

But the trim lawns, the well-kept flowers of Tarla's garden blossomed and flourished like racketeers in a famine. (p. 85)

The suggestion that wealthy social workers flourish at the expense of the poor they profess to assist is reinforced by a skilful telescoping of Lady Ram Prashad Khanna's speech to imply that it contained nothing of real value:

She said how good everybody was and how hard they worked;

how their efforts were appreciated; how this Minister had
said to her only yesterday and that Minister had told her
only last week; how pleasing it all was and how
commendable; and then, with a flourish and the air of one
giving a treat long held in store, she read out a message from
the Prime Minister. (p. 86)

In *Amrita*, Ruth Jhabvala's interest is still focused on Indians
in India rather than on Western visitors, happy or unhappy.
The contest of wills that develops between Prema and
Mrs Anand is a subject she will take up again in many novels
and stories as lust, cruelty and envy, with the power-struggles
they set going, continue to attract her curious and observant
eye.

But we are still on the sunnier side of her fiction, and it is
not until *The Householder* closes on what is likely to be the
moment of the purest happiness in the married lives of Indu
and Prem that clouds begin to gather over the very pleasant
prospect that is her view of India.

Notes

1. All references in this chapter, and in this book as a whole, to Ruth
    Jhabvala's first novel are to the American edition, which (though both
    are out of print) is easier to obtain today than the British one. Despite
    the change of title, there is no difference between the two editions as
    regards text beyond the re-phrasing of a few sentences, e.g., 'Out of
    three sisters she was the only one who owned no motor car' in *To
    Whom She Will* is altered in *Amrita* to read 'Of three sisters ...'; 'a clutter
    of tastelessly chosen objects d'art' in the Saxena household is altered
    to read 'objects'; 'looking discontented' is altered to read 'discontented'
    (pp. 9, 12, 16). *Amrita* was published without the list of characters
    that preceded the text and a glossary of Indian words with a selection
    of recipes for the preparation of Indian foods that immediately followed
    it in the British edition.
2. Santha Rama Rau, *Remember the House* (Gollancz, London: 1956),
    p. 161.
3. The title is drawn from a tale in the translated Indian story-cycle of
    the *Panchatantra*:

    If she remain a maiden still
    She gives herself to whom she will.
    Then marry her in tender age,

So warns the heaven-begotten sage.

The change of title to *Amrita* suggests a deliberate shift of emphasis from the elements of social comedy and criticism in the novel to the character of the heroine as the book's true centre.

4. Renee Winegarten, "Ruth Prawer Jhabvala: A Jewish passage to India," *Midstream*, March 1974, pp. 72-9; quoted in *Contemporary Literary Criticism* (Detroit, 1975), p. 258.

5. H.M. Williams, "English writing in free India," op. cit., p. 9.

6. *Glasgow Herald* review.

7. *Yorkshire Observer* review.

8. Even, surprisingly, by Haydn Moore Williams, who (writing in 1971) found 'the sudden switch at the end of the book, when Amrita falls in love with Krishna Sen Gupta ... both sentimental and incredible': See "Strangers in a backward place: Modern India in the fiction of Ruth Prawer Jhabvala", *Journal of Commonwealth Literature* 6:1 (1971), p. 63.

9. Few Indian mothers would run the morals of their only daughter down before other members of the family: yet Radha complains to Tarla and Mira that Amrita 'does not lead a good life' (p. 12). These are flaws in Ruth Jhabvala's characterisations of Indians that disappear in later novels. In *Esmond in India*, for example, Madhuri disapproves of her daughter Shakuntala but does not disgrace her in public, enlisting her daughter-in-law Indira's help in taming Shakuntala with the utmost tactfulness — and only after Indira has shown herself to be a loyal supporter of Madhuri's intentions for the family. In *The Nature of Passion* the proposal that Nimmi cuts her hair short originates with her Parsi boy-friend, epitome of fashionable 'modernity', and shocks her conservative family.

10. E. de Souza, "The blinds drawn and the airconditioner on: The novels of Ruth Prawer Jhabvala", *World Literature Written in English* 17:1 (April 1978), p. 222.

11. Ibid., p. 221. It should be noted that Eunice de Souza finds in Ruth Jhabvala's work 'no progress towards a deepening of insights about the social forces at work in the country, no striving to understand these' (p. 219), no 'insight, analysis, or psychological depth' (p. 221). This article, which attributes to Ruth Jhabvala 'observations which always remain superficial, and a mind which consistently fails to analyse what it observes" (p. 224) adopts an approach to her fiction that I consider unrewarding and expresses a point of view with which I do not agree. It is, however, very forcefully written, and puts strongly and well a good number of the criticisms Ruth Jhabvala's work has provoked in India.

CHAPTER

III

The nature of passion
1956

If people were to talk of Usha's wedding for years to come, the memory of Nimmi's they should carry with them into their next birth. A hundred cooks and confectioners would be sitting in his house day and night to prepare for the feasting: six bands in red and gold uniforms to serenade the guests; whole streets lit up by the illuminations from his house; Delhi drained of chickens and rice and spices and sugar and ghee ... And after the wedding — for he could not stop there — after she was married, he would make her life a paradise. She should have a motor car of her own, every day a new sari, lakhs worth of jewellery, dozens of servants. At every step someone should attend her, every wish to be fulfilled before she had wished it.

> And when she went out, all the world should turn its head
> and ask 'Who is this Queen?' to be answered, 'she is the
> daughter of Lala Narayan Dass Verma'.[1]

An ability to slide her narrative voice in and out of her
characters' thoughts, imbuing it with the colours and rhythms
of their distinctive manner of speech, was a feature that
contributed much to Ruth Jhabvala's lively portraits of Radha
and Hari in *Amrita*. It is most skilfully used in *The Nature of
Passion* to explore the various aspects of the personality of
'Lalaji' (Lala Narayan Dass Verma, the Punjabi businessman
to whom belongs 'the nature of passion' which gives her second
novel its title). He is the true source of the book's vitality, his
thoughts and memories giving it warmth and vigour as he
reflects now on the way children supply 'the sounds and the
smells of a home, its soul' (p. 196), now on the life he will make
for his beloved daughter, Nimmi. His egotism frequently takes
the form (as in the passage quoted above) of sentimental
affection, endearing him to the reader. He is one among many
characters in the novel who find themselves trapped in
difficulties, and for whom the reader feels sympathy; even
occasionally, pity. His patience, sagacity and resourcefulness
invite admiration. That she is able to make him the 'hero' of
her novel and ironically locate in his morally flawed personality
the criteria by which her other characters may be judged or
exposed, indicates a considerable advance on Ruth Jhabvala's
writing of *Amrita*. For Lalaji is conspicuously guilty of the gross
dishonesty for which the idealistic Krishna Sen Gupta so
passionately 'hated' India in the earlier novel. In her portrayal
of him Ruth Jhabvala displays for the first time the sustained
ironic narrative tone that has become characteristic of her
mature style.

The Nature of Passion presents a fictional world that is,
though rich in humour, colour and interest, a symbol of
rapacity on a universal scale. The author's ironic observation
follows the corruption generated by Lalaji as it spreads to stain
every other sphere of Indian life, from officialdom (as
represented by his second son, Chandra Prakash) to the sphere
of art and culture (as represented by the friends of his youngest
son, Ved). Although there are moments in the novel when finer

feelings manage to break through the carapace of selfishness
that their life has formed around the soul of every character,
the Indian world Ruth Jhabvala pictures is morally,
intellectually and aesthetically bleak. The admirable objectivity
with which she isolates and dissects its several parts makes
it possible for us to see *The Nature of Passion* as a satiric
exposure of worldliness on the one hand, and as a celebration
of India's indestructible vitality of spirit on the other.

Objectivity is possible because the standpoint from which the
novel makes its judgments is not merely personal to its author.
Its title implies an attempt on Ruth Jhabvala's part to penetrate
the Indian psyche and express it in its own, rather than in
imported terms. The passage from the *Bhagavad Gita* that
prefaces the work, together with Dr S. Radhakrishnan's
commentary upon it, furnishes authority and a basis for her
characterisation of Lalaji as a personality inclined towards
worldliness (*rajasa*: 'the nature of passion') and therefore
engaged continually in a restless struggle to increase his share
of life's material benefits. It is her theme that the rajasa nature
leads its possessor to activities 'tainted by selfish desires and
as her plot reveals, Lalaji enjoys and deliberately works to
increase these 'tainted' activities. A moral standard of a kind
is perpetually before his eyes in the form of the clerk who works
in his city office, a restrained and calm old man

> who had steeped not only his mind in the wisdom of the
> Vedas and the Gita and all the old writings, but also his whole
> life. He was pure, withdrawn, detached. (pp. 238-9)

This is the novel's only 'yogi' who contrives, while assisting
Lalaji's business activities, to keep himself unstained by their
corruptions. His example is respected, sometimes even envied,
by Lalaji, but only as an ideal to be aspired to and perhaps
achieved ... some day. Despite occasional twinges of conscience
that remind him that 'One should be content with, indifferent
to, what one had and concentrate one's life only on spiritual
things' (p. 239), Lalaji's ruling passion emerges in an eagerness
to extend his influence and power through a growing network
of family and business connections, and an unfailing interest
in the worldly advancement of his children, whom he sees as
extensions of himself. Ruth Jhabvala creates in her crooked
businessman one of the great characters of contemporary

fiction, a 'Godfather' ahead of his time, who enlists our unwilling admiration and amused respect for the determination with which he rules his wayward family, remaining true to his own 'practical' values while brushing aside as irrelevant the universally accepted standards of law and morality:

> 'Bribery and Corruption'! Foreign words, it seemed to him. Here in India ... one did not know such words. Giving presents and gratifications to government officers was an indispensable courtesy and a respectable, civilised way of carrying on business. (p. 54)

The structure of the novel and the deftness with which its plot is made to gather complications which will be as deftly resolved in a happy ending remind us, as did *Amrita*, of eighteenth century English comic drama. Here too, characters are listed as in the *dramatis personae* of a play, and introduced in a fictional equivalent of the opening scene in a three-act comedy. The birth of a daughter to Lalaji's eldest son Om brings the family and its clan connections together in a spirited display of community loyalty and jubilation, and introduces the principal characters. By setting the scene in a nursing-home rather than in the family house, Ruth Jhabvala is able to depict without any hint of contrivance the fierce determination with which family traditions are preserved and maintained by Punjabis, even when they find themselves in an unfamiliar environment. This traditionalism, it is implied, is the source of the clan's innate strength and resilience, and guarantees its continued prosperity. Since it is expected that the family presents itself in strength on such occasions as births, marriages and funerals, absence from the scene or a lack of proper interest in it on the part of any member of the family denotes a lack of feeling or a faulty upbringing, symptomatic of disrespect and indiscipline at best, and at worst of a reprehensible 'modernity'. Since Ved and Nimmi show by their behaviour on this occasion that they are in revolt against the family traditions that threaten their individuality, and Chandra Prakash his resentment at being treated by his relations as a mere appendage of his father, the reader is unobtrusively shown the sources from which conflict (and comedy) can be expected to arise: the children's desire for independence will clash in turn with their father's wish to direct their future along paths chosen by himself, and with the wishes of their family to see them 'settled in life' and contributing actively to the numbers and prosperity of the clan.

Lalaji believes he has erred in educating his son Chandra abroad. As a result he has acquired, instead of a respectful and biddable extension to his family, a 'modern' Indian daughter-in-law who despises his business activities and plans to educate her children 'beyond any point of contact' (p. 195) with his family. Chandra himself, obsessively preoccupied with his status as an English-educated, 'gazetted Government Officer', is becoming increasingly uneasy about his father's growing reputation for dishonesty which threatens his own career as a respectable civil servant aspiring to promotion. These complicated emotions are balanced by the more straight-forward rebelliousness of Nimmi, who yearns to be elegant and cultured and longs for romance, only to find herself continually frustrated by the earthiness and conventionality of her family. Ved fancies the bohemian life of a poet, and despises the dedication to business of his father and his elder brother, Om: 'Money, money, money,' [Ved] said. 'That is all anyone thinks of in this house' (p. 61). As a Government inquiry into bribery and corruption in Delhi's business circles gathers momentum and begins to threaten Lalaji's empire, and as his children's unruliness involves him in ever-increasing family disputes, Ruth Jhabvala 'fascinates us with the chess moves by which Lalaji struggles to emerge from check.'[2] He brings Ved under control by means of a planned, methodical play on the boy's weakness for luxury that eventually leads him back to his father, to fellowship with his loathed elder brother, and to a junior directorship in the family firm. By threatening Chandra with a stoppage of the generous allowance that pays for the upkeep of his comfortable house and for the holidays enjoyed by his wife and children in the fashionable hill-resorts, Lalaji induces his son to extract an incriminating letter from a Government file and thereby escapes public exposure. His greatest (and perhaps only real) affection is for Nimmi, and his sympathy for her conflict with his business interests. But even here luck is with him, and his path is smoothed by the shallowness of his daughter's character. The betrothal he arranges for her turns out, most fortuitously, to be with a young man to whom Nimmi is only too ready to transfer the affections

that have been disappointed by her first 'love', a Parsi playboy.
Their marriage will, when it takes place, extend the family
further in suitably wealthy and influential directions and brings
with it a contract for Lalaji worth twenty-five lakhs of rupees.

As the resolution of the plot indicates, there is little idealism
in *The Nature of Passion*. On the contrary, its picture of a world
in which the good things of life are seized and enjoyed with
rapacious greed is filled with an abundance of intensely physical
detail. When Lalaji and his prosperous relative Dev Raj discuss
the marriage proposal for Nimmi that will so profit them all,
these details are significantly stressed:

> They bulged over the sides of the deckchairs, stretching the
> canvas tight with the weight of their backs and rumps. Both
> wore white kurta-pyjama, of finest muslin freshly laundered,
> which thinly veiled their immense amount of flesh .... Their
> voices droned soft and lazy in trivial conversation. From time
> to time they yawned and shifted their broad thighs. (p. 140)

Om's wife Sushila sings a lullaby to the household's newest
baby with the reassuring lyric: 'Butter, sugar, meat, sleep baby
sleep' (p. 116). Lalaji's elder daughter Rani is plump and sleekly
prosperous, 'her ample bosom' encased in 'a tight shining
blouse,' her person redolent 'not only directly of scent and hair
oil, but also indirectly of good living and a rich husband'
(p. 215). The Delhi society of which Rani is a part is seen as
greedy and self-indulgent; at a restaurant to which Ved goes
in his pursuit of high life,

> Well-fed people were piled on gilt chairs and damascened
> sofas which looked too fragile to hold them. A few couples
> were dancing, but most people concentrated on eating.
> Bearers swayed under overladen trays and thrust vast
> steaming dishes between closely packed shoulders.
> Preoccupation with food and drink had swamped the dainty
> western-style elegance of the interior decoration, and even
> the dancers and the band, its jazzy little tunes so bravely
> played, could not hold out against the bulging bearded
> cheeks of chewing men. (p. 191)

Ruth Jhabvala's diction sensuously celebrates the solidity and
substance of middle-class India, through the concentrated use
in these passages of images that recall food in its marketable

state — 'the weight of their backs and rumps', 'plump', 'ample',
'flesh', 'broad thighs' and 'closely packed shoulders'. They are
immediately qualified, however, by words such as 'bulged',
'stretch', 'tight', 'piled' and 'overladen', which suggest an
accompanying unhealthiness and disproportion, an impression
supported by the description of furniture, clothes, servants,
platters and music that seem 'too fragile', and weak for the
Indian 'preoccupation with food and drink' and 'good living' that
strains and threatens to overwhelm them.

Minor characters who appear momentarily on the edges of
the bourgeois action of the novel unobtrusively lodge, through
their fleeting presence, an ironic criticism of such indulgence.
Among these are the numerous servants who minister to the
needs of the principal characters and the affluent, uncaring
society of which they are a part: the bearers who 'sway' under
the weight of the food ordered by intently chewing customers
in restaurants; the servants of Lalaji's household who are only
thought of by their master and his family as 'wasting coal or
making havoc with the sugar and the ghee' (p. 21); the servant
who crouches near Lalaji and Dev Raj, waiting only to appear
when called (p. 140); the 'gardener in a loincloth' who
unexpectedly crosses Nimmi's line of vision as she parades her
finery in a college corridor (p. 45). A 'long ... thin ... and
mournful' refugee from the Punjab appears as a supplicant in
Lalaji's office, and is physically intimidated by the brutal Om
(p. 53). 'Big disasters must always leave small wrecks behind'
is the 'philosophical' comment made on this incident by the
prosperous Lalaji, who later 'arranges' the erection of a group
of sweepers' hutments as a convenient occupation for the idle
Ved (p. 121). 'Tattered figures' lie 'curled up in their doorways'
as Ved meditates on the expenses incurred in giving a lavish
party to establish himself as a man of style (p. 230); a beggar's
'whining ragged figure' rises out of the dark as Nimmi and her
Parsi admirer, elegant in evening dress, park their car at Kutub
Minar, to be given two annas by the sophisticated Pheroze who
'did not want to be pestered' (p. 136).

As the novel nears its end on the high note of Lalaji's triumph,
and his family celebrates Nimmi's betrothal by feasting richly
in the gardens of an ancient mausoleum, a figure of this kind
appears for the last time. As Nimmi, the spoiled 'queen' of her
father's fondly indulgent thoughts, meditates complacently on

the luxurious future opening before her,

> in the distance, out on the barren plains, the broken flight
> of steps of a vanished palace led to nowhere and a man with
> a stick and a loincloth walked behind two yoked and shabby
> bullocks. (p. 259)

The days of India's greatness are gone, her palaces have
vanished, the approaches to them and all that they stood for
are broken and decayed. The maharajas and princes have been
replaced by Lalaji and his kind, whose money rules Indian
society. The shadowy and deprived, often derelict, figures on
the fringes of the novel's action (and the consciousness of its
principal characters) represent what Ruth Jhabvala has called
'the great mass of India', inescapably part of the lives of all who
live there.[3] The indifference of the affluent to the fate of India's
very poor is one aspect of the theme of betrayal that Haydn
Moore Williams sees as a constant element in all Ruth
Jhabvala's fiction prior to 1969.[4] The seemingly casual
manner in which these figures are introduced and the comic
effects they sometimes help to create serve to highlight the
tragedy of a society that is dislocated and lacking in standards
and moral leadership, in which greedy exploitation of the poor
has replaced concern and social responsibility for them; as
when Bahwa, a playwright who writes problem plays about
callous employers and distressed widows and orphans, chases
out of the auditorium 'some ragged children' who 'stood gazing
up at (him)' and his company of amateur actors (p. 162).

In the context of monumental indifference such as this
towards those who are in real need of succour, the accusations
of selfishness that fly back and forth among the members of
Lalaji's luxury-loving family yield exquisite, if somewhat grim,
comedy. Worried by thoughts of the file in which his letter
reposes, and which Chandra is reluctant to disturb, Lalaji turns
mentally on his family: 'They were ungrateful, they had no love
for the father who did everything for them' (p. 119). Chandra's
wife Kanta is convinced that their demands on the father-in-
law she despises are 'really far too modest' (pp. 196-7). When
Chandra finally does remove the letter from the file, he does
so in order to protect his own comfortable way of life and not
from a sense of gratitude nor of duty.[5] In the great scene that
follows Rani's summons of her father and brother from the office

to deal with the rumours of Nimmi's affair with Pheroze, the
entire household turns on Lalaji and accuses him of selfish
prevarication (pp. 221-3).

Although limited areas of the novel's world are presented
alternately through the eyes of Lalaji's self-centred children,
the reader views the whole as Lalaji sees it: a world in which
bureaucrats exist merely to clear his path to bigger and better
business successes, and whose human society appears to have
been created with no other purpose than to provide a suitable
setting for his adored daughter. It is a world which Lalaji sees
himself as ruling, surrounded by those 'queens' and 'pearls',
his daughters and grand-daughters. It is his personal desire
(and one endorsed by the traditions of the joint family system)
that his sons should follow in his footsteps, and seek their
independence only in the license and privileges his money
bestows on them. Ruth Jhabvala records with delight the
shrewdness and warm sentimentality of this energetic
personality, who displays ruthlessness in his business
transactions and a comical helplessness when his womenfolk
unite against him, who glories in his status as community-
leader and head of a large and increasingly prosperous family,
yet humbles himself before the austere saintliness of a lowly
clerk in his own office. Lalaji's immorality and dishonesty are
played off against his endearing quirks of character to create
an engagingly human personality in contrast to which several
representatives of respectability in the novel are ironically
exposed as the selfish hypocrites they are.

'Honour' and 'status', for instance, are words that are
constantly on the lips respectively of Lalaji's widowed sister
Phuphiji and his son Chandra. Phuphiji (whose angry activity
on Lalaji's behalf recalls that of Mrs. Norris on Sir Thomas
Bertram's in Jane Austen's *Mansfield Park*) attempts in the
name of 'honour' and 'duty' to subject the younger women in
the family to a series of petty restrictions and reproaches.
Chandra is much concerned with his own status as 'a gazetted
Government officer'. It is evident, however, that the moralistic
attitudes of both these characters stem from egotism. Phuphiji
(who has never been beautiful, and never known love)
denounces the attractive Nimmi in a voice that shakes with
the passion of a moral indignation indistinguishable from sexual
frustration. She uses inappropriately violent public prayer as

a form of moral blackmail (resembling in this Mr. Anand's mother in *Amrita*) and disputes the running of the household with her sister-in-law. The joint family system appears to breed and encourage such neuroses as Phuphiji's, endowing egotism with cruel authority: 'This was right, this was as it should be' (p. 148). Chandra, for his part, is wedded to the idea of self-advancement, beside which all other concerns fade to nothing. Yet, as the novel indicates, the 'honour' and 'status' Phuphiji and Chandra represent (as, indeed, the considerable comfort in which both of them live) arise directly from Lalaji's shady business dealings. Which, the novel seems to ask, is the more reprehensible: Lalaji, who considers bribery 'a respectable, civilised way of carrying on business' (p. 54)? Phuphiji, who wants the youth, beauty and individuality of her niece Nimmi sacrificed on the altar of family 'honour'? Or Chandra, who moralises about 'this evil' of corruption (p. 255), having personally helped to tighten its grip on India's political life and who is living, even as he speaks, in luxury derived from it?

By comparison with Lalaji, who brings a generous warmth to every aspect of his private life , both Phuphiji and Chandra seem callous and cold. When, while discussing Nimmi, Phuphiji cries vengefully, 'A girl of that age has no right to *enjoy* herself! She should be managing a household and bearing children, and looking after a husband', Lalaji responds with mild pity, 'It will come to her soon enough' (p. 89). When Chandra seeks to excuse his children's embarrassment in their grandfather's presence by remarking that they become shy in the company of 'other people', Lalaji inquires simply: 'The grandfather is also other people?' (p. 193).

The phrasing of Lalaji's rebuke to his son, like his definition of 'Bribery' and 'Corruption' as foreign words unknown in India, is an instance of the irony with which Ruth Jhabvala presents the world of *The Nature of Passion* as a society which seems to have lost its standards. The adoption of foreign words and expressions in catch-phrases denoting elite status appears frequently enough to suggest that traditional values are under threat: the artistic world inhabited by Ved's friends talks meaninglessly of 'depth', 'vision' and 'emotional form', the social set to which he would like to belong rejects as 'dull' and 'vulgar' everything it does not like or comprehend. Those who (like Nimmi) aspire to cultured elegance behave as if all 'education' flowed from 'Cambridge, England', and the 'modern' Kanta refers to her children as 'kids' and calls her husband 'darling', or even (to the astonishment of her father-in-law) by name. Side by side with these imported expressions are the richly indigenous, ranging from the contemptuous and colloquial 'Pearl-shearl' and 'dowry-showry' to the formal 'Yes, Sahib, please command me' and the sententious 'They know only how to take. How to give they have not learnt.' The incongruous effect created when the same speaker uses both registers satirically points up affectation; for example, Nimmi, who in the course of her literary studies anxiously seeks to know the difference between the words 'sensual' and 'sensuous' and asks at a party for 'French sherry,' unconsciously and habitually omits the use of the definite article: 'I am taking Honours course, she is taking General.' Her uncultured relations, who do not aspire to elegance, use only one register: 'You are arranging marriage for him?' 'You go to visit in their houses also?' 'All of you eating my life up.'

Ruth Jhabvala has a quick ear for the way the use of the imperative mood in Indian speech reverberates in contexts of hospitality, and she puts it to ironic purpose. 'Sit, sit,' 'Take rest,' 'Eat, son, eat' and 'Take, child, take' are employed in situations that betoken family unity and even affection, but subtly indicate that the apparently kindly speaker intends to brook no refusal: the last expression is used by Lalaji's wife as she offers complexion ruining nuts to a niece she dislikes. Especially interesting and amusing are the many instances in the novel in which the word order of Indian speech is sustained in translation for special effects so as to convey, for example, a note of querulousness in a complaint against a servant in 'Even the fire he has not lit,' and the robustness of the personal compliments with which Lalaji and Dev Raj are accustomed to greet each other: 'Like a pregnant woman in the last month he looks!' 'Like a tub of ghee he is only!'

Such innovative use as this of the linguistic resources opened to her by her predecessors, Kipling and Forster, and by her own increasing knowledge of India and Indians shows that Ruth Jhabvala has been able to go beyond her early models. The ability to look to sources located in actual experience (her own observations of Jewish and of middle-class Indian family life) that makes itself felt in Amrita is thus carried a stage further.

But it should also be noted that in satirizing selfishness in the
members of Lalaji's materialistic family, Ruth Jhabvala turns
for the last time to eighteenth century fiction for her models.
Phuphiji's striking resemblance to Mrs Norris (whose meddling,
bullying and petty tyrannies make life a burden for poor Fanny
Price at Mansfield Park) has already been remarked; to this
could perhaps be added the resemblance of Ved Prakash to the
younger Branghton in Fanny Burney's novel *Evelina*, who

> disdains his father for his close attention to business, and
> love of money, though he seems himself to have no talents,
> spirit or generosity, to make him superior.[6]

Similarly, selfishness and a feverish enthusiasm for social
climbing unite with ambition on her husband's behalf to
produce in Kanta an Indian avatar of Fanny Dashwood in Jane
Austen's *Sense and Sensibility*. Like Fanny, whose constitution
is so extremely delicate that she never feels quite well enough
to call on her sisters-in-law, Kanta avoids social gatherings at
which her husband's relations will be present in large numbers,
and is easily 'exhausted' by the preparations for a mere dinner-
party (pp. 64-6). In an extended passage that recalls the well-
known dialogue between John and Fanny Dashwood in which
Fanny manages by degrees to convince her husband that his
father had 'had no idea of your giving [your mother and step-
sisters] any money at all'[7], Kanta coaxes Chandra out of
gloomy fear and into a mood of smug self-assurance. 'Anyone
in your position would have had to do the same thing,' Kanta
assures her timorous husband, who is agitated by the thought
that the unexplainable disappearance of Lalaji's incriminating
letter from a file which has been in his own keeping must
inevitably come to light (p. 249); 'No one will ever know about
it' (p. 250); 'It is only your father who has acted dishonestly'
(p. 252); 'What could you do when your own father came to
you and blackmailed you?' (p. 253); 'It is very bad ... that a
man like your father should have so much power through
bribing people' (p. 254). At last there comes the moralising
comment: 'It is a terrible thing ... bribery and corruption'
(p. 255). Although they are in a position to help Ved and Nimmi,
Chandra and Kanta give them no more assistance than John
and Fanny Dashwood vouchsafe to Elinor and Marianne. To
Ved's appeal for help, Chandra replies coldly: 'I cannot interfere,

I have my own life to lead and my own family to care for,' while
Kanta takes the position that 'The less I have to do with [Ved
and Nimmi] the better it will be for me and my children.' The
final word on the subject is Kanta's: 'It is very selfish of them
to ask us' (p. 256).

The males of Lalaji's family (with the significant exception of
Chandra, who lives outside the family circle and is neurotic
and tense) are vigorous, forthright and hearty in their
enjoyment of life. They pride themselves on the size of their
families and on their own girth ('Like a tub of ghee he is only!')
as the outward and visible signs of their sexual prowess and
financial prosperity. Daughters are sentimentally welcomed into
their world and showered with luxury and affection: 'A little
sister you have got, a little sister like a pearl,' says Lalaji to
his grandson, announcing the birth of yet another baby (p. 15).
But the true worth of daughters lies in the fact that they will
eventually be married off as a profitable investment for the joint
family. Life in the women's quarter is at best dull, monotonous
and lonely; at worst it can be fearful, frustrating and vicious.
But, as Lalaji reflects comfortably,

> This was right, this was as it should be. A family was not
> a family, a home not a home, unless there was a women's
> quarter in which the women could lead their own lives.
> Demure daughters-in-law, stern mothers-in-law, widowed
> aunts, all pounding spices, sifting rice, scolding servants,
> washing babies; the stone jars of rice and lentils, the vat
> of boiling milk, the barbecue, the pump in the courtyard;
> quarrels and recriminations and occasional songs, nostalgic
> peasant songs or plaintive hymns winding round the
> ceaseless kitchen noises — these constituted the necessary,
> if unconsidered, background to a man's life. (pp. 148-9)

Lalaji's youngest daughter Nimmi, whose beauty, immaturity
and wilfulness arouse the reader's interest and concern for her
welfare at the start of *The Nature of Passion*, has no desire to
become (as her mother and her sister-in-law Shanta have done)
part of the 'unconsidered background' to the life of any man.
She disdains the women of her family as ignorant and ill-
mannered, and resents the gossip and recrimination her most
trivial action seems capable of arousing among them. Her
feelings on this subject are so strong that she loses the power

to discriminate. She has little but contempt for her quiet sister-in-law Shanta whose whole existence is concentrated on Om, but is ignored and belittled by him; yet it is Shanta who, braving the anger of her own mother, defends Nimmi herself against the insinuations of jealous, mischief-making relatives (pp. 217-8). Nimmi ridicules and callously upsets her sister Usha, who loves her with a tender and generous affection:

> 'I am so proud of you ... When you first came to the College and I was still there, how proud I was when I saw you walk down the corridors and I could tell everybody: this is my sister.' (p. 209)

Despite Nimmi's claims to superiority, her own standards are superficial: she plans merely to be more fashionable than her 'modern' sister-in-law Kanta, and marry someone better-looking than Chandra Prakash. Her feeling for Pheroze Bhatliwala, her first 'love,' is based on curiosity rather than on affection or respect. She wishes to be admired and envied, and picks Pheroze as a 'boy-friend' because he is more presentable and good-looking than anyone else in her limited circle. When he kisses her in the moon-light at Kutub Minar, she does not think of love:

> She kept her eyes wide open and thought: So this is how a man kisses — and next: What would they say at home? — and next: How excited Rajen will be when she hears! (p. 137)

Nimmi does not really return her father's affection, and is easily consoled for Pheroze's eventual defection by the attentions of another young man whom she eventually marries. Despite her wish (as a student of Keats' poetry) to appreciate the difference between sensuality and sensuousness, Nimmi does not really understand what is meant by love or (as her relationship with her college friend Rajen Mathur shows) by genuine friendship. By the end of the novel she has learned nothing of value: her new-found maturity and sophistication amount to no more than a self-confident expertise in monopolising the mirror in the Club ladies' room, and the prospect of marriage finds her preparing merely to astonish her Cambridge-educated friends with 'the elegance of her clothes and manners' (p. 258). Not even the reader's pity for Nimmi, punished for her brief flirtation with

Pheroze by being incarcerated in the women's quarters at the
behest of her tyrannical aunt Phuphiji until her wedding may
be duly celebrated, can obliterate the impression created by
her portrayal as a whole that she (like her three brothers in
their various ways) is a true inheritor of 'the nature of passion.'

Nimmi's brother Ved composes 'erotic' verse, the weakness
and incompetence of which (he mistakes suggestiveness for
eroticism) is obvious to every one but himself. When he wearies
of his artistic friends and seeks entry into fashionable society,
he can look no higher than the 'set' of unmarried Delhi social
butterflies who move from party to party, bored and (eventually)
boring. There is little promise for India's cultural future here,
and Ruth Jhabvala crisply satirizes bad art in the persons of
Tivari, a journalist who spends his time idling in restaurants,
and Zahir-ud-din, an artist who, in the regrettable absence of
other connoisseurs, admires his own work with enthusiasm:
'(Those murals) have depth and vision' (p. 37). Their friend
Bahwa, a playwright, claims to have 'steeped (himself) in our
great National Heritage, in our Culture which is 5000 years old'
(p. 226), assertions that ring quite as false as Lady Ram
Prashad Khanna's vague gestures in the direction of Indian
cultural history in *Amrita*. The 'problem plays' that flow from
Bahwa's pen are grossly over-stated, and ludicrously 'balanced'
with comic and romantic 'relief.' They are quite remote from
the real life around him, and consequently Ruth Jhabvala's
handling of genuine social problems in *The Nature of Passion*
(among which are the position of women in the Indian joint
family, corruption in business and in the Indian bureaucracy,
and the 'instinctive subservience' of servants to superiors) offers
continuous implicit criticism of the 'literature' produced by
Bahwa and his like.

These young men believe quite seriously that they possess
among themselves 'all the talent' required for such enterprises
as forming a film company (p. 77) or a professional touring
theatre group (p. 75). Lalaji, as might be expected, has no
interest in the activities of these aesthetes; to him they are no
more than a bunch of idling scroungers whose influence over
Ved is distracting him from following his proper path in life
— which, of course, leads directly into the family business! But
they are deeply interested in *him*: when Zahir-ud-din offers to
paint a portrait of the grossly fat Lalaji which will be, he

promises, 'a beautiful picture' (p. 42), Ved learns with disgust
that his father's money is the key to the world of Indian art
just as it appears to be the key to every other Indian world.

The only voice to be raised occasionally in overt or ironic
criticism of the values that rule the fictional world of *The Nature
of Passion* belongs to Tivari, Ved's journalist friend. Tivari refers
with irony to Bahwa's 'lively social conscience,' and exposes
the superficiality of Ved's literary 'knowledge': 'Lately you have
learnt a lot about literature' (p. 226). Money, he reminds Ved
when he complains of his family's mercenariness, 'is not a bad
thing to know about' (p. 34). He declares provocatively that
Lalaji must be 'a very interesting man' (p. 36), and points out
the undeniable fact that Lalaji has no need 'to read and write
and speak English. He pays people like us to do it for him'
(p. 36). But Tivari's credibility as a critic of society is somewhat
undermined by the fact that he holds 'a well-paid government
post,' and proves to be quite as eager as Ved's other associates
to make money out of him and (if possible) out of Lalaji himself.
Ultimately, Tivari is hardly distinguishable from Bahwa and
Zahir-ud-din, and though his function in the novel is to deflate
pretentiousness and romanticism, he substitutes cynicism for
the ironic idealism of such characters as Krishna Sen Gupta
in *Amrita* and Sudhir Banerjee in *A Backward Place* and is too
vulnerable to the reader's judgement to occupy the judicial
bench himself. Any impulse felt by any of the novel's characters
towards selflessness or genuine sympathy for others is either
quickly stifled or reasoned away. Thus Usha's affection for
Nimmi and Shanta's defence of her go unregarded, and are
brushed aside by her as typical of sentimental, ignorant women.
Chandra Prakash feels briefly guilty when his children fail to
greet their grandfather affectionately; Lalaji mourns inwardly
when he is forced to negotiate a marriage for Nimmi that will
inevitably take her away from his own house. But (as with
Nimmi's feelings for Pheroze) these emotions are quickly
soothed: Chandra supports Kanta whole-heartedly in her
determination to keep the children away from the
contamination of his family, and Lalaji characteristically
reconciles himself to life's realities:

> There is great sorrow both in wealth and in beautiful
> daughters. Since the one has to be kept up, and the other

given away. (p. 241)

Only one Western character appears in *The Nature of Passion*. Ved visits a nightclub, and there finds that

> the leader of the band was a European; an oldish man with a bald head, but very gay, he made encouraging gestures to the dancers, flexed his knees and shouted things at the band which made them all break into smiles at once. Kuku said 'He has been in India twenty-five years and now he wants to go home, but he has no money.' (p. 191)

The comic, slightly pathetic figure of the expatriate bandleader is the second in a procession of displaced Westerners whose recurrence in Ruth Jhabvala's fiction has been considered in Chapter 1.[8] Like his predecessor, the Viennese violinist in *Amrita* (see Chapter 2), like the beggar who startles Nimmi and Pheroze at Kutub Minar or the Punjabi refugee Om turns out of his father's office, the European bandleader is one of those whom fate and circumstance have betrayed, and whom no individual cares to succour. Like them, he illustrates Lalaji's practical philosophy: 'Big disasters must always leave small wrecks behind' (p. 53), and his personal tragedy contributes yet another to the succession of fine brushstrokes with which Ruth Jhabvala builds up her picture of India.

Although it is seen and described as if from within, the Indian world of *The Nature of Passion* is not one with any part of which its author can identify herself, but one from which she remains detached. It is from this detachment, from the actual experience of living as 'a permanent expatriate' in the Indian world[9] without being absorbed into it, that Ruth Jhabvala's characteristic irony has become the precise, double-edged authorial instrument that is now familiar to readers of her novels and short stories, and to viewers of the films for which she has written the screen-plays. In *The Nature of Passion*, her clear-eyed observation of Indian life at many levels adds astringency to her delight in its comic variety:thus we perceive that there is no genuine concern for India's political health evinced by any of the ambitious civil servants who attend Kanta's dinner-party, and no real elegance or distinction of mind manifest in the limited conversational ability and superficial social graces of Pheroze Bhatliwala that so impress Nimmi. A.R. Humphreys's remarks on the novels of Fielding and Smollett are very applicable to the 'true comedy' of *The Nature of Passion.*

> Satire is to abound ... but it is not the novel's major purpose, which is to bring its readers to a healthy and resilient frame of mind through good humour, and that is best found in the recognition of the true comedy that lies around them.[10]

Ruth Jhabvala portrays the characters of this novel with a verve that calls the eighteenth century comic novelists and the engravings of Hogarth to mind, recording with affectionate detail the quirks and oddities, the weaknesses and strengths of each individual in the extended (and continually extending) family of Lala Narayan Dass Verma. And in her anti-hero's character with its blending of endearing and repulsive qualities, we may see both a symbol of his creator's conflicting feelings for India, and evidence of her ability to externalize them in her art.

Notes

1. R.P. Jhabvala, *The Nature of Passion* (Allen & Unwin, London: 1956), p. 261. All references in this chapter and in the book as a whole are to this edition.
2. Haydn Moore Williams, "The Yogi and the Babbitt," op. cit., p. 83.
3. 'I haven't lived among the very poor, so obviously I can't write about them directly. Although I like to think that they are there *indirectly* — the great mass of India beneath these middle class lives — as they are there indirectly for all of us who live here' — R.P. Jhabvala, quoted by R. Agarwal, op. cit., p. 34.
4. 'The tragedy of modern India as depicted in Jhabvala's novels is the total failure of communication between the Babbitt and the Yogi' —H.M. Williams, ibid., p. 89.
5. See H.M. Williams on this point, ibid., pp. 83-4.
6. Fanny Burney, *Evelina*, ed. E.A. Bloom (Oxford University Press, London: 1968) p. 51.
7. See Jane Austen, *Sense and Sensibility*, vol. I, Chapter 2.
8. These characters are examined in detail in P. Stiles, "India and the western sensibility in the fiction of R.P. Jhabvala," unpublished M.A. dissertation, Macquarie University, New South Wales.
9. H.M. Williams, "R.K. Narayan and R. Prawer Jhabvala: Two interpreters of modern India," op. cit., p. 1153.
10. A.R. Humphreys, 'Fielding and Smollett," *The Pelican Guide to English Literature* IV: — *From Dryden to Johnson* (Penguin Books, Harmondsworth: 1970). p. 318.

CHAPTER

IV

Esmond in India
1957

Ruth Jhabvala's novels characteristically focus on the world in which she finds herself at the time of writing, and *Esmond in India*[1] is no exception. Published in 1957, it depicts an urban upper-class India in which, ten years after Independence, life has adjusted itself to the realities of *Swaraj*. The former revolutionaries, though still respected, are somewhat out of date and their places are being taken by others. Among these others is Har Dayal, a middle-aged gentleman of cultural interests, who had in his youth been attracted by the 'madness' and 'danger' of the struggle for Independence (p. 210) but, guided with gentle firmness by his wife Madhuri, had followed the cautious course he now likes to term 'the life of the spirit' (p. 195). The practical benefits of his having done so are revealed in the novel's opening pages, as his indulged young daughter Shakuntala wakes to a house swimming richly 'with clear pale yellow light,' its well-kept garden 'an extension of the room: sunlight and flowers' (p. 10).

The fact that *Esmond in India* ends as it begins, by focusing on Shakuntala's girlish enthusiasm for life and (later on) for love, usefully demonstrates that Ruth Jhabvala's novels are neither 'historical' in the generally accepted sense, nor an imaginative rewriting of historical incident. Her characters exist in the shadow or the aftermath of great events, and her attention is held by their lives and not by the events themselves. In both *Amrita* and *The Nature of Passion*, the reader is introduced to characters who have come to Delhi as refugees from the Punjab, their lives disrupted by Partition; in *The Householder*, Prem is made indignant by the idea that India's Independence can be dismissed as unimportant and irrelevant to philosophical discussion; and in *Esmond in India*, the hunger-strikes and jail-sentences of the Independence struggle live on only in the memories of some of the characters. The chief interest of these novels lies in the inward perceptions of the characters rather than in any historical role they can be said to have played in the shaping of modern India; in their capacity for self-knowledge and self-deception, and their impulse towards self-fulfilment or self-destruction.

The struggle for freedom is recalled by those of the novel's characters who were actively involved in it, only through intimate, 'domestic' details. A distinguished patriot who had given his life for the cause is remembered by his wife Uma not in his final, heroic moments but in vigorous life, 'tearing an oven-baked chicken with his hands and eating it with superhuman relish' (p. 219). Uma recalls with particular pleasure, not the meetings with the Mahatma (of which there must have been several, and which a writer of historical novels would not think of passing over) but the cooking of a memorable meal on the day her brother Ram Nath came out of jail. She cannot quite remember the year of this event but, touched momentarily with greatness, she recalls that 'Never in my life have I cooked so well as on that day!' (p. 225). Her own solitary remembered act of heroism has a touch of farce about it, when

she had sat upon a folder of incriminating papers and pretended
to police searchers that her labour pains had begun. It is
evident that these were times during which traditional codes
of restraint and modesty had been dispensed with, and life lived
to the full (pp. 225-6). No member of Har Dayal's family has
experienced (or been permitted by Madhuri to even approach)
the 'atmosphere of greatness' symbolized in the novel by
memories of Uma's dead husband, a vital, vigorous giant
'bursting with health and strength,' who had done 'everything
on a vast scale' (p. 219). In the company of such heroes, Uma
and Ram Nath had known greater freedom of spirit in jail than
they do now, in the aftermath of Independence. For then
circumstances had been 'never ordinary; life was always lived
at a different pitch from that of people with no purpose' (p. 219).
Uma feels sadly that the fiery enthusiasm for life that they had
known has now died out in her and in her brother, that life
itself has 'withdrawn from her and her house and her family'
(p. 220).

Esmond in India spans a period of five months, from February
to May or June of an Indian year in the late 1950s, in effect
the time that elapses between Shakuntala's graduation from
college and her foreshadowed marriage with the son of her
father's friend and associate, Professor Bhatnagar. But though
the novel begins and ends with Shakuntala in view, she is of
rather less interest and importance in the novel than her
seniors: her parents, their friends, and of course Esmond
Stillwood, the Western stranger in their midst. The principal
characters are grouped in four 'households,' as follows:

A — Har Dayal and Madhuri, with their son Amrit, their
     daughter Shakuntala and their daughter-in-law, Indira;
B — Ram Nath and his wife Lakshmi, and their absent son
     Narayan, a physician working in a village outside Delhi;
C — Uma, alone with her memories, the old maid-servant
     Bachani, and a resident Swami;
D — Esmond Stillwood, his Indian wife (Uma's daughter)
     Gulab, and their son Ravi.

The plot brings these four households into alternate association
and conflict, as Gulab (starting from C, as Uma's daughter)
becomes engaged to Amrit (A) and then marries Esmond (D),
returning at the end of the novel with Ravi to (C); as Shakuntala

(A) is thought of by Uma (C) as a suitable wife for Narayan (B) and has a love-affair with Esmond (D). Gulab (C, later D) and Narayan (B) are first cousins; Har Dayal (A) and Ram Nath (B) are old friends and Cambridge associates; Uma (C) and Ram Nath (B) are not only siblings, but share memories of the Independence struggle — which are, however, very different from those of Madhuri (A) and Lakshmi (B). Several circles of activity intersect in the course of the novel: Shakuntala seeks the excitement of adult life, and finds what she believes is 'love'; Narayan needs a wife, and asks his father to find one for him; Esmond, nearing the end of his endurance after several years in India, is ready to go to pieces; Uma is determined, after five years of inactivity, to bring Gulab and Ravi back home; Madhuri and Har Dayal are looking out for a suitable husband (or a vocation) for Shakuntala.

The principal theme Ruth Jhabvala explores through these shifting, turning circles of activity is the dilemma of the Westerner for whom initial delight in India turns into a trap: the novel is her first detailed study of a subject, preliminary hints of her interests, which may be seen in both her previous novels[2] and which she has taken up repeatedly in subsequent novels, stories and scree-plays, thus making it a major literary preoccupation for a considerable period of her writing life. To examine Esmond closely, she isolates him: he is the only Westerner among the Indian characters in households A, B, C and D. They are inter-linked by blood, shared memories or old association, while he is only linked with C by the formal bond of a marriage of which they all (and especially Uma and Ram Nath) disapprove. Although he associates with other Westerners in Delhi, Esmond is isolated even among them: he is alone in having no plans to leave India, and is thus set apart from his English mistress Betty and the members of the Western Women's Organization. He is also one of the very few characters in the novel who possess some sensitivity to India, and a genuine appreciation of her culture and history. His very professional and thorough knowledge of the subject is contrasted with the indifference and superficiality evinced by other Westerners in Delhi, and it is an ironic reflection on the amateurishness and ignorance of the 'cultivated' literary lion Har Dayal that he employs the European Stillwood to tutor his daughter in Indian classical literature.

Esmond is contrasted in different ways with other characters in the novel. Despite his growing distress of mind, Esmond is much more intelligent and sensitive than the stupid, pompous Amrit whose prospective wife he has married. Narayan, on the other hand, would regard with contempt the luxurious life led by Har Dayal's family, which Esmond would like to make his own. Gulab, who in her initial attraction for Esmond and her later opposition to him becomes a symbol of India as far as he is concerned, adopts a way of life that is in appropriate conflict with Esmond's own representation of Western civilisation:

> He was trapped, quite trapped. Here in this flat which he had tried to make so elegant and charming, but which she had managed to fill completely with her animal presence. His senses revolted at the thought of her, of her greed and smell and languor, her passion for meat and for spices and strong perfumes. She was everywhere; everywhere he felt her — in the heat saturating the air which clung to him and enveloped him as in a sheath of perspiration; in the sugarcane juice, which the people in the streets were drinking and which he could almost taste, filled with dust and germs and too much sweetness; in the faint but penetrating smell of over-ripe fruit; everywhere, she was everywhere, and he felt himself stifling in her softness and her warmth. (p. 207)

By tracing Esmond's rapidly accelerating journey from comparative calm to mounting hysteria during the five months covered by the action of the novel (which represent the climax to several years during which Esmond has grown steadily disillusioned with both Gulab and his life in India), Ruth Jhabvala is able to plot the stages by which the 'experience of India' affects the Western sensibility.

Esmond has begun to realize that 'he had to get out ... quickly' (p. 207), that it is only the prospect of leaving India for good that can ever again make him feel 'young and free' (p. 255). His admiration for Indian art, architecture and literature is genuine, and he believes that in giving the lessons and lectures on Indian classical culture that earn him his living he has found his 'true vocation' (p. 230). But he has found that his intellectual and aesthetic approach to her culture is no protection against India. Despite his conscientiousness as a teacher (and as father to Ravi), Esmond's personality begins to disintegrate along with his marriage as 'the strain of living with Gulab (becomes) more and more intense' (p. 230). His growing distaste for India merges with contempt for his lovely and slow-witted wife until she becomes, in his overwrought imagination, the living embodiment of all he resents and despises about India: her 'animal sleep' seems to oppose his alert rationality, her lethargy his energetic activity, and her quiet complaisance his need for lively companionship. Esmond is proud of his self-image as a man of culture, and is shaken and distressed by the violence of his own revulsion and the behaviour it brings out in him. He finds occasional relief from his problems in his relationship with the brightly British Betty, and in the activities of the cultural group that provides him with publicity, payment and a regular audience. His later attempt to console himself with Shakuntala, however, amusingly backfires on him. Temporarily fascinated by Esmond's Shelleyan aspect of tragic melancholy, the romantic Shakuntala offers him her love and devotion in a quite unexpected reversion on her part to the traditional outlook that holds Gulab captive. Her enthusiastic resolve to 'adore you and to serve you and to be your slave' (p. 184) is yet another trap, from which Esmond finally flees to England and safety,

> where there were solid grey houses and solid grey people, and the sky was kept within decent proportions. (p. 252)

Ruth Jhabvala's study of Esmond is not untouched with irony. His personal dilemma, though agonising for him, for Gulab, and for their little son Ravi, is part of the novel's comic pattern: he is a disgruntled, consciously superior (and therefore comic) Jaques in an Indian *As You Like It*, who attempts to distance himself from a rapidly-moving sequence of events in which he is caught up against his will. Despite Shakuntala's romantic desire to see her lover as 'cool ... handsome and ... distinguished' (p. 22), a being apart from the grotesque Westerners she meets at Delhi parties, Esmond is often most comic in his stance of conscious superiority, since it does not deter him from telephoning the wives of Western diplomats in order to 'pick up' invitations to lunch or dinner (p. 42). The complacency with which he speaks a Hindustani that his Indian

bearer cannot understand, nor even identify as an Indian
language, reminds us of Professor Hoch in *Amrita*. The
fastidious grace with which he consumes a delicate cheese salad
'alone at his smart little dining table in his smart little dining
corner' (p. 41) strikes a note that is genuinely comic. The blend
of comedy and pathos which marks his appearances in the
novel is never better exemplified than during a visit to Agra
when his shoes are stolen in the heat of the day, and he stands
in comic , yet dignified isolation,

> he and the hot sun, and behind him, a fitting background
> to his monumental tragedy, the Taj Mahal. (p. 171)

As the passages quoted indicate, the climate and weather
conditions of north India contribute to Esmond's growing
unease. Little signs unobtrusively chart the passing of the
seasons: Madhuri is brought hot chocolate by Har Dayal on
page 25, an indication that the weather in Delhi is still wintry;
Esmond's lecture on the Indian love-lyric is delivered on an open
terrace at sunset, when the weather is becoming warm — 'the
season was changing, soon now it would be summer' (p. 100);
the Western Women's Organization visits the Taj at Agra in high
summer, and Esmond is annoyed by Betty's delay which makes
the morning heat unavoidable (p. 166). Back in Delhi, the heat
becomes oppressive in his little flat and soon has Esmond
'screaming' with anger (p. 202), viciously savaging his own
beautifully arranged home (p. 203). Ruth Jhabvala's treatment
of weather and atmosphere builds to a climax in the moments
before Gulab, left alone with Ravi in the flat, becomes the victim
of attempted rape:

> It was very hot; all the noonday heat had accumulated into
> a solid mass which lay heavy in the air and pressed on the
> walls and ceiling, so that they seemed almost to bend and
> close in under its weight ... It was so hot and so still; all
> the world seemed to have swooned into a stupor. (p. 245)

Despite the obvious links between this climatic passage and
Ruth Jhabvala's description in "Myself in India" of her own
response to Delhi's hot season[3], her characterization of
Esmond resolves itself in comedy as her study of Etta in *A
Backward Place* (published some eight years later) does not.
The reader of *Esmond in India* can savour the irony implicit

in Har Dayal's plan to prepare his daughter for an arranged marriage by engaging her seducer to tutor her in art history. Nor is Esmond exempt from his creator's depiction of the human race as incorrigibly inclined to self-deception: he believes he needs a wife who will be his equal, but Betty, who knows him to be a bully, keeps her hold on him by never giving into him. The novel ends on a final picture of Esmond as gay deceiver: his hand clasped in Shakuntala's, he gazes smilingly into her trusting, confident eyes and thinks with longing and increasing pleasure of escape to England, and to freedom.

While Esmond struggles to liberate himself from India, Shakuntala wakes up each morning in her elegant, well-appointed home to an intoxicating sense of freedom:

> The whole day was hers and she could do whatever she liked with it. And anything might happen during the course of it. It was a fact brought home to her anew every morning, and every morning newly exciting. (p. 10)

Ruth Jhabvala's third novel could well have been sub-titled 'The Nature of Freedom,' for Shakuntala is in reality (like Esmond and many other characters in the novel) still in bondage although living in 'free India' ten years after Independence:

> The magazine was called *Advance: a Monthly review of the Arts*. It looked very interesting. She fluttered the pages; sometime when she was free she would read it. Daddyji would advise her which articles to read first. (p. 12)

'*Sometime when she was free*' Shakuntala might imagine 'that life was very beautiful and all open before her' (p. 16), and Har Dayal (the significantly Westernised 'Daddyji' of Shakuntala's thoughts) might regard himself as 'a free agent' (p. 210), but they are both invisibly bound by the silken strands of *tanha*, materialistic desire, which emanate from the discreet, yet powerful personality of Shakuntala's mother, Madhuri. Amrit and Indira look 'happy, healthy and vigorous, like an ideal couple in an advertisement for vitamin pills' (p. 212), but they too are bound, by their own conventionality and their limited aims in life. Indira is convinced that 'it is only natural' for everybody to enjoy, if they can, the pleasures of good food, pretty clothes, servants, a car and a comfortable home (p. 215); Amrit exudes self-confidence and self-approval. Living a life of leisure

in his beautiful house, at the heart of which Madhuri tranquilly
distils an 'air of elegance and refinement that ... pervaded the
whole ... growing more and more concentrated the nearer one
drew into her presence' (p. 25), Har Dayal occasionally suffers
a twinge of guilt: especially when he compares his own style
of living with the austere existence chosen by Ram Nath,
veteran of the Independence struggle and his own former
Cambridge friend and hero. But such moments of doubt and
self-disgust soon pass, and Har Dayal is content on the whole
to regard his own and Shakuntala's liking for comfort and the
superficial social life of Delhi as inclinations natural to those
who care deeply for 'the refinements of life, the beauties that
come with sophistication' (p. 215).

Shakuntala's ideas of personal freedom (like Nimmi's ideas
of elegance in *The Nature of Passion*) are comically limited and
superficial. Infatuated with Esmond, never guessing that his
picturesque melancholy goes far deeper than mere
disappointment in a dull wife, she thinks divorce (for Esmond
and Gulab) the perfect answer to her own hope to marry him.
Unconventionally, 'fearlessly' holding his hand in a crowded
Indian shopping street, Shakuntala (still undeceived by reality)
tells herself she 'knows' life to be 'more wonderful, a hundred
times more wonderful, than even she had suspected' (p. 256).
To the reader, who has been admitted by Ruth Jhabvala to the
secret plans of Shakuntala's parents and of Esmond himself,
it is of course only too clear that real life will not lend itself
to Shakuntala's arrangements: she does not know it, but the
six months of glorious freedom she has enjoyed since her
graduation are about to end in a socially approved marriage
to the Harvard-returned son of one of her father's friends.
Shakuntala, who had pitied her sister-in-law Indira at the start
of the novel ('How dull it must be to have no longer any choice:
all possibilities to be irrecoverably lost in the certainty of Amrit'
— p. 11) will soon find all choices and possibilities, including
her romantic dream of finding a purpose in life through a
'daring' marriage to Esmond, end as does Indira's description
of a girl she had known at college

> who wanted to be an artist ... but afterwards ... was married
> to an Under-Secretary in the Ministry of External Affairs and
> now she has a baby and lives on Aurangzeb Road. (p. 27)

So end artistic ideals in 'free' India.

Much in the manner of the heroine of Jane Austen's novel *Emma*, Shakuntala ('handsome, clever and rich') simplifies the life around her into patterns she can comprehend. 'Love and fate and sorrow — that I understand very well,' she cries with amusing certainty (p. 228), but the complex characters and relationships of her family and friends are quite beyond her inexperienced grasp. She believes implicitly in her father's pretensions to culture, and does not realise that the Western guests at a party they attend together are laughing at Har Dayal rather than with him (p. 77). She does not begin to perceive the iron resolve beneath her mother's refined elegance and fragile appearance, and amusingly mistakes the polite hostility with which Madhuri and Ram Nath treat each other for the self-control she imagines necessary to star-crossed lovers (p. 87). She never suspects the nature of the terrifying chasm that has begun to open between Esmond and Gulab (p. 107). Most especially is she unaware of the intensity — and the implications — of her own feelings: as when she considers that 'the company of Indira would have been a hindrance rather than an asset' at a lecture Esmond is to give (p. 100). These errors of judgment are closely bound up with Shakuntala's delight in role-playing: she loves 'slipping on a new and untried personality, and always liked to experiment with new personalities' (p. 11). This aspect of her character creates amusing complications in the novel's plot, as when her passionately expressed desire to work for India's 'Prosperity and Greatness' (p. 120) and emulate the self-sacrifice of Narayan (p. 92) misleads both Uma and Ram Nath into thinking her a suitable wife for him. They are quite unaware that Shakuntala is merely 'experimenting', voicing an idealism that happens to fit her current 'personality' as an artist while childishly grabbing an opportunity to get back at her smug elder brother, Amrit. Shakuntala delights in shocking staid , conventional Indira — 'I must keep up my painting and my poetry, I cannot live without these things' (p. 197); tells herself it is 'even rather glamorous and advanced to be a divorcee' (p. 208); and after her expert seduction by Esmond even supposes herself 'reborn' (p. 191) and impelled, like her 'own Daddyji' before her, to 'the life of the spirit' (p. 195).

Esmond's cynicism undercuts Shakuntala's romantic

memory of the night on which, as she puts it, 'we ... consecrated
our love' (p. 233):

> 'Do you call our love an awkward position?' she sadly asked.
> The position is ridiculous, he thought, and the pleasure
> short. (p. 233)

Unlike Emma Woodhouse, Shakuntala does not grow up into
good sense and a liberal outlook. At the end of the novel she
is very much what she was at its beginning, spoiled, self-centred
and a little obtuse. All that her 'wonderful' experience of life
has given her is a romantic memory of her love affair with
Esmond to carry into the safe, conventional life she will lead
as young Mrs Bhatnagar, Delhi socialite.

The fact that such seasoned political campaigners as Uma
and Ram Nath are so misled by Shakuntala's transient
enthusiasms that they see in her a mirror-image of their own
idealism casts a somewhat dubious light on that idealism, and
on their judgment. Both Uma and her brother compulsively
question and mull over the past. Was it really what it had
seemed? Was it genuine inspiration or merely youthful
enthusiasm that has now run out on them, leaving them ill
at ease, discontented, and unwilling to face the realities of the
India they had worked so hard to set free? Liberty appears to
exact hard penalties from those who give all for its sake. Uma
lives alone in a decaying mansion, Ram Nath in an overcrowded
tenement, Narayan in an isolated village, Gulab (who has
married according to her own inclinations) in a cramped,
conventional flat. The 'refinements of life, the beauties that
come with sophistication' (p. 215) appear ironically to be the
reward only of those who keep, like silkworms in a box, safely
within the conventions.

In this connection, Ruth Jhabvala's portrayal of Ram Nath
is especially interesting. The old freedom fighter's dry wit
provides *Esmond in India* with some of its best comic moments,
as when he leads Amrit on to greater and greater stupidities,
finally seeming to agree wholeheartedly with the young man's
impudent assessment of Narayan:

> 'I think my son has no ambition — is it not dreadful to have
> such a son? He is a doctor but he dare not aspire to a
> fashionable practice; and worst of all, not only has he no

money in the bank, he is not even ashamed of this fact. Have
I not reason as a father to grieve for him?' (p. 90)

We are reminded of Mr. Bennet in *Pride and Prejudice*, who
listened to (and encouraged) Mr Collins's absurdities 'with the
keenest enjoyment, maintaining at the same time the most
resolute composure of countenance'[4]. But although he has
withdrawn from public (and indeed, almost entirely even from
private) life, and though, like Mr Bennet, he prefers the
company of books to that of people and derives wicked
amusement from irritating and thwarting a stupid wife, Ram
Nath is aware (as Mr Bennet too often is not) of his own
inadequacies:

Once he had known ... very well, all the different values
belonging to different classes and different people. In rejecting
those of his own class and position in life, he had not acted
blindly. Heknewthat it was pleasant and comfortable to have
money, privacy and privilege; only he had exchanged these
things for others which to him personally meant much more.
But he had never lost his knowledge of what the rejected
values still meant to other people, to people like Har Dayal.
(p. 161)

Ram Nath had hoped that retirement would bring him a better
understanding of life through reading and contemplation
(p. 242), but his self-critical and ironic eye notes that his

soul had shrivelled. In old age there should be some
greatness, some wisdom ... instead of expanding and taking
in all the world, he had narrowed and could only see himself
and his own path. (p. 162)

Ram Nath's rational approach to life causes him to cut through
sentiment and 'cloudy talk of God,' substituting an honest
realism for the mindless worship of 'primitive myths' (p. 98). It
is therefore one of the novel's ironies that Uma assigns to her
brother the task of persuading Gulab to leave Esmond. 'When
... differences go very deep, it is better for husband and wife
to part, because otherwise they will begin to hate one another
and that is very ugly,' says Ram Nath (p. 164), whose own
domestic life with Lakshmi is one of perpetual bickering and who
has, in fact, long withdrawn from her in spirit if not in person.

Ram Nath and his son Narayan are characters of moral principle, whose acts accord with their deepest feelings and convictions. Ram Nath will not, for instance, write the letters of reference that help to maintain the Indian system of 'personalities and personal recommendation' (p. 61), and respects his son's decision to work among the rural poor in preference to growing prosperous in a Delhi practice. Such characters as they, Ruth Jhabvala seems to suggest, are rare indeed; and she establishes their rarity and worth by means of effective contrast with such characters as Har Dayal and Shakuntala, who are happiest when they are indulging false sentiment. In Ruth Jhabvala's fiction the character of worth is known not only by his genuine consideration for others, but by his willingness to act on their behalf; and a clear dividing line is frequently drawn between those who act with a decent concern and those who merely talk about doing so.[5] Uma and Lakshmi, despite their respective limitations, belong with their menfolk in this regard. Uma is one who, 'in her time, had both talked a lot and, when it came to the point, done all she could without hesitation' (p. 121). Lakshmi, impatient as she is with the idealism of her husband and her son, does not lack concern for Ram Nath. Under all her complaints is a sad, bewildered affection for the old man who taunts and disregards her: 'He never eats, so I too have to starve with him' (p. 40).

Genuine self-awareness is another characteristic that distinguishes the personality of worth in Ruth Jhabvala's fiction. In the light of her confession in "Myself in India" to 'a deplorable tendency to constant self-analysis,'[6] it becomes evident that in Lalaji of *The Nature of Passion*, Gopi of *A New Dominion* and other 'successful,' worldly-wise characters she is exploring personalities unlike her own, persons possessed of cheerful, practical natures who waste no time on self-doubt or introspective pondering. Those who are her 'likes' appear to be the shy, retiring, thoughtful characters in her novels who all too frequently lose life's battles, or whose rare successes are fraught with irony or deprivation: Prem in *The Householder*, who 'starts out with a desire to be noticed for his talents, and ends hoping simply to be allowed to keep his joy,'[7] Krishna Sen Gupta in *Amrita*, whose decision to marry arises from a mature realisation of his own inconsistencies; Sudhir Bannerjee in *A Backward Place*, whose conscience and intelligence are perpetually at war; the narrator in *Heat and Dust*; Raymond in *A New Dominion*; Sarla Devi in *Get Ready For Battle*; the sensitive, observant Natasha of *In Search of Love and Beauty*; blindly idealistic Michael Wishwell in *Three Continents*; Hari Mehta in the film BOMBAY TALKIE; Ram Nath in *Esmond in India* — 'losers' all in life's materialistic struggle, but all of them characters who represent their creator's moral positives of sensitivity, decency and integrity.

Closely linked with the examination in *Esmond in India* of 'freedom' in 'free India' is an inquiry — conducted at an ironic, rather than a reformist level — into the social and mental conditioning of upper-class Indian women. Although *The Nature of Passion* presents numerous female characters who are physically confined, due to Punjabi convention, to the inmost chambers of their homes, most of these ladies show themselves capable of getting their own way in what they consider the major affairs of life. *Esmond in India* depicts a spiritual and mental bondage that is far more difficult to break through than the petty restrictions Nimmi brushes impatiently aside in her search for excitement in *The Nature of Passion*. Gulab, Uma and Shakuntala have left mere convention behind them, yet appear to be more effectively bound by their upbringing and their instincts than by any formal rule of *purdah*. Despite his irritation with Lakshmi, Ram Nath understands the inescapable dilemma of Indian women:

> That was a hard thing for women, he thought, to have their lives warped by circumstances to which they could not submit because they could not or would not understand them. As his own wife's had been. (p. 63)

His 'logical and emancipated mind' (p. 36) distrusts sentimentality and circumlocution. He describes the Indian ideal of feminine duty with revulsion, and in terms that significantly foreshadow Ruth Jhabvala's own opinions on the subject, in "Myself in India"[8]:

> Our women are so ... like animals, like cows ... Beat them, starve them, maltreat them how you like, they will sit and look with animal eyes and never raise a hand to defend

themselves, saying 'do with me what you will, you are my
husband, my God, it is my duty to submit to my God.' (p. 97)

While her brother is amused and irritated by women's 'cloudy
talk' of religion, and refers her coldly to the assistance of 'your'
God (p. 35), Uma counters disillusionment with personal
generosity and religious fervour. She warmly welcomes a motley
crew of visitors who bed down in any available corner in her
rambling old house, and finds 'great spiritual comfort' in a
Swami who is her permanent guest (p. 66). The true centre
of her life is, however, her daughter Gulab whom she worships
with love and offerings of food as she worships the images in
her shrine-room. The energy Uma poured into the freedom
struggle is now directed against Esmond; in her battle to get
Gulab and Ravi away from him she uses every weapon in an
extensive armoury, emotional blackmail and arguments both
practical   and   spiritual.   Her   affectionate,   comradely
understanding of her brother is one of the most attractive
features of a novel in which many of the family relationships
presented are characterised by insincerity and selfishness
rather than by warmth. Selfish preoccupations of different kinds
lurk behind Shakuntala's demonstrative affection for her father,
Gulab's dependence on Uma, Madhuri's approval of Amrit and
Lakshmi's defensive advocacy of Narayan. Uma is set apart from
these by her idealism and the genuine warmth of her nature.
Yet, once the unusual stimulus of the freedom struggle is
withdrawn, even this vigorous, apparently liberated female
personality reverts to type, wasting her uncommon energies in
hostility towards her son-in-law and unbridled indulgence of
her daughter and grandson, and needing (as Ram Nath is
perceptively aware) religious sanction to do the things that
obviously need doing.

Gulab, who had defied convention in marrying Esmond,
remains loyal to him because of the prompting of that tradition
according to which a woman's husband is her God. Even
Shakuntala, dreaming of a 'brave' and 'fearless' future with
Esmond, can only talk of her love in conventional terms:

'Esmond, I know you are married and also you have a child,
but I tell you all this means nothing to me. Only I know you
have come into my life and now it is my duty to give
everything I have to you, to adore you and to serve you and

to be your slave.' (p. 184)

These three women, who consider themselves (and are considered) 'free' are in reality quite as much slaves to tradition as Madhuri and Indira, two characters representative in this novel of well-bred respectability. Madhuri

vaguely knew the Saxenas and the Srivastavas and knew them to be respectable families of the right class. That was the sort of thing about which one could trust a girl like Indira: she would make friends only with girls of the right class. (pp. 24-5)

Caught unhappily between these two groups of women, longing to emulate and rival Madhuri but forced to live at a level below even Uma's, is Lakshmi, her domestic setting expressing the overturning of her life's expectations. She occupies, with Ram Nath, the ground floor and courtyard of a large house, and is constantly irritated by the two tiers of upper galleries inhabited by 'very ordinary lower-middle-class people' who overlook her and her activities:

Had it not been for misfortune and an obstinate husband (she) would certainly have lived (as she often assured herself and her neighbours) in a large house of her own with many servants. (p. 33)

The simple outlook that lets Lakshmi comfort herself with prayer and domesticity, pounding spices, making pickles and tending her linen (p. 240) renders her insensitive to the idealism of Ram Nath and Narayan. She

had not been prepared for a husband who gave up his career before he had even entered on it, forfeited his property —and hers — and went in and out of prison for the sake of a cause for which she herself could find neither understanding nor sympathy. (p. 64)

A victim of self-deception like so many other characters in Ruth Jhabvala's novels, Lakshmi tells herself that Narayan's exile in a remote village is not self-imposed but brought upon him by necessity 'since his own father has not sufficient love in his heart to help his son' (p. 137). She expects the match projected between Narayan and Shakuntala to compensate her at last for years of privation, and entertains absurd hopes of ruling a house like Madhuri's when Narayan should finally take up a Delhi practice. Yet, though she contributes substantially to the comedy of *Esmond in India* through her over-reaction to Ram Nath's ironic barbs, her own misguided actions, and her wilful blindness to the facts that govern her life, Lakshmi participates (as her husband concedes with something like envy) 'wholeheartedly in the affairs of life' (p. 240). Her horizons are limited, but she is no fool. A materialist herself, she understands the materialists in her circle and sees far more clearly than Uma or Ram Nath into Shakuntala's heart:

> 'All her life she has lived in a big house with many servants, she has had all the jewellery and saris she wants. Should she now want to give up these things because you tell her not to care for worldly possessions?' (p. 137)

The single character in *Esmond in India* who appears to have found true 'freedom' of spirit is the absent Narayan, Ram Nath's brilliant young son, a physician who has given up wealth, comfort and the satisfaction of pleasing his querulous mother in order to work among the poor. Gandhian ideals of selfless service seem to live on in the austerely simple way of life chosen by father and son; indeed, Uma sees in her nephew a continuation of the family tradition of patriotic self-sacrifice. Yet both Narayan and his father have had to sacrifice comfort and honour in order to remain free in spirit. The moral stature of these two remarkable men goes quite unappreciated by Lakshmi, who can only perceive (and resent) the fact that those persons who 'only sat quiet and did nothing (during the Independence struggle) ... are now getting the prizes' (pp. 40, 39). Narayan's example may be admired by the 'prize winners' in Har Dayal's family, but hardly imitated. Amrit inquires:

> 'And how is old Narayan? ... You know, I cannot understand him. He is such a clever chap, yet why does he go out there in the jungles when other doctors are making a good pile in the cities and also leading a comfortable life among civilised people? ... I am sure he has ten times the amount of grey matter that I have. But where has this got him in life?' (pp. 89-90)

Har Dayal pays lip-service to Narayan's nobility of spirit and

Madhuri resents the young man's virtue, which opposes and
shadows all she represents and works to achieve for herself
and her children. The mention of his name provides Shakuntala
with yet another star to which she can hitch her temporary
enthusiasms·

> 'If only there was something for me to do,' said Shakuntala
> ... her voice quivering with a longing to prove herself. She
> ... thought of Uma in those days and she added: 'In your
> time, Auntieji, all of you who wanted could help, you could
> all go to prison, but now — what can I do, when I am not
> a doctor nor a social worker now,' she laughed as she said
> it, sounding not at all dispirited, 'good for anything at all.'
> (p. 121)

Ram Nath is humiliated by his inability to find Narayan a
suitable wife; Lakshmi comforts herself in cooking mango
chutney and lime pickle for him. The indifference with which
Narayan is treated outside his immediate family circle is true,
the novel implies, to the facts of contemporary life in India.[9]
Another such absent character of worth is Uma's dead
husband, whose remembered vigour and idealism stand in
permanent contrast to Har Dayal's effeminacy and Ram
Nath's thorny cynicism. Death has set *him* 'free', preserving
his heroic image intact and preventing his dwindling (like
so many of his contemporaries) into ineffectiveness, out of
touch with the India they helped to create.

The 'free' India in which these characters move in conflict
and occasional, uneasy association, is itself ideologically
unsettled and confused. Har Dayal, who is very much in
touch with official thinking on cultural matters, talks
privately of internationalism but is carefully chauvinist in
his public utterances. 'Nowadays everything is international,
all the old distinctions are going,' he informs Madhuri when
their younger son Raj announces his engagement to an
English girl. 'In marriage no one cares very much any more
about caste or nationality' (p. 210). Yet, planning one of the
speeches he loves to make,

> his mind hovered round a quotation from Mathew Arnold,
> which he decided after all to leave out; whatever quotation
> he might use would have to come from the Indian classics,

preferably from Sanskrit; only such would be well received.
(p. 156)

Shakuntala regards herself as deliciously free, and knows her
brother to be an uncultured materialist, but there is the weight
of a whole social tradition of male superiority and female
subordination in Amrit's complacent reply to Indira's news that
Shakuntala wishes to marry Narayan:

> 'She may wish,' said Amrit, 'but that is a long way away
> from what she will get.' And for some unknown reason he
> laughed. (p. 213)

The old struggle of Indian nationalism *versus* British
imperialism has given place to a new conflict. India strives now
(as Shakuntala says, with unconscious truth) no longer to be
free, but to be great — or rather, to regain and keep her
greatness of spirit. The conflict between Har Dayal's family and
Ram Nath's over the projected marriage that is to bring them
together is a conflict between personalities that brings
fundamental approaches to life into opposition. For a short time
a possibility exists that culture and action, idealism and
practicality might be reconciled and modify one another to the
benefit of all, but the possibility passes. Ruth Jhabvala sees
India as spiritually divided[10], her potential for greatness
unfulfilled and her destiny thwarted. Individual fulfilment
is achieved here and there, and from time to time. But
despite the fact that it is an amusing novel, pessimism
weighs heavily on *Esmond in India*, and happiness, except
of the most limited kind, seems permanently out of reach.

The distinctive vision of the Indian landscape that becomes
a recurring motif in Ruth Jhabvala's later fiction[11] appears
in *Esmond in India* for the first time:

> Imperceptibly, dust unto dust, village and shops faded
> again into desert landscape, and sometimes there was a
> ruined mosque among the withered shrubs and stumps
> of trees. The sun became hotter every minute, making of
> sky and earth one vast white bowl of dust. (p. 145)

In most of Ruth Jhabvala's fiction this is a vision peculiar,
indeed apparently reserved, for only the most sensitive of
Western eyes. It is as if by responding to the fifth element

(*vyom*, the sky) that Indian tradition adds to the four (water, earth, air and fire) it shares with the West, characters such as Esmond Stillwood, Raymond in *A New Dominion*, and the narrator of *Heat and Dust* reveal their openness — and therefore, vulnerability — to India. Looking about him with discontented, disenchanted eyes, Esmond sees

> always, encompassing everything and holding it in its vast bowl, the Indian sky — an unchanging unending expanse of white-blue glare, the epitome of meaningless monotony which dwarfed all human life into insignificance. (p. 252)

Within the comic pattern of the novel, Esmond's 'vision' of India is seen as idiosyncratic and eccentric. It is Uma's house, in its flaking beauty and decayed grandeur, its memories of past heroism, its vestiges of feudal social relationships and religious fervour, and its atmosphere of a spacious but neglected and unregulated Paradise, that furnishes the novel's metaphor for India. The garden has run wild, the pond is covered with slime, the fountain plays no longer. The servants' quarter has been let and sublet, for 'there were always poor people desperately in need of a corner to live in' (p. 95). Significantly, this is a house that Esmond, though he longs to 'love India ... feel at home there and never want to go away' (p. 235) never enters, preferring the elegant — and empty — refinements of Madhuri's drawing room (p. 234).

Religious ritual is conspicuous by its absence in Har Dayal's house, where the only ceremonies permitted to exist revolve around Madhuri — her bath and massage at ten o'clock each morning, her chocolate (brought to her by her adoring husband) at eleven. The Nataraj and Ganesha figures in her drawing room are merely ornaments, not objects of worship (p. 153). Books replace religion in Ram Nath's life, and despite her regular prayers, cooking and worrying about Narayan are Lakshmi's real spiritual consolations. There is no place for religion in the smart little flat occupied by Esmond and Gulab. And though Uma's household seems to be the exception to this rule (for Uma reads the scriptures and meditates upon them, seeks advice from the Swami upstairs and regularly renews garlands around portraits of the dead), even here the real object of worship is Gulab, Uma's 'gorgeous slattern' of a daughter[12], to be fed 'offerings' of buttermilk, sweets and fruit by her

mother and her maid-servant Bachani, as she sprawls dreamily,
like an untidy houri, under the cracked plaster of a frescoed
ceiling. These are all households of the new India, and the place
assigned in each of them to religious observance indicates the
rapidity with which old traditions are being discarded and new
ones tried on for size. Old values seem to be in retreat,
modernity, rationalism and 'culture' replace the old myths.

As the principal representative in the novel of that 'culture',
Har Dayal attracts Ruth Jhabvala's most withering satire. His
mind revolving continually around the speeches he is frequently
called upon to make, he appears to be entirely made up of
platitudes. A conversation concerning the happiness of his
beloved daughter cannot entirely distract him from the pleasant
task of formulating phrases to be used in that afternoon's
address. His thoughts run in well-lubricated grooves: a mention
of the Taj Mahal brings an automatic response: 'that noble pile
which is not only a monument to a great queen but also to
a great culture' (p. 157). Har Dayal positively enjoys the futile
'busyness' of his life: ' "I will be so busy this morning," he would
say with a happy sigh' (p. 49). He welcomes an endless stream
of visitors and fellow committee members with 'enthusiasm' and
'a radiant smile' (p. 50). Treated by both the Western and the
Indian sections of Delhi society as a cultured intellectual, Har
Dayal exudes an aura that misleads Shakuntala into believing
'that she was really living in the midst of great cultural activity'
(p. 14). His appreciation of cultural values is, however, much
more a matter of sentiment than of intelligence or taste. His
would-be witty sonorities are frequently nipped in the bud, by
his creator herself, by Ram Nath, and even by Amrit and
Shakuntala:

> 'Get up at once — people have come to see your father,
> what will they think if they see you sitting there?'
> 'Oh,' Shakuntala said, and laughed, 'they are too busy with
> their committee to be able to think.' (p. 52)

The femininity of Har Dayal's nature is duly noted: affectionately
by Shakuntala (pp. 28-9), and with scornful wonder by Lakshmi
(p. 177). His life is ruled by his iron-willed wife, and she has
few illusions about him:

Madhuri had at one time feared that he might follow the

general madness and throw himself into the Independence
movement, go to jail, give up his property and social standing.
Certainly, given Har Dayal's predilection for making speeches
and gestures, the danger had not been negligible; it had only
been by exerting all her influence and bringing it to bear on
the side of his other predilection for comfortable living, that
she had managed to counteract it. The balance had been
precarious for many years, but she had always contrived to
keep it. Now, of course, all the danger was over, and she
could enjoy the satisfaction of having successfully steered
him into a safe and comfortable harbour. (p. 210)

Har Dayal is, despite his claims to live 'the life of the spirit,'
quite as materialistic as Madhuri. He would prefer to see
Shakuntala married to Professor Bhatnagar's Harvard-returned
son than to the impecunious (if brilliant and idealistic) Narayan:
the high status of the Bhatnagars in 'free' India outweighs by
far the years of friendship and all Har Dayal's much talked of
admiration for Ram Nath. A cruelly comic study in Ruth
Jhabvala's early style, Har Dayal is another of the 'interpreters'
of Indian culture that she pillories in *Amrita* and *A Backward
Place*, with the added refinement in his case that when it comes
to interpreting India to his own daughter, this Indian man of
culture calls on the 'expert' knowledge of Esmond Stillwood,
her English lover. Har Dayal's character is caught in all its
comic weakness when Ram Nath sees through his affectionate
protests to the embarrassment the proposal has caused him:

> 'Yes, he has come to tell us that it will not be possible for
> Shakuntala to marry Narayan ... Is it not so?' Ram Nath
> asked Har Dayal, who looked at the ground and said in a
> muffled voice: 'My friend, please let me explain what I have
> come to say.'
> 'Why explain — what is there to explain? You will tell me
> that she is too young and that they do not know one another
> and that you want her to have more education. And I will
> say yes, you are right, and so it is finished.' (p. 223)

In the world of shifting values Ruth Jhabvala sets herself to
depict by making India her subject, certain elements are
selected by her and presented as being of permanent and
untarnishable worth. Indian classical music and literature,

devotional songs, dance, art and architecture stand in her
novels and stories for the essential and most valuable aspects
of Indian civilisation, and her characters frequently reveal
themselves to the reader according to their capacity to respond
fully to them. This is the test to which Har Dayal, member of
many cultural committees, is put and found wanting:

> Poetry had such an ennobling effect, it made one realise all
> the beauty in the world and in one's own soul. But somehow,
> when he felt beauty moving in his soul, his thoughts always
> turned to Ram Nath. (pp. 192-3)

It will be Har Dayal's punishment to live with the knowledge
that his materialism has led him to deny the 'beauty moving
in his soul': he has 'failed Ram Nath and refused him the only
thing he had ever asked from him' (p. 225).

Ruth Jhabvala displays in this novel, as in *The Nature of
Passion* and much of her other fiction, a characteristic
sensitivity to the social condition of the 'nameless faceless'
domestic servants of India (p. 41). Madhuri takes unquestioned
possession of the lives of her well-trained servants (p. 209) and
Shakuntala, despite her high idealism, is not above venting her
feelings viciously, on occasion, on her father's chauffeur
(p. 123). Lakshmi (who has none) regards the employment of
'many servants' as one of the necessities of civilised life (p. 136),
as do Amrit and Indira (who have a great many). Gulab pays
the price for her indifference to the humanity of what her
creator has called 'the great mass of India'[13] when she is
nearly raped by a servant:

> (Gulab) never even noticed him; so many servants had
> come and gone since her marriage that for her they had
> ceased to have individual personalities, being no more
> significant than any other piece of property around the
> house. (p. 41)

In contrast to the shifting urban population of 'nameless
faceless' servants is Bachani, who regards herself as a part
and extension of Uma herself, and not merely of her
household. Both women are as one in honouring Ram Nath,
spoiling Gulab, worshipping Ravi and despising Esmond and
all his concerns. They grumble at one another, but the bond
between them is strong. The domestics in *Esmond in India*

exhibit personal feelings of which their employers are unaware,
and which provide an unobtrusive critical commentary on the
pleasures they are paid to service. Even the driver of the coach
in which the Western Women's Organization makes its
expedition was

> used to taking parties to Agra. He kept his eyes stolidly on
> the road and never turned round to see what the Sahibs and
> Memsahibs behind him were doing. When they stopped for
> any reason, he tactfully disappeared. (p. 144)

The novel as a whole displays Ruth Jhabvala's developing skill
in the manipulation of dialogue to project conflict, not merely
between individuals (though *Esmond in India* is rich in scenes
of domestic friction) but between cultures and civilisations.
Particularly interesting as a kind of Indian set-piece is the
exchange between Lakshmi and Madhuri (pp. 171-8) during
which Lakshmi attempts to propose a marriage between
Shakuntala and Narayan, only to find herself completely
outwitted and subtly humiliated: the proposal never even gets
mentioned, and Madhuri even manages to suggest (quite
outrageously, from Lakshmi's point of view) that Shakuntala
— already a college graduate — is unlikely to be married until
her 'education' is complete. On pages 186-90 there is a sad,
revealing little conversation between Lakshmi and Ram Nath
that uncovers their feelings for their son and for each other:
'They had never understood one another nor much cared for
one another; but they had been married a long time' (p. 189).
The exchange is unexpectedly touching, because pity for
Lakshmi awakens anger in Ram Nath that he had thought long
disciplined into tranquillity (pp. 188-9). His anger causes him
to act in a way that awakens her concern for him and wins
the grudging admission of affection: 'I have no wish yet to be
left a widow' (p. 188). The battle between Uma and Esmond
over Ravi's upbringing (pp. 140-4) is no mere domestic tiff but
a cultural confrontation that is additionally fuelled when
Gulab's dutiful loyalty to Esmond conquers her filial attachment
to Uma. On pages 210-17 Madhuri exerts her hidden power
over Har Dayal, Amrit and Indira, and Shakuntala's fate is
sealed.

Equally interesting are the occasions on which conflict is
submerged in apparent accord. The result is usually ironic,

frequently broadly comic; as when Har Dayal and Shakuntala
walk in the garden in a mood of mutual satisfaction:

> Each felt truly understood by the other, and as
> understanding also implied justification, Har Dayal
> experienced great relief. (p. 196)

Their 'satisfaction' is comically mistimed and quite unfounded,
since each has been deceiving the other. Har Dayal has been
made uneasy by his unfulfilled obligation to Ram Nath,
Shakuntala is in a state of secret rapture over her love for
Esmond, yet both declare themselves dedicated to 'the life of
the spirit,' to 'things beautiful ... gracious living and the arts.'
They are at one only on a single issue: both wish to pursue
their selfish ends and avoid any real contact with Narayan's
nobility of purpose. Yet both rationalize these impulses very
satisfactorily. Misunderstanding and mutual incomprehension
make comedy of a less complex kind out of the many meetings
Shakuntala has with Esmond and with her dutiful sister-in-
law Indira; and out of the exchanges that take place between
Lakshmi and Uma (pp. 235-8).

In many of these conversations, as in the dialogues of *A
Backward Place*, the nature of India is a recurrent theme. A
number of different views are contrasted, each revealing as
much about a particular speaker as it does about India.
Madhuri is not overly concerned with the political or cultural
future of India as a free nation; but she is very interested in
maintaining her present style of living within the very
comfortable setting India provides for her. Mention of Uma's
husband by Har Dayal as 'a giant — in body and in mind and
in spirit' (p. 31) brings her sharp rejoinder: 'How you always
exaggerate'. Madhuri's views on India and what is of true value
in it are practical and straightforwardly materialistic:

> Europe, England, even America, were all right for education
> or sight-seeing, but one had always to come back to one's
> own dear India. It was here that one's roots were, here that
> one could get the best position, here that one enjoyed one's
> money and property and one's proper social status. It was
> safe here, comfortable. (p. 28)

For Uma, idealistic as always, India remains 'Our Country ...
Our Cause' (p. 39). For Esmond, India is many faceted,

retaining his admiration for her high culture, attracting his
hatred and fear as he feels himself in danger of being engulfed
by her. To most of the other Westerners in the novel, India is
largely incomprehensible. They make gestures in the direction
of Indian culture, poetry, art and music, but as their small talk
makes clear, they secretly despise any one who either does
know something about these subjects or admits respect for
them: thus, Esmond is something of a joke among the Western
community in Delhi though he is often called upon by its
members to advise, lecture, and generally make himself useful:
'He's come specially to India to teach you people all about your
own country' (p. 81). India is more a subject for humour among
the members of the Western Women's Organization than for
respect or interest. Betty's quip, made on their expedition to
Agra to see the Taj Mahal — 'On the left you will see a pee-
house for jackals' (p. 148) — causes much amusement, some
of it subtly directed at Esmond, who is their guide to the
architectural treasures of India.

   Esmond in India, which includes numerous characters with
cultural interests or pretensions, allows occasional scope for
a literary joke. The over-blown romanticism of Har Dayal's
'translations' elicits Esmond's scorn at Betty's party; and when
Uma's quotation from the *Bhagavad Gita* is capped by Har
Dayal's quotation from a Shakespeare sonnet, Ram Nath enjoys
a gentle jibe at both of them: 'It was written by a very holy
swamiji called Shakespeare' (pp. 223-4). An occasional glimpse
of an amused author behind the scenes is possible for the reader
who is alert to the ironic self-satire in the comment:

> In those days it had been thought expedient to marry young
> men before they left for their studies abroad. Nowadays it
> was different; one took the risk even of a foreign daughter-
> in-law. (p. 29)

The words are the narrator's, they describe a situation central
to the author's personal experience[14], but they have taken on
the colours of Madhuri's mind. The passage illustrates the
remarkable detachment with which Ruth Jhabvala conducts
her study of post-Independence India. Her objectivity in the
process of writing makes it possible for the novel to
accommodate the change of attitude to her central character
that she detects in herself in recent years:

With *Esmond in India* the first European intruded on her
fiction. She thought it an anti-European book, and hostile
to Esmonds. But with the relentless shifts of feeling over the
years, she has come to think herself quite like him.[15]

The flaws in the novel seem to me to centre on the
personality of Gulab and on the circumstances of her
marriage with Esmond. It is difficult to credit, given the
Indian cultural situation, that Madhuri would ever have
permitted the arrangement of a marriage between her eldest
son and a girl whose way of living is so much at odds with
her own elegantly ordered existence, and whose family she
actively disapproves of and distrusts. Again, harbouring the
resentment she does over Amrit's broken engagement with
Gulab, it is hard to believe that she would not recollect the
name of Esmond Stillwood, to marry whom Gulab withdrew
from her engagement with Amrit. The manner of Gulab's
marriage to Esmond is unclear: we read of jewels given to
her only daughter by Uma, but of no wedding ceremonies.
Gulab's reasons for eventually leaving Esmond are explained,
but not very convincingly: She 'had to return, as was the
custom, to her own people' (p. 248). Gulab's almost
pathological fear of being looked at by any man other than
her husband (pp. 247-8) does not fit the personality of a girl
who has flouted convention in order to make a love marriage
with a Westerner, and who has, moreover, spent her
formative years in Uma's traditional but extremely
progressive household, frequented as it must have been
during the years of the struggle for India's Independence,
by scores of eager, patriotic men of all ages.

But perhaps it is an error to apply to Gulab the rational
criteria one would apply to the novel's other characters, since
she inhabits a world of her own as a creature both sub-
human and super-human. Ram Nath, sitting near his niece,
has 'the sense of being near a great amorphous mass of
sensuous life, of softness and sweet cloying tastes' (p. 163).
And there is, too, something of the goddess in Gulab, as her
eyes flash 'a wonderful fire' (p. 19), and she accepts oblations
from her mother's hands, reclining at her ease like a deity
on a frescoed temple ceiling while Bachani prepares more
offerings in the kitchen (p. 20). On these levels Ruth

Jhabvala succeeds in making Gulab symbolic (in Esmond's increasingly disturbed imagination) of India. She has a sensuous, instinctive awareness of reality, and acts habitually by instinct rather than by ratiocination. Where her creator fails is in fitting this animal-goddess believably into the patterns of everyday life, where she must fill the roles of wife, mother, daughter and housewife. Our first view of Gulab is of someone trying to exist in an impossible situation; and although it becomes clear to us as the novel progresses that her mother's house is her appropriate setting, we are left with the suspicion that there is no real-life building in which Gulab could conceivably find a niche, except a temple[16]. In the character of Gulab, Ruth Jhabvala projects for the first time a mystic vision of India that she will develop and re-state with much greater success in her later fiction.

Notes

1. R.P. Jhabvala, *Esmond in India* (Allen & Unwin, London: 1957), published in the U.S.A. in 1958 by Norton. All references in this chapter and in this book as a whole are to the British edition.
2. See Chapters II and III.
3. Quoted in Chapter I.
4. Jane Austen, *Pride and Prejudice*, vol. I, Chapter 14.
5. In *Amrita*, Hari Sahni is full of gushing feeling, but proves wanting when it comes to actually caring for, and supporting, Amrita; while Krishna Sen Gupta keeps his feelings under control yet acts always with her welfare in mind. Usha in *The Nature of Passion* 'never talked to anyone of her feelings,' but has more genuine concern for others than Nimmi, who loves nothing better than talking about hers. In the film BOMBAY TALKIE, Lucia Lane is selfish and self-centred, but a woman (so she is fond of saying) of intense and passionate feeling. She lays waste wherever she goes, grabbing 'happiness' at the expense of the helpless and the sensitive, Hari and Mala. In *A New Dominion*, the boat ride in the second part of the novel clearly distinguishes Gopi's shallow sentiment from Raymond's intense and self-sacrificing (though hidden) concern for his friend's welfare. Yet Gopi accuses Raymond of coldness, and a lack of 'feeling'. In *Get Ready for Battle*, Kusum and Brij Mohan are two characters who continually overflow with sentimental feeling, but act invariably from completely selfish motives. Like Hari in *Amrita*, Nimmi, Gopi and Lucia, they prey on the weakness and generosity of others.
6. R.P. Jhabvala, "Myself in India," op. cit., p. 8.

7.   Renee Winegarten, op. cit., p. 75.

8.   Op. cit., pp. 19-20. 'Sometimes it seems to me how pleasant it would
     be to say yes and give in and wear a sari and be meek and accepting
     and see God in a cow.'

9.   R. Agarwal records the following interesting exchange in his "An
     interview with Ruth Prawer Jhabvala," op. cit., p. 35.

     Q: It is ... said that you present only one aspect of Indian society ...
     There are Indians who are working quietly and unpretentiously.
     You have stayed in India for over two decades. Haven't you met
     such people? If yes, why don't they figure in your work?

     A: Yes, I know Indians who are working quietly and unpretentiously
     — quite a few of them — but would you say they are the most
     representative of India and Indian life today? And doesn't a writer
     always take the most representative aspect of his subject — that
     which will bring out its principal, its most striking feature of Indian
     life today — Indians working quietly and unpretentiously? Would
     you really?

10. See Chapter III; see also note 4 to the same chapter.

11. Notably in A Backward Place, A New Dominion, Heat and Dust and
     the story "An Experience of India."

12. A. Hamilton, "The Book of Ruth," op. cit.

13. See note 3 to Chapter III.

14. The reason why I live in India is because my strongest human ties
     are here. If I hadn't married an Indian, I don't think I would ever have
     come here for I am not attracted — or used not to be attracted —to
     the things that usually bring people to India.' See "Myself in India,"
     op. cit., p. 80.

15. A. Hamilton, op. cit.

16. Questioned by R. Agarwal on 'a shade of exaggeration' in the
     characterisation of Gulab, R.P. Jhabvala replied:

     I think novelists can be classified into two schools, or sects: (1) those
     whose characters are as large as life — here the high priests are
     writers like Tolstoy and George Eliot; (2) those whose characters
     are larger than life — the high priests being Dickens and Proust.
     I am a follower of the second school.

     See "An interview with Ruth Prawer Jhabvala," op. cit.

CHAPTER
V

The householder
1960

The title of Ruth Jhabvala's fourth novel, *The Householder*[1],
provides its own frame of reference. The dominant Hindu view
of life, which took shape during the ten centuries that are
generally believed to have elapsed between the composition of
the Upanishads and the formulation of the codes of Manu and
Kautilya (roughly 500 B.C. to A.D. 500), classifies the life of
the 'householder' as the second of four *Asramas* or stages in
Aryan life: preceded by the period of studentship, it is followed
by one of retirement and calm reflection, and at last by the
renunciation of all worldly interests.[2]
Prem is an underpaid teacher at a private college in Delhi.

A new arrival in the capital, he is newly married and lives with his wife Indu and their single domestic servant in a small flat for which he is paying more rent than they can afford. Prem seems to be achieving nothing: his employer and his landlord are obviously exploiting him, his students do not respect him, his friend Raj appears to have outgrown the interests they shared in earlier days, and Indu seems not only bored and unhappy but inclined to deliberately thwart his wishes. The plot of the novel humorously traces the process by which Prem, who was until very recently a carefree student, gradually takes on the responsibilities of the householder's life, shedding his adolescent dependence on parental props and developing (through an improving relationship with his wife) self-respect and an increased confidence in some, at least, of his abilities.

In building a novel around Prem's experiences, Ruth Jhabvala demonstrates her awareness 'that what is ludicrous on the surface may be tragic underneath'.[3] The comic side of Prem's story is chiefly contained in his creator's deft exposition of his early immaturity. Shy and uncertain of himself, the very youthful Prem displays an amusing pomposity. He takes himself very seriously indeed — is he not, after all, a Professor of Hindi, the son of a distinguished college principal, an employer (even if it be only of a single servant-boy), the married head of a household, and even a prospective father? But he is taken seriously by no one. The first thirty-one pages of the novel follow Prem through a typical day: he spends Sunday evening correcting essays, reflecting on the loneliness of his own home in comparison with the noisy activity at the Seigals' downstairs; goes next morning to the college at which he teaches, has an abortive conversation with Mr Khanna, its principal, on the subject (which he never succeeds in mentioning) of his need for an increase in his salary, visits his landlord Mr. Seigal, quarrels with Indu over letters they have received from their respective mothers, and ends the day in loneliness. The companionship of two people, an ex-college friend named Raj and a colleague of Prem's named Sohan Lal (both of them 'householders' of some years' standing) yields Prem some chequered consolation for his disappointment in life, and in himself.

Life often seems too much to cope with alone (for Indu, still almost a stranger to him, is no source of strength), and

inexperienced Prem seeks guidance from those who have
travelled further than he has in 'the round of life'. The
'successful' persons of his acquaintance are Mr Khanna,
Mr Seigal, his married friend Raj and Mr Chaddha, a senior
colleague at the college. From time to time Prem attempts to
emulate one or other of these persons, creating comedy for the
reader of The Householder and disillusionment for himself.
Occasionally he resorts in addition to the memory of his late
father's example. Striving to model himself on this paternal
pattern,

> 'Strive and strive and strive again!' (Prem) exhorted himself,
> with a show of bravery; and turned promptly to the wrong
> person for advice and encouragement. (p. 51)

This 'wrong person' is Sohan Lal, 'wrong' as a guide to worldly
success because his lack of means proclaims him incompetent
and a failure in life, doomed to be forever subservient to such
worldly, 'successful' persons as Mr Khanna and Mr Chaddha.
Sohan Lal is the only character in The Householder who is not
a source of comedy. Sensitive, habitually 'despondent' as a
result of the discouraging life he leads, Sohan Lal's remarks
convey deep-reaching criticism, not only of the Indian system
of early arranged marriage which has deprived him of freedom
to live the spiritual life to which his temperament calls him,
but of the Hindu view of life of which such marriage is a part:

> Who would not turn to God and take pleasure only in
> thinking about Him, if he could? ... It is easy for a young
> man whose marriage has not been made to vow himself to
> God ... What burdens has he, what responsibilities? He is
> free to do as he pleases*... Here in our India ... it is so that
> while we are still children and know nothing of what we want,
> they take us and tie us up with a wife and children ... So
> ... when we are old enough to know what the world is and
> God is, then it is too late, for we have a burden on our back
> which we cannot shake off for the rest of our days. (pp. 133-4)

Unlike Ved Prakash in The Nature of Passion, Sohan Lal is no
spoiled, self-indulgent boy. Early marriage has deprived this
thoughtful, sensitive young man of all joy and of any purpose
in life beyond that of deferring endlessly, for security's sake,
to Mr Khanna and his equally rapacious wife. Since Sohan Lal

has a moral delicacy similar to Prem's, the reader perceives that
Prem's future may unhappily come to resemble Sohan Lal's
present existence when life has sported further with him and
multiplied his cares.

Mr Khanna and his wife are chief among a number of
characters in the novel whose behaviour alternately encourages
or thwarts Prem's progress to maturity, and whose personalities
indicate, usually by contrast, the direction in which his is
developing. Outwardly a dedicated educationist proud of his
'most distinguished and reliable teaching staff' and the
'excellent discipline' they keep (p. 169), the jovial Mr Khanna
is in reality a practical businessman who exploits the poorer
teachers in his pay quite outrageously and expels no student
since 'he could not bear to refund the fees' (p. 12):

> The Khanna Private College was not cheap. Mr. Khanna
> specialized in boys from well-off families who were not clever
> enough to get admission into the better colleges. He kept
> them for a year or so, during which time he ostensibly trained
> them to get past the admission tests. That most of them did
> so was perhaps due less to their own hard work than to
> Mr Khanna's contacts, which were very good. (p. 48)

Noticeably easy-going on educational standards and methods,
Mr Khanna is interestingly full of theories about food. 'You
should always take plenty of salt with your food. It quickens
the energies' (p. 14) is a characteristic remark of his that
contrasts with the attitudes to food necessarily adopted by such
members of his staff as Sohan Lal, who cannot afford the luxury
of 'English breakfasts of eggs and toast' and eats his meagre
meals in shamed isolation from his colleagues. Mr Khanna's
greed — he eats with concentration, 'shovelling a great amount
of food into his mouth' (p. 70) — and indifference to the
problems of Prem and Sohan Lal give the lie to his pretensions
to culture and sensitivity. He and his principal auxiliary in the
Private College, Mr Chaddha, affect a formal, flowery mode of
speech that is entirely removed, not only from Indian English
idiom and from ordinary English expression, but from common
life itself:

> Mr Chaddha said, 'The society of ladies is said to have a
> very softening effect ...'

'It is not for nothing,' suggested Mr Khanna, 'that they are known as the gentle sex ... It is good sometimes to break off in the midst of toil ... and enjoy an hour's leisure and ease in their charming company.'

'As our heroes of old,' said Mr Chaddha, 'withdrew for respite from their battle to have their wounds dressed and their brows soothed by the hands of their consorts.' (p. 98)

Messrs. Khanna and Chaddha support each other's point of view and applaud each other's turns of phrase. Their 'cultured' insincerities contrast effectively with Prem's honest simplicity and, comically, with Mrs Khanna's inelegant directness.

Much of the dialogue in *The Householder* is worded in an artistic adaptation of Indian English idiom that shows how far (and fast) Ruth Jhabvala has progressed in this regard since the writing of *Amrita*. Indian English provides writers who need to convey in English the thoughts and words of people who do not normally think or speak in English or behave according to Western convention, with a good many expressions that have been 'Indianized' through the repetition, addition, omission or substitution of certain words and through alterations in conventional word-order. Of all of these Ruth Jhabvala made judicious use in *The Nature of Passion*, and in *The Householder* she refines her technique. At one end of her scale are Messrs. Khanna and Chaddha, whose formally 'correct', elaborate phrases betray their insincerity. At the other is Mrs Khanna, whose brash behaviour occasionally embarrasses her husband, but whose blatant bullying of the college staff is a source of powerful support for his attitudes. Her flamboyant assertions of her own generosity and her use, alternately, of simulated rage and humility to inspire fear in 'her husband's employees', (p. 17) are expressed in Indian English forms whose crudeness gives all that she says the effect of comedy:

'Finest Darjeeling tea I serve to them!' she shouted. 'At what a loss to myself every month God only knows! ... Like a servant I wait on them,' she said ... her gold ear-rings ... shaking with indignation. (p. 16)

'What is the use of my cooking, cooking, cooking,' Mrs Khanna demanded, 'if you don't eat properly?' (p. 71)

'What is the use of telling,' said Mrs Khanna. (p. 146)

Such loudness contrasts finely with Prem's extreme delicacy of feeling, especially in those moments at which the Khannas' self-righteous assertions of their sense of 'justice' remind Prem that he has been less than just to Indu (p. 71), or Mrs Khanna's furtive interest in her neighbours' sexual activities embarrasses him:

> Mrs Khanna and three other ladies ... sat in a close circle, each one stirring in a tea-cup; one lady was talking and the others leaning eagerly towards her. Their eyes were gleaming. 'Every afternoon from two to five when her husband was in office,' the lady was saying. The others swayed their heads and clicked their tongues. They did not notice Prem. 'And the children in the house all the time,' the lady said in a shocked gloating voice. 'Hai-hai,' said Mrs Khanna with another click of the tongue. The teaspoons went round in the cups in quick agitation. (p. 145)

The Khannas' tea-party for the college staff, during which the pregnant Indu stuffs herself compulsively with sweetmeats, permits us to observe many of these characters in action. Mr Khanna's stream of platitudes is closely followed by Mr Chaddha's sycophantic speech of thanks, sentences from which strike with ironic effect upon Prem's consciousness as, horrified but helpless, he watches the irate Mrs Khanna advance on Indu (pp. 100-103). The speeches are empty and insincere, Mrs Khanna's 'hospitality' is a mere matter of form. Indu has been the only reality in the garish room, her straightforwardness in vivid and endearing contrast to the pretentiousness of the whole occasion.

Despite his innate politeness and respect for others, Prem instinctively disapproves of the Seigals. Their good humour cannot, in his eyes, excuse their self-indulgent indolence. There is an amusing element of self-righteousness in Prem's attitude to Mr Seigal who, when called upon after six o'clock in the evening, seems 'to have only just got up from his afternoon sleep' (p. 53). The Seigals are comfortably off, and thoroughly enjoy their

> nightly card-parties ... lights and ... noise and ... radio, the whisky, the cups of tea and the plates of sweetmeats so freely circulated. (p. 26)

Prem would like to be comfortably off himself, but does not admire the Seigal's way of living:

> He did not think that such ease was conducive to a really noble life. (p. 26)

The humour with which Ruth Jhabvala traces Prem's 'progress' is thus given a delicate ironic edge by the disillusioning evidence yielded by every stage of his experience, that worldly 'success' does not depend on moral worth or integrity. Indeed, both Prem and Sohan Lal already possess qualities of character that raise them (though of course they would not presume to think so themselves) above the ostentation and vulgar self-consequence of the 'mature' and 'successful' persons they seek to placate and emulate. Since experience seems (sadly) to teach him that in the world of men the areas of 'sense' and 'sensibility' are mutually exclusive, Prem has learned by the novel's end to keep these aspects of his life apart. Sharing the spiritual side of his life with Sohan Lal, Prem looks to Raj for advice in such worldly matters as bettering his financial position. In responsibly coming to terms with what is 'tragic underneath' the circumstances of his life, Prem advances to maturity:

> He knew that, whatever it might cost him, he had to hold on to his job. He had to do everything, accept everything, for the sake of holding on to his job. (p. 171)

His decision to protect Indu from the knowledge that 'insecurity ... would for ever threaten them' (p. 172) gives him greater dignity than all his anxious self-assertion in the early days of their marriage. Significantly, it is not with the spiritual-minded Sohan Lal, but with an evening on which Prem and Indu entertain Raj and his family at dinner, that the novel ends. A Government official in the Ministry of Food, married and head of a young family, Raj will be Prem's model for worldly advancement, regarded by him 'as an expert on all matters relating to adult life' (p. 155). Although Raj's behaviour suggests that success as a householder can turn a pleasant youth into a pompous and selfish, even brutal and hypocritical prig, it is unlikely that Prem and Indu will ever again experience such a moment of joy and mutual satisfaction:

'Very nice,' Raj's wife pronounced, after her first few mouthfuls, swaying her head from side to side in appreciation.

Indu glowed, but she murmured, 'It is only our plain home food.'

Raj had his mouth full of rice. He said, 'It seems your wife is a very good cook.' Then Prem felt really proud. (p. 192)

It is a scene that finely concentrates the varied aspects of Ruth Jhabvala's approach to her subject: her sympathy and pity for Prem, her amused admiration for Indu, her ironic scorn of the complacent Raj, her sense of comedy and, underlying them all, her awareness of the transience and fragility of the satisfaction being experienced by hosts and guests alike, shadowed as it so clearly is by the insecurity that threatens Prem and has already engulfed Sohan Lal.

While Prem strives to establish himself in the linked roles of husband, breadwinner and householder, Indu finds some difficulty in accommodating her individual, lively outlook to the requirements of her role as married woman and housewife. She comes from a fun-loving family, and though she wishes to be a credit to her parents and to Prem, she cannot help being amused by the very idea of herself as the dignified 'lady of the household.' Indian tradition lays down time-honoured rules for a wife's conduct[4] and Indu finds that there exist certain ideals according to which her husband and her mother-in-law expect her to behave.

Indu and Prem are little more than children, innocents (like the embracing cherubs carved on their bed) doing their best to conduct themselves according to the traditional 'rules' governing the adult world to which marriage has brought them. Unfortunately, their good intentions often place them in comical opposition to each other; as when Prem's plan to assert himself in the role of authoritative husband collides with Indu's intention to prove herself a model housewife:

He would have been quite pleased if his food had been slightly delayed, but Indu was very prompt with it ... She kept bringing him more hot chapattis ... Maybe he was a successful husband already. (p. 67)

When she is annoyed with Prem, Indu might serve his food to

him with 'a defiant little slam' (p. 79), but she will still prepare
it with care and serve it to him herself. Prem, a teacher of Hindi
well versed in the classics, whose ideas about marriage have
been shaped primarily by his mother's exemplary deference to
her late husband, applies ancient rule and childhood memory
to present experience with amusing results. Returning home
rather late to find the house dark and silent and Indu asleep,
he reflects that

> it was not right for a wife to go to sleep before she had served
> her husband however late he might come. He considered for
> a moment whether to wake her up and tell her so. (p. 62)

These incidents are typical of the misunderstandings which
punctuate the early months of their married life. Neither likes
nor understands the other very much to begin with. Both have
stubbornly individual personalities which resist the merging
that marriage requires of them, and a good deal of comedy
arises out of the efforts of Indu and Prem to fit themselves (and
each other) into the traditional roles of housewife and
householder. Indu talks with assumed wisdom about marriage
and its problems with Mrs Seigal (pp. 109-10) though married
but a few months herself; Prem nods sagely when Sohan Lal
criticizes the Indian system of arranged marriage which has
'burdened' the lives of them both (admitting privately to himself
that despite occasional misunderstandings with Indu, he rather
enjoys his 'burdens'). By the end of the book discord has been
resolved in harmony. Having learned first to love and be loved
by each other, Prem and Indu take their places as members
of adult society.

Part of their education consists in learning to value each
other's individual foibles and personal preferences. Indu's
earthy practicality confounds modest Prem, whose idealistic
concepts regarding the nature of 'girls' have not prepared him
for feminine directness:

> 'I told you, all girls go home when they are in this
> condition.'
> 'You talk as if it is my fault that you are —' Before he could
> finish, she had asked, 'Then whose fault is it?' This struck
> him as definitely indelicate. He frowned, for he did not like
> girls to be indelicate. They should be remote and soulful;

like Goddesses they should be. 'It is not nice to talk like that,'
he reproved her.

'What did I say? Only what is true.'

He would have explained to her that it is not always right
for a girl to say what is true; but what use was explaining?
A girl should understand these things by herself. (p. 31)

The earthy language Indu uses when addressing the
washerman ('What do you use for washing clothes — cow-
dung?') makes that individual grin appreciatively, while Prem
writhes in embarrassed annoyance (p. 44). Her personality
transcends daily domesticities, and Prem's education in life and
in love begins when he learns to value this delightful quality
in his wife instead of resenting it:

Her eyes were modestly lowered and she appeared intent on
preparing dough for parathas. But the way her hands moved
so swiftly and her bangles jingled and a strand of hair which
had escaped from her big coil fluttered merrily on her cheek
as she kneaded and pounded the dough: somehow her whole
figure expressed laughter. He wanted to be angry with her,
and yet also he wanted to laugh with her. (p. 46)

The character of Prem's mother adds substantially to the
comedy of the novel, while aiding the development of its main
theme. A middle-aged widow, she directs towards her only son
a smothering maternal affection in which the natural expression
of her personal feelings is heightened and sanctified by tradition
and convention. Ruth Jhabvala manages to convey through
comedy not only the frustration and irritation caused in Prem's
household by the old lady's behaviour, but the pathos of her
situation. Bitterly self-pitying, her life rendered lonely and
purposeless by the death of her husband and the marriage of
her children, her longing for regard shows itself in constant
attempts to compete with Indu and denigrate her in Prem's
eyes. Her ceaseless reflections on Indu's alleged lack of looks
and education, and supposed inadequacies as a housewife
(p. 85) create a 'rather strained' atmosphere in the small flat
during her visit (p. 86), and Prem learns from Raj, whose
gloomy sigh seems 'to come from out of the memory of a deep
experience' that 'it is often difficult when a wife and a mother
meet' (p. 94). The domestic quiet of Prem, Indu and their

cheerful servant-boy vanishes before her complaints. In a
typical incident, his mother's grumbling that Indu prefers
Mrs Seigal's company to hers, that the servant is never at
home, and that her afternoon cup of tea has been forgotten,
causes the usually gentle Prem to scold and shake the servant-
boy and reprove Indu who, deprived by tradition of the right
to defend herself against her mother-in-law's insinuations,
shouts in her turn at the servant and threatens him with
terrible punishments — whereupon 'Prem's mother took the
hairpins out of her mouth and said, "She has bad temper also.
My poor son." ' (p. 96)

His mother's presence and her solicitude for him make private
conversation between husband and wife impossible in the tiny
flat:

> 'Son!' his mother called from the next room. Prem could
> not help emitting a small sound of impatience, and that made
> Indu laugh. 'Son?'
> 'Yes, please!' Prem called back, rather too loudly. Indu
> threw the end of her sari over her face and laughed from
> behind it.
> 'What are you doing, son?' his mother asked rather
> plaintively.
> 'Nothing, Mother!' Indu rocked herself to and fro on the
> bed.
> 'Why do you leave me to sit here alone?'
> 'Keep quiet,' Prem urgently whispered to Indu, who was
> making choking sounds. 'I am just coming!' he called to his
> mother. 'I am only changing my shirt!' (pp. 106-7)

Annoying as all this naturally is to Prem, it is a necessary stage
in his development. He realizes that he 'wanted to be looked
after not by his mother but by Indu. And he wanted to look
after her' (p. 173). Prem's new-found maturity emerges as he
decisively arranges for his mother's tactful removal from his
home to that of his sister; and the innate courtesy and delicacy
that are characteristic of Ruth Jhabvala's personalities of worth
appear in the patient affection with which he sees the old lady
off at the Delhi railway station:

> 'Your sister needs me, son. I will have to leave you.'
> ...Prem looked crestfallen, but he said bravely, 'Of course

if she needs you, you must go.'

'... I did my best for you, son. We chose the girl as carefully as we could ... Try and bear up, son ... What help a mother can give, I have given ... I tried to teach her your favourite dishes, son ... But she does not learn well ... If your sister had not needed me, I would have stayed with you a much longer time ... Try and bear up, son !'

Prem waved and said, 'Please don't worry at all,' though it was not likely that she could any longer hear.

He did not wait till the train was out of sight but turned straightaway and made his way to the exit. He was so excited that he hardly noticed the crowds milling round the station-yard ... He thought only of gettiang home as quickly as possible, where Indu would be sitting waiting for him. (pp. 160-3)

The old lady has been tactfully disposed of, still secure in her illusions of her own indispensability to Prem. The fundamental change that has taken place in Prem's relationship with her emerges only indirectly, and most entertainingly, in a song Indu sings to Raj's little daughter in the last pages of *The Householder*:

> 'My granny's gone to market ...
> For four bowls she did pay,
> But one got broken on the way
> Oh, how angry granny got!
> She stamped her foot and home she trot!'

which gains additional spice from the fact that her mother-in-law has indeed been sent 'home' by Prem, and cannot be present to cloud or take credit for Indu's undoubted triumph as housewife and hostess (pp. 191-2).

Both Prem and Indu have been brought up in a tradition that taboos open displays of love between husband and wife, resulting in their mutual reluctance to admit, even in private, their affection for and need of each other. The conflicts thus created are both comic and touching; as when Prem, anxious to avoid impropriety and the risk of amusing or shocking Indu's family by telling her in a letter that he misses her, writes to her instead about the weather and the current price of mangoes, only to find these formalities melting unexpectedly into words of passion:

> The house is empty without you and my heart also is empty
> ... I want to stroke you and kiss you everywhere with my
> mouth and then I want to be inside you. When I think of
> this, I feel I shall die with longing so much for you. (p. 142)

The letter is never dispatched; ashamed at the thought that
his mother may read it, Prem burns it. When Indu returns from
her visit to her parents' house she appears remote and cold.
Finding that in her absence her mother-in-law has usurped
her position as 'the lady of the household,' she is trying hard,
by not showing her feelings, to act the part that tradition
demands: quietly submissive to Prem's mother, making no
demands on her husband, she is determinedly *not* 'angry'. But
her feelings (like Prem's) are too strong for the rules, and
emotion forces her at last into an oblique confession of love:

> 'Yes, now you have important letters to post! But when I am
> away, not one line could you write to me, though I waited
> and waited —' (p. 150)

She has told Prem in words, for the first time, that she loves
him. Their growing sympathy and affection for each other help
to disperse the guilt they feel about 'what he did with her at
night in the dark' (p. 9). When she accepts his first gift of sweets
and he kisses her, 'she did not push him away, nor did he feel
at all ashamed, though it was daytime' (p. 81). The monsoon
rains and a starlit night bring Prem and Indu out on the roof,
laughing with the freedom of the children they are, but also
as lovers (pp. 163-4, 179-80) in the pastoral tradition of the
Gita Govinda. As their sexual relationship steadies, Prem and
Indu begin to present to the outside world a united front that
accords with accepted tradition. On a long bus-ride to Mehrauli
to attend a wedding, they behave with meticulous propriety
though they have been making passionate love in private all
week long:

> They did not talk all the way, for they would have felt it to
> be indelicate to have a conversation together in public. They
> were also careful to sit far enough apart never to come into
> contact with one another, however much the bus rattled and
> shook them. (pp. 180-1)

Arriving at the wedding-house, they separate: Indu joins the
women guests, Prem the men (p. 182). These are established
customs, and conforming to them no longer creates conflict with
the young couple's private desires. On the contrary, it is done
(like their invitation to Raj and his wife to eat with them) by
mutual consent and helps to establish their right to respect
and 'dignity', not only as wedding guests but as adults.

Ruth Jhabvala selects a mode of Indian English expression
for Prem and Indu that, while occasionally admitting comedy,
indicates their dissociation from the extremes of insensitivity
represented by Mr and Mrs Khanna. Prem is a young man of
real feeling and sensitivity. Sitting in a green space in the still
unfamiliar city of Delhi, he notices the beauty of the sunset
sky, reflects on the beauty of nature, and is ready to find
meaning and philosophy in the significance of that beauty for
mankind (p. 39). He has high moral standards, the result of
a strict parental upbringing, and his thoughts fall naturally into
the form of quotation or reminiscence, often turning towards
self-analysis and misgiving. Very early in the novel the
occasional merging of the narrative with Prem's Indian English
meditations marks him out as above mere satire, a character
whose thoughts, even when immature or amusing, merit
sympathetic attention:

> Soon he would have a family and his expenses would mount;
> but his salary at Mr Khanna's college was only 175 rupees
> a month. *How to manage on that?* (p. 9)

> (Prem) knew that, in order to retrieve the situation, he ought
> to say at once *it is for myself I am asking.* (p. 15)

> (Girls) should be remote and soulful; *like Goddesses they
> should be.* (p. 31)

A 'norm' is established for his conversations of a simple, direct
English idiom stripped of complicated or Latinised words:

> 'My mother is coming to visit us,' Prem said.
> Indu said, 'Then she will be able to look after you here
> when I am gone.'
> 'How can you go away when my mother is coming to visit
> us?'
> 'Why not?' (p. 29)

It is an idiom that can accommodate without strain the common Indian English expressions that denote, for the purpose of fiction written in English, the speaker of Hindi or Urdu. It can also admit an occasional formality (very necessary to Ruth Jhabvala's needs in characterising Prem, who is given to invoking the 'rules') and a sententious expression:

He was at once ashamed of his longing: like a child, he thought, I crave for sweets. If one wishes to control others, one must first learn to control one's own senses. (p. 69)

When Ruth Jhabvala presents Prem in conversation with others, such as his friends Sohan Lal or Raj, nearly every phrase he utters brings out his distinctive qualities of character:

'It is a very nice place,' (Prem) added quickly. 'Only a little far.'
'It is very far,' Sohan Lal said. 'But where else could I get a place for my whole family for only 15 rupees?'
Prem sighed and said, 'When once one becomes a father of a family, one has to make many sacrifices.'
Sohan Lal smiled in rapturous agreement ... But all he said was 'When is your wife expecting?' (p. 19)

Here Prem's sudden switch from the simple English of his first utterance to pompous formality in his second has the desired effect of making the sentiment expressed in the second ring as false as Mr Khanna's flowery phrases. The reader receives the author's signal that these ideas, like the style in which they are expressed, are assumed rather than Prem's own. But since Prem's 'normal' mode of expression has been established very early in the novel as being, like Sohal Lal's, a simple, occasionally 'Indianised' one — 'How to manage on that?' (p. 9); 'So much?' (p. 17); 'It is for myself I am asking' (p. 15); 'I have been thinking what we were talking the other day' (p. 33) —it is only of an amusing and immature sententiousness that the reader convicts him, and not of insincerity.

Ruth Jhabvala invests the use of Indian English expression by both Prem and Indu with meaning that occasionally affects the alert reader at levels beyond those of linguistic propriety or of comedy. Indu's 'You want?', uttered as she holds out a sweetmeat to her penitent husband is moving because the word 'want' gives unobtrusive and unconscious expression to the

physical desire that begins to flow between the lovers in this
scene (p. 81). The word 'bring' used instead of the more correct
'buy' helps to channel sympathy of a different kind when Prem
gives his elderly mother the pink satin blouse material he had
bought for the absent Indu, around which (symbolic in its
colour, and soft, smooth texture of her physical appeal for him)
his thoughts have been hovering sensuously for several days:

> 'Yesterday I brought a present for you,' Prem said. 'I wanted
> it to be a surprise for you.' He went into the bedroom, opened
> the drawer and took out the piece of pink satin.
> Her eyes lit up as soon as she saw it. 'You brought this
> for me?' She stroked it, held it up to the light, touched it
> against her cheek. 'What is the use of bringing such a thing
> for an old woman like me?' She held it in front of herself.
> 'For your wife you should bring.'
> 'I brought it for you.' (pp. 136-7)

It is an important moment in the novel, establishing once and
for all that Prem has come of age. Even before she has spoken
them, he has experienced the truth of his mother's words: 'What
is your mother to you now?' Indu has replaced his mother in
Prem's heart, fills all his thoughts, and has become the centre
of his affection and his desire. The giving of the gift involves
some sacrifice for Prem, not all of it financial: in her absence
it has become a kind of substitute for Indu, and Prem has been
secretly dreaming of the occasions on which, sewn into a blouse,
'she would put it on and it would fit tight and gleaming over
her breasts' (p. 134). His action brings out the unselfishness
of his nature; but the words that accompany his action are
especially touching in the context of his new-found maturity
because the substitution of 'bring' for 'buy' (standard in Indian
English idiom) transforms his afterthought into what is, from
his mother's point of view, a tender memory of the past since
she can, as a widow, make no present use of the pink satin.
The inappropriate 'present' hastily thrust at an old woman by
the independent male who no longer needs her recalls (and,
for a fleeting moment, becomes) the loving 'surprises' planned
by Prem as a child for his young and beautiful mother.

Prem's aspirations to live 'a noble life' raise his thoughts from
time to time above the mundane existence he shares with the
Seigals and the Khannas, and focus them on a higher 'reality',

embodied in 'a bearded swami in an orange robe' (p. 73) to
whom he is introduced by Sohan Lal. The swami brings a new
beauty and joy into Prem's disappointing life, teaching him to
see in nature 'how God sports with flowers and fish and birds
in his playful mood' (p. 130). The music to which the swami
and his devotees dance ascends 'on spirals of joy', causing Prem
to tremble at the mere thought of the happiness that would
be his if only he were free to join them (p. 132).

The personality of the swami (the first member of his tribe
to make an appearance of some length in a Jhabvala novel)
is of particular interest in view of characterisations of religious
teachers still to come in Ruth Jhabvala's later fiction. He uses
a conversational idiom with his followers that resembles
Swamiji's in A New Dominion suggesting a relationship more
physical than spiritual:

> The swami affectionately tousled Sohan Lal's hair and said,
> 'You have been neglecting me.'
>   Sohan Lal said, 'If only I could, I would like to be with you
> all day and all night.'
>   'This is exactly how the lover speaks to the girl he has been
> neglecting,' the swami said. Everybody laughed, including
> Sohan Lal and the swami. Someone said, 'We are all your
> lovers', and the swami replied, 'And you all neglect me,'
> which brought more laughter ...
>   Prem came forward, and he too touched the swami's feet.
> 'Oh-ho,' said the swami, 'so good to me already.' (p. 73)

The swami's words, however, are not empty of truth or
significance. They captivate even the dark, intense
Vishvanathan, 'fierce with love for God' (p. 133), scornful of the
outer trappings of 'temples or priests or bells' (p. 131). His tale
of a broken glass trinket over which some villagers fight bitterly,
unaware of its worthlessness in comparison with a prince's
diamond ring puts into the form of a fable the central paradox
of The Householder: that Prem in his youth, innocence and
modesty, undervalues himself, seeking to emulate 'successful',
assured people to whom he is morally superior. The fact that
his true worth is overlooked by all but a few is a further
illustration of the swami's parable.

The presence of the swami imparts to those who come within
his aura those 'intimations of heaven'[5] that Ruth Jhabvala

considers part of the Indian experience, apparently transforming and uniting them in love. After his first meeting with him, the idealistic Prem is so overwhelmed that he wishes to abandon the householder's life immediately for that of the *sanyasa*:

> He felt lightheaded, and kept laughing to himself. Probably people who met him thought he was drunk. In a way that was how he felt ... He thought yes, this is how one must live — with love and laughter and song and thoughts of God. All his former worries about his rent, his rise in salary, his lack of authority as teacher and husband, were nothing but a thin scum floating on top of a deep well of happiness and satisfaction. Nothing, he thought, would ever trouble him again. (p. 78)

From this moment on, decides Prem, he would live 'in contemplation only of spiritual things.'

Such joyous floating in the rarefied upper air of spiritual consciousness, however, does not — cannot — last long. Leaning over Indu that night to tell her the happy news of his revelation, that in future 'he would love her as a sister and both would sit at the feet of the swami and think of God and indulge in happy, innocent play' (p. 78), Prem instantly (and amusingly) forgets everything but the 'unutterably sweet' sensations released in him by her physical presence. Later, thinking over his failure to return to the swami despite all his wishes and sincere intentions, Prem arrives at a maturer understanding of himself and his role in life:

> The swami seemed to ask for nothing, yet afterwards one realized that he asked for almost everything and expected one to forget, for his sake, all the things one was used to and thought important.
>   Prem told himself that he was not ready for that yet. (p. 105)

Prem's decision stems not so much from a considered acceptance of the views of philosopher-sages such as Manu and Kautilya[6] as from a mature acceptance of his own personality, his desires and his limitations. The swami will become for Prem what he has plainly already become for Sohan Lal: a present escape, and a future hope. Embittered by experience, disillusioned and beaten into submission by the circumstances of his life, Sohan Lal finds that he can transport himself occasionally through the swami to a world of 'gaiety and carefree abandon' (p. 105), far from the unpleasant and pressing realities of an existence dominated by such people as the Khannas.

The Householder is a study of human life and aspirations that is delicately poised on the fine line between comedy and tragedy. Ruth Jhabvala's satiric exposition of Raj's unprepossessing personality is part of the analysis undertaken in the novel as a whole of the cramping effects of Indian social convention upon the young and hopeful. Once a young student himself, Raj now dismisses young men who have not yet found an occupation as mere 'loafers' (p. 21). He is much better off than Prem, but chafes at the price of a bus-ride, ignores the appeals of beggars, and lets Prem pay for his tea. A brief exchange between Raj and Prem's German friend Hans Loeuwe (the first of Ruth Jhabvala's Western self-seekers to appear in a novel) demonstrates his creator's amused, yet compassionate view of Raj:

> Hans beamed at him: 'So you are a cog in the vast machinery of the Government?'
> 'No, I am a sub-officer, Grade Two.'
> 'By cog I mean one little screw in a big big wheel. It is a joke.' Raj continued to stare ahead of him but now he wore a look of tight-lipped disapproval. Quite obviously he did not regard his job as fit subject for a joke. (p. 157)

Hans's remarks reflect his own preoccupations (Prem's encounters with a group of Western 'spiritual seekers' in Delhi contribute a good deal to the comedy of The Householder), but they also expose Raj's increasing materialism, and a pompous self-consequence that is not unlike Prem's. Raj's pomposity is amusingly pricked by Hans, but at the level at which Raj exists, a job is indeed no 'fit subject for a joke'. Pursued by fears that he will lose his job at the college, Prem himself is hoping for employment as a Government service officer. He knows that the choice before him is limited, and aspires to the security of a Government job and the possession of one of the 'rows and rows of hutments, each one with an oval door, a little veranda and a tiny rectangle of grass in front' (p. 90) allotted to

Government officers such as Raj. Parenthood will only too surely
increase the 'doctor's bills and income-tax forms and all the
other horrors the world has in store' for Prem (p. 173). The
novel ends while insecurity has not yet clouded Prem's ability
to feel joy in simple things. The 'tempting and rapturous' vision
yielded to Prem by his visit to the swami (p. 176) is one of the
high moments life grants him, his 'satisfaction' at seeing
reflected in his mirror 'a man's face, no longer a boy's' (p. 178)
is another. His uninhibited and passionate lovemaking with
Indu (p. 178), the friendly condescension with which he regards
a young and gloomy bridegroom (p. 184), his dignity as a
wedding-guest (p. 182), his secret enjoyment of the respect
shown by others to his pregnant wife (p. 182), his new
confidence in facing the future with Indu beside him to support
and be protected by him (p. 188), and his pride in playing the
host to Raj and his family (p. 191) are all similarly touched,
even in their amusing aspects, by his creator's sympathetic
seriousness.

Hans Loeuwe is a member of a group of Westerners who
provide *The Householder* with more sources of amusement. In
this novel more than in any other work of fiction, Ruth Jhabvala
treats Westerners in India as subjects for unalloyed humour.
There is even an element of caricature in her presentation: an
European woman Prem meets at a party 'had big teeth like a
horse and a long neck thrust slightly forward round which she
wore a bead necklace,' while to emphasise her opinions she
'drew back her lips and bared her long yellow teeth' (pp. 87-9).
Another Western woman is described as 'a wizened white lady
in a cotton sari, who was recounting her experiences with a
very advanced yogi in Lucknow' (p. 90). Hans Loeuwe has 'pale
eyes' and 'moist colourless gums' (p. 40), his legs and feet being
'large and naked and white like chicken-flesh' (p. 59). At the
party Prem attends Hans is seen to be 'wiping the saliva from
his lips which had gathered there in the excitement' of
conversation (p. 87). Kitty, a British resident in Delhi of many
years' standing and a student of yoga, has a face that is 'square
and red' (p. 57). She bends over a tea-tray 'with her big bottom
in its black and white cotton dress stuck out at one end and
her head at the other; her lips were moving slightly and she
looked preoccupied and even a little sinister' (p. 61).

The general effect of such descriptions as these is to convey an impression of grotesque ungainliness, even of mental and physical weakness. Their grotesqueness is due partly to the fact that these characters are seen through Prem's eyes, and assessed by his limited experience of the world. Their conversation, which generally concerns their quest for spiritual fulfilment in India, perplexes Prem, who 'had always thought that Europeans were very materialistic' (p. 62) and whose own mind cannot rise easily above the practical matters that make his life miserable: his inadequate salary and the exorbitant rent he is paying Mr Seigal. The result is a series of conversational exchanges in which the participants are comically at cross-purposes:

> The lady thrust her head forward at Prem and told him, almost viciously, 'You may be Indian by birth, but we are all Indian by conviction.' She pulled back her head and looked complacent.
> ...Prem cleared his throat and began to speak. 'All through our long struggle for Independence, our convictions —'
> 'Don't drag politics into it!' cried the lady. 'What does it matter, Independence or no Independence?' Prem was horrified. Was she suggesting that India should not be free? All his patriotism bristled up. (p. 88)

These misunderstandings increase when Prem befriends Hans Loeuwe, who is apparently in Stage One of Ruth Jhabvala's cycle of Indian experience.[7] India to him is 'beautiful' (p. 9), 'one big feast' (p. 40), 'spiritual', and 'marvellous' (pp. 40, 41). Hans believes Prem to be 'intellectual' (41) and 'very advanced' in 'spiritual matters' (p. 60). Preoccupied with his spiritual aspirations, Hans ascribes his own philosophical thoughts to his young Indian friend — whose mind, alas, is invariably busy with quite unspiritual thoughts about Hans's ugliness and unnecessarily loud voice. Hans is comically mistaken in his estimate of Prem at such moments, but in terms of the novel's implied code of values he is quite right: Prem *is* a more thoughtful, even spiritual, person than most of the other characters. Hans's preoccupation with spiritual advancement renders him often comically insensitive to the practical difficulties of those around him, but his remarks frequently carry more than a ring of truth. 'Friends reveal a person's character,' he says, just before Prem introduces him to Raj,

the friend he regards as his mentor (p. 156); and of Raj himself
a little later, 'He has a good face ... but I think he has been
neglecting the spiritual side' (p. 156). Hans's scorn for mere
appearances —

> What does it matter if people look? ... What we are talking
> is not a secret thing but the Truth which everyone must
> know if he is to lead a good spiritual life (p. 158).

— shows up pettiness and pretentiousness in many of the
Indians he innocently finds so 'spiritual'. His inner conflict
illuminates Prem's difficulties in distinguishing the false from
the true, and the worthless from the valuable:

> I forget the source of my being and so I become attached
> to friends and other things which are only Maya. (p. 187)

Since the writing of *The Nature of Passion* in which the
technique was first successfully tried out, we have seen that
Ruth Jhabvala frequently employs servants and other members
of India's poor as silent commentators upon the actions of her
middle class characters. The servant-boy employed by Prem and
Indu in *The Householder* serves the emotional needs of his
master and mistress. His presence in the flat is in itself a
necessary prop for the insecure Prem, who thinks that the wife
of 'a man of education and some standing' such as himself
should have a servant to scour pots and wash floors (p. 36);
when Indu needs to demonstrate her housewifely skills or vent
her irritation with Prem, she shouts at the servant-boy who
on these occasions stands 'quite still and stares into the
distance with a patient look' (p. 28). Ruth Jhabvala develops
the character of this domestic servant to a degree unusual in
her early fiction, for even old Bachani in *Esmond in India*
regarded herself as an extension of Uma's personality rather
than as an individual in her own right. The servant-boy, who
appears to have no family of his own, attaches himself with
particular affection to Indu who, sorely tried by Prem's lack of
understanding and her mother-in-law's open hostility, needs
moral support very badly. It begins to seem to Prem that the
boy perpetually intrudes when he scolds, or is about to scold,
Indu (p. 64), and regards him reproachfully when they quarrel
(p. 68). The boy defends Indu's cooking when Prem slights it
(p. 79), and mourns her departure (pp. 113-14); takes a marked

personal interest in her letters to Prem (p. 12), and pays her
special attention when she returns (pp. 147-8). When he allies
himself with Prem in defending Indu against her mother-in-
law's attacks, the servant-boy becomes part of Prem's real
'household' of care and affection. When Indu is nervously
preparing for her debut as a hostess, she screams impartially
at both Prem and the servant. And he, like everyone else, is
transfigured on this occasion. 'He was wearing a new shirt and
looked proud and dignified'; serving the guests, he watches
them 'with an air of importance' (p. 192). His merry insouciance
and his warm partisanship distinguish him from the novel's
other domestic, Mohammed Ali (Kitty's bearer) who 'was
unshaven and visibly dirty, and ... wore and expression of
profound melancholy' (p. 60). Ali wears the remains of a once-
splendid uniform with mere traces of red braiding and tufts
where gilt buttons had been. According to Kitty, his eyes reflect
a sadness caused by the passing of British India (p. 60);
according to Hans, they mirror Eternity (p. 60). It is evident
that, like Prem's servant-boy, Mohammed Ali serves his
employers' emotional needs, depending upon them (as Prem
and Sohan Lal depend upon Mr Khanna's college, and Raj upon
his Government job) for a livelihood. The raggedness and misery
of Indian servants and the insecurity that permanently haunts
their lives serve Ruth Jhabvala well in *The Householder*,
providing links or points of contrast with her principal
characters, especially Prem. This is a technique that reaches
its most sophisticated expression in the characterisation of
Shyam and Bulbul, the domestic servants in *A New Dominion*.

As in *Amrita*, *The Nature of Passion* and *Esmond in India*,
certain oblique criticisms of Indian society are expressed in *The
Householder* through ironic reflection. The students at the
college, who (significantly) have no taste for poetry (p. 124),
cunningly turn the task of describing an actual event into the
far simpler exercise of repeating parrot-wise the moral
sentiments of a high order that will get them through
examinations. Of India's Republic Day Parade,

'How beautiful to see our Country, our Bharat so feasted and
loved' they wrote; or 'Thus was offering of thanks given to
God and our good and great Prime Minister for our Freedom
and Independence' ... (Prem) was often surprised ... at the

deep thoughts and feelings his students expressed. In the classroom they seemed such callow young men, one would never have credited them with any of these finer sentiments. (p. 8)

The students' phrases have much in common with the platitudes to which Messrs Khanna and Chaddha treat their colleagues at the college staff party. When speech and writing appear to be admired for their impressiveness rather than for substance and originality, and considered important only for the status and material rewards they bring, it is implied that genuine scholarship and literary sensitivity go unappreciated. Prem's mother, a simple soul, is impressed when her son appears to have 'some writing work to do':

> While he was writing she walked round the room on tiptoe. Once she rushed out into the kitchen to admonish the servant-boy who was cheerfully singing: 'My son is doing writing work and you bellow here like a jackal!' (p. 148)

The 'finer sentiments' in which teachers and students at the Khanna Private College specialise are similarly impressive at this limited level. Prem, on the other hand, despite his shyness and his youthful inhibitions, uses words that come from the heart: there is a difference, even in his 'petition' to Mr Khanna and especially in his letter to Indu, between his style and that of the others. Yet the petition is entirely ignored by Mr Khanna, and his passionate love-letter is destroyed by Prem himself in shame and fear of what his mother and Indu's family would say were they to see it. His deeply-felt remarks on the four stages in a man's life are hardly heard by Mr Seigal and his son, who are interested only by film-music, and thoughts of food or ribaldry. Although Prem's problems are a source of humour in the novel, it is significant that the substance of what this sensitive and serious young man has to say, whether in speech or in writing, is ignored or disapproved of by his society.

The novel demonstrates Ruth Jhabvala's increasing skill in the handling of dialogue for purposes additional to the comic. *The Householder* abounds with conversations that reveal the speakers in seeming accord, but in reality at cross-purposes or in opposition: when Prem is one of them, such dialogues contribute materially to his unhappy sense of getting nowhere and achieving nothing. Each such exchange, however, seemingly futile and inconclusive, increases the reader's respect and affection for Prem, who is seen to care about others in the midst of his own desperately pressing problems, whose idealism emerges in contrast to the Seigals' crass self-indulgence, and whose delicacy and restraint are demonstrated by means of contrast with the Khannas' practised bullying on the one hand, and Hans Loeuwe's unexpectedly crude talk of female beauty on the other.

In his quarrels with Indu, Prem strives to adopt an adult, responsible manner but is often amusingly thrown off balance by her potent physical attraction for him. Ashamed of his 'unworthy' thoughts about her body (p. 56), the conflict between Prem's idealism and his healthy maleness is presented humorously, yet with sympathetic understanding. Their disputes, which often end in deadlock, and in which Prem and Indu overtly assert their claims to respect as householder and housewife respectively, express in reality their need of each other as friend and as lover.

Once Prem felt 'sad because Indu was there; now he felt sad because she was not there' (p. 145). After their mutual (if indirect) avowal of love for each other, Indu becomes Prem's main source of consolation: a failure apparently, on every other front, he feels he has achieved something as a husband and a lover. Her extreme youth and her dependence upon him for support call forth all the tender 'protectiveness in Prem's sensitive nature. His status in the college ceases to matter so very much. He has tried to raise it, but fate is clearly against him. Prem is adult enough to find happiness in what he does have, his wife and his confidence in his role of householder.

Notes

1. R.P. Jhabvala, *The Householder* (John Murray, London: 1960; 1973). All references in this chapter and throughout this book are to the 1973 edition.
2. See R.C. Majumdar (ed.) *The History and Culture of the Indian People*, Vol. I: 'The Vedic Age' (George Allen & Unwin, London, 1951; 1957), pp. 493-4:

The Brahamanas' supreme genius for compromise and adjustments
of difference probably led later to the formulation of the ... theory
of *Asramas* or different stages of Aryan life. (1) In the forest one
lives with a teacher and learns the Veda as a *Brahmacharin*;
(2) as a householder (*Grthastha*) he next founds a household, begets
children and himself offers sacrifices or has them offered; (3) when
grown old, he leaves his house and village for the forest, where as
a *Vanaprastha* (forest-hermit) he offers only a minimum sacrificial
service and devotes himself mainly to meditation ... The oldest
Upanishads speak of these *Asramas* only as three types or branches
of life, but not as successive stages. It is only in the late Upanishads,
the Great Epic, and the Dharmasastras, that the theory of
successive stages of life is formulated and is developed further by
the addition of a fourth stage, that of the *Sannyasin* who gives up
even sacrifice, in fact, all good works, and as an ascetic, renounces
the world to meditate on the Absolute (*Brahman*), with a view to
realize it or achieve union with it.

3.   Quoted by R. Agarwal, "An interview with Ruth Prawer Jhabvala," p. 34.
4.   These traditional rules, communicated through song, story and many
      a sermon are diffused throughout Asia. Quoted below are extracts from
      'A Brahmin's advice to a daughter on her marriage' from the Sinhala
      poem *Kavyasekara* (adapted from a translation by L.C. van Geyzel and
      Harold Peiris, in "Ceylonese writing: Some perspectives," *Community*
      5 (1963), pp. 11-18):

> 'Conduct yourself like a maid-servant.
> To your husband's kinsfolk and his parents ...
>
> Sweep your house and courtyard each day.
> Don't sit still when you notice filth and dirt,
> And light the lamps in your dwelling
> Without fail when the sun rises and sets ...
>
> Learning how to prepare every nourishing dish
> That is your husband's favourite,
> Regularly making them you must feed him,
> Looking like a fond mother to his joys and sorrows ...
>
> Permitting no change in your love
> Do nothing bad for your husband's well-being ...
>
> Even if your husband is enraged,
> Giving utterance to no bitter words
> Waken kindness within his heart.'

5.   'If you live, or see others live, in what sometimes seems like hell, you
      may begin to believe in heaven — of which, by the way, India does
      not leave you without some intimations ...
          And once there is news of such a superior place, it is only natural
      no longer to care very much about what happens here. Or what
      happens now, for one's sense of time also seems to change' — R.P.
      Jhabvala, "Moonlight, jasmine and rickets," op. cit.

6.   While some authorities allowed that a student might omit the stage of the householder and enter directly into forest-life or asceticism, Manu and Kautilya stressed the importance of married life, if begetting progeny and engaging in economically productive activity before seeking spiritual liberation. Manu said: 'Because men of the three other orders are daily supported by the householder with gifts and food, the order of the householder is the most excellent.' See G.N.S. Raghavan, *Understanding India* (Indian Council for cultural Relations, Delhi: 1976), p. 17

7.   See Chapter I, pp. 6-7.

CHAPTER
VI

Get ready for battle
1962

While wondering at their own attitude, my Western characters wonder still more at that of the Indian characters. One of these Western characters may be invited to a wedding — a festive scene where fairy lights twinkle, the tables are loaded with pilaos and kebabs, and the guests with ornaments and brocades; the bandsmen play.

No one seems to notice that the bandsmen have no shoes, that gazing in at the front there is a rabble of children suffering from rickets and eye disease while at the back, where the waste food goes, a rabble of grownups is holding out old tins. Don't Indians *see*? my Western character asks.[1]

The immense disparity between the rich and the poor of India,
her awareness of which has shadowed every piece of writing
produced by Ruth Jhabvala after 1960, is the overriding subject
and theme of her fifth novel, *Get Ready for Battle*.[2] In its
contrast of the luxurious world inhabited by a wealthy
businessman with that other world of sickness and destitution
which his wife Sarla Devi, a woman of conscience, struggles
to alleviate, Ruth Jhabvala projects a fictional equivalent of
'what one has to see here every day,'[3] a common example of
which she describes in the newspaper article quoted at the
beginning of this chapter.

The novel opens with a description of the behaviour of the
guests at a lavish party hosted by Gulzari Lal, a Delhi business
magnate among the members of whose family the chief 'battles'
of the novel's title will be waged. The materialistic interests of
those parent are etched in acid:

> ... no one was bored, for almost everyone in the room could
> be of use to someone else and this was stimulating. There
> was a Commissioner who was stimulating to a number of
> fairly high-ranking civil servants, who were in their turn
> stimulating to a number of middle-ranking civil servants, and
> so on, down to the municipal engineer for whom the party
> was made by the presence of the vice-chairman of his Board.
> An overall stimulus was provided by a Maharaja, an imposing
> figure who, now that his kingdom and a good deal of his
> income were gone, was taking an interest in business affairs;
> he was really of no importance to anyone, but his presence
> made everyone feel they had got into good company and had
> come a long way from where they had started. (pp. 7-8)

By her use of the sexually suggestive words 'stimulus' and
'stimulating' and her provocative repetition of them in
connection with the various categories of guests at the party,
Ruth Jhabvala turns Gulzari Lal's entertainment into an orgy
at which the hope of personal gain provides the principal
aphrodisiac and spur to activity. Against this background, the
novel's main characters are pictured as driven by ruling
passions that appear to vary from one personality to another
but amount in the end to different aspects of the same self-
regard. The plot of *Get Ready for Battle* appears to centre on
the efforts of Gulzari Lal's middle-aged and kittenish mistress,

Kusum, to bring him to the point of divorcing his wife and marrying her. By the end of the novel these efforts have proved successful, and Kusum (having eliminated her future husband's daughter-in-law as well as his wife, and provided herself with an ardent unofficial admirer in Brij Mohan, Gulzari Lal's brother-in-law) prepares to enter into her kingdom. Other patterns intersect with this main plot. Gulzari Lal's only son Vishnu wants a life independent of his father, and of a clinging wife who has lost the attraction she once had for him. Gulzari Lal himself is opposed to the idea of a divorce, which militates against his 'favourite dream ... of himself as a successful family man' (p. 153), and which distracts his attention from his main interest in life, the profitable development of land.

In striking contrast to these anxious 'seekers' is the novel's only apparent 'giver', Gulzari Lal's estranged wife Sarla Devi, who has abandoned the world for a life of religious contemplation. 'How I admire your mother,' Vishnu's friend Gautam says enthusiastically:

> She has shaken off everything, all the things that due to her station in life had been piled on her ... Your mother is for me the ideal of all women. (p. 20)

But opinions differ on the nature of Sarla Devi's 'sacrifice'. Her daughter-in-law Mala declares that Sarla Devi 'has never cared for anyone, only herself' (p. 14). This might seem to be an unreasonable remark in view of her determined efforts on behalf of Delhi's underprivileged people; and yet it is soon clear that she delights fiercely in her self-chosen isolation, and in the austere simplicity of her life. Gautam's admiration appears somewhat misplaced when we learn that Sarla Devi regards her separation from her husband and her family as a form of self-indulgence, for which her periodic forays in support of the colonists of Bundi Busti and of various other causes are in the nature of penance.

The novel takes its title from the advice given by the god Krishna to the heroic prince Arjuna on the field of Kurukshetra:

> Treating alike pleasure and pain, gain and loss, victory and defeat, then get ready for battle

urges Krishna as recorded in the *Bhagavad Gita*, as Arjuna prepares to withdraw from the field, daunted by the sight of the array of kinsmen before him whom he must slay in order to achieve victory. One day, Sarla Devi hopes, she will never again have to 'engage' herself in battle, but for the present her active social (and private) conscience will not let her rest. As her efforts to prevent the take-over and development by her husband's firm of the land occupied by a colony of poor people in whom she takes an interest brings Sarla Devi into open conflict with the members of her family, she becomes a character of considerable and complex interest. Austere and high-principled, she alone knows what it is to be 'most intensely alive' (p. 169), and in this ability to live every moment to the full she contrasts strongly with the lethargic Vishnu and Mala, and with most of the novel's other characters who are, in the moral sense, only half alive in comparison with her:

> Sarla Devi was very displeased with herself. This was not a new sensation for her, for she had always made high demands on herself and had always, in her own estimation, fallen short of them. By way of penance she would then set herself some unpleasant task and the discomforts she thus forced on herself — and often on others — were sops to a conscience which nevertheless hardly ever ceased to trouble her. (p. 175)

This pattern renews itself throughout the reader's acquaintance with Sarla Devi: passionate involvement in her private religious life, loss of control, self-disgust, contrition, followed by penance (invariably taking the form of some kind of social involvement) performed until she is ready once again to resume her pleasurable isolation. She is the symbol and epitome of what Ruth Jhabvala regards as the 'opposite reaction' to the Indian greed and callousness she describes in her article — 'That Indian spirituality — not grabbing at the world but wanting nothing whatsoever to do with it'[4] — that is quite as much a part of Indian experience. Like that other symbol of an aspect of the Indian experience, Gulab Stillwood in *Esmond in India*, Sarla Devi is somewhat 'larger than life.'[5] At the end of *Get Ready for Battle*, she takes upon herself the blame for the expulsion of Bundi Busti's slum dwellers, and walks away towards Delhi's red light district to compensate Tara the prostitute for the treatment she has received from Brij Mohan. As a woman of conscience (and in Gautam's opinion, if no

one else's, a latter-day saint), Sarla Devi is an excellent foil for
the novel's other characters, none of whom pursue any ideal
higher than the advancement of their own prosperity. Everyone
(with the exception of Vishnu, who loves her) is made extremely
uncomfortable by her presence and behaviour. In the
luxuriously appointed drawing room of that dedicated social
worker, Mrs Bhatnagar, Sarla Devi strikes 'a discordant note'
(p. 176), and the tone in which she addresses her is only too
plainly 'disrespectful' (p. 162). When Mrs Bhatnagar informs
her that American jeeps will take social workers out to the new
site to which the colonists are about to be moved, and Sarla
Devi inquires if jeeps are also to be provided to transport the
inhabitants of homes at the new site to their workplaces in the
city, both Mrs Bhatnagar and her aide Mrs Dass realise that
they have 'someone very unpractical to deal with' (p. 162). Sarla
Devi is most effective in indirectly exposing the cunning and
calculation hidden under Kusum's exuberant warmth and
charm, an exposure the more complete because so entirely
unconscious and unplanned:

> (Kusum) followed (Gulzari Lal) out on to the veranda and stole
> her hand into his. 'It is for our sake,' she said softly ... 'If
> you don't do something about Bundi Busti, she will refuse
> to give you divorce,' she said, very close to him and in a
> persuasive, urgent whisper.
>
> Gulzari Lal puffed his cheek round his cigar and stared
> out into the garden through a haze of fragrant smoke.
>
> 'She will revenge herself like this on you, and who will be
> the ones to suffer but you and I?'
>
> 'She is not like that,' he said.
>
> 'How you talk! Everyone is like that. If she has a weapon
> against us, she will use it to gain her own ends, that is only
> natural.'
>
> 'It may be natural, but she is not natural.'
>
> 'I see. She is a monster. A very fine way to talk about the
> mother of your son!'
>
> Perhaps she was better than natural. But he did not want
> to think about that. He himself was no better than natural
> and he needed a woman who was no better either. 'She
> doesn't think like other people,' he said. ·
>
> 'You have lived with her for so many years and still you

don't know her. And I, after seeing her for only half an hour,
can read her mind exactly.'

'It is not *her* mind you are reading, it is your own.' He did
not know how to explain to her; except to say she is nobler
than you are. (pp. 183-4)

Nobility of spirit such as Sarla Devi's is, in the context of
materialistic Delhi, both 'unnatural' and insane. It is significant
that the colonists' only defender is thought 'unnatural' by the
wealthy members of her own social class, and that the two
characters in the novel who call her a 'mad woman' are
themselves among the most selfish in outlook: her brother Brij
Mohan, and her daughter-in-law Mala. Her idealism, the
largeness of her pity for the under-privileged, and the constant
reproach to them embodied in her selflessness and self-
discipline make it difficult for the members of her family to think
complacently of their own virtues. Turned inside out (although
quite unconsciously) by her, such 'virtues' begin to look
remarkably like greed and self-indulgence.

It is one of her son Vishnu's claims to the reader's respect
that he appreciates Sarla Devi. He 'liked visiting his mother;
he had always liked her company better than anyone else's'
(p. 23). Vishnu is approaching a time of decision. Married by
his father to a beautiful, conventional girl from a suitable family
five years before the novel begins, his wife and small daughter
do not by any means occupy all his thoughts. He does not as
yet understand his own character, and the strong, conflicting
impulses of his own nature continually take him by surprise.[6]

Our first view of Vishnu at his father's party amusingly
underlines what seems at first sight to be a markedly sensual
nature. An English girl entertains him.

with her impressions of India while he looked down at her
with much charm and gallantry and wondered to himself
at her flatchestedness. (p. 9)

In sexual matters Vishnu appears to be excited by the unusual.
The provocative behaviour of Gogo (a Delhi socialite) sets up
a characteristic reaction: 'his eyes shone, his nostrils were
slightly dilated: he had the poised expectancy of a hunter'
(p. 82). A later scene that melts quickly into sexual frenzy
begins with Mala's waiting upon him at table and is prefaced

by his own amused allusion to the unexpectedness of this: 'Today you are behaving like a model Indian wife' (p. 186). His uncle Brij Mohan's sensuality is in Vishnu's nature ('Mala knew her husband's tastes, and poor little Sumi was hardly the girl to appeal to them,' p. 41), reinforced by an appreciation of the pleasures and comforts of life, inherited from his father. But despite Brij Mohan's urgings to 'only follow on your father's golden road' (p. 28) and his inclination to laud his handsome nephew as the Don Juan of Delhi, Vishnu is not particularly interested in women, or even in sex. It is significant that when he drives Gogo home after a party at which she has made her interest in him obvious, he is thinking not about her or the fact that they are alone together on a balmy summer night, but of 'fountain-pens and how exactly they were made' (p. 86).

In his relationship with Gautam's young relative, Sumi, Vishnu without much difficulty submerges and sublimates his attraction to her in the time-honoured Indian way, by treating her as his sister (p. 98). His occasional moments of lust for the wife who bores him need, it appears, to be triggered off by the possibility of discovery or of social embarrassment. On one such occasion, Mala's conventionality makes her 'sit rigid ... careful not to give a sign' as Vishnu communicates with her by physical sexual signals in the presence of a third person (Sumi) under cover of the gathering dusk (p. 186). The nearness of servants, the imminence of his father's appearance in the room, the possibility of discovery, or the anger of his wife contribute the elements of danger that Vishnu seems to require for the whetting of his sexual appetite. Although, at the end of the novel, Mala succeeds in making him promise to take her and Pritti with him when he leaves Delhi for Chandnipat, the reader senses that this triumph over his will is unlikely to be permanent. It would appear that the untapped energy within Vishnu has been correctly interpreted by his mother:

It is necessary for him to roam about ... he is *my* son ... He will never let himself be tied down by ordinary worldly things but will soar above them. That is his nature. (p. 90)

Sarla Devi calls Vishnu to a life similar to her own, of compassionate involvement with the troubles of the poor, and is disappointed when he decides to venture, not into idealistic striving, but into a business of his own devising. She had hoped

he would not take his father's materialistic path, and he knows
he has failed her (p. 222). But she has also failed him, by a
lack of understanding if not of love. Vishnu has to free himself
from claims upon him that are far more powerful than the
merely materialistic, for as Gautam notes acutely, Vishnu's
materialism is acquired rather than ingrained:

> From birth you have been on the one track your father put
> you on, the key has been turned and you run round and
> round. (p. 21)

Many possibilities beckon to Vishnu, the most tempting arising
out of his own nature. Gautam wants him to help in the
establishment of a school for free spirits, an attractive proposal
since the intelligent and sensitive Vishnu has become rather
'tired of comfortable and prosperous people' (p. 19) and longs
to escape the secure slot in life that his father has designed
for him. Mala wants to possess him utterly, Sumi to make him
the centre of her life, Gogo and her 'set' want him back in their
fashionable group. Ignoring all these claims upon him, Vishnu
must find his own path in life. In the sense that he must choose
his own future, a 'battle' lies before him as it does before his
mother, a war that takes courage and singlemindedness to fight
and to win. He is not, therefore, as unlike Sarla Devi as he had
first seemed to be; he, too, will shake off 'everything, all the
things that due to (his) station in life had been piled on (him)'.
But Vishnu is his father's son as well as his mother's. His spirit,
although as free and aspiring as hers, has no religious bent;
he will make his bid for independence and for personal
fulfilment, but his choice when it comes will be for a life lived
within established conventions, organizing a business that will
probably be as successful as his father's, though of a different
kind, and independent both of it and of him.

Gulzari Lal is no *nouveau riche*.[7] His family background is,
or has been, aristocratic: his forefathers 'lived stately lives in
large country houses and dispensed charity and justice to their
villages' (p. 33). He possesses an 'inbred courtesy, a dignity'
that lend grace to all his relationships, including those
pertaining to his business and his wayward family. To these
qualities   he adds (in his own opinion) other

virtues — that is, his realism, his capacity for hard work,

his shrewd business-sense, his balanced view of life. (p. 49)

And yet, despite all this, Gautam tells Vishnu that Gulzari Lal seems to him to be

> the worst type of man, attached to money and money-making and existing not as a man but only through the things he possesses, like his car, his house, his mistress. Women and gold, as Sri Ramakrishna has said, these are the worst temptations in the life of man, and your father has not only tasted of them but has swallowed them whole. (p. 21)

Such a judgement of Gulzari Lal might seem extreme. But *Get Ready for Battle*, although more firmly rooted in the realities of Indian life than any other of Ruth Jhabvala's novels, is paradoxically not a study in realism but a book that concerns itself with the difference between reality and illusion on a moral level. In practical terms Ruth Jhabvala's exploration of this theme emerges frequently as a satiric comparison of her characters' illusion about themselves with what they really are. In no other among her novels are the lines of demarcation between saint and reprobate, and what is 'natural' and 'unnatural,' noble and worthless, so clearly and uncompromisingly drawn. Her spokesman on moral matters is usually Gautam. Genuinely free in spirit, unlike every other character in the novel including Sarla Devi, his view on most matters is likely to be the most morally penetrating, and his insight reliable:

> 'As for me, wherever I shall be and whatever I shall do, I shall always be a rich man'.
> 'A millionaire,' said Sumi. Yet he did not sound or look ridiculous, in spite of his shabby clothes and his cracked dirty feet. He stretched himself, luxuriously like a real millionaire, and said: 'Tomorrow I am off.' (p. 212)

Gautam's analysis of Vishnu is closer to the truth than those made by Vishnu's relations and his other friends. Sarla Devi is, for Gautam, an 'ideal,' since she has taken nothing and wants nothing from life (p. 20); here again, his words illuminate her continuing problem. So remote is she from ordinary everyday concerns that her efforts to alleviate or redress the injustice she sees around her invariably misfire, plunging her repeatedly into distress and near-despair. He sees clearly that on her marriage, Sumi will inevitably be ground down into the domestic drudge her sister has become. His opinion of Gulzari Lal is, unhappily, the correct one, a fact that becomes quite evident during their interview over breakfast early in the novel, when the monetary implications of the word 'tendered' reveal the speaker's true interests:

'(Vishnu) has always been used to this kind of life,' Gulzari Lal tendered respectfully. 'It may be difficult for him to change.'

'This is exactly why he must change,' Gautam said. 'He will sink into sloth and luxury if he carries on in this way and all higher life will be lost to him.'

Gulzari Lal pretended to be listening with serious interest. He could afford to be tolerant: he had lived longer in the world than Gautam and had learnt that, in spite of fine words, the end, the goal of life, towards which all men strove, was to be rich and comfortable. (p. 34)

Gautam's views on the subject of religious swamis are of interest, since they illuminate Ruth Jhabvala's own ironic approach to it in *A New Dominion* and *Heat and Dust*:

'... there is always a danger,' said Gautam. 'Especially for our women ... Often they mistake what is lower in themselves for a higher manifestation. How many of our women do we see hanging around healthy young swamis, they swoon with love and speak words of ecstasy — to whom? To God? Or to the swami?' (p. 150)

These remarks, which have arisen from Sumi's singing of a passionate devotional song in Vishnu's presence, appear to go ignored. They are certainly unanswered. Vishnu, at whom they are directed as a kind of warning, seems at the moment of their utterance to be studying a photograph of the father of his host, Gautam's cousin Shankar. The subsequent conversation is structured, however, to convey unobtrusively the fact that Gautam's warning has been heard and taken to heart by Vishnu:

'Your father?' Vishnu asked Shankar, turning from his study of the photograph.

'May he be in peace and happiness,' Shankar
acknowledged.

'And even when there is no swami ... All these expressions
of love and longing — come to me, I await you, ravish me
— who knows whether they are meant to fly straight up to
God or whether perhaps they are not meant for someone
nearer to earth?'

'There is some resemblance,' Vishnu said, looking at the
photograph and at Shankar and back again. (p. 150)

When a few minutes later, Sumi makes a direct appeal to
Vishnu under cover of the chatter of the children he is driving
around the colony in his car, he indicates 'firmly' that their
relationship is over:

'I don't want anything, only friendship,' Sumi said ... 'You
will come tomorrow?'

'There is Pattu's house! If only he could see us now!'

'Then should I come to your house? Would Mala be angry
with me?' Vishnu turned firmly once more by the cinema
hoarding. 'She was such a good friend to me.'

'Just see, children,' explained Vishnu, 'now I wish to stop,
so I take my right foot off the accelerator and put it on the
brake. Like this.' Gautam opened the door for Sumi and the
children to get out. (pp. 152-3)

Ruth Jhabvala's handling of seemingly trivial dialogue and
seemingly commonplace incident to expose the inner landscape
of her characters' minds and souls is (as the passages quoted
above show) one of the features of her characteristic technique
that is well advanced in *Get Ready for Battle*. She has come
a very long way from the arguments that took place among the
daughters of Pandit Ram Bahadur Saxena in *Amrita*, which
were lively, entertaining, and illustrative of aspects of conflict
in Indian upper-class society in the 1950s, but of limited
significance in relation to the psychology of the characters
involved. Similarly, the somewhat intrusive narrative voice of
Amrita, which commented freely on both character and motive
in that novel, is replaced by a far subtler and more effective
technique: the interiors of houses and offices become instinct
with symbolic life and share the functions of an ironic observer
with the narrator. Both aspects of her developing style are well

illustrated in her presentation of 'sophisticated' conversation among a group of 'Bright Young People' in Delhi:

> 'I think we ought to concentrate more on our cottage industries,' said Premola Singh, a very intelligent and well-educated girl (she had a higher degree in Home Science). 'I was reading such an interesting article the other day on village handicrafts.'
>
> 'Village fiddlesticks,' said Pitu. 'That's all sentimental rubbish,' He made a sound of disgust, waved his hand in the air and stumbled over a hand-loomed rug. (p. 84)

The rug, an example of the handicrafts to which Premola has referred, has tripped Pitu up in the very moment of his rejection of it. The scene provides a foretaste of the much more complex ironic effects Ruth Jhabvala will gain in later work from the furnishings of Karim's Knightsbridge flat in *Heat and Dust*, of numerous houses, apartments and institutions in *In Search of Love and Beauty*, or the Maharaja's portrait in the film 'AUTOBIOGRAPHY OF A PRINCESS.'

Ruth Jhabvala exposes self-interest and self-preoccupation through her handling of conversation in *Get Ready For Battle* by using a cutting and splicing technique that her work in the cinema after 1960 has extended and developed. A striking example of her method in this early novel occurs when Vishnu and Mala are shown while in the act of passionate lovemaking, to be in reality miles apart from each other:

> He shut his eyes and tasted her again with his lips. Wanting only to lie still and drown in her, it was some time before he felt like talking again. 'No, not to Bombay —' Then he told her, briefly and in short disconnected sentences, with his face still pressed into her, about Joginder and his factory at Chandnipat.
>
> 'Chandnipat,' she said.
>
> 'It will be very dull and there will be nobody.'
>
> But she was smiling. She thought of the three of them, he and she and Pritti, in a dull place. There would be nowhere for him to go and he would have to be with her and they would lie like this every day and all night.
>
> 'And the house we shall live in will be nothing like this. No comforts, nothing.' But she was hardly listening, thinking

only of how completely she would possess him there. (p. 188)

Ruth Jhabvala uses the idiom of spoken Indian English in these conversations to an extent and with a lack of inhibition unprecedented in her fiction. *The Nature of Passion* and *The Householder* are of course, each in its own way, special cases, since the principal characters in these novels are represented as being for the most part habitual speakers of Indian languages. In *Amrita*, while certain characters such as Radha and Mira were permitted to express themselves comically in the spoken idiom, Ruth Jhabvala was careful to see that her hero and heroine, Krishna and Amrita, generally expressed themselves in a mode as pure and unblemished as their natures. The educated Indians of *Esmod in India* (even Uma, who has apparently never heard of Shakespeare) express themselves in a fluent standard English which has very little that is 'Indian' about it. *Get Ready For Battle*, perhaps because it followed the successful linguistic experiments of *The Householder*, is more daring and more honest in this regard, including the well-educated Vishnu among the users of the spoken idiom:

> 'You are not listening to Gautam,' (Vishnu) reproved her, 'and he is using such fine long words. How will you ever become clever and educated if you don't even listen when *people talk clever things with you?*'
> '*What to listen*,' said Sumi. '*All day I hear him.*' (pp. 98-99)

With a suppleness and flexibility carried on from her earlier novels, Ruth Jhabvala's narrative voice takes on from time to time the distinctive speech-rhythms and even the phraseology of her characters. This is especially effective in conveying the words and thoughts of Kusum:

> Kusum realised his embarrassment so she said, simply and with feeling: 'I am your mother, Vishnu, and you are my son, I can say, no, it is my duty to say everything before you.' But then *she got a bad conscience* which made her add: 'Of course, you have your own mother also, I know no one can take the place of the real mother.' (p. 12)

It was in an effort to make him understand that Kusum stayed away from the house. She wanted to be missed and

she was; and not only by Gulzari Lal. *Every day Mala
telephoned her: 'Please come,' she said always.* But Kusum,
while protesting her love over the telephone *for Mala and
Pritti and Vishnu and, yes, for all of them,* nevertheless stayed
away. (p. 13)*

Get Ready For Battle, as I have noted earlier, is not a novel
remarkable for the complexity of its characterisation, an
exception being made in this regard of the characters of Sarla
Devi and her son Vishnu. The reader is assisted by the author
to see clearly into the shallow souls of Gulzari Lal, Kusum, Mala
and Brij Mohan. None of these make, or are capable of making,
moral progress. Their advances are made exclusively in the
material worlds of economics, social respectability, personal
aggrandisement or sexual satisfaction. Even Brij Mohan's
dismissal of Tara and her bawd is not, at its root, the
determined attempt at self-discipline he likes to think it, for
it has become increasingly obvious in the novel's last pages that
the newly respectable Kusum will be more than willing to
deputise (in a socially acceptable way, of course) for the paid
prostitute Brij Mohan has thrown out. The genuine idealism
of Gautam, the vigorous, earthy practicality of Joginder, Rattan
Singh's raucous bullying and Tara's practised complaisance are
equally well observed and defined. Ruth Jhabvala's
compassionate study, in the character of Sumi, of a playful
adolescent surprised by the intensity of her own feelings who
learns to accommodate those feelings — and her developing
sexuality — to the requirements of the arranged marriage
prescribed by social custom, is one of the most attractive
features of the novel. Its delicacy provides a welcome contrast
with the broad satiric strokes reserved for the social service
committee-ladies of Delhi:

> Mrs Bhatnagar said: 'It is not for reasons of private
> speculation that the colony is to be shifted but as part of
> a larger programme of rehabilitation.'
> 'Rehabilitation and resettlement of sub-standard housing
> groups,' said Mrs Dass with an earnest and important face ...
> 'Let me repeat again,' said Mrs Bhatnagar, with her eyes
> shut as if in pain, 'that whoever is or is not buying the

* The italics in the passages quoted above are mine.

adjoining land has nothing to do with the question in hand
... Our line of policy on slum rehabilitation ... has already
been thoroughly thrashed out in committee.'

'I will send you a copy of the minutes of our meetings on
these subjects,' said Mrs Dass.

'And we shall be happy to incorporate you on the relevant
committee. We are always glad to welcome sincere and willing
workers to help us in our task.' (p. 179)

The novel as a whole reflects a view of India that has altered
profoundly from the comic vision that inspired Ruth Jhabvala's
earlier works. What had previously seemed 'always a little bit
ludicrous'[8] even in its excesses, has ceased to amuse. To Lalaji
in *The Nature of Passion*, bribery had seemed an 'indispensable
courtesy and a respectable, civilised way of carrying on
business.'[9] The effect of such a passage is, as K.R. Srinivasa
Iyengar has justly noted, to make the reader 'laugh, or at least
smile.'[10] The callous indifference to human needs and human
suffering displayed by Mesdames Bhatnagar and Dass is,
however, beyond laughter. Ruth Jhabvala's writing about India
could well have stopped here, arrested by the disillusionment
that warps creative vision. Alternatively, her writing could have
limited itself to bitter satire in which people appear merely as
types and exempla thrown up by an irreparably damaged
society. The latter possibility is evident in *Get Ready For Battle*,
with its lack of ironic shading (a loss especially noticeable after
the richly humane acceptance of life's realities in *The
Householder*) and its numerous two-dimensional characters.

Fortunately, neither of these eventualities occurred. The
grimness that her satire takes on in *Get Ready for Battle* is
never, however, quite lost in Ruth Jhabvala's later fiction,
although as *A Backward Place* demonstrates, irony does on
occasion modify without diluting it.

Notes

1. R.P. Jhabvala, "Moonlight, jasmine and rickets," op. cit.
2. R.P. Jhabvala, *Get Ready for Battle* (John Murray, London: 1962, 1978).
    All references in this chapter and throughout the book are to the 1978
    edition.

3. 'We may praise Indian democracy, go into raptures over Indian music, admire Indian intellectuals — but whatever we say, not for one moment should we lose sight of the fact that a very great number of Indians never get enough to eat. Literally that: from birth to death they never for one day cease to suffer from hunger. *Can* one lose sight of that fact? God knows, I've tried. But after seeing what one has to see here every day, it is not really possible to go on living one's life the way one is used to.' See "Myself in India," op. cit., p. 8.

4. "Moonlight, jasmine and rickets," op. cit.

5. See note 16 to Chapter IV. R. Agarwal's question was worded as follows: 'Don't you think that Gulab in *Esmond in India* is a little too sluggish or Sarla Devi in *Get Ready for Battle* is a little too unworldly? Don't you think there is a shade of exaggeration in the depiction of characters and situations in your novels?'

6. I find it interesting — and puzzling — that K.R.S. Iyengar describes Vishnu as the 'worthless' son of Gulzari Lal and Sarla Devi, a judgement that seems to me superficial and unsupported by the author's characterisation of him. See K.R.S. Iyengar, *Indian Writing in English* (Bombay: 1962; 1973 ed.), p. 455.

7. Haydn Moore Williams terms him such in "R.K. Narayan and R. Prawer Jhabvala: Two interpreters of modern India," op. cit. p. 1149.

8. K.R.S. Iyengar, op. cit., p. 460.

9. R.P. Jhabvala, *The Nature of Passion*, p. 54.

10. K.R.S. Iyengar, ibid.

CHAPTER
VII

A backward place
1965

'Oh do stop it, Franz!' Etta interrupted. 'India, India, India, all the time, as if there was anything interesting to be said! One has the misfortune to be here, well all right, let's leave it at that, but why do we have to keep on torturing ourselves by talking about it?' (pp. 36-7).

The 'backward place' of Ruth Jhabvala's sixth novel[1] is India. Despite Etta's assertion that there is nothing interesting to be said about it, India is the avowed or unconscious theme of nearly every conversation that takes place among the novel's characters. Etta, a Hungarian expatriate who longs to return

to Europe but cannot, has constructed a life for herself in Delhi
that is, in effect, a tiny European island set in an unfriendly
Indian sea: 'so elegant, so continental, in such good taste,'
thinks Etta's friend Judy on her visits to Etta's flat (p. 6).
Trapped by time and circumstance, growing increasingly
desperate, Etta calls the land of her exile 'this primitive society,'
declares it to be possessed of a 'primitive morality' (p. 5), and
wages a bitter war against both India and the spectre of
approaching age which seem to her to be different aspects of
the same antagonist. 'Don't you know that the Indian sun has
been put specially into the sky to ruin our complexions?' (p. 7)
is a characteristic comment that concentrates her resentment
and her fierce resolve to preserve her individuality, her
Europeanness and her good looks in spite of all 'India' can do
to her.

Another Westerner stranded in India is Clarissa, an Englishwoman of good family who declares that she, unlike Etta, is
in India 'out of conviction and idealism' (p. 26). She manages,
with a fervour not entirely unmixed with expediency, to find
beauty in everything around her; but her superficiality is
exposed by her comments to Sudhir Bannerjee, a sensitive
young Bengali intellectual, on the 'splendid work' being done
by him and his assistant, Judy, at the Cultural Dais (p. 122),
an institution at which, despite the high hopes attending its
establishment, 'there was nothing much going on' (p. 17).
Clarissa's enthusiasm strikes Sudhir as unpleasantly
reminiscent of the British era:

> The hand laid on his shoulder seemed to him the pseudo-
> paternal hand of the British Raj, and his instinctive reaction
> was to want to shake it off as rudely and violently as possible.
> (p. 123)

Here lies, possibly, the seed of an idea that germinated four
years later, in the novel *A New Dominion*, as spiritual 'seekers'
like Clarissa and casual Western travellers fall willing captives
to the attractions of the country their kind had once ruled.
Sudhir listens as Clarissa delightedly disclaims any right to be
referred to as 'an English lady,' and

> felt sad for her. He imagined how she must have come out
> to India first, spurred on by Romain Rolland and the Light

of Asia and the Everyman edition of the Bhagavad Gita, and
intent on a quest in which notions of soul and God played
a prominent, if vague part; and how valiantly she had kept
up this quest, or at least the pretence of it, though she was
getting older year by year, and lonelier, and more ridiculous,
and soul and God perhaps no nearer. (p. 126)

Clarissa is a pseudo-liberal, trying hard to live up to liberal
ideals that, deep down, she does not hold with at all. Her
hypocrisy and class-consciousness are revealed by her snobbish
remarks, almost instantly disclaimed, on Judy's lower middle-
class origins and lack of education (p. 122). Her comments on
India's social system resemble the nostalgic, sentimental views
of medievalists who take no account of the personal and
psychological damage done to the Indian citizen who must
suffer the adverse effects of the institution of caste:

> I'm very very anti-untouchability and all that, I think it's
> simply horrible, but I can see all the same that there's
> something beautiful about the caste system. Beautiful and
> right. Every man in his own rank, doing his own work, there's
> a divine harmony there which is entirely lacking in the West
> today. (p. 123)

Two other Westerners in India, Dr. Franz Hochstadt and his
wife Frieda, short-term residents in Delhi on a university
exchange programme, adopt a tone of lofty idealism when
discussing India:

> 'India gives us so much,' Mrs Hochstadt said, 'What joy
> to be asked to give a little in return.' (p. 115)

The satire to which Ruth Jhabvala subjects the Hochstadts
transcends in depth and seriousness her presentation of those
other foreign 'experts' on Indian civilisation, Professor Hoch in
Amrita and Esmond Stillwood in *Esmond in India*. These several
characterisations have many points in common, however.
Dr. Hochstadt adopts a lecturer's stance when talking about
India that recalls Esmond's manner when instructing the
Western Women's Organization, and his views resemble those
aired by Professor Hoch in Tarla Mathur's drawing room. He
talks of 'the humbler people of this land' as the true source
for an 'understanding of India in all her depths', supported by

his wife's enthusiastic assertion that 'the real India' is to be found in the villages (p. 36). These are opinions that were expressed by Professor Hoch while planning a cultural pageant for Lady Ram Prashad Khanna's garden party. Etta points out with acid humour that Clarissa holds similar views, but 'takes good care' to associate only with wealthy sophisticates. She accuses Clarissa of hypocrisy (p. 36), and we cannot miss the implication that the Hochstadts are hypocrites too.

But Ruth Jhabvala's attitude to the Hochstadts is more complex than Etta's, as her exposure of them is far subtler. Though Dr. Hochstadt is 'an economist of some standing' (pp. 33-34) he studiously avoids making any comment on India's pressing economic problems, evidently preferring to focus his attention on her cultural achievements. The two-year limit on the Hochstadts' sojourn in India sets them apart from other Westerners in Delhi; while Etta, long-term resident and avowed 'prisoner' of India can be driven into 'a frenzy of irritation' by the incompetence of Indian post-office clerks, Mrs Hochstadt can say tolerantly and with positive affection, 'It is one of the many charms the country has for us' (p. 34). They are, unlike Etta and Judy, 'cultured people and had of course prepared themselves thoroughly before coming out to India' (p. 35) intellectually and aesthetically, so that they are ready on any occasion with an appropriate quotation from Forster, Coomaraswamy, Vivekananda, or from India's translated religious texts that (in their view, at least) instantly sets the immediate problem in its correct perspective. Given to theory and generalisation, they miss reality, an obtuseness that takes on very serious implications when they comfortably fit Etta into their theories regarding 'the effect India has on a certain type of European' (p. 38), insensitive to the fact that their friend is on the brink of a mental breakdown. Delighted to be able to quote Forster at an apparently appropriate moment, Dr. Hochstadt explains to the distraught Etta that 'Life plays itself out to a different rhythm here,' adding pleasantly — and in unconscious prophecy of Etta's coming attempt at suicide — 'It is fatal to come to India and expect to be able to live to a Western rhythm' (p. 34).

Although kindly and sympathetic people at heart, Franz and Frieda Hochstadt have designed a programme for their stay in India that is not unlike the 'lines' of demarcation deliberately

adopted by the Minnies and Crawfords in *Heat and Dust*: while
they 'contact' India, they are careful (as the Minnies and
Crawfords are careful) not to step in too far, or to cross the
dividing lines that keep them safe. Their policy of ignoring the
unpleasant aspects of life in India, justifiable to some degree
in relation to matters arising out of cultural differences (p. 98),
is less acceptable when they extend it to more serious problems:

> She and Franz had discussed the problem of beggars too,
> and had come to the conclusion that it was no use giving
> any of them anything ... So, come lepers in handmade carts,
> starving mothers with starving babies, crippled children or
> deformed old men, Frieda hardened her naturally soft heart
> against them and refused to see or hear. (p. 99)

Ruth Jhabvala's pleasantly civilised dissection of the Hochstadts
shifts to a different satiric level after Etta — in despair at her
fleeing youth and her recent rejection by her Indian protector,
Mr. Gupta — insults Judy's Indian husband Bal at the
Hochstadts' *alfresco* picnic. The Hochstadts, we are told,

> discussed (Etta's) case fully and had many interesting things
> to say to each other on the subject of ageing beauties, on
> the one hand, and on the adaptations the Western con-
> sciousness has to make to the Orient, on the other.
> Dr. Hochstadt had some fascinating comments on the latter
> subject in particular, he went right back to racial archetypes
> and quoted Jung, and held his wife spellbound. (p. 198)

Ruth Jhabvala's satire here may derive some of its fire from
her sense of helplessness and rage (never crudely explicit in
her fiction, but often detectable beneath the surface of her
studies of human callousness in its varied Indian mani-
festations) at a phenomenon that profoundly altered the path
of her own life: the insensitivity to human individuality that
made it possible for the Nazis to contemplate unmoved, and
attempt to bring about, the methodical extermination of the
Jewish race. It is significant that Judy, who speaks the language
of the heart and not that of the intellect, finds the Hochstadts'
analysis of her friends too objective, too impersonal, too easy
(p. 38). Franz and Frieda Hochstadt represent not only
ignorance and insensitivity in cultural matters relating to India,
but — and it is in this that Ruth Jhabvala's satiric exposure

of them transcends her earlier work in this area — a conscious, quite deliberate denial of human imperative and human need.

In striking contrast to these several Western attitudes to India is Judy's joy in her Indian family life, a powerful reaction to her memories of her girlhood home in England, where she had lived with her parents,

> just the three of them, in that tight little house, with the doors and curtains firmly shut to keep the cold and the strangers out. (p. 42)

After Judy's marriage to Bal, a young and not very successful Indian actor, and her father's death of lung cancer, her mother 'left alone in her clean house with the household bargains and the closed doors' (p. 42) had hanged herself. Like the much better bred and educated narrator of Heat and Dust, Judy finds in the home Etta contemptuously calls 'an Indian slum' (p. 35) a refuge from loneliness, insularity and the psychological disintegration that has overtaken her mother in Britain, and presumably awaits Etta in her lonely flat. The contrast between Western ways of living and the Indian joint-family system is effected by following an early description of Etta's flat with one of Judy's household, one of two related by kinship that occupy a single house 'in a sidestreet leading off from a road of shops' (p. 9). Here there is to be found none of the friction that characterises the joint-family households in Amrita, The Nature of Passion, 'A Loss of Faith," "The Interview," and "The Aliens". Judy gets on very well with her pleasant sister-in-law Shanti (a name that appropriately signifies 'Peace'); amicable relations exist between their husbands, and they share a delightful elderly aunt Bhuaji in much the same way that their children take it for granted 'that both parts of the house were theirs, to eat, play and sleep at will in either' (p. 10). Shanti's tranquil outlook, her husband's capacity to think independently and responsibly, and aunt Bhuaji's genuinely religious and benevolent nature contribute a good deal to the impression that this quite ordinary middle-class Indian household is a haven of peace when compared with the nervous tensions generated in Etta's flat.

The views of these Western expatriates and foreign visitors are contrasted with other opinions about India, expressed by Indians. Sudhir Bannerjee thoroughly despises his job as

general secretary of Delhi's Cultural Dais, and regards with
amused contempt the efforts of that institution to 'draw in the
cultural threads of all nations' (p. 63). Sudhir and his elderly
friend Jaykar (a veteran freedom-fighter of the struggle for
India's independence) discuss unceasingly, but

> with humorous nonchalance such topics as corruption in
> high places ... the failure of community development
> schemes and the impossibility of raising the basic wage level.
> (p. 74)

Their 'nonchalance' masks deep feeling, verging on anger.
Jaykar speaks with mild irony of a scheme for a professional
theatre in the capital put forward by Bal, but

> his eyes ... glittered with a suppressed fury which, old and
> dimmed as they were, was very characteristic of them.
> (pp. 75-76)

Sudhir's criticisms of India's backwardness arise, unlike Etta's,
out of genuine concern for the condition of his native land.
Well-bred, highly intelligent, sympathetic and self-critical,
Sudhir is well fitted (as was Krishna Sen Gupta in *Amrita*) to
be his creator's occasional mouth-piece. His career, presented
in quietly ironic outline (pp. 39-41), suggests that there is no
place for high principles in middle-class India. In accepting his
futile job at the Cultural Dais, Sudhir has temporarily admitted
defeat; which is why he despises his work, and later abandons
it to become a teacher in a Literacy Institute in a remote part
of India. Sudhir resembles Narayan, the young physician in
Esmond in India who gives up the comfort and consequence
of a Delhi practice to heal the sick in a remote province. He
shares with Krishna Sen Gupta a Bengali background of
gentility, education and idealism, together with sensitivity to
others' needs. Sudhir reflects (and occasionally expresses in
words) his creator's consciousness of the poverty and
backwardness of the 'great animal' she rides.[2] Through his
alertly observant eye the reader becomes aware of significant
contrasts in the Indian world of *A Backward Place*: for example,
that striking gap between appearance and reality conveyed as the
domestic servants of Mrs Kaul, Honorary Secretary of the Dais,

> glide about with such discretion and good manners that it

was hard to grasp that they had perspiring bodies under those starched uniforms or that, like other people's servants, they lived eight to a room in some unsanitary quarter, drowned their troubles in drink and beat their wives. (p. 107)

Comparison of this passage with Ruth Jhabvala's description, written ten years earlier, of a similar social occasion at Tarla Mathur's house in *Amrita*[3] will show how far she has progressed from the satiric simplicities of that novel. Sudhir's thoughts frequently blend with the narrative, and his opinions when verbally expressed adopt, like the narrator's, a tone of understated irony that occasionally rises — when he is most irritated or aroused — to satire. His nasal imitation, an outrageous parody of the style of an address delivered at the Cultural Dais is, as Judy rightly says, 'Very funny':

> ... it is worth bearing in mind ... that under such conditions cultural themes develop their own criteria so that it might develop under scrutiny that Huguenot poetry of the seventh century is not absolutely incompatible with Hottentot poetry of the ninth ... (p. 18)

Like Etta, Sudhir finds in humour an occasional relief from an abiding sense of helpless frustration. Their wit is a genuine expression of the satiric sensibility that laughs so that it may not weep. But Sudhir's satire is of a higher order than Etta's, possessing no tinge of self-pity. He and Jaykar use humour to mask their sorrow and anger at corrupted wounds in the body of modern India that they diagnose with skill and precision, but are unable to cure.

In contrast, Etta's remarks about India are never genuinely comic. The value of her observations is continually undermined by insufficient knowledge, superficial values and obvious unhappiness, all of which combine to make most of her comments seem — even when they come close to the truth —to reflect strong feeling rather than a discriminating mind.

The events of the novel unexpectedly reveal the India Etta alleges is 'backward' to be a region where material concepts of 'backwardness' have no real relevance, since there good and evil, beauty and terror are to be experienced with an intensity unknown elsewhere. The 'India' of *A Backward Place* is a universe complete in itself, where the human spirit is

strenuously tested, to be sometimes generously blessed and
rewarded, sometimes utterly destroyed. As events run their
course and characters meet and part in conflict or accord
against the background of Delhi in the 1960s, India annihilates
Etta, increases poor Clarissa's confusion of mind and eludes
the Hochstadts, yet fills Judy with new confidence, the bestows
on Sudhir a quiet heroism and a purpose in life. Travelling by
train out of Delhi as the novel nears its end, Sudhir recognises
in the conversations he hears about him:

> a manifestation of all the variety and unexpectedness of the
> fertile lives that sprang out of this soil, which was in itself
> so various and unexpected and was now desert and now
> flourishing fields and now the flattest plains and now the
> highest and highest most holy of mountains.
>
> He thought about all the discussions he and Jaykar and
> other friends were forever having about India, and indeed
> how every one always talked about it, incessantly,
> compulsively, and yet never said anything that was in the
> least conclusive or that could not be instantly and
> authoritatively contradicted ... It seemed to him now ... that
> perhaps the paradox was not a paradox after all or, if it was,
> was one that pleasurably resolved itself for the sake of him
> who accepted it and rejoiced in it and gave himself over to
> it, the way a lover might. (p. 248)

Sudhir is one of those blessed by India; for Sudhir, as for Judy,
true 'lovers' both, the paradox resolves itself. They abandon
their jobs at the Cultural Dais and leave Delhi, Judy bound
for Bombay with her husband, her children and the religious-
minded Bhuaji to live a life resembling that of birds and fishes,
'drifting without thought or effort or fear, aerial and at ease'
(p. 216); Sudhir for a humble job as teacher in a Literacy
Institute in Madhya Pradesh. In contrast to them, the
Hochstadts (platitudinous to the last) leave India congratulating
themselves on all they have gained through their (extremely
superficial) 'contact with this fabled land' (p. 255), while Etta,
convalescing after a nervous breakdown and a suicide attempt,
has Clarissia (who has moved into her flat) draw the curtains
and shut India out of her view altogether.

Backgrounds and settings in A Backward Place frequently
yield intimations of present reality or future events. As was the

case to a limited degree in *Get Ready for Battle*, they take on
the functions of silent commentators and prophets, so that the
actions of individuals begin to seem, after a while, not only to
be dominated by the Indian milieu, but subtly influenced by
and interwoven with it. Thus the narrative reinforces Ruth
Jhabvala's projection of India as protagonist who — under the
illusory disguise of 'backwardness' —methodically strips its
opponents of their cultural supports and psychological balance,
exposes the emptiness at the heart of their intellectual
pretensions, and either demoralises them (as in the case of Etta
and Clarissa) or dismisses them (as in the case of the
Hochstadts). The segment of India's landscape that is to be seen
from Etta's terrace offers certain features to the eye that are
unchanging and permanent in a sinister, even threatening way:

> ... this was not Europe ... Vast barren spaces, full of dust
> and bits of litter, flowed around and between the smart new
> houses; there was not a tree in sight, and the only growth
> to spring spontaneously out of this soil was, here and there,
> little huts patched together out of mud and old boards and
> pieces of sacking. The whole area was intersected by a
> railwayline for goods trains, and there were two prominent
> landmarks: an old mausoleum of blackened stone and no
> architectural value (but with a curious air of permanence
> about it: one felt that when all the pretty houses and all the
> makeshift huts had gone, this at any rate would still be here),
> and an enormous brightly coloured advertisement hoarding
> for rubber tyres. Most prominent of all was the sky, which
> covered and dwarfed everything, was electric blue and had
> black kites wheeling slowly round and round against it. (p. 7)

Dust, aridity, a tomb, and a sky filled with birds of prey: these
'flow' round, outlast and 'cover' the signs of progress and
modernity, of spontaneous life and commercial success. Silent,
unchanging, they are reminders of the inevitability of death and
the transience of human vanity and desire that make Etta's
efforts to make time stand still seem petty, irrelevant and quite
futile. Significantly, it is the sight of such a reminder — 'a bit
of too blue sky and the black wings of some birds of prey
flashing against it' (p. 250) — that makes Etta insist on her
curtains being drawn at the end of the novel.

As the plot develops, bringing Etta ever closer to the point

at which she loses control, suggestions of menace and
desolation cluster thickly about her. Her chic flat — the
expression of her 'European' sophistication — becomes 'stale
with cigarette smoke, untidy and dusty, closed in like a cage'
(p. 229). Around the Rangmahal, a week-end resort conceived
as an imitation palace of pleasure to which Etta is brought by
Mr Gupta, there stretches a landscape that is empty and silent,
redolent of transience and decay:

> Beyond the cottages, the countryside stretched far and wide
> and empty into the darkness. No sound came from it, no
> smell except of dry dust. The sky seemed equally endless
> and desolate. There was no moon visible, though it must have
> been lurking somewhere, for the clouds that drifted slow as
> ghosts across the sky seemed faintly shadowed with light.
> This was just sufficient to outline a few ruins that stood far
> apart on little mounds. Now and again the jackals howled.
> (p. 129)

The revellers who patronise the Rangmahal are middle-aged,
and their delights — from which all gaiety has fled — are
conventionally sordid rather than amusing or aesthetically
pleasing. It is in this desolate setting, where the Rangmahal's
derelict swimming-pool and bandstand and an encounter with
another couple (the man middle-aged, the girl young, shrill and
determinedly lively) sadly foretell the future of Etta's
relationship with her admirer, the he informs her of his plans
to visit the glamorous capitals of Europe — and treats as a
joke her desperate appeal that he should take her with him
(p. 133).

Ruth Jhabvala frequently employs descriptions of an interior
setting to expose, and sometimes dissect, hidden truths about
individual character. The suite of rooms occupied by the
Hochstadts in a government hostel quickly takes on 'a very
comfortable European atmosphere'. Here, as well as in their
'expert' interpretations of India to each other and to their
friends, the Hochstadts manage 'to put their own touch on
everything' (p. 35). With India shut out of it, everything in Etta's
bedroom

> was as it should be. The room was dim and apricot-coloured;
> her jars and lipsticks glittered on the white rosewood

dressing-table; the flowers Mr Jumperwala had brought still
lay, elegant in paper and ribbons, across the bed ... In the
next room Clarissa was clinking with glasses and bottles;
she had also put on a record and Piaf was singing *La Vie
En Rose*. (p. 251)

In his own eyes the suite occupied by Mr Gupta in the hotel
he owns

looked nice and, what was more, had been very expensive,
and so could not be changed just because it did not suit
the whims of one particular woman. (p. 90)

In contrast to these interiors, the room Jaykar occupies in his
son's house has

nothing in it except a string cot to sleep on, the lectern to
write on and two wooden shelves; a room as bare and clean
as the life that was lived in it. (p. 164)

Jaykar advocates the life of the unhoused pilgrim, and though
too old to make heroic decisions himself, he lives simply,
inspires others to do so, and brings out what is best in them.
Clarissa, however, who also preaches the joys of the simple life
and claims to live it, spends as much of her time as possible
in the houses of wealthy Indian friends, and whatever is left
in a 'bleak untidy room' in an office building, feeding herself
on scraps of shop-cooked food and growing older and lonelier
and dirtier year by year' (p. 81).
   The Cultural Dais, an organization that is more pretentious
than useful, is appropriately accommodated in

a handsome house, though not quite on as grand a scale
as the huge portico in front might have led one to believe.
(p. 20)

It is in the old-fashioned, paved courtyard of this house, in
which Sudhir tells Judy of the poverty of his struggling students
(p. 61) that 'the real life of the family' had been carried on in
former times, not in the 'grand long hall' occupied by the Dais.
Jaykar's son, a minor government official, lives in one of a group
of weather-beaten houses in 'a remote new housing colony'
which

were all identical and stretched row upon row ... their yellow

plaster was peeling off, their ledges were sagging and there
were cracks in the cement-work. (p. 16)

The houses are defective, and potentially dangerous; in this they
symbolise the administration which created them, as the
insecurity felt by the inmates in their shoddy, gimcrack
surroundings reflects the still greater uncertainty they feel in
their work. Jaykar's son labours 'under the constant
apprehension that ... he might be dismissed' at any moment
and therefore keeps 'very quiet and out of harm's way' (p. 162),
protesting at the conditions neither of his work nor of his life.
The fact that these are new houses is evidence, as Jaykar's
conversation with Sudhir reveals, of the dishonesty rampant
in Indian public life, a theme taken up earlier by Ruth Jhabvala
in both *The Nature of Passion* and *Get Ready for Battle*. The
contractor who built the quarters has lined his pockets at the
expense of the residents; and in doing so has weakened the
structure of the building, as well as that of the administration
it represents.

Other descriptions of the Indian milieu, and especially of the
sky in its changing moods, indicate the author's sense of the
existence of a spiritual, mystic side to India's complex
'personality' that strengthens human virtue, blesses and guards
it. The same 'too blue' sky with its distinctly menacing kites
that disturbs Etta can, at times, reveal subtler aspects of itself
to which some of the novel's characters respond, while others
do not. The business-like Mr Gupta, for instance, walks up and
down Etta's terrace with his mind on financial affairs.

never once looking up at the sky, which was a pale pearly
grey with one last lilac streak still fading in the west. (p. 48)

In shutting out the intimations of death and age yielded by the
Indian sky, Etta is also shutting out its 'intimations of heaven'.
Mr Gupta, on the other hand, notices neither. But the sky
speaks to others, one of whom is Judy: she is baffled by the
pseudo-intellectual discussions of India that the Hochstadts
delight in, but her own response to India is instinctive,
imaginative and full of feeling. Her decision (momentous
because it defies her Western middle-class conditioning, the
caution and insularity that have been her parents' legacy) to
accompany Bal to Bombay is made in a moment as beautiful

as that in which the beggar-woman Leelavati finds death in
Heat and Dust:

> She looked up now and found the sky, in its first dawn of
> night, a smooth soft surface of pale silver ...
> She couldn't ever remember having looked up at the sky
> in England. She must have done, but she couldn't remember.
> There had been nothing memorable: nothing had spoken.
> So one locked oneself up at home, all warm and cosy, and
> looked at the television and grew lonelier and lonelier till it
> was unbearable and then one found a hook in the lavatory.
> Judy could not imagine ever being that lonely here. In the
> end, there was always the sky. Who spoke from the sky here?
> Why did it seem to her that someone spoke? (pp. 240-41)

Another character in the novel to whom the sky speaks is
Sudhir who, on his journey out of Delhi, remembers with the
clarity of a vision an earlier experience that now makes sense
to him and gives him new hope:

> He remembered how once he had wandered through an
> abandoned slum colony, where the pitiful shreds of pitiful
> lives lay scattered over the cracked and filthy earth and an
> old woman dug hopelessly in a heap of ashes, and suddenly,
> it was sunset and the sky blazing with the most splendid,
> the most royal of colours and everything — the old woman,
> and the ashes, the rags, the broken bricks, the split old
> bicycle tyres — everything burst into glory. (p. 247)

It will take more than the beauty of the Indian sky at sunset
to improve the worldly lot of the destitute old woman it touches
with such 'glory'. Sudhir's vision is not offered as a solution
to the problems of poverty and insecurity that burden India's
poor; it is merely part of the personal reward, even blessing,
that India gives to those who see into her soul and are prepared
to give themselves to her as Sudhir has done. Abandoning the
security of living (as Jaykar puts it) like one among so many
'mice in holes' (p. 203), Sudhir leaves Delhi and the Cultural
Dais to their empty intellectual and aesthetic pretensions, to
devote his considerable intelligence to assisting Indian
education at its lowest level in a part of India remote from the
fashionable capital. Announcing his decision, Sudhir is sardonic
rather than heroic:

I'm going to teach in a Literacy Institute. I think my level
of culture doesn't really rise higher than to neoliterates.
(p. 228)

His 'vision' is personal to him, and symbolises the fact that,
in his creator's view, beauty and 'glory' are as much a part of
India as her poverty and backwardness, to be perceived only
by those who have thoughts and time for more than their own
comfort and material advancement.

Sharing with the elderly Jaykar both his idealism and the
detached cynicism with which he masks it, Sudhir (like Krishna
Sen Gupta in *Amrita*) has been born too late for the glowing,
openly expressed patriotism that lit up the lives of Ram Nath
and Uma (of *Esmond in India*) during the Independence struggle.
Jaykar, however, whose revolutionary career in those years had
led to his spending some fifteen years of his life in jail, has
known the disappointment of seeing that fiery idealism turn
to ashes. Like Ram Nath, like Nirad Chakravarty, the heroine's
father in *Amrita*, he is distressed by the activities of the
Government he 'had fought so hard to install' (p. 73). His
comments to Sudhir on the present realities of Indian life and
politics are deeply felt and passionately spoken, but when
printed in his paper, *Second Thoughts*, they sound empty and
rhetorical. Nor can Jaykar be taken entirely seriously, even
when he is most deeply concerned. Defending the Indian
character from the superficial generalisations of foreign
observers, he falls into the same trap himself: 'As if the Indian
character could be summed up! ... yes indeed, we are a slippery
lot.' (pp. 189-90). Yet, though events have passed Jaykar by,
he provides a bridge between the idealism that had attended
and inspired the Independence struggle and Sudhir's as yet
unchannelled feelings for his country; between the ancient
Indian tradition that honours the houseless, unburdened
pilgrim and the real need of Bal and Judy to cut loose from
the purposeless lives they are leading in Delhi.

A Backward Place covers a period of approximately ten
months, a fact unobtrusively conveyed to the reader in the
information that the Rs. 475 ('nearly five hundred rupees') in
Judy's fixed deposit savings account at the start of the novel
has grown (at the rate of Rs. 25 each month) to the Rs. 725
she draws out of the bank before leaving Delhi. During this

period, Etta, Judy and Sudhir struggle for survival in hostile
and unpromising circumstances. Etta strives vainly to keep her
personality whole, Judy to reconcile the warring impulses in
her own nature that impel her now towards love and self-
abandonment, now towards caution and self-preservation, and
Sudhir to keep his mind uncontaminated by obsequiousness
and cynicism, and directed towards some worthwhile goal. They
have all known desperation before finding the fragile security
they enjoy at the start of the novel, Etta as Mr Gupta's means
of 'relaxation', Judy and Sudhir in jobs at the Cultural Dais.
They are all three 'dispensable', and know it: 'It'll be like that
other place I had,' Judy tells Sudhir,

> 'One fine day it was needed for someone else so out I went.
> And there wasn't a bean in the house.' And she added in
> quiet agony, 'Oh gosh.'
> 'You're alive, isn't it?' (Sudhir) said dryly. (p. 151)

The experience of watching Mrs Kaul dismiss a young female
employee reminds both Judy and Sudhir (as her 'encounter'
with the Anglo-Indian girl at the Rangmahal reminds Etta) how
close they are to dispensability, and how poorly equipped they
are to cope with it. In its fear and 'agony' their situation
resembles the experiences that the Jewish refugees of 'A
Birthday in London' have lived through, and Sudhir plainly feels
(like Mr Lumbik in that story) that the fact of survival is a
success-story in itself. The gap between the dreadful realities
of their struggle and the aesthetic abstractions that 'stimulate'
the Cultural Dais is indicated through grim comedy, when a
desperate Judy appeals indirectly to the Hochstadts for help
by informing them that Bal is more interested in the film than
in live drama. She is met by reproachful reminders from the
Hochstadts that 'it is in the drama that the fuller artistic
expression must reveal itself':

> 'There we will find what is new, the work of young Indian
> play-wrights moved by the contemporary predicament, and
> hand in hand with it also the revival of the great Sanskrit
> dramas of the past —'
> 'The *Shakuntala*, the *Mricchakatika*, the *Mudraraksasa*,'
> said Dr Hochstadt, pronouncing the Sanskrit with a great
> flourish, sharply enunciating each vowel and consonant and

baring his teeth in the process. 'There lies India's glory!' cried
Mrs Hochstadt, clapping her hands together and quite beside
herself with enthusiasm.

Under these circumstances, Judy was ashamed to tell them
that it was not the relative merits of cinema and drama as
mediums of artistic expression that particularly exercised her,
but rather their relative merits as sources of income. (p. 200)

It is a moment that might recall to some readers the bitter
allusion made by the accomplished governess Jane Fairfax in
Jane Austen's novel *Emma* to employment offices as agencies
'for the sale of human flesh', only to be met by complacent
Mrs Elton's cheerful inquiry as to whether she had intended
a satirical 'fling at the slave trade?' The moment passes in Jane
Austen's novel, but in Ruth Jhabvala's it expands until it
overshadows other concerns. Survival in its various forms is
perhaps the major theme of *A Backward Place*.

It is, in these circumstances, only to be expected that the
Hochstadts provoke some of the finest and most sustained
displays of Ruth Jhabvala's satiric wit. The description of the
'world premiere of Ibsen's *Doll's House* in Hindi' on which
(together with the Hochstadts' complacent reflections upon it)
the novel closes is especially interesting; for the skilful blending
of narrative with the Hochstadts' characteristic expression,[4]
and for the manner in which the passage gathers together the
themes of cultural confrontation and analysis of the nature of
India that are interwoven in the novel as a whole:

But these were petty details, and the Hochstadts had, after
mature reflection, no difficulty in rising above them: which
left them free to contemplate the larger issues and applaud,
with all their hearts, the courage and daring of the enterprise.
Here was a true attempt, on the one hand, to revive the
theatre and rekindle in the people a love of that great art
which they had lost but which had once, in ancient days,
been so triumphantly theirs; and, on the other, to weld this
ancient heritage to what had since been achieved in countries
of the West and so bring about a synthesis not only of old
and new but also — and what could be culturally more
fertile? — of East and West. (p. 255)

As the platitudes roll relentlessly on, gaining momentum until they culminate in the novel's final devastating paragraph, Ruth Jhabvala exposes not only the sterility of the Cultural Dais and of its endeavours in the sphere of art, but the stupidity of the foreign experts whose 'contact' with India has been so superficial that they can claim to recognise in such endeavours a cultural renaissance.

Mrs Kaul, the Honorary Secretary of the Dais, is neatly summed up by Sudhir:

> Mrs Kaul, bless her, cares for none of our noble abstracts but, on the contrary, for some very solid concretes: the Cultural Dais for her stands for social advancement, a place where you can meet nice and interesting people and be in touch and be important, also an opportunity perhaps to wangle a trip abroad. (p. 94)

Mrs Kaul's plans for extending the activities of the Dais centre round a well-publicised dramatic production. She is not sure what the play will be, but that in her eyes is a matter of the most minor importance. Directors, actors, playwrights are merely 'such people' to her — the chief consideration is to set a date for the production and notify the guest of honour: 'This is how a great country like ours is built!' (p. 193). Human suffering, too, is unimportant to Mrs Kaul. To a dismissed employee of the Social Development Board, a young woman who supports a whole family on her small salary, and who cries out in appeal to her, 'I *need* the money!', Mrs Kaul, sitting elegantly at ease in her luxurious drawing room, replies 'You can see I am busy. I am in conference' (p. 110). She runs the Dais as if it were an extension of her own mansion, and would dismiss Judy from her post as assistant as she would dismiss a domestic servant if Sudhir were not there to deter her. The Dais provides Mrs Kaul with an interest in life, as social service activities compensate Tarla Mathur for an unsatisfactory husband in *Amrita*. 'Without this work, what is there in my life?' she cries to Sudhir; 'I'm like a bird in a gilded cage' (pp. 228-29). It is when she decides to draw the actors for the projected play from her select social circle of 'people we know', declaring them to be 'all deeply interested in the advancement of the theatre movement in our country' (p. 227) that Sudhir decides at last that he has had enough.

Ruth Jhabvala's description (pp. 55-64) of a typical evening

at the Dais confirms our worst fears regarding the utter futility
of its activities. As the meeting breaks up and the guests (dull,
pretentious people drawn exclusively from the 'cultured' section
of Delhi society that is 'well-dressed, spoke good English and
had been abroad' — p. 58) scatter for refreshments and
conversation, the gap between appearance and reality is made
clear by visual and aural means:

> The groups of figures, *clear in outline but blurred in details,
> looked charming and well composed*, the ladies in their
> coloured dresses and saris, the men all in white. And their
> conversation too, *when one did not hear what was being
> spoken, sounded lively* and blended with the twitterings of
> the birds. (p. 63, my italics)

Bal's idea of a theatre project, elaborated by Sudhir into an
impressive document as a means of giving Bal a break in life
(and perhaps, too, of keeping Judy in Delhi), is quickly taken
over by others. Mrs Kaul is 'excited' and 'really stimulated' by
the idea (p. 110), the word 'stimulated' carrying ironic
implications similar to those generated by its use in Ruth
Jhabvala's description of Gulzari Lal's party in *Get Ready For
Battle*. She sees in it, according to a cynical forecast of Sudhir's
that he does not stay long enough in Delhi to see most
accurately fulfilled,

> the speeches, the bouquets, the best saris, Mrs Kaul
> receiving the Prime Minister and leading him up the aisle
> to usher him into his seat, while the cameras click and the
> flashlights flash. Marvellous. (p. 76)

Clarissa professes to see the project as a 'rallying point for all
those hundreds — nay thousands — of people who're burning
themselves up with their own energy', pressing even the doctor
who owns the building that houses the Dais (and who has no
other interest in life except maintaining it) into a new and
unexpected role as 'another one looking for a cause' (p. 127).
The Dais provides an admirable focus for the novel's action.
It attracts such diverse personalities as Clarissa, Etta and the
Hochstadts, and keeps their minds circling around the
definition of the true India that is one of the main themes of
A Backward Place. Self-deception, a favourite subject for study
with Ruth Jhabvala, is much in evidence among the supporters

of the Dais. Sudhir perceives that, quite apart from Judy and
Bal for whose sake he formulates the project, 'there were other
people too who expected something from it' (p. 127). In tracing
these various expectations, and the extent to which they achieve
or fall short of fulfilment, Ruth Jhabvala charts in microcosm
the particular weaknesses of modern India.

Ruth Jhabvala's portrait of Kishan Kumar, a male film idol,
sheds light on her attitude to the Bombay motion picture
industry and its place in modern Indian life. When *A Backward
Place* was published, Ruth Jhabvala had been working for five
years with Merchant-Ivory films, and had written screen plays
for THE HOUSEHOLDER and SHAKESPEAREWALLAH. The first of
these subtly indicates the difference between film fantasies and
real life as it is lived by a typical pair of youthful middle-class
newly-weds, the second traces the process by which cheap film
art and star personality cults coarsen the sensibilities of India's
theatre-going public. Her work in *A Backward Place* bears
comparison with R.K. Narayan's picture of the commercial film
as the enemy of the creative imagination, in both his novel *Mr
Sampath* and his essay, "The Reluctant Guide". On Kishan
Kumar's casual promise, 'Stick with me and you'll be okay'
(p. 155), Bal builds the dream castle in Bombay towards which
he, Judy and their two children are moving when the novel
ends. While Bal and his actor-friends are filled, each with the
excitement generated by his own ideas and hopes of success,
Kishan Kumar too

> under the stimulus of their enthusiasm and admiration
> coupled with the drinks he had had ... saw himself — no,
> he *was* the great actor-producer, the colossus of the Bombay
> film world. (p. 105)

The film-fed vanity that helps to make a monster out of the
boyish actor Vikram in a film Ruth Jhabvala scripted in 1970,
BOMBAY TALKIE, finds a fictional parallel in Kishan Kumar's
behaviour:

> When he was asked ... for his autograph, he gave it with
> a kind of professional humility which was rather at odds with
> the huge portentous squiggle in which he wrote his name
> on the proffered scraps of paper. (p. 103)

Ruth Jhabvala's portrait of the star gains depth from an

unexpected sympathy, directed towards the youth and
vulnerability of the young man in Kishan Kumar. For he is in
all essentials, merely a magnification of the appealing and
vulnerable Bal, differing from Bal and his fellow-admirers only
in being 'taller than any of them, handsomer, more charming,
more expensively, more beautifully dressed' (p. 102). When fired
— as Bal is, in the course of the novel, often fired — by the
excitement of an idea, Kishan Kumar

> looked wonderful ... happiness shone on his face, which was
> not only superbly handsome but also very young so that it
> became, now that he was excited and his film star
> affectations had fallen away, the perfect mirror for the perfect
> boy's heart. (p. 106)

When the reader sees Kishan Kumar again (on a second visit
to Delhi), the image has coarsened, the mask of generosity
slipped away, revealing a self-absorption so intense that, in
contrast with the humble Bal, Kishan Kumar appears gross:

> Kishan Kumar came out of the bathroom stark naked.
> Drops of water still glistened on his smooth, healthy, olive-
> coloured skin. He showed no surprise at Bal's presence and
> perhaps he was even pleased to have company (he always
> liked company). And he liked to be watched, the way Bal was
> now watching him, as he slowly, with loving luxurious
> gestures, never taking his eyes off his image in the mirror,
> began to dress.
> Bal got plenty of time and opportunity to unfold his case.
> He was glad he had come back. From time to time Kishan
> Kumar gave him an encouraging nod and once he asked for
> a cigarette to be lit and stuck between his lips.
> ... 'How do I look?'
> 'Very nice', Bal said and had the tact to leave a moment's
> respectful silence.
> Kishan Kumar was pleased. He turned his head to see
> himself in profile and smoothed back the hair over one
> temple. (p. 154)

This scene follows one in which Sudhir becomes aware of Judy's
complete dependence upon him (and his continuance in his
post at the Dais) for the support of her family. It is itself
immediately followed by a scene set in Mr Gupta's hotel suite,

in which Etta appeals to her protector, and is repulsed. All these characters are, in effect, pleading their right to survive; they are the weak, the expendable, dependent for their existence on the whims of the 'strong', the powerful Kishan Kumars, Mr Guptas and Mrs Kauls of this world, their dilemma much the same as that of Prem in *The Householder* as he writes his 'petition' to Mr Khanna. The grotesque vanity of the film-star is apparent to the reader, if not to Bal; and not the least of the fears created by this scene in the reader's mind is the premonition — not only of what will happen to Bal's family if Kishan Kumar does not keep his promises, but of what will happen to them if he does, and if by some chance Bal's dreams of financial success in the film industry come true. It is hard to overlook the possibility that waiting for them in Bombay is a subtle form of corruption which will inevitably turn the passionate enthusiasm Judy loves now in Bal into a monstrous vanity. The change that has taken place in Kishan Kumar's personality between his first and second visits to Delhi (a comparable development is traceable in Vikram's personality in the film BOMBAY TALKIE, and also in Gopi's in the novel *A New Dominion*) indicates the speed and effectiveness of the degenerative process. It cannot be thought likely that the charming but essentially weak-charactered Bal will resist it.

Kishan Kumar carries around with him some of the cinema's fantasy and magic. He is able, by his mere presence, to make Bal and his friends feel that 'life was beginning for all of them' (p. 106). It is worth comparing his portrait in *A Backward Place* with such treatments of related subjects by Ruth Jhabvala as the reactions of Hari to film romance in *Amrita*, and of the narrator in "The Interview" to the Bombay film. In each of these studies she lays stress on the fantasies and unreal escape-routes opened by the commercial film, which coarsen Indian sentiment until it is indistinguishable from cheap sentimentality, and do nothing to improve conditions in India, either of life or of thought.

Although looking at first sight somewhat similar to her satiric studies of Mrs Kaul and Kishan Kumar, Ruth Jhabvala's characterisation of Bal strikes a delicately placed median note between irony and sympathy which relieves what might otherwise seem a very grim comedy:

It would not be true to say that Bal did not worry. But he worried on a higher level. He knew that the present state of their affairs was so entirely temporary that there was no need to waste any energy thinking about it. He was thus left entirely free to speculate on what was to come. That this would be to the highest degree satisfactory he never for one moment doubted, and the only questions to give him pause were ones of how and when. (p. 151-2)

Bal is treated by his creator (and by his wife, Judy) like an appealing child. His 'brilliant idea', once conceived, must be communicated; and as he searches for a listener, the reader receives an impression of his immaturity. He idles the morning away while everyone else in the household is busy at work (pp. 65-66), spending the rest of his day partly at the radio station talking to a junior administrator who had once been one of his unemployed cronies (pp. 66-8), and the rest in a coffee-house, discussing his idea with others like himself (pp. 69-70).

The sickness of his son Prithvi exposes the strains within the little family: Judy's efforts to waken Bal to a responsible adult view of his parental obligations, and to make him see the worthlessness of his idol, Kishan Kumar; Bal's tendency to use his charm to sidestep all such efforts. Bal's irresponsibility amounts to cruelty, and in this he resembles Hari Sahni in *Amrita*, another charming young man who causes, through the weakness of his character, intense anguish in the mind and heart of a superior female personality. Unlike Hari, however, Bal has deep feelings that can be aroused, and an outlook capable of maturing. He becomes ashamed when Jaykar classes him with the idlers, the 'apes and loafers' in the coffee-house (p. 136), and Etta's accusation that he is living on his wife's earnings finally gets him up and out of Delhi, with a definite goal in view:

'From now on, you will see, I shall be a different person. And no one will ever dare to say to me again' — and his eyes blazed dangerously — 'that I can't support my own family. No one shall ever insult me like that again.' (p. 217)

Bal's unquenchable optimism renders him 'happy most of the time ... which was more than could be said for Mukand' (p. 84), his hardworking and reliable elder brother. This optimism finally conquers Judy's doubts and fears, and moves the family, with its tiny stock of worldly possessions and Judy's meagre savings (but with new faith and hope in the future) to a new life in Bombay. Bal's conversation with Sudhir (pp. 213-7) recalls a somewhat similar interview between Hari Sahni and Krishna Sen Gupta in *Amrita*, with the significant difference that Bal (unlike Hari) is determined to assume responsibility for the future, and Sudhir (unlike Krishna) experiences a desire to emulate his companion's cheerful approach to life:

> Sudhir ... felt heavy and sullen and earthbound beside Bal. Bal seemed to him like one of those birds floating on the sky — drifting without thought or effort or fear, aerial and at ease. (p. 216)

A Backward Place abounds, satiric studies such as those of the Hochstadts, Kishan Kumar and Mrs Kaul included, in satisfying characterisations, executed in depth. The somewhat stage-managed scenes of *Amrita* and *The Nature of Passion* are replaced by a narrative that flows with naturalness and ease, bringing characters into seemingly casual association or contrast that enables the reader to observe them from many angles, catch subtle modulations in their ways of addressing different people, and watch their behaviour in a series of challenging situations. One particularly interesting characterisation is that of Mr Gupta, 'a hotel owner, a rich but self-made man, a vigorous fifty' (p. 45) who

> had married all his daughters and settled his sons, his business was doing well, and there was time now, as there had never been before, for a little relaxation. Etta was this relaxation: she was feminine, sprightly, spoiled and kittenish for him. (p. 46)

The terms of his description subtly link this modern ruler of industry with the wealth, energy and power associated with the Gupta dynasty of ancient India. When Clarissa tells him that he has 'a real conqueror's face ... the *veni vidi vici* type' (p. 50) she is close to the truth, for he is 'a bold and self-willed man, who took everything he wanted' (p. 47); although he indulges Etta and Clarissa, he is swayed by no one. Etta calls her powerful protector 'Guppy' or 'Gup', a characteristic example of her deliberately challenging approach to India, and of her defiant attempts to assert herself and her 'Europeanness' at the expense of all things Indian. Mr Gupta is quite unaffected by this, but the reader registers the nickname and its diminutive as a down-grading of the vigorous, energetic associations of an ancient name.

Guppy is majestically detached from most of what is going on around him, and even in situations other men would find most trying, he can display both wisdom and interest. When Etta and Clarissa squabble in his presence, the reader has an opportunity to view Etta's pretensions to European elegance from an unexpected perspective:

> His own women were very much more subtle: generations of purdah living had sharpened their wits and made them adept at insinuation, at neatly turned, finely veiled personal insults. Clarissa and Etta, on the other hand, were crude enough, he felt, to come to blows ... He judged it wiser to put a stop to this quarrel, though it rather interested him. (p. 53)

Etta cannot 'afford to lose' Guppy (p. 49), Clarissa attempts to establish a relationship with him by means of flattery (p. 51). For a large part of the novel, the two women are involved in a vicious power-struggle for the amused (and largely indifferent) Guppy. On one occasion their conflict emerges in an open quarrel that all the Hochstadts' tact cannot control (pp. 141-6). On another, they dance to frenzied gramophone music while Guppy looks on, amused by their drunkenness and their grotesque movements (pp. 54-55). The latter scene ironically recreates, with deliberate unpleasantness, the descriptions in Indian classical poetry of erotic scenes in the harems and drinking-halls of mediaeval Indian rulers. Guppy, like the Indian sky that oppresses Etta, is a part of India that may seem to alter from time to time, but is essentially changeless and unchangeable. (He has been 'taught' by Etta to give up wearing ostentatious jewellery, but she has no effect on his inner life, nor, indeed, any influence even on the decoration of his hotel suite.) Etta represents for Guppy merely a minor incident in his active life, subject to termination at any time he should wish it ended; he, however, is the part of unchanging India that will finally cause the disintegration of her brittle personality.

The novel provides many opportunities for the reader to see Guppy as a man of power, accustomed to doing as he pleases. When he decides to spend an evening at the Rangmahal (which Etta heartily dislikes), the evening moves as he wishes it to move (pp. 128-33). But perhaps the most unequivocal expression of his character occurs when his new mistress, a plump, pretty Indian teenager, unexpectedly meets Etta, the ageing European mistress he is preparing to discard. Guppy begins at a distinct disadvantage in the scene that follows between him and Etta, making obviously invented excuses 'in a loud, jovial voice' (p. 157). But as Etta makes use of her advantage to coax him kittenishly to take her with him to Cannes, his essentially ruthless personality begins to show itself until the end leaves the reader in no doubt (despite Guppy's expressions of polite hospitality) as to how things are to stand between them in the future:

> He wasn't listening. He was thinking of some important matters waiting for him down in the office and, determined to get there, he used rather more of his strength than he would have done if he had not been so preoccupied. Of course, with this he loosened her grip easily and even made her tumble some distance away, so that she lost her balance and would have fallen if she hadn't supported herself on an arm-chair.
> ... 'Oh sorry,' he said; not much concerned, though, for obviously she wasn't hurt and it was, after all, her own fault. 'I'm going down now. If you are staying, please order anything you like — coffee, tea, anything ... Or you could order whisky, gin, beer, whatever you like. Be quite comfortable while I'm gone.' (pp. 160-61)

The interest and forcefulness of Guppy's personality gain a good deal from Ruth Jhabvala's implicit contrast of it with that of Mr Jumperwala, who succeeds him as Etta's admirer. Unlike Guppy, Mr Jumperwala is a product of the European sophistication Etta worships, but he also represents a step down for her, in physical terms, from Guppy's undeniable, if uncultured, vigour. Mr Jumperwala is a target for Ruth Jhabvala's satire, with his 'polished English manners', his superior background — 'We are all Cambridge people,' he says modestly (pp. 139-40) — and his inexpressibly tedious anecdotes about his life in England. His dated English slang, his affectionate reminiscences of the English friends who used to call him 'Dusky', and his memories of Brewer Street and London cabs and of breathing the Knightsbridge air look forward, interestingly, to the far more complex and compassionate portrait, created ten years later, of the Princess in the film AUTOBIOGRAPHY OF A PRINCESS. He represents, at the same time, a mature version of another Parsi character, Phiroze Batliwala, the superficially sophisticated, philandering tennis-player with whom Nimmi falls briefly in 'love' in *The Nature of Passion*.

The characters of Etta and Clarissa, too, have close connections with Ruth Jhabvala's other work, providing among other things two carefully contrasted studies of the Western sensibility under stress in India. Indications are given quite early in the novel that Etta, despite her poised appearance, is under severe strain: Judy's appearance in a sari makes her 'angry' (p. 6), and her servant's forgetfulness makes her 'hiss' furiously at him. She is aware of her own condition, and frightened by it — 'I'm smoking too much,' she added, as she lit another cigarette with slightly agitated fingers' (p. 36); this incident occurs when Etta is reminded that the Hochstadts, unlike herself, are short-term visitors to India. Her abrasive conversational manner, regarding which the Hochstadts are 'wise and understanding' and theorise in the most interesting way (p. 38) is a symptom of a condition, the seriousness of which she masks with her flippant, worldly manner and her much-vaunted self-sufficiency. She is not only smoking too much, but is soon found (by Guppy) to be relying on sleeping pills (p. 46). She drinks too much, too fast (pp. 50-51). Although not yet too despairing or proud to study the dress and manners of transit passengers in hotel lounges — 'these brief emissaries of a Europe she had left over twenty-five years ago but still looked to for everything that was valuable to her' (pp. 88-89) — Etta is ageing rapidly; seizing a moment when Guppy takes a refreshing catnap to relax her own body and her face, she is quick, as soon as he awakes, to slip 'her feet back into her shoes and her face back into youth and sprightliness' (pp. 89-90).

She begins to lose control over her emotions. Her reaction to the news that Clarissa is trying to enlist Guppy in the cause

of the theatre project is violent and hysterical (pp. 111-16).
Invited by the Hochstadts to join their *alfresco* picnic among
the Lodhi tombs, she vents her frustration at Mr Gupta's neglect
of her on Bal, who happens to remind her of the legions of
handsome young Indians she had attracted when she was
young and beautiful. Clarissa tells her, 'I think you're going
crazy' (p. 205), and Etta seems indeed to be set on a course
of self-destruction, laying waste in addition all that comes in
her way. The novel follows her through every stage of the
process of deterioration. Her smart flat turns into a squalid
'cage', and Etta begins (like Mrs Saunders in *Heat and Dust*,
who has also lived too long in India) to scream at her Indian
servants and suspect them of dishonesty (p. 231). As a last
resort, she even suggests to Judy that they go away to Europe
together (p. 234), a gesture reminiscent of Esmond's hopes
concerning Betty in the last pages of *Esmond in India*. Etta's
violence, unlike Esmond's (who turns on his Indian wife, Gulab),
is ultimately vented on herself, and her attempt at suicide
(averted at the last moment by the Hochstadts) provides the
novel with its climax.

Clarissa, too, is caught up in the process of change that
affects Etta, although she is Etta's opposite in appearance,
convictions and background. Of British upper-class origin,
Clarissa has lived 'many years in India' (p. 25); her accent has
lost 'some of its local colour and idiom, and her complexion,
once probably rosy and redolent of English skies, had taken
on the withered pallor of all Western women too long in the
East' (p. 25). Despite her declared abandonment of material
values in her pursuit of the eternal, Clarissa is inclined (as Etta
mercilessly points out) to sponge on her wealthy friends, and
adopts a frankly physical and sensual approach to young men
like Bal (p. 82). Not over-burdened with a self-critical spirit,
Clarissa rationalizes most of these inconsistencies by calling
herself 'a free-and-easy mixture of sadhu and artist' (p. 82).
One inconsistency, however, surprises Clarissa herself. 'I don't
know what came over me', she wails to Mrs Hochstadt, after
she has struck a beggar-child in the street, 'I'm not that sort
of person! ... I respect people!' (p. 101). Her failure to keep to
her liberal 'principles' reduces Clarissa to hysteria, in a scene
that looks forward to the distress of the narrator of *Heat and
Dust* on finding that she too has begun to consider the human

beings around her as 'dispensable'.[5]

It will be seen that in *A Backward Place* as a whole, setting, dialogue and incident are exploited daringly for their symbolic significance, a technique developed in Ruth Jhabvala's last three novels, and given added economy and subtlety by experience evidently gleaned from the disciplines of short-story and screen-play writing. Most striking of all is the fact that the novel indicates a fundamental change of direction. Indian characters are now replaced at the centre of Ruth Jhabvala's fictional stage by Westerners caught up in the disillusionment with India that is part of her own experience. And although the characters of *A Backward Place* are effectively realized as personalities in their own right, and though the subject of *their* thoughts and discussions is constantly — inescapably — the endlessly fascinating, puzzling and infuriating phenomenon that is 'India', the novel as a whole heralds a change of interest. 'I must admit,' Ruth Jhabvala wrote in 1966, a year after the publication of this novel,

> 'that India no longer interests me as a subject. What I am interested in now is myself in India.'[6]

Notes

1. R.P. Jhabvala, *A Backward Place* (John Murray, London: 1965), pp. 36-37. All references in this chapter and throughout the book are to this edition.
2. 'All the time I know myself to be on the back of this great animal of poverty and backwardness.' R.P. Jhabvala, "Myself in India", op. cit., p. 10.
3. The relevant passage from *Amrita* is quoted in Chapter II.
4. See the discussion of this passage in Chapter I.
5. R.P. Jhabvala, *Heat and Dust*, pp. 109-13.
6. "Myself in India", op. cit., p. 8.

CHAPTER

VIII

A new dominion
OR, *Travelers*

1972, 1973

'... this is not a place that one can pick up and put down
again as if nothing had happened. In a way it's not so much
a country as an experience, and whether it turns out to be
a good or a bad one depends I suppose on oneself.'[1]

The keys to the extension of Ruth Jhabvala's kingdom of fiction
that opens in her seventh novel, *A New Dominion*, are held by
four characters who are described as follows in a list that
prefaces the volume:

Raymond : a tourist
Lee   : a girl on spiritual quest
Asha   : a middle-aged princess
Gopi   : a student

The list is divided neatly into 'Indian' and 'Western' sections,
an arrangement that prepares the reader for a novel that will
bring Indian and Western values into colloquy through the
conflict or association of characters of differing origin. Further
structuring (which may owe something to the Forsterian
example of A Passage to India) may be observed in the division
of the novel into three parts titled 'Delhi', 'The Holy City', and
'Maupur' respectively. The adoption of a plot that tells the story
of a quest (or quests) and the careful balancing of the characters
invest A New Dominion with the atmosphere of a morality play.
Each major character has his good and bad 'angel': Raymond
is drawn alternately towards self-indulgence and towards morai
responsibility, by Gopi and by Miss Charlotte ('a Christian
missionary') respectively; Lee is attracted now to the ashram
under the influence of Swamiji, 'a spiritual guide', now (under
Miss Charlotte's influence) to the life outside it; Asha wavers
between the life of a recluse in imitation of Banubai, 'a
prophetess', and the life of a libertine when tempted to it by
Bulbul, her maid; and Gopi is 'educated' by Raymond and Asha,
who assume responsibility for shaping, respectively, his artistic
tastes and his sexual skills.

In its American edition, A New Dominion was re-named
Travelers, a title that connects plot with theme as, linked by
their weaknesses and their sympathy for one another, the four
major characters journey from Delhi to the holy city of Banaras,
and thence to 'Maupur', moving deeper into India and further
into experiences that put their personalities to unexpected and
severe tests.

The India through which they travel in their quest of self-
fulfilment or self-knowledge is, as the title 'A New Dominion'
suggests, no longer the British colony that provided the setting
for E.M. Forster's A Passage to India. Forster's India was a land
in which Indian and Westerner were separated from each other
by a political situation, by mutual insularity and
misunderstanding and, symbolically at least, by the landscape
of India itself. With the dissolution of Empire, Raymond and

Lee can move in the Indian society of the 1970s with a freedom
that would have been unthinkable a mere thirty years earlier
and, unshielded by officialdom of any kind, experience joys and
sorrows of unexpected intensity, the 'heaven' and 'hell' that
India's variety encompasses. Contemporary India is symbolically
represented by the hospital to which Raymond and Lee take
Margaret (another of Swamiji's spiritual devotees) when she falls
sick at the ashram. The block they see first is only a splendid
facade. It has

> been built with the aid of foreign aid, but when it was finished
> there wasn't any money left for furnishing and equipment
> so now they were waiting for more aid. Meanwhile, they
> carried on in the old buildings. These were very old and
> rather grim, built partly of stone and partly of brick; inside
> they needed painting and plastering very badly ... There were
> an awful, awful lot of people. (p. 196)

Old and grim, overcrowded but still managing to survive, efforts
to modernise and improve ending only too often in a mere
superficial 'outside' job, this is India. In the background are
the tombs and monuments, the 'beautifully laid-out old
gardens' (p. 107) with their grass and flowerbeds and
channelled waterways that are reminders of the past. Also
included in the picture are numerous aspects of India's variety
of scene and situation, as the action of the novel moves from
the elegant, sophisticated parties and diplomatic receptions of
the capital to Banaras with its swamis and temples, and its
congested street 'populated by people who had come to the holy
city in order to die there' (p. 142); and thence to the desert
state of Maupur, where Asha looks out over a view dominated
by symbols of death, violence and destruction:

> She could look out over the dead garden and, beyond that,
> across the whole wide landscape lying broiling in the sun,
> up to the wooded hills from where the tigers sometimes
> roared ... Nothing moved ... except the birds of prey circling
> around and around in the dun-coloured sky. (p. 213)

Ruth Jhabvala's picture of contemporary India includes an
incisive indictment of an Indian chauvinism that has replaced
British imperial arrogance, with equally damaging effects upon
what it contacts and controls. The assertion of 'a new dominion'

takes place at many levels, but most strikingly in its effect on
the sensibilities of the Westerners in India. Lee, Evie and
Margaret (female 'self'-seekers at Swamiji's ashram), a German
professor who humbles himself before Banubai, and a
Norwegian girl described by a woman Minister of State are all
'subjects' of this new imperialism: the 'self'-seekers are crushed
by it as Indians were overwhelmed by British imperialism in
the past, the visitors from Germany and Norway abandon their
cultural loyalties for what they take to be a superior set of
values and customs. Both Banubai and the Minister are quite
certain that it *is* superior, and they trumpet their claims with
Macaulay-esque vigour and self-satisfaction. Their view is most
clearly expressed in Banubai's reproach to Raymond in
Banaras:

> For two hundred years you tried to make us believe that you
> are superior persons. But now the tables are turned. Now
> that your culture is bankrupt and your lives have become
> empty and meaningless, you are beginning to learn where
> truth has been hidden and stored away throughout the
> centuries. (p. 161)

Banubai repeats this aggressive chauvinism with Lee (p. 173),
who is left wondering whether she really is 'a polluting influence'
on 'truly spiritual Indians'. Even the far less impressionable
Raymond begins to doubt the reliability of his own judgment.
Indian chauvinism is neatly and ironically 'placed' by Ruth
Jhabvala when she has Gopi weigh in tipsily with his
characteristically limited (and single-track) version of it:

> It's all just propaganda. You don't know anything about sex
> — none of you know, you're all frigid. (p. 185)

As a counter to the impulse towards 'dominion' — whether
of the British or the Indian variety — the developing action of
the novel suggests that differences of race matter little when
the deepest needs of human nature seek utterance and
fulfilment. Asha and Raymond are both fascinated by Gopi, and
both hide their 'unnatural' love for him under other, more
acceptable, masks — Asha of mother love, Raymond of
friendship. Both Lee and Asha surrender themselves to the
guidance of a guru, Lee to Swamiji, Asha to Banubai. Raymond
and Gopi both find comfort in a maternal presence, and their

relationships of this nature (Raymond with his cultured,
affectionate mother in England, Gopi with his 'spiritual' mother,
Banubai) are intimate and warm. On a less personal level,
Banubai's philosophy (which she asserts is the product of
oriental spirituality) is unexpectedly reminiscent of
fundamentalist anti-humanist Protestantism in the West:

> Such things are not may — they are not perhaps! They cry
> out like a trumpet! With a royal sound! A godly sound! They
> cry out yes! And again, yes! (p. 131)

Religion, in the persons of Miss Charlotte and the charitable
Hindus of Banaras, makes provision for the derelicts of West
and East alike: when Raymond observes the dying pilgrims
being fed in Banaras, his thoughts naturally move to
Mrs Grenfell and Mr Tompkins, aged English people whom the
retreat of Empire has left stranded in India, and whom
Miss Charlotte is settling in Madras. Death seeks out Margaret
and a young Hindu wife without distinction of race; love and
jealousy trap Asha and Lee; Gopi and Lee become the willing
victims of experienced predators. The baseness of Bulbul is
matched by that of an ancient British Struldbrug, Miss Peck,
and the lively conscience of a British Council wife by the
idealism of the 'Founder-President of the University for
Universal Synthesis'. The 'India' in which these people interact
is 'not so much a country as an experience': indeed, a metaphor
for the experience of living itself. The uniqueness of India (and
its appropriateness to Ruth Jhabvala's exploration of human
psychology through her fictional characters) lies in the fact that
it provides conditions which render inescapable the experience
of facing the mysteries of the self, and of living with the
consequences of doing so.

Despite *A New Dominion*'s discouraging picture of massive
neglect and irresponsibility at the political level, its celebration
of the 'supreme ... gifts (India has) to give those ... ready to
take them' (p. 75) is, though often ironic, fully realised and
assured. In the 'new dominion', art and idealism still (though
with difficulty) survive. There are still musicians who string and
restring their notes 'like pearls and each pearl ... rounded by
generations of artistry', whose music requires for its
appreciation 'a quality of the ear as refined and a sensibility
as delicate as the music itself' (p. 86). The 'University of

Universal Synthesis' is housed in one humble room, and possesses in its Founder-President its single faculty member, yet does not lack idealism or fervour for all that. There is grandeur in the ideas that soar so far above the reality in which the 'lonely and frequently hungry old man' (p. 99) lives in austere and uncomfortable conditions. His aim, 'to educate the mind in the language of the heart and the heart in the language of the mind' (p. 140) is 'noble and beautiful in its conception' (p. 141); it is a reflection on modernity (of both East and West) that these ideas are neglected by all except their originator, while Swamiji's visions of jet-propelled travel and air-conditioned ashrams seem only too likely to become a reality. Raymond receives exquisite aesthetic enjoyment through his delight in Indian art and music; Lee's experiences at the ashram change her outlook on life and educate her emotions; Miss Charlotte's activities in healing the sick and assisting the poor yield her happiness and a purpose in life.

But, again at a personal level, India can also take a terrible toll. In accordance with the theory of a cycle of experience on which Ruth Jhabvala bases her studies of Westerners in India[2], the period of time in which the intense effects of a full turn of the 'wheel' of torture and disillusionment can be experienced provides the time-span of *A New Dominion*. Raymond and Lee are brought by the sensitivity of one and immaturity of the other closer to ecstasy and despair during that short time than they have ever come before. In the final outcome, it is not the travellers who 'see', 'enjoy' or 'understand' India, but India that absorbs and dominates them. Lee is submerged in the life of Swamiji's ashram, and Raymond retreats wounded to England, as his gallant forebears had done in earlier times. As for the Indian characters, it is evident that Asha cannot break out of her pattern of moral extremes and will either continue to move between Banubai and some young lover, or meet a tragic end when Gopi discards her (as he inevitably will) for some younger or wealthier patroness. The action is unobtrusively designed in such a way that each character receives a clear warning of what is to come. Just before she enters Delhi, Lee witnesses the funeral of a young woman who has been murdered. She recalls the incident when she observes Evie's arrangements for Margaret's funeral (p. 206), yet does not heed the warning and returns of her own will to the ashram. Asha knows the history of her father's desert lodge, 'The Retreat', but when Raymond suggests that she release Gopi before he becomes as bored as her father's Anglo-Indian mistress had become with him, she cannot bring herself to do so. When Raymond abandons his pose of detachment and pleads with Gopi to leave 'The Retreat', Gopi ignores — or does not understand — Raymond's urgency. Of the four, Raymond alone recognises and accepts the warning when it comes. At the start of their rivalry for Gopi's affection, Asha has told Raymond the story of an English tutor's infatuation for a young, 'uncultured' Indian clerk. When, at Maupur, she informs him that the tutor had tried to kill himself, Raymond leaves India with anxious haste, horrified by the violence of his own intense emotions. His precipitate flight at its end contrasts with his leisurely, sensuous enjoyment of India's romantic beauty at the beginning of his stay. In this way all four characters are given opportunities to retrace their steps or take a new path, before they move in their chosen directions out of the novel and out of the reader's view.

A New Dominion is the first of Ruth Jhabvala's novels to do without the authorial aid of a recognizable persona, although Raymond from time to time (as in the polite scepticism with which he regards Banubai — pp. 130-31) expresses an inward thought we might feel to be his creator's. It is also the first of her works to put to fictional use the technique she had had to learn in writing for film: of devising action or dialogue that is constantly cut, to dissolve into another scene. The first four 'scenes' introduce the reader to the four main characters, the next four rapidly put them in touch with one another. In the ninth 'scene', the narrative is taken up by Lee, who is the only character permitted to double as narrator throughout the novel, although both she and Raymond write letters which invariably advance the plot in addition to disclosing details of character and motive. Since the bulk of the novel is narrated in the third person, the occasions on which Lee (directly, or in a letter) and Raymond (indirectly, in a letter) take up the narrative have an effect similar to that created in a film by a shift of camera angle. The reader is permitted to observe the action from varied points of view that promote understanding of the action as a whole. A good example of this occurs in Part Two, 'The Holy City', when a shift that transfers the narration to Lee lets the reader

perceive for himself how much she is under the control of
Swamiji. Her former friends, Raymond and Miss Charlotte, now
appear comic and ill at ease to Lee:

> She looked funny sitting there perched up on her chair with
> her hands folded in her lap and her ankles crossed. She was
> wearing one of her awful frocks ... She was prim in the same
> way Raymond gets prim and terribly polite when he's
> embarrassed or put out. Actually, the two of them sitting
> there seemed to sort of belong together —if only because they
> were so different from the rest of us ... Their faces were
> different too, I can't quite say how but they didn't have that
> *look* that everyone else in the ashram has ... I suppose it
> comes from meditation and all of us feeling the way we do
> about him. (p. 152)

The 'him' of the last sentence is, of course, Swamiji, and since
it is Swamiji who regards the visit to his ashram by Raymond
and Miss Charlotte as unwarranted interference in the lives
of his devotees, the reader infers that the change in Lee's
attitude to her friends has been brought about by the fact that
her thoughts are no longer her own, but his.

Although Raymond is not the author's persona in *A New
Dominion* as Krishna Sen Gupta, Sudhir Bannerjee and Gautam
fulfil that function in *Amrita*, *A Backward Place* and *Get Ready
For Battle* respectively, Ruth Jhabvala has in him her most
reliable and perceptive observer. Raymond's respect for the
feelings of others makes him react strongly against the ruthless
egocentricity and callousness he perceives in Swamiji's
exploitation of Evie, Margaret and Lee. His own love for Gopi
turns him into a most sensitive recorder of other people's
emotions, identifying the hidden sexuality in Banubai's
'motherly' caresses of the boy, and in Lee's worship of Swamiji.
The self-control and stoicism 'he had grown up with and used
all his strength to develop' (p. 176) provide Raymond with
armour that successfully deceives the would-be analysts around
him. Lee accuses him of being a mere tourist in India, with
a tourist's superficial approach to the spiritual wealth around
him (p. 61). Asha tells him he understands nothing, and is 'cold
and unfeeling' (p. 140). Gopi calls him stupid and materialistic
(p. 24), Banubai declares that he 'doesn't feel love in his own
heart and ... sneers at the love in other people's' (p. 141), and

even the Founder-President of the University of Universal Synthesis feels called upon to say (unconsciously echoing Forster) that Raymond is 'not unfeeling ... but rational, rational. For the Westerner the mind comes first, then the heart' (p. 140).

As we watch Raymond racked by his unconfessed and unrequited love, and observe the exquisite torture to which he subjects himself by offering his company to Asha and Gopi in order to wrest an occasional, furtive pleasure from Gopi's beauty of eye and limb, we see that these confident analyses are very wide off the mark. What begins as a visit to India by a cultured tourist of unusual sensitivity to beauty and age in buildings, and to purity of form in the arts, turns into struggle and suffering. By the time he leaves Banaras for Maupur, Raymond is mortally wounded in spirit. It is only his concern for Lee and his fears for her fate at Swamiji's hands that take him to Maupur at all (pp. 176-9), and while there his thoughts turn constantly 'home'. Associated with Raymond's courage and his powers of endurance are other qualities that do not, however, escape his creator's ironic eye: at Banaras, his attachment to Gopi takes priority over friendship and responsibility, over other loves, and over human need (p. 136). But there are times when, in the face of Asha's deliberately cruel provocation, his self-control amounts to heroism. Like the narrator of *Heat and Dust*, Raymond is one of those courageous English people whose forbears died in India, and whose own experience there continues the tradition of living (and suffering) to the full.

Raymond's delicacy and restraint contrast strongly with the lack of these qualities in Lee, Asha and Gopi. Unlike them, he never — even when most hurt or distressed —takes refuge in self-deception without being ironically conscious that he is doing so. His scepticism and and clearness of vision isolates him so often from his companions that he sometimes doubts his own judgment (p. 130). His response to Banubai is one of embarrassment, not the joy and wonder she is used to inspiring in her visitors (pp. 130-31). He perceives her significant resemblance to Swamiji, and he is uncomfortably aware of dark sides to the personalities of both that his friends, more susceptible or credulous, appear to miss. Raymond is often forced to take a lonely stand against a majority opinion: he insists that Margaret's illness is serious and needs immediate treatment, while both Lee and Swamiji dismiss it as a minor

indisposition (pp. 132-6); he is alone in considering Swamiji's
book less important than Margaret's health (p. 133); he is
Miss Charlotte's only advocate with both the Government of
India and the British High Commission; he is alone in
attempting to separate Lee from Swamiji, and Gopi from Asha.

Ruth Jhabvala's portrait of Raymond has connections with
her work in other novels, in stories and in screen-plays. His
extreme sensitivity links him with Cyril Sahib in the film
AUTOBIOGRAPHY OF A PRINCESS, and with Harry in *Heat and Dust*;
as do his suppressed homosexuality and the struggle with India
that leaves him wounded and suffering, so that his departure
from India is not so much the inevitable end of a tour as the
instinctive withdrawal of an animal to its lair to lick its wounds
and regain health and strength. In Raymond's first girlish,
gossipy letter to his mother, Ruth Jhabvala does not merely
convey essential information about Indian life to her Western
reader in an easily assimilable form, but provides early evidence
of the intimacy of his relationship with her, of his observant
eye for significant detail, and of his capacity for self-criticism
and self-satire. By this means she inspires in the reader an
amused sympathy for Raymond and respect for his judgment
that will be called for later in the novel when Raymond is writing
home about matters more important than afternoon tea:

> The crockery too seemed to have been borrowed and none
> of it matched and some of it had cracks with dirt ingrained
> in them. Yes I know, unforgivable of me to notice these things
> — but I promise I didn't make what you call my *fastidious*
> face, I really watched myself and did my best to be
> enthusiastic over everything. Perhaps I overdid it a bit —an
> awful lot of 'delicious' and 'divine' and 'most kind' and 'thank
> you so much' — but I dare say you would call that erring
> in the right direction. And I smiled, I think, continuously.
> (p. 34)

The details Raymond notices are those that would be noticed
by a fastidious spinster; and the same critically observant eye
will later find the British High Commission compound

> so tremedously clean — you can't help thinking that no place
> in India has the right to be that clean ... Mr Taylor ... a
> counsellor ... gets a special bungalow, fully airconditioned

of course and with fitted carpets. (p. 71)

It is Raymond, and he alone, who will perceive the true meaning of Lee's dejection (p. 146), and discover that the 'love and bliss' radiating from Evie's face is due entirely to Swamiji so that, as far as she is concerned, Margaret and every other created being can die in the utmost pain, whether they ripen into their 'fullest possibility' thereby or not (p. 134).

Raymond's experience of India resembles Esmond Stillwood's in *Esmond in India* and Etta's in *A Backward Place* in being a fictional illustration of Ruth Jhabvala's conviction that Western characters of sensitivity are, by being in India,

exposed to another dimension and (begin) to open up in response to it. But this is often a painful process and not everyone can stand it, especially not for any length of time.[3]

His American fellow-traveller, Lee, holds the key to a second theme: that of self-deception. Lee is essentially

truthful, with others, of course, but first of all with herself. She wanted her whole life to be based only on truth found and tested by herself. (pp. 216-7)

Such an approach to life and to the Indian experience should make Lee, one would think, as reliable an observer as Raymond. She is enterprising and adventurous, has come to India 'to try and learn' (p. 32), and moves freely and unconventionally at all levels of Indian life in order to do so: Lee will sleep in the house of a chance acquaintance met on a train, or dine by invitation at a maharaja's mansion as the spirit moves her. 'Learning', however, is associated by Lee with the feelings rather than with the intellect, so that her search for the meaning of life turns into a process of emotional, rather than intellectual, education. It is certainly very far from being the spiritual progress for which she mistakes it. Lee scorns Raymond's aesthetic and intellectual approach to India:

Who wants guide-books? Either a place has good emanations or it doesn't. If you don't have feeling for that, then what's the use of knowing facts? They just blunt you. (p. 24)

Her youth and emotional inexperience (she has, as she tells Asha, never been in love — 'and I don't want to be either' —

p. 32), coupled with her studied avoidance of anything even remotely intellectual, make her very vulnerable indeed, as her response to the magic of an Indian evening makes clear:

> I feel restless, I don't know what to do ... They garden is wild and overgrown and full of exotic bushes with very strong scents. There's something sinful about these scents and also about the too bright moonlight that comes in through the window and falls on the whitewashed wall and the icon of Christ hanging there. It's so disturbing out there in the garden ... I keep thinking there must be tigers behind those bushes ready to spring, and surely there must be snakes in all that uncut grass. (p. 28)

The subconsciously sexual nature of her imaginings shows that Lee is physically and emotionally ready for love, despite her desire to rise above 'these small things that engulfed people' (p. 61) to a spiritual plane. Her preconceptions and self-absorption blind her to the truth about herself and those around her. Amusingly, she writes off the agonisingly sensitive Raymond as a mere tourist, and acquiesces to Gopi's egotistic sexual demands in a charitable spirit! — 'She was glad to be doing this for him' (p. 42). When love comes to her at last, in the shape of the '*phenomenal*' (her word — p. 74) and predatory Swamiji, she does not recognise it:

> I drag myself around. I've never been like this before. Everything is so strange, so dismal; it's as if there's no light in the sun, and those glorious Indian nights ... are dark and drab to me. (p. 157)

Raymond notices her jealous misery when Margaret basks in the warmth of Swamiji's regard (pp. 144-6), but Lee cannot understand her own condition. When, after a prolonged period of deliberate neglect of her by Swamiji, Lee initiates a nocturnal interview with him in the course of which he has sexual intercourse with her, her life subtly alters. It is, however, characteristic of Lee that she must still see her changed condition in 'spiritual' terms; lamenting what she still interprets as her own 'low stage of development', she does not guess that she resembles all lovers in finding that she has only to think of the beloved

and then I feel everything is all right — no not all right but marvellous, marvellous! as long as he is there, I don't have a thing to worry about. (p. 166)

Lee withdraws from the ashram and visits Asha and Banubai at Banaras in an attempt to become her independent self again. 'From now on I'll do without anyone' (p. 172). But both at Banaras, where she ignores Banubai's hints regarding Swamiji's sinister activities (p. 173), and at Maupur, where she finds her thoughts continually turning to the ashram (pp. 183-4), her feelings soon go beyond her control. Self-deception has Lee in its grip: 'I always felt good in the ashram' (p. 183). When the sick and dying Margaret appears at Maupur, Lee briefly regains command of her mind and perceptions. She overrides Evie (p. 195), and under Miss Charlotte's soothing influence, sees Swamiji and all that is connected with him in a different —and disgusting — light (p. 208). She is ready to leave India. But this does not last long. Asha's passion for Gopi stirs an answering tremor in Lee: 'I don't want to go' (p. 216). Lee has indeed 'learned', but only the language of the heart. In the novel's closing paragraphs, she travels once again: no longer forward in search of fresh adventure and further education but back along the path she has recently traversed, to Banaras from Maupur, to obedience from independence, re-tracing in her imagination the steps and stages that will restore her at last to the person she sees as the true centre of her existence.

The pathos of Lee's situation — and that of the other 'little mice' in Swamiji's trap (p. 178) — is offset by her misplaced confidence in the truth of her own perceptions. Even Raymond, fighting gallantly on her behalf despite his own terrible wounds, has to accept the inevitable: wherever Lee's path may lead her, she is convinced that for her there is no other. But she is one among several characters in A New Dominion whom convictions deceive and lead astray, or over whom Ruth Jhabvala's irony plays continually as they seek refuge from the truth about themselves in a variety of self-deceptions. Raymond refers to his dalliance with Gopi as 'fascinating research' (p. 107); Asha and Gopi sanctify and idealise their relationship by quoting her husband's Urdu verses rapturously to each other (p. 59); Gopi tells Raymond that under Banubai's influence, Asha has begun to regard him as her son (p. 129); Banubai herself professes to worship the lord Krishna in Gopi when she caresses him

(p. 129). It is in the 'Holy City' of Banaras that these self-deceptions are most in evidence, as the characters briefly assume a variety of roles in attempts to avoid facing the painful truth about themselves: Gopi tries on the role of bridegroom, Asha of mother, Lee of independent traveller, Raymond of affectionate, resigned friend. These are transformations, indeed! and last only until Banaras is left behind for Maupur and its stark, exposed desert landscape patrolled by circling vultures: here self-deception becomes unnecessary and irrelevant and the characters, turning in directions dictated by their true sensibilities, move out of our view along paths that are unlikely to permit a return.

A good deal of comedy in *A New Dominion* stems from the self-deception practised by nearly everyone, from the highest to the lowest. Raymond and Lee meet during their travels in India. A cabinet minister whose muslin dhoti exposes his unlovely legs reminds Lee severely that 'maidenly modesty' is the first necessity in a young girl (p. 16); a female minister of state masks aggressive chauvinism in what she expects to pass as pleasant small talk:

> We had a Norwegian girl at Shantinivas, she learned to speak our language so beautifully. How she took to our ways! She always wore our sari and ate our vegetables cooked in our Indian way ... (p. 83)

Asha's brother, ex-Maharaja Rao Sahib who is standing for election in his home state of Maupur, finds it hard to express in words the '*affinity*' he feels with the people (p. 204) who, he pretends not to know, are extremely likely to shift their loyalties by the time elections are held again to the son of a *bania*, a moneylender. Raymond finds that Gopi's mother and sisters, living 'in the upstairs part of a crooked little house in a very crowded locality' can complain of their neighbours' 'impudence' (pp. 34-5) and that his servant Shyam, who lives in 'one airless room in a tenement facing a service land' (pp. 48-9), can resent an insult to his honour. Gopi, who, as his creator dryly remarks, 'was not much used to self-analysis' (p. 114), is a particularly rich source of satiric comedy. He makes 'heroic' love to Lee, choosing to overlook (and later forget) her obvious lack of interest in him (p. 42); his romantic 'resignation' to the inevitability with which life is sweeping Raymond and himself

apart is comically destroyed when Asha interposes her very
physical presence between them and recalls Gopi to an
awareness of his sexual desires (pp. 162-5); his heated defence
of his highly dubious 'filial' relationship with Banubai gives the
theme of self-deception what is possibly its most comic
exposure:

> You don't know anything. You have no idea of our culture.
> In your culture there is nothing — only sex, sex, sex —so
> how can you understand what it means to be mother and
> son, what a beautiful relationship it is for us. (p. 129)

Gopi treats his own mother with brusqueness and irritability,
yet professes to regard Banubai with traditional respect and
'beautiful' reverence; he also forgets, or chooses to ignore (since
he knows of it) Raymond's deep attachment to his own mother.

While Raymond and Lee experience in different ways the
intense intimations of hell and heaven that India offers the
visitor to her shores, Gopi meets experience of a different kind,
and at a different level. The shy student from a 'distinctly third-
rate' college 'run by private enterprise in some outlying suburb'
(p. 7) whom Raymond asks to tea learns quickly from him (and
later from Asha) how to manipulate people in order to get what
he wants out of life. Gopi's wants are, without exception,
materialistic. He is disappointed to discover that Raymond has
no 'imported' possessions, and when he sees Raymond's
clothes, 'finger(s) the material with approval and desire' (p. 10).
His egotism is hard to appease, as Raymond finds during a
quarrel Gopi has with Shyam (pp. 47-8), and Lee discovers in
a bedroom over a Delhi kebab house (pp. 37-8). The theme of
moral education explored in Ruth Jhabvala's portrait of Lee
receives a secondary exposition in the character of Gopi; and,
as with Lee, the approach adopted is ironic.

Gopi's crass mind runs on status and money. Since it is
closed to everything that does not relate to himself and his own
limited interests, it is open to 'education' only in limited ways.
When Gopi's suggestion that Lee accompanies him upstairs to
look at a 'very nice' hotel room fails to get a reaction from her,
he makes a second suggestion that shows how rapidly his
education is progressing:

> 'There's a very good view' ... How these people cared for views!

> Gopi had learned this lesson from Raymond. What it was
> they saw so much in a view God only knew. (p. 38)

He 'educates' his taste for luxurious living at Asha's expense,
buying expensive clothes and indulging in exotic food and drink
(pp. 58-9). Gopi's association with Raymond and Asha improves
only his outward appearance and his sexual skills. Their
company merely deepens the selfish egotism that flaws his
character, without improving it in any way. By the end of the
novel, he is a shy student no longer:

> Gopi was a very handsome man now. He had filled out
> somewhat and, though still slender, he seemed broader, more
> manly. The ruby studs on his kurta were open in a studiedly
> casual way, revealing his olive skin matted with hair in which
> nestled the end of a fine gold chain he wore around his neck.
> (p. 211)

Inviting the artistic Raymond to praise his kurta studs (made
from Asha's family jewels, and of considerable value), Gopi
demonstrates what he has 'learned': 'You can't get workmanship
like this nowadays' (p. 211). His praise of an inferior picture
immediately afterwards shows that though he has learned to
parrot the 'right' phrases, and to wear clothes that set his good
looks off to advantage, the ignorance of his undiscriminating
mind remains inviolate. His sentimental insincerities as they
part leave Raymond anguished and ashamed, for Gopi is almost
as much his creation as he is Asha's.

So well does Ruth Jhabvala build up Gopi's squalid moral
being that she can use his behaviour, his thoughts and his
words to establish indirectly the virtues or failings of other
characters in the novel. His behaviour to Shyam underlines by
contrast the scrupulous delicacy with which Raymond treats
this servant (p. 47); his egotistical exploitation of Lee's body
helps to establish by contrast her own open and generous
approach, both to him and to every one she meets (p. 41).
'Physical mishaps to others always amused him' (p. 21), and
he has no sense either of gratitude or of loyalty: he punishes
Raymond by pettishly preferring Lee's company to his (p. 35),
and while with Lee he criticises and ridicules the man who has
bought the clothes he is wearing (p. 36). The fact that Gopi calls
Raymond materialistic, insensitive and stupid (p. 24) indirectly

establishes Raymond as being none of these things; his
uncritical acceptance of Swamiji's ashram literature as 'holy,
good and true things' (p. 64) argues against its being so; and
his unstinting praise of Banubai (p. 131) confirms the reader's
doubts regarding her 'sanctity' and holiness. Devoid of affection
for anyone, worshipping only the good things that money can
buy him, his education receives its finishing touches during
the hours he spends in dissipation and drinking with Asha at
Maupur. By the time Raymond is ready to leave India, the work
of art upon which he and Asha have spent so much time,
emotion and labour is complete. Gopi has turned under their
tutelage into a vicious and cunning parasite whose striking
beauty of face and body only masks inner depravity and
emptiness.

'Yes there is something higher and we all want to reach it.
Only who are we to say which is the right path?' (p. 217) asks
Asha at the end of *A New Dominion*, having in the course of
the novel sought for this spiritual goal in a number of what
seem to be quite contradictory, even opposed, directions. Her
variable state of mind and inconsistent habit of life have been
most accurately described in a major text of India's religious
literature:

> Look at him!
>
> Having conquered the forest of desire,
> he runs to the forest of new desires;
> freed from the forest of desire,
> he runs to the forest of new desires
> — All in vain; for he runs into bondage.
>
> Like the spider woven in its own web
> is the man gripped by his craving.
> Wise men renounce craving and leave the world,
> wise men do not grieve, having discarded sorrow.[4]

Asha is most emphatically not to be numbered among 'the wise'.
Plunging backwards and forwards from self-indulgence to self-
disgust, from exhilaration to deep depression, her behaviour
distresses her brother, irritates her sister-in-law, amuses her
spiritual teacher Banubai, and troubles herself. For although
she finds self-control difficult, Asha rarely deceives herself; and
if she does, it is not for long. She is aware of her weaknesses,
and although inclined to justify them from time to time as the
natural accompaniments of an incurably romantic nature (one

of the novel's constant sources of ironic comedy), she tries to
do better. Ruth Jhabvala interweaves an analysis of Asha's
moral weaknesses with a compassionate study of an ageing,
still beautiful woman of strong feeling, and achieves another
successful exposition — of *rajasa*, the personality inclined
towards worldliness, comparable with, yet a clear advance on,
her depiction of Lalaji in *The Nature of Passion*.

Ruth Jhabvala's characterisation is both just and
sympathetic, giving full value to Asha's affection for her weak
brother, her spirited 'patronage' of a group of neglected
musicians at Rao Sahib's party with a style and grandeur that
recalls her royal heritage, her munificence to Gopi, her scorn
for the political place-getting of Delhi. Each of these virtues is,
however, flawed. Asha's affection for Rao Sahib is sentimental
rather than sensible; her regal patronage of the musicians
stems partly from mere impulse, partly from a desire to irritate
her sister-in-law, and is not, in any case, long sustained; her
generosity to Gopi contributes to his degeneration, and stems
from her own weakness for him rather than from any positive
virtue; and she resents her brother's pre-occupation with
politics chiefly because it distracts his attention from herself.
Ruth Jhabvala steeps Asha's 'romantic' activities in irony that
strips them of their glamour and exposes them as the fruits
of lust, and she underplays neither the cunning with which
Asha stalks and captures Gopi, the cruelty with which she
tortures and humiliates Raymond, nor the comedy of her
occasional essays in self-deception.

Ruth Jhabvala's portrait of Rao Sahib is a half sympathetic,
half satirical study of a weakened royalty adapting itself to new
conditions. Already an M.P., and bound (he hopes) for a seat
in the cabinet, Rao Sahib and his ambitious wife Sunita are
comically embarrassed by Asha's grandly individualistic
behaviour (pp. 18-19). In the scene titled 'Brother and Sister'
(pp. 201-4) it becomes very obvious that what vigour still
survives in this dying royal line is to be found in Asha rather
than in her brother. Bulbul's story of the terrible punishment
meted out a century before by a Rao to the lover of his erring,
passionate sister throws into comic relief the ineffectualness
of the present Rao, who is engaged in wheedling people into
voting for him, who is selling his ancestral lands to a developer,
who goes in for talk rather than for deeds, and whose orange

turban needs straightening by *his* erring and passionate sister
(pp. 203-04). Further ironic comedy is provided by Ruth
Jhabvala's exposure, through Rao Sahib, of the wordy inactivity
of much Government policy in India (and elsewhere). Indeed,
when Rao Sahib discusses Miss Charlotte's mission problems
with Raymond, he so far forgets himself as to speak in his
official capacity not on behalf of, but '*as* a secular state' (p. 72).
His smooth platitudes make it clear that although the
Government of India has no sympathy for 'the individual efforts
of foreigners' (p. 72), the 'people of India' — as represented
by the hungry lepers and cripples who crowd Miss Charlotte's
back veranda, and the sweepers' children she educates —will
have no one else to whom they can turn for help until the
'giant machine' of state relief begins to move ... if it
ever does.

Ruth Jhabvala's view of such representatives of the new India
as Rao Sahib, the cabinet minister at his first party, and the
female minister of state at his second is critical and
contemptuous. Art and idealism may survive, and the individual
Indian citizen find succour and fulfilment, but not with the
assistance of such as these. The skilled musicians have only
the English tourist, Raymond, to appreciate and applaud them
as they deserve, the pamphlet dedicated 'To the Soul of
Mankind' finds no reader except Raymond, and the needs of
Miss Charlotte's disadvantaged patients are swallowed up in
Rao Sahib's large phrases: all three of these are understated
but nonetheless effective comments on contemporary India, and
are reinforced by the opulence of the entertainments organised
by Sunita to assist her husband's political career, and by the
futility of the women's meeting Asha irresponsibly (but
comically) breaks up.

Certain recurrent images in *A New Dominion* imply a conflict
between forces of good and evil which, together with the
theme of a quest for a spiritual goal, can be traced back in
time not only to the moral literature of Europe but to the
religious literature of Asia. The English medical missionary
Miss Charlotte is described in terms of churchbells and flowers.
Lee notices that when Miss Charlotte laughed, 'she *rang* like
a bell, a very clear one' (p. 26), and Raymond compares her
with the fresh English flowers he finds growing in Indian
gardens: larkspur, phlox, pansies and sweet-peas —

Whenever I see them, I get a strange feeling and wonder what they are doing here, how did they grow, and how are they managing to survive. I get the same feeling with Miss Charlotte. (p. 62)

The secret of Miss Charlotte's survival lies in her approach to life and to her work. She is an example of what her creator has described as 'a strong person who plunges in and does what he can as a doctor or social worker'[5]. As sound in heart, body and mind as the bell she resembles, her 'faith and joy' do not blind her to the beauty produced by other faiths, and by non-Western cultures. She thinks the Taj Mahal more beautiful on each visit (p. 143), and finds the religious festivals at Fatehpur Sikri 'moving' (p. 143). She appears blind only to the baseness of human nature, and either ignores or fails to perceive the way ordinary human selfishness and spite in the 86-year-old Miss Peck seem to be made more grotesque by advanced age (p. 71). When Miss Charlotte arrives at Maupur, humanity and love return to Lee:

Everything changed ... Then the body on the bed was not only someone who had died and had been expected to die — but was Margaret! Margaret! (p. 205)

It is almost as if Miss Charlotte's presence and Margaret's angelic appearance in death (p. 207) have exorcised Swamiji's evil power. Lee rejects the promptings of Evie, Swamiji's agent (p. 207), and decides to leave India. It is only after Miss Charlotte has left Maupur that Lee's resolution falters, and she follows Evie to Banaras and to Swamiji.

Ranged against Miss Charlotte in her efforts to succour and save are the 'sensitivity' of the Indian Government to foreign missionary endeavours, the delicacies of British diplomacy, and, on a more immediate level, the polite but nevertheless powerful antagonism of Swamiji. Their respective functions as the good and evil angels of the novel are not immediately obvious, for Miss Charlotte's appearance is comic and unheroic as she wages her desperate battle for Margaret's life (p. 152), while Raymond finds Swamiji 'cheerful and amusing company, a relaxed person though giving an impression of tremendous energy' (p. 120). Every time Swamiji makes an appearance in the novel, Ruth Jhabvala ensures that there exist two possible

interpretations of his behaviour: mysticism and spirituality on
the one hand, charlatanism and opportunism on the other.
There are areas of mystery in Indian life, indeed in all life, which
do not yield their secrets easily; Ruth Jhabvala's irony permits
her to traverse these areas, charting their boundaries, without
pretending to unravel their mysteries. The reader might, with
Raymond, identify Lee's attachment to her swami as a symptom
of the joy and pain of first love, and suspect both the purity
of Banubai's motives and the spirituality of her message. But
irony admits the existence of an alternative view; the adoration,
respect and gratitude both Swamiji and Banubai inspire in their
disciples suggest that a reality exists to which Raymond's
scepticism renders him blind. 'Who are we to say which is the
right path?' Ambiguity surrounds Swamiji's activities:

> The ashram was not actually in Banaras but about ten miles
> outside it. This was deliberate policy on Swamiji's part: he
> did not wish to batten on the holiness of the past but to
> inspire new souls with a new spirit. It was also convenient
> that land was going cheap in that area. (p. 65)

The portentous phrasing of the last sentence but one contrasts
startlingly with the colloquialism of 'land was going cheap', and
the validity of Swamiji's 'policy' is consequently qualified and
questioned by it. In the chapter 'Swamiji Eats Lunch' (pp. 118-
23) Ruth Jhabvala's subtly ambiguous use of language ensures
that throughout the 'scene', Swamiji's holiness is
simultaneously demonstrated and undermined. Her phrases
function at three levels, the spiritual, the material and the
sexual. Thus, Swamiji tells Raymond,

> The old Lee must be broken before the new Lee can be
> formed, and we are now only at the first stage of our task.
> (p. 121)

Raymond blushes — to him, who is so delicate in his reluctance
to intrude physically on Gopi despite the fact that he is deeply
in love with him, this seems the height of sexual crudeness,
and carries a distastefully inhuman overtone implying that men
and women are mere machinery. Yet, according to Swamiji, he
has used the phrase in a spiritual sense, referring to the soul,
the spirit and the mind.

Since this conversation is being conducted in an

airconditioned hotel dining room, in which Swamiji is helping
himself generously to lunch at Raymond's expense, eating roly-
poly pudding with intense enjoyment '— a great favourite with
me' (p. 123) — and practising his table manners in preparation
for his projected world trip, the spiritual value of his disciplines
must, necessarily, be in some doubt. Indeed, other features of
the scene — such as Swamiji's alacrity in accepting Raymond's
polite invitation to lunch, and his unfolding of his plans for
spreading his message — suggest that Swamiji is quick to
exploit others for his own, very material, gains. This, unlike
the Founder-President of the University of Universal Synthesis,
is no old-fashioned innocent idealist but an opportunity quick
to take advantage of modern technological developments:

> He would travel everywhere by aeroplane and helicopter, and
> also multiply his presence by means of television
> appearances. (p. 120)

His impudence is highlighted by allusions to the aerial chariots
used by Vishnu and other Hindu deities, and to Krishna's ability
to manifest himself before (and enchant) Radha and her
companion milk-maids individually and collectively. 'Without
effort' Swamiji dismisses his devoted disciple Evie 'as nothing'
(p. 120); accepts the reverence paid by the hotel servants to
his orange robe, and regards the curious and admiring Western
tourists about him 'in a sort of easy, speculative manner as
if one day perhaps, if he wanted to, if he cared to, they would
all be his' (p. 123).

Lee's imaginings of tigers and snakes lurking in the mission
garden are ironically fulfilled by the animal imagery Ruth
Jhabvala employs in building up the personality of Swamiji.
His eyes 'rove' and 'dart' about the hotel dining-room (p. 123),
and Lee recalls their sexual encounter in bestial terms (p. 169).
As he tells Raymond of his (seemingly spiritual) desire that Lee
should return to him, Swamiji's feverishly bright eyes and his
gesture of running 'a broad, pale tongue swiftly round his lips'
(p. 179) create associations of animality that are in clear
opposition to those surrounding Miss Charlotte, of churchbells
and flowers. These images join with others used in other
portraits to establish the moral structure on which Ruth
Jhabvala bases *A New Dominion*. Raymond, trying to restrain
Asha in a mood of passionate frenzy 'felt her body pulsating

with strength and fury; it was like clasping a demon' (p. 159).
Bob, the 'go-ahead young man' who combines Indian subtlety
with American expertise in a blend that seems guaranteed to
bring him prosperity in the new India, 'estimates the size and
possibilities' of the Rao garden at Maupur with 'a devouring
glance' (p. 194), recalling Swamiji's 'speculative' assessment of
tourists at Banaras. Bulbul's voice is 'hoarse and grating and
rather wicked' (p. 171) as she sings the suggestive ballad that
Asha finds 'delicious', and tempts her back from the life of a
recluse to one of sensual indulgence with Gopi (p. 171).

The conflict between good and evil in *A New Dominion* is not
capable of a simple resolution into — let us say — a battle
between Christianity and Hinduism for Lee's soul, or even
between modern science and Indian spiritual disciplines for
Margaret's life. It is both of these; and more. 'Good' characters
show themselves to be occasionally both flawed and ridiculous,
'evil' ones are attractive and disarmingly polite; seriousness and
comedy are inextricably blended in incident after incident. Good
and evil co-exist, in fact, at every level and in every character
in *A New Dominion*, just as they have a habit of doing in real
life; and although Ruth Jhabvala supplies her readers (and her
characters) with signposts and resting places along the path
of their pilgrimage, her characteristic irony ensures that we
each make our own way to that personal celestial city wherein,
if we have read the signs carefully enough, puzzlement ceases
and understanding is complete. For herself, however, one
suspects that the pilgrimage continues, and that the sustained
ironies of *A New Dominion* have made possible yet another stage
on its author's journey towards a better understanding of India,
of life and of herself.

An examination of some of the incidents that make up the
plot of this novel helps to indicate how Ruth Jhabvala turns
personal experience into art, and why her ironic detachment
is indispensable to that art. Her essay "Myself in India" resorted
to 'exaggerated images' in order to 'give some idea of how
intolerable India — the idea, the sensation of it — can
become'.[6] The passage, in which we can observe Ruth
Jhabvala at a preliminary stage in the process of turning
experience into imaginative fiction, is important to *A New
Dominion* and to her mature writing as a whole:

Sometimes, when I think of my life, it seems to have

contracted to this one point and to be concentrated in this
one room, and it is always a very hot, very long afternoon
when the airconditioner has failed ... India swallows me up
and now it seems to me that I am no longer in my room
but in the white-hot city streets under a white-hot sky ...
here comes a smiling leper in a cart being pushed by another
leper; there is also the carcass of a dog and vultures have
swooped down on it. The river has dried up and stretches
in miles of flat cracked earth ... We come to a jungle in which
wild beasts live, and then there are ravines and here live
outlaws with the hearts of wild beasts ... Now it is no longer
hot but terribly cold, we are in snow and ice and here is
Mount Kailash on which sits Siva the Destroyer wearing a
necklace of human skulls. Down in the plains they are
worshipping him ... They are killing a boy ... There is a priest
with them ... reciting some holy verses ... to bless and
propitiate.[7]

These images, which are perhaps 'exaggerated' but nonetheless
drawn from the realities of life in India, are explored in *A New
Dominion* at the levels, simultaneously, of experience and
symbol. The oppression of a Delhi summer 'when the
airconditioner has failed' is captured at the level of experience
in the terrible heat of Maupur when the electric fans fail to
work but is, at the same time, symbolic of the sense of
oppression Raymond feels as Asha gathers herself, like the
'heavy dark birds' that hang in the sky above them, to strike
death into his heart with her story of Peter, her brother's
English tutor (p. 187). Gopi's enjoyment of the physical mishaps
of others and his casual torture of Raymond link him with the
'outlaws with the hearts of wild beasts' described in Ruth
Jhabvala's essay, who 'make raids into the village and ... rob
and burn and mutilate and kill for sport'[8] while Swamiji could
be seen without strain as a fictional version of the priest who
unctuously recites holy verses over the body of a murdered
child. The list of correspondences is almost without end, due
to the range of Ruth Jhabvala's observation, the intensity of
her gaze, and her ability to fuse experience with art. But even
this brief selection suggests the strenuousness of the
experiences that lie at the heart of *A New Dominion*, and
indicates why a technique that allows her to maintain a certain

distance from what she is describing is essential to the maintenance of balance in her writing.

Ruth Jhabvala's irony has developed, it seems to me, into a technique chosen as much from necessity as from inclination. It has many aspects in *A New Dominion*. A double view is made possible, for instance, by her progress from the technique of concentrating her attention on a single character (as she did in *Esmond in India*) to that of balancing Raymond's experiences with Lee's, contrasting his disillusionment with her sense of fulfilment, and including both characters in a quartet with two Indian characters who are also engaged in making decisions that will affect their future lives. Secondly, Ruth Jhabvala achieves ironic effects by interweaving comedy of incident or dialogue with the most serious of moral issues: for example, one of Swamiji's most sinister assertions of his power over Margaret and Lee is part of a chapter in which his enjoyment of luxurious hotel-living makes a comic contrast with his orange robe and his aura of sanctity. Raymond's tenderest moments with Gopi are interrupted (and shown to have been based on self-deception on both sides) by Asha's comic intrusion into their boat. Ruth Jhabvala's ironic viewpoint is steadied by these contrasts, which make detachment and impartiality possible not only at such moments, but throughout the novel as a whole.

The reader feels sympathy for Raymond when Gopi deserts him, but is also aware of the (partial) justice of Asha's claim that in keeping Gopi from Raymond, she is keeping him from what is 'unnatural'. At the same time, he is aware (because of the delicacy of Raymond's nature) how predatory and 'unnatural' on both sides is the relationship that begins between Asha and Gopi. Similarly, the reader shares Raymond's concern for Lee in what seems to be a situation headed clearly for disaster; and yet Lee is herself convinced that she has never been happier, and that she has found at last the 'truth' she has been looking for. Names and titles furnish further sources of ironic truth and humour: 'Shantinivas' ('The House of Peace') is apparently inhabited by makers of most unholy noise, if the minister of state's singing is any indication (pp. 87-88). Swamiji's ashram calls itself the 'Universal Society for Spiritual Regeneration in the Modern World', a title which gains in irony as we follow the adventures in it of Evie, Margaret and Lee. The week-ender built by Asha's father in the 1930s rejoices in the name of 'The Retreat'. The late Rao had been ostensibly seeking relief from the pressure of state duties in pleasure and relaxation; in reality he had been retreating from a conventional (and luxurious) life to luxuries of a less conventional and licit kind. The religious associations of the name ironically expose Asha's self-deceptions as well as her father's: she thinks of her own 'retreat' to Maupur as providing a brief spell of happiness before she abandons the world for the life of a recluse, but in fact the house affords her privacy in which to debauch Gopi without let or hindrance (p. 182)

A number of connections can be traced between Ruth Jhabvala's writing in *A New Dominion* and her experiences as a writer of screen-plays for Merchant-Ivory films. Their permanent interest lies not in the fact that they exist but in what they reveal of her technique in turning real life into fiction. James Ivory's book about his experiences as a film-maker in India[9] includes a description of Maharaja Umaid Singh's retreat at Sada Samand, twenty miles from Jodhpur, a house which made Ivory feel 'as if I had arrived at the farthest edge of civilisation'.[10] This is, presumably, the house which reappears in *A New Dominion* as 'The Retreat'; but the lake inhabited by flamingoes described by Ivory as flanking the house disappears in Ruth Jhabvala's recreation, and in its place we are given the deliberately constructed desolation, with remarkable effect, of a

> house rearing up ... in the middle of the desert. There was no water and the sun beat down on a landscape inhabited by jackals and vultures. (p. 182)

Ivory's search for a palace in which the 'Buckingham Players' could present a Shakespeare play for a Maharaja's pleasure in the film SHAKESPEAREWALLAH ('the representative of one dying order saluting that of another'[11] as Ivory puts it) is turned in *A New Dominion* into the magnificent scene at Rao Sahib's party in which Asha, the last daughter of a royal line, temporarily provides two courtly musicians with a tattered travesty of the royal patronage they can no longer claim and she has no longer the right to bestow in the new India. Ivory also reports an incident that occurred during the filming of THE GURU at Bikaner in 1968 involving two of the actors who starred in the film, which appears to lie behind Raymond's anguished self-control when Asha playfully but deliberately tortures him at Maupur[12]; and a particularly grisly incident involving a dangerously sick actress and a carrion crow that can perhaps be glimpsed through Ruth Jhabvala's descriptions of birds of prey in a still sky that create an atmosphere of brooding fate and inescapable evil around Margaret's sickness and Asha's loneliness in *A New Dominion.*

Beyond the four main characters and their 'good' and 'evil' angels there move a number of other personalities whose presence brings Ruth Jhabvala's settings to life, and whose actions either influence the behaviour of the main characters or comment upon them. There is a sustained social comment (as well as comedy) for instance, in the fact that the classical musicians — although patronized by 'royalty' in the shape of Asha — are forced to display their skill in a remote part of Rao Sahib's garden, while the singers of rousing religious hymns bask simultaneously in the glare of the electric lights and the approbation of a minister of state. This is a comment that is given further ironic development when the musicians are deserted by their fickle patron, and a foreign tourist gives them the attention and appreciation they deserve. The piece of dried chappati on which the Founder-President of the University of Universal Synthesis refreshes himself, the poverty of Raymond's servant Shyam, and the under-nourished Indian children who crowd Miss Charlotte's back veranda point up by contrast the opulence and unconcern displayed by the wealthy and powerful. At Rao Sahib's party, Lee helps herself to food from

> an endless succession of dishes piled with pilaos, curries, kebabs, salads, baked chickens, stuffed eggs, pickles and curds ... full of delicate flavours and essences. (pp. 16-17)

A 'stout, richly dressed Indian lady' tells Raymond with gluttonous pleasure about the 'marzipan dessert ... coloured green and in the shape of a fish' (p. 55) that had been a talking-point at a Delhi party she had attended the week before. The sketches of middle-class deprivation and prosperity that *A New Dominion* provides are effective, and precisely yet unobtrusively illuminate the themes of the novel. The preoccupation of Gopi's newly-rich relations with their brand-new house in Banaras contrasts neatly with the 'crooked little house' in Delhi in which Gopi's mother and sisters live. His

preference of the former to the latter is an early indication of
his materialism, and a sign that he will soon desert even the
prospect of connection through marriage with these rich
relations' sugar mills for the greater luxuries to be enjoyed as
Asha's lover. Bob, the 'go-ahead young man' educated in the
United States, whose father is a Maupur moneylender, is
vigorous proof that in the new India the maharajas are going
down before a new plutocracy of young business moguls. There
is no character who is so minor that he may not influence the
novel's action in unexpected and profound ways. When Lee
leans forward and bites at a chili held out to her by Gopi, the
intimate sexual connotations of the gesture (of which, typically,
she is unaware) cause a sensation in the crowded restaurant:

> Even the party of Sikhs at another table — huge burly men
> who had seemed totally absorbed in eating — even they had
> seen, and their mighty jaws stopped chewing in wonder.
> (p. 37)

A comic moment, memorably expressed: but the expectations
generated in the Sikhs and their fellow-diners create a highly
charged atmosphere in which Gopi begins to feel he owes it
to himself to seduce Lee. And so begins Gopi's spectacular
career as acolyte and minister of Love[13].

Beyond even these are a selection of absent characters who
live in the novel through the thoughts and memories of others.
Raymond's mother, constantly evoked through her son's
affectionate letters to her as a fastidious, sensitive and subtly
domineering woman, is particularly useful to *A New Dominion*
on the technical side by providing the novel with its most
perceptive observer, her alter ego Raymond. Miss Hart, Asha's
English governess, who 'hated everything Indian' (pp. 43-4) is
a useful contrast to Lee and Raymond, visitors from the West
who find painful the mere thought of leaving India. The English
people, long dead, whose graves Raymond studies during the
making of arrangements for Margaret's funeral, have histories
that offer parallels with the experiences of Margaret and Lee.
The experiences of Peter, Rao Sahib's English tutor, recounted
to Raymond by Asha in cruel detail, give Raymond an infallible
signal that the time has come to leave India. This is a technique
Ruth Jhabvala first used in *Esmond in India*, with the character
of the absent physician Narayan[14], and employs again in

writing *A New Dominion* to create a novel in which nothing is irrelevant, no character superfluous, and in which every aspect of her art blends with every other to create a rich and organic whole.

Two years after the publication of *A New Dominion*, its author was still recovering from the strain and exhaustion that had attended its writing: 'I don't think I can write another novel for a long time,' she told an interviewer in 1974[15]. The book represents a high point in her career, encompassing and improving upon the literary lessons taught her by seventeen years of writing fiction, incorporating an artistic distillation of the new experiences brought her by writing for film. The future still unknown, Ruth Jhabvala appears to have had no doubts about the comparative value of her past achievements. 'Which, according to you, is your best novel?' Ramlal Agarwal asked her in 1974[16]. Her answer was: '*A New Dominion*'.

Notes

1. R.P. Jhabvala, *A New Dominion* (John Murray, London: 1972; 1974), p. 107. This novel was published in the United States (1973) by Harper and Row under the title *Travelers*. All references in this chapter and throughout this book are to the 1974 British edition.
2. See Chapter I of this book.
3. "Moonlight, jasmine and rickets", op. cit.
4. Stanzas 344 and 347 of the *Tanhavagga*, the Buddha's Discourse on Craving, in *The Dhammapada*, trans. P. Lal, Noonday Press, New York: 1967, p. 159.
5. R.P. Jhabvala, "Myself in India", op. cit., p. 9.
6. Ibid., p. 17.
7. Ibid.
8. Ibid.
9. James Ivory, *Autobiography of a Princess: Also Being the Adventures of an American Film Director in the Land of the Maharajas* (Harper & Row, New York: 1975). British edition published by John Murray, 1976.
10. Ibid., p. 101.
11. Ibid., p. 107.
12. Ibid., pp. 127-8.
13. See other, much less complex, descriptions of Indians at table in *Amrita* (p. 56), and *The Nature of Passion* (p. 69)
14. See pages 99-100.
15. R. Agarwal, 'An interview with Ruth Prawer Jhabvala', op. cit., p. 35.
16. Ibid.

CHAPTER

IX

Heat and dust

1975

India always changes people, and I have been no exception.[1]

With these words the narrator of Ruth Jhabvala's eighth novel, *Heat and Dust*, initiates the most moving study to date of a theme which has been at the heart of every novel or story the author has written that has taken up the subject of individuals uprooted from an European background and planted, however temporarily, in India. It is evident that in her exploration of such characters as the young English civil servant Douglas Rivers and his wife Olivia; the Minnies', Crawfords and Saunders', long-term residents in India; the narrator and the

Christian missionary she encounters in Bombay; Harry, the
Nawab of Khatm's English friend and companion; Chid, a
would-be ascetic who cannot lose his flat Midlands accent; and
a young English couple who come to India to seek Universal
Love and find only dishonesty and disease, Ruth Jhabvala is
externalising and probing through fiction certain aspects,
painful, exhilarating, puzzling and comic, of her own experience
of India.

Her characters are seen by the reader in many situations,
and viewed from varied angles. Douglas Rivers, for example,
is admired and loved by his wife, approved of immensely by
his seniors in the British administrative service and by British
residents in Satipur, ignored and dismissed as insignificant by
the Nawab. He is seen at various points in the novel as host,
as guest, as tender and sympathetic husband, as a dutiful and
conscientious British official, and as a patronising and
impudent intruder into the Nawab's private life. From a
technical point of view, one of Ruth Jhabvala's most impressive
achievements in this novel is her maintenance of a scrupulously
detached narrative tone which works in harmony with parallels
of character and incident throughout the novel, to create an
atmosphere of objectivity in which certain major thematic
concerns can be fully explored.

Five main themes, each of them closely connected with the
other four and explored through an extremely skilfully managed
series of parallels, run through *Heat and Dust*. The first of these
examines the experience of Europeans in India, using
flashbacks (from the narrator's continuous experience, as
recorded in her journal, of India in the 1970s) to incidents that
occurred in the 1920s, in order 'to add an extra dimension of
time for the confirmation of a pattern ... so far traced only in
terms of contemporary India'.[2] The reader is presented with
a series of case studies of Europeans of both periods who are
at different points on the wheel of change — change, both of
principle and behaviour — that Ruth Jhabvala has suggested
as being an inevitable part of the experience of living in India[3].
The narrator, an Englishwoman in her twenties who has come
to India in the hope of finding out more about the life led in
India by her grandfather's first wife, Olivia Rivers, both before
and after her elopement in 1923 with the Nawab of Khatm, is
at 'stage on' when she matter-of-factly accepts the sick and

deformed citizens of Satipur as part of the 'landscape' (pp. 78-9), and notes without further comment that her share in the bathroom facilities of her lodgings include 'the little sweeper girl who is attached to them' (p. 6). Olivia is at 'stage one' herself, when she casually accepts the idea that

> there's always something like that going on in the quarters. Someone dying or getting born or married. (pp. 129-30)

The same insistent drumming and chanting that she dismisses as being merely a part of life in India have, however, begun to seem 'like brain fever' to the Nawab's friend Harry, who is in the grip of 'stage three', and feels he cannot 'stand it another day' (p. 129). Mrs Saunders, the wife of the British Medical Superintendent of Khatm in 1923, is clearly at 'stage three' when she begins to shout like a madwoman, see haunting visions in the fireplace, and nourish sexual fantasies about her Indian servants.

Some Europeans in the novel manage to resist total change, but invariably pay a price for such immunity: the missionary's selfless social work is one approach to the problem, though it makes of her a 'paper-white, vaporous ... ghost' (p. 4). Major Minnies' refusal to immerse himself in what he calls 'the other dimension' of life in India is another (p. 148). Beth Crawford wife of the British collector, knows 'where lines had to be drawn, not only in speech and behaviour but also in one's thought' (pp. 168-9). Neither she and her husband nor the missionary, nor Major and Mrs Minnies, however, can penetrate to India's intimations of heaven and spiritual fulfilment, of which even the Major's appreciation of Indian poetry reflects only a pale and unsatisfactory shadow. Douglas Rivers, stoically resisting changes of principle, cannot escape physical change: Olivia finds that his face has become 'heavier, even somewhat puffy, making him look more like other Englishmen in India', and finds the discovery unbearable (p. 116). Some Europeans take to the hills, the time-honoured British way of bearing (or avoiding) the strains placed upon them by the Indian climate. Chid, in the throes of 'stage three', wants 'to know and see nothing; just to lie there and wait' in hospital until he can return to Britain (p. 29). Some kind of confirmation of these experiences, and of the author's theory as expressed in "Myself in India", is voiced by an Indian character, overworked Dr Gopal, who looks briefly

up from his task in the hospital to say, 'I think perhaps God
never meant that human beings should live in such a place'
(p. 158). The narrator is quick to contest the point, and by her
own decision to stay on in India eventually contradicts, or seems
to contradict, it. But the problem is examined from many points
of view, and the novel's detached narrative tone, though
occasionally modulating to irony, never ceases to be objective
and sympathetic.

A second theme, which attains prominence because of Ruth
Jhabvala's decision to set part of her story in the India of the
British Raj, takes up the destructive effects of the imposition
of one culture upon another. Her satiric eye, which observed
the excesses of Indian chauvinism in *A New Dominion*, now
focuses upon an earlier period and another 'domination'. The
British way of life in India is presented in *Heat and Dust* as
restrictive, both of Europeans in their contact with Indians and
their experience of India, and of Indians such as the Nawab.
Inheritor of a noble and warlike tradition, the Nawab must now
confine himself to orderly paths clipped for him by the British
out of the scrub. The Raj is also seen, at any rate in its 1923
issue, to have been unnaturally, gloomily 'moral'. Dr Saunders,
supported by a grim Scottish matron, is the novel's principal
representative of British morality. So condemnatory and
revengeful is he towards heretics and backsliders from his moral
code, that Olivia flees precipitately from all that he represents
to the unknown (and for all she can guess, perhaps equally
terrible) mysteries of the Palace. There is something 'musty and
dark' about the morality of Dr Saunders and his wife, which
emerges in the atmosphere that hangs about their house, a
dwelling that has harboured death and a sickness that never
sees recovery or the light of day. The narrator shivers as she
enters it fifty years later, and reflects on the remarkable fact
that Mrs Saunders had looked out every day from her back
veranda upon the graveyard in which her baby was buried
(p. 24). There is a suggestion here that Mrs Saunders'
hallucinations are the result, not only of the length of time she
has lived in India, but of the sick morality she and her husband
have brought to their life there.

In its political aspect the British Raj is seen to have been
dishonest and deceitful, encouraging a similar dishonesty and
deceit in its subjects. The tranquillity Olivia finds on her arrival

at Satipur is, she soon discovers, entirely superficial. Everyone puts on an act. Olivia watches the Nawab as he responds with seemingly courteous amusement to a racist joke made by Major Minnies at his own dinner-table: she felt 'he was putting it on: she was almost sure of it' (p. 17). She finds, on accompanying Mrs Crawford to the Palace in order to call on the Nawab's mother, the Begum of Khatm, that

> everyone played their part well — the Palace ladies as well as Mrs Crawford — and gave evidence of having frequently played it before. (p. 29)

Douglas turns to Olivia after what had seemed to her to be a particularly affable meeting with the local Indian magnates, and remarks with enjoyment and 'benign amusement': 'What a pack of rogues they are' (p. 37). Olivia's honesty in her relationship with the Nawab is in direct contrast to the subterfuge that goes on all around her. She stands alone in this matter, except for the somewhat wavering support of Harry, who sees no difference in the way his countrymen handle their Indian subjects and servants, and their treatment of the weaker, defenceless members of their own society. He calls it 'bullying', and remarks that he had had plenty of experience of it at the public school he had attended as a boy.

A third theme in *Heat and Dust* suggests that personal relationships can provide an occasional resting-place on the wheel of experience and disillusionment; an oasis in the desert of life. Amid the tensions created in the Nawab's mind by the frustrations of British rule, Olivia's love and sympathy provide relief, they are 'a small miracle' (p. 46), a spring in a desert grove. The house she lives in and fills with her personality is called 'The Oasis' by Harry (pp. 33-4); and the shady grove with its perennial spring in the middle of the desert to which the Nawab brings her (pp. 42-3) is symbolic in the novel of the personal relationships that offer sanctuary to them both across the barriers of political or social prejudice. Later, across the additional barrier of time, the grove affords its refreshment to another pair of lovers, the narrator and her Indian landlord, Inder Lal. The British attitude to India and to Indians is, of course, a negation of this point of view. Major Minnies' projections of 'dimensions' and Mrs Crawford's firmly drawn 'lines' deny the possibility that wholesome relationships can form across the divisions they establish. Olivia's beliefs and actions, on the other hand, give it their frail but courageous support: 'People can still be friends, can't they,' she asks, 'even if it is India?' (p. 103). At a memorable moment in the 1970s story, an old beggar-woman, Leelavati, is saved from death on a dust-heap and is instead cradled at the moment of her passing in the arms of the narrator's motherly Indian friend, the widow Maji. At the very end of Leelavati's miserable life she has found an oasis, and the narrator, who is present, experiences the miracle of refreshment (pp. 114-5).

A fourth theme, familiar to readers of Ruth Jhabvala's novels, is the expression of her conviction that India conveys impressions of hell to those who live there, but that it also conveys intimations of heaven.[4] *Heat and Dust* expresses a sense of India as a universe in itself, encompassing death for an Indian widow after a lifetime of humiliation and beggary and unguessable degradation for the European derelicts outside A.'s Hotel who seem to the narrator to be 'like souls in hell' (p. 6), but also emcompassing visions of perfect joy:

Unable to see, I imagine mountain peaks higher than any I've ever dreamed of; the snow on them is also whiter than all other snow — so white it is luminous and shines against a sky which is of a deeper blue than any yet known to me. That is what I expect to see. Perhaps it is also what Olivia saw: the view — or vision — that filled her eyes all those years and suffused her soul. (p. 180)

A fifth theme that one cannot doubt is deeply personal to the author is an inquiry into the means of living (in India, and presumably outside it, too) with passion and deep feeling. Ruth Jhabvala distinguishes very clearly between genuine feeling and mere sentimentality in her contrasted character studies of Krishna Sen Gupta and Hari Sahni in *Amrita*, Ram Nath and Har Dayal in *Esmond in India*, Sudhir and Clarissa in *A Backward Place*, and Raymond and Gopi in *A New Dominion*. She has consistently selected for the partial representation of her own point of view characters who combine intelligence with a delicate sensitivity to the predicaments of others: Sudhir Bannerjee of *A Backward Place* is one of these, the narrator of *Heat and Dust* another. Her exploration of this theme is not, however, confined to — or by — her own personal problems.

One type of passionate feeling considered in *Heat and Dust* is religious ecstasy, the joy experienced by Maji in *samadhi* (meditation), and which Chid seeks to experience; by the novel's end the narrator too is moving (she hopes) towards some such fulfilment.

While religious ecstasy is enthusiastically endorsed by India, there are other kinds of deep feeling that run their possessors into dangers and difficulties. Olivia, both sensitive and passionate, is (according to Major Minnies, whose theories about India and the Western sensibility are comparable to those of Dr Hochstadt in *A Backward Place*) bound to be peculiarly vulnerable to the destructive effects of the Indian experience. Another type of passionate individualism is explored by Ruth Jhabvala in her portrait of the Nawab, a personality with heroic potential, a very prince ('No other word for him,' admits Major Minnies, p. 149). Possessing the character, intelligence and ability to rule absolutely as his ancestors have done, the Nawab degenerates under the idleness and the petty economies forced upon him by British rule. Under the pressures exerted upon him by British administrators, he loses the innate delicacy that has always governed his relationships with those he loves and honours as friends. He turns on Harry and taunts him cruelly, even considers the idea of using his child by Olivia to mortify Douglas and his other tormentors. The inevitable deterioration of his character is further underlined when, fifty years later, his nephew Karim informs the narrator that the Nawab had sold treasures belonging to his state to maintain the dignity of his court. Tales of the Nawab's fiery ancestor, Amanullah Khan, are contrasted with the half-comic, half-pathetic picture of the Nawab himself at fifty, prematurely aged, fat and flabby, devouring cream cakes in a London restaurant and carrying about in his pockets the telephone numbers of Foreign Office officials from whom he is expected to beg funds for his expenses (pp. 175-7).

Other aspects of this theme include comments on the narrator's unconventionality of dress, attitude and behaviour which (though it might seem almost conventional to the Western reader of today) seems like eccentricity to India's conservative middle-class as represented by her landlord; and also the need of the individual to hold on at all costs to a personal identity, which can often be answered only by the

extreme and not entirely satisfactory device of a self-imposed
isolation. Olivia and the narrator both choose this path,
although their creator's experience has shown her that it
invariably brings 'retribution' with it[5]. Olivia's dilemma is
complicated by the fact that hers, like her creator's, is a creative
personality. She finds, after a short time spent in Satipur, that
she ceases to play the piano — she finds it does not 'harmonise'
with the rhythm of life in India (p. 130). Later she takes up
embroidery; and when, fifty years later, the narrator climbs up
to the mountain residence in which Olivia spent her last years,
she finds an embroidery frame in the embrasure of the window
through which Olivia must have looked out at the skies and
the mountain snows that made up her view — 'or vision'. There
are implications here that an artist's commitment to the creative
experience must be followed at the expense of all òther claims,
physical, professional or personal, a theme that has also been
very movingly explored in one of Ruth Jhabvala's short stories,
"The Housewife".

As these concerns weave and interweave with deceptive
naturalness in *Heat and Dust*, a matter-of-fact simplicity of
diction natural to the narrator's temperament is linked with
an apparently casual narrative tone to create an ironic
instrument of remarkable flexibility:

> After a while Olivia said in a contrite voice, 'I don't know
> what's wrong with me.'
> 'I told you: it's the heat. No Englishwoman is meant to
> stand it.'
> 'You're probably right.' (p. 117)

The hot season in Satipur is, at plot-level, real and tangible:
real dust blows into the Assistant Collector's house during a
dust-storm to settle on Olivia's piano and cushions, and the
grove affords shelter from very real heat. In the context of the
novel's themes and interests, however, the heat and dust of
its title become symbolic of passion that is intense enough to
destroy the human personality. The prudent Memsahibs of
Satipur flock to Simla to avoid the heat, but Olivia (who believes
that she loves her husband Douglas, and is failing in love with
the Nawab) stays behind to meet it. Like the lovesick ladies of
the Kangra miniature paintings, who toss on their lonely
embroidered couches while dust-storms gather threateningly

overhead, she is racked by the delicate fire of a passion that
her affectionate but unimaginative husband fails to recognize
although 'he had seen a lot of Indian fevers' (p. 19).

The narrator's habit of noting the seasonal changes in what
is for her still a foreign land is most skilfully used by Ruth
Jhabvala not only to reflect the passage of real time and by
this means support the progress of the plot, but to provide a
setting that reinforces her depiction of the moods and
personalities of certain characters. The moisture of the rainy
season delicately matches the sadness of Harry's mood as he
comtemplates departure from India (p. 160). Landscape as
described by the narrator, who brings fresh eyes to it, subtly
develops mood and theme. There is a notable moment in the
novel in which the Nawab, passionately declaring his right to
rule as an autocrat in Khatm, seats himself by a window in
his palace:

> His profile was outlined against gardens and sky like the
> portrait of a ruler painted against the background of his own
> dominions. (p. 145)

Never has he seemed more truly royal than at this moment,
when inroads are being made upon his independence and
authority by the agents of British rule and his power is already
on the decline. The disintegration of a Khatm house leaves a
blank space at which Olivia gazes during the abortion that robs
her of the Nawab's child, a melancholy incident that is
amusingly balanced and compensated for when the narrator's
pregnancy is confirmed amidst the flashing light of a seemingly
jewelled landscape (p. 165); a parallel that brings out the fact
that the narrator's child by Inder Lal will be born to a more
liberal inheritance of freedom and understanding than the child
of Olivia and the Nawab could have succeeded to in the
inauspicious conditions of British rule. When Olivia drives in
the Nawab's Rolls Royce 'past the Crawfords' house, past the
Saunders's, past the church and cemetery' and out into the
'open country' between Satipur and Khatm (p. 41) she is leaving
behind her forever those divisive 'Civil Lines', the symbols of
British authority and respectability, and venturing into
unknown and perhaps dangerous territory where her lover will
be her only guide and support.[6]

Ruth Jhabvala's use of a cutting and splicing technique

developed in writing for the cinema gives *Heat and Dust* its distinctive character, and sustains both its interest as fiction and the objectivity of its view of the events described. The novel is divided into 23 sections of varying length. A 13-page section set in the 1970s begins the book, followed in turn by a 7-page section set in 1923 and a 5-page section set in the 1970s. The two periods of Satipur 'history' fifty years apart are in this way made to alternate and interweave, the sections representing Olivia's experiences in 1923 and the narrator's in 1973 keeping (after the fourth section) to approximately the same length, never exceeding 10 pages, never falling below 6. They then begin to shrink, occupying from 2 to 4 pages each, until in the 23rd and final section (which is of approximately the same length as the first and is also set in the 1970s) the stories of Olivia and the narrator are brought together through Major Minnies' monograph 'on the influence of India on the European consciousness and character' (which applies equally to them both) and run finally into one as the narrator pauses by Olivia's last home on a mountainside to complete her journal before continuing her climb towards the truth she seeks, and to which she believes Olivia's experience points the way.

By this method of strictly controlling the length of her 'flash-backs', Ruth Jhabvala creates the impression —essential to her theme — that the experiences of the two women, which seem to begin from points set very far apart both in time and as regards their apparently different personalities, start to run parallel from the time they reach India, and become at length indistinguishable from each other. There are two carefully contrived 'flaws' that introduce variations into this symmetrical design. The first is section 4, a 23-page section set in 1923, the second is section 18, 13.5 pages long and also set in 1923. In the first of these, Olivia's special relationship with the Nawab is established during their first visit together to the green grove in the desert, with its shrine and its little spring of water; and in the second — in which the 1923 plot reaches its climax —the Nawab's princeliness, his reckless association with the dacoits, and his love for Olivia are given full play. Ruth Jhabvala has 'cut up' her manuscript as if it were film[7] so that each section sets the other off to the best advantage, introducing into her material and her design the variety that is essential if interest and verisimilitude are to be maintained.

The use of fictional 'flashbacks' between 1923 and 1973 is
a device Ruth Jhabvala has adapted from the screenplay she
wrote in 1973 for James Ivory's film AUTOBIOGRAPHY OF A
PRINCESS,[8] in which a self-exiled Indian princess relives
through documentary footage of her idolised father's royal days,
a past that she remembers with pleasure and regards as
valuable. In *Heat and Dust* Olivia's letters replace the Princess's
reels of photographic film, and since they are described and
interpreted to the reader by the narrator, the narrative must
accommodate (and does so with great naturalness) the technical
devices by which Olivia's experiences are made to parallel and
contrast with those of the narrator. In AUTOBIOGRAPHY the
Princess while reconstructing her father's career and the quality
of the life she has known, unconsciously lays bare the
limitations of her outlook and the emptiness of her own life.
In *Heat and Dust* the narrator while researching Olivia's life
is simultaneously reliving it and revealing her own personal
history.

As the story of *Heat and Dust* moves backwards and forwards
in the telling, the experiences of Olivia and the narrator, the
Nawab and his modern avatar Inder Lal, Harry and Chid are
linked by the use of certain objects and incidents, phrases and
experiences as fixed points upon which parallels between
different aspects of the two eras can be established: an Italian
angel in a British cemetery, looking very 'Indian' in 1973 with
its 'headless, wingless torso' (p. 24); a spring of water in a green
grove that makes a weary traveller feel she is 'being received
into Paradise' (p. 124); the miniature paintings at the palace
at Khatm, a festival, an excursion and a picnic, the sickness
of a friend, a pregnancy and its termination are woven into a
complex pattern. The effect of such a structure is to emphasise,
very delicately indeed, one of the novel's main themes: that
human nature in its aspects of warmth, love and friendliness,
and the possibility of spiritual regeneration are constants
unaffected by the flow of time and history.

The close connection between the film AUTOBIOGRAPHY OF A
PRINCESS and *Heat and Dust* may be seen in the matter of the
carefully selected details by means of which Ruth Jhabvala
builds up her picture of the Nawab and of palace life. The
childish parlour-games and the expensive cars (the Nawab
travels in a Rolls, an Alpha-Romeo and a red open sports car),

the elaborate picnic food and complicated drinks, the chandeliers and silver, crystal and candelabras are based on material drawn from the biographies and photographic records of Maharajas, notably of Jodhpur and Jaipur, that were accumulated and worked from during the making of a number of films directed by James Ivory and set in India, for all of which Ruth Jhabvala either wrote, or collaborated on, the screenplays. The evocation of the life led by the Nawab's nephew Karim and his wife Kitty in their London flat is based on interviews with dispossessed Maharajas, selected excerpts from which are made use of by Ruth Jhabvala in the screenplay of AUTOBIOGRAPHY. In matters of characterisation as well as of theme, significant parallels can be observed: Karim and Kitty's friends, like the Princess in AUTOBIOGRAPHY, sentimentalise the past; Harry closely resembles, in the characteristic weakness of his personality and his affectionate dependence on the Nawab, the character of Cyril Sahib in AUTOBIOGRAPHY, who was called a degenerate by visiting Mrs Grundies and was alternately loved and tormented by the Princess's late father. Finally, there may be recognised, perhaps, a connection between Maji in *Heat and Dust* and the 80-year-old court singer whose performance ends the film: both women retain their gaiety and their control of their art despite the changes taking place around them, becoming symbolic of all that is permanent and changeless in India, representing traditions that will still be vitally alive when Maharajas and British India alike have slid into oblivion.

AUTOBIOGRAPHY OF A PRINCESS enjoys, in effect, the assistance of three 'narrators': the viewer sees the films as the Princess runs them for Cyril Sahib's entertainment and hears, alternately, the comments and very different reminiscences of the two characters as they watch the films. A novel cannot, without running to far greater length than does *Heat and Dust* (and doing so at the possible expense of both unity and interest), employ multiple narrators in quite the same way. *Heat and Dust* employs a single narrator, whose function is not only to relate two stories — her own and Olivia's — but to present characters in such a way that they reinforce, without strain or loss of objectivity, this double exposure of event and experience. Rather than double characters, Ruth Jhabvala chooses to repeat inner, hidden characteristics in different personalities that link them together. She then doubles the patterns in which these

personalities are made, by the novel's plot, to move: patterns
which seem to be contrived (even, sometimes, pre-determined)
by forces from both within and outside themselves. Thus, where
the Nawab is clearly born to command, Inder Lal is doomed
to take orders from others. Yet they are alike in possessing an
inner sensitivity; in finding their marriage partners
unsatisfactory and for similar reasons; in valuing above all
things the 'miracle' of a personal relationship. Both are
poetically sentimental about the past; and in modern India and
in British India alike, the peace of mind of each is menaced
by slander, envy, and destructive, malicious bullying. Harry and
Chid, with little in common beyond a weakness that makes
them depend on others for support, reach a point at which
further existence in India becomes physically intolerable. Where
Olivia surrounds herself with elegant and stylish possessions,
the narrator strips herself deliberately of all but absolutely
essentials; yet they resemble each other in their sensitivity to
atmosphere and to people, and their experiences run parallel,
merging finally into one. The effect of this very detailed and
careful structuring is to suggest that time, like history,
endlessly repeats itself, thus reinforcing the sense the novel
transmits of India as a divine essence transcending human
concerns while including them in its totality.

The entire substance of *Heat and Dust* is filtered through the
consciousness of the narrator, who becomes (through Ruth
Jhabvala's subtle adaptation of the cinematic technique of
flashback) both the instrument and the subject of her creator's
ironic view of life. Her effectiveness as a tool of social analysis
depends to a great degree on the firmness with which her
character is established in the opening sections of the novel
as honest and reliable, and her approach to recording the events
of Olivia's life and her own established as serious. This is
effectively managed through an unobtrusive accumulation of
detail that gradually builds an impression in the reader's mind
of a personality at once self-aware and generous. The narrator
is herself the grand-daughter of the stoic, self-controlled,
idealistic Douglas Rivers; her quiet remark that Chid has no
family connection with India reminds the alert reader that she
is herself the last of a line of English men and women who have
lived in India, some of whom fought and died for her. The
narrator does not openly discuss her own feelings on this matter

of family tradition (since this, as she writes with characteristic self-effacement at the start of her journal, 'is not my story, it is Olivia's as far as I can follow it', p. 2), but reveals them unconsciously. She presents Douglas to the reader with the comment 'He was upright and just' (p. 1), and when Karim refers to his uncle the Nawab as 'a naughty boy' she refrains from contributing gossipy revelations about her own grandfather's relations with Olivia. She is thus revealed (in contrast to Karim) as a morally fastidious person, with a background and outlook of such sturdy, if understated, idealism that we are not surprised when the end of *Heat and Dust* finds her ready to strive towards a dimly glimpsed, unknown spiritual goal. She is, in fact, a worthy inheritor of the stoic and single-minded Rivers family tradition, though her heroism takes a different path and a different form in a world that has changed with the dissolution of Empire.

The narrator belongs to a new generation of liberal-minded, educated travellers from the West who consciously strive to communicate with India, rather than to patronise or belittle her. Hence her concern when Dr Gopal criticises India (p. 158), and her awareness of the Indian point of view:

> I suppose we must look strange to them, and what must also be strange is the way we are living among them — no longer apart, but eating their food and often wearing Indian clothes because they are cooler and cheaper. (p. 9)

No longer bedevilled by the need to act as her great-aunt, 'Memsahib Crawford', had done in 1923, the narrator draws no divisive lines to separate herself from those around her. She can refer naturally to Maji and her fellow-widows as 'my friends', and extend her affection to Inder Lal with no consciousness of dividing barriers of race or even (and here one recalls Clarissa, in *A Backward Place*) of class. If her words and actions sprang merely from a guilty liberal conscience, an urge to compensate in some measure for British injustices in the past, the reader would not be quite so ready to trust the narrator's reliability as a recorder of events. But her obvious lack of enthusiasm for Kitty and Karim and their circle of familiars and parasites (although with characteristic good manners she doesn't call them such), and her determined attempt to bring Leelavati's desperate condition to the attention of fellow-citizens and the hospital authorities are among the points that indicate her awareness that Indians are by no means perfect.

The narrator's is, above all, an educated sensibility. Unlike others among Ruth Jhabvala's female Westerners seeking fulfilment in India (Lee in *A New Dominion*, Katie in the story "How I Became a Holy Mother") she tries to avoid being or becoming the plaything to impulse. She has made careful preparations for her journey to India, examined memoirs, letters and prints of the 1920s and earlier (p. 2). On arrival, she wastes no time in setting to work directly on her journal and the imaginative recreation of the experience glimpsed through Olivia's letters. She shapes her days to 'a steady routine' (p. 48), and strips her life of all but the barest essentials so that she will not be distracted from her task or from the Indian life about her which is part of her subject (pp. 6-7). Her decision to stay in India is not an immature enthusiasm born of *guru*-worship (as is Jenny's in James Ivory's film, THE GURU, for which Ruth Jhabvala collaborated with Ivory in writing the script in 1968) but arises in part out of a considered rejection of Western values that she has tried and found wanting. Her writing style (unlike Olivia's, which is heavily italicised, and full of vivacity and enthusiasm) is quiet, direct and thoughtful, devoid of emphases critical, satirical or emotional.

At the close of the novel, however, when Olivia's letters have come to an end and the narrator must piece together other kinds of evidence, reflect on the picture as a whole and reach her own conclusion and decision, it becomes evident that her writing has begun to lose its objectivity: she begins to seek, not illumination or truth, but confirmation of her own wishes. When Dr Gopal remarks, half-jokingly, that India's hell — like her heaven — is for Indians only, the narrator reveals her heart directly for the first time:

I don't want to admit it; I don't want it to be so. (p. 159)

In an unexpected burst of passion, she lists examples to support her claim that Europeans have stayed on in India of their own free will; but since these include an anonymous Englishman doing religious penance, an adventurer who was murdered, and the Christian missionary already met in Bombay whom the reader has judged to be somewhat unbalanced, they can hardly be considered auspicious precedents. The exception is Olivia, whose example — like the house in which she died — 'stands quite by itself on a mountain ledge' (p. 174). The nature of Olivia's experience is, however, shrouded in mist like the mountain itself. The narrator can only guess and speculate, fitting together the information that Olivia had specifically desired cremation and had never accompanied the Nawab on his visits to Britain, with her own impression of the house as retaining Olivia's distinctive ambience in its furniture and decoration and her observation of a chair and an embroidery frame set in a window embrasure. Do these details support the narrator's evident desire to see Olivia as having been (or become) heroic, spiritual and creative, in some way 'special'? Or do they provide us with a final picture of Olivia as a tragically isolated Lady of Shalott, weaving into her embroidery frame a shadow world of remembered and reflected figures drawn from the real world she has left behind her and to which she (like the narrator) perhaps 'rarely look(ed) down'? (p. 180). The question cannot be answered on the facts available, and is in fact never answered by the narrator, whose journal becomes in the context of her stated decision to keep climbing, a last gallant communication from the field of action made before her voice falls silent.

The narrator's shift from objectivity to a determination to see only one point of view — her own — is skilfully caught by Ruth Jhabvala in the narrator's description of, and comments on, Major Minnies' monograph:

Although the Major was so sympathetic to India, his piece sounds like a warning. He said that one has to be very determined to withstand — to stand up to — India. And the most vulnerable, he said, are always those who love her best. There are many ways of loving India, many things to love her for — the scenery, the history, the poetry, the music, and indeed the physical beauty of the men and women —but all, said the Major, are dangerous for the European who allows himself to love too much. India always, he said, finds out the weak spot and presses on it. Both Dr Saunders and Major Minnies spoke of the weak spot. But whereas for Dr Saunders it is something, or someone, rotten, for the Major this weak spot is to be found in the most sensitive, often the finest people — and, moreover, in their finest

feelings. It is there that India seeks them out and pulls them
over into what the Major called the other dimension. He also
referred to it as another element, one in which the European
is not accustomed to live so that by immersion in it he
becomes debilitated, or even (like Olivia) destroyed.
(pp. 170-71)

The narrator distinguishes carefully here between Dr Saunders'
remarks and the Major's, recognises the warning to herself that
is embodied in the latter, and does her best to present it fairly
and truthfully. But the subject is too close to her heart to permit
her to maintain her objective stance: going on to remark that
the Major warns against an excess of feeling and love for India,
she exclaims, 'He who had loved India so much, knew her so
well, chose to spend the end of his days here!' (p. 171). So
unusual in the narrator is this kind of direct critical comment
that the remark reveals at once the intensity of her feelings
and the violence of her disagreement with the Major's view.
Indirectly, our belief is confirmed in the sensitivity and self-
control that have between them given us *up to this point* a
recorder whose objectivity we can trust.

The first pages of *Heat and Dust*, like the last (all that section
of the novel which is not, as it were, underpinned and stabilised
by constant reference to Olivia's letters) need to be seen in the
light of the narrator's description of her own altered condition:

> (My early impressions) are no longer the same because I
> myself am no longer the same. India always changes people,
> and I have been no exception. (p. 2)

Viewed in this way, the entire record made by the narrator of
Olivia's experiences and her own may be regarded as an exercise
in self-analysis. Ruth Jhabvala has referred in "Myself in India"
to her own 'deplorable tendency to constant self-analysis'.[9]
Since she has also stated that her Western characters 'of course
include myself',[10] we may, if we wish, link the impulses to
self-disgust and self-isolation, and the intense sensitivity to
atmosphere and seasonal change Olivia shares with the
narrator, with their creator's frank description of her own
experience in India.

This grand-daughter of Douglas Rivers, inheriting from him
an inclination to conceal and control her feelings, is 'quite a

shy person' (p. 51), given to self-criticism. Olivia, she remarks, 'was everything I'm not' (p. 7). The narrator describes herself (to Inder Lal) as one of those Europeans who come to India 'in the hope of finding a simpler and more natural way of life' (p. 95), a personal statement that includes — as did Gulliver's self-abasement before the Houyhnhnms — a judgment upon her own society and the civilisation of which it is a part. She sees her life as 'lacking in essentials' (p. 127) and although she tries to efface herself while imaginatively recreating Olivia's experience, it cannot be forgotten that the determined honesty and detachment she brings to this task are born of her urgent need to understand it as fully as possible, so that she may move from understanding towards a more satisfying life for herself. The shift already noted in the novel's last pages from objectivity to emotion confirms the impression given by an accumulation of self-critical notes such as those just quoted, that the narrator of *Heat and Dust* is not merely an unusually sensitive person who shies away from vanity and self-congratulation, but one who is ceasing to see herself as a whole and integrated personality.

The narrator's record fills with references to her own inadequacies (even while the judgment she displays in writing it gives evidence to the contrary). Her impulse to increased self-isolation in order to find spiritual fulfilment combines with her tendency to idealise Olivia's 'vision', to suggest a growing psychological imbalance. Has the awareness with which she caught the process of change in herself — when she realised that she was beginning to regard pain and horror 'with the same indifference as everyone else' (pp. 112-13) — disappeared by the end of the novel, and the detached narrator become a deluded one? She may be on the way to becoming what she had herself once thought Chid — 'a little mad' (p. 64). She may even, like the Western derelicts outside A.'s Hotel, end her story as 'a soul in hell'.

The growing awareness inspired in the reader of the narrator's psychological condition while *she* continues to direct her desperately objective gaze at Olivia creates an ironic double-view. A mist of ambiguity gathers about her opinions and her judgments. The holy men she described as 'randy' during her early days in Satipur (and amusedly satirised in her retelling of the adventures of two English devotees of Universal Love —

pp. 22, 63-64) have become by the end of the novel a group
of virtuous ascetics whose way of life she intends to explore.
From what we have seen of Lee in *A New Dominion*, and of other
characters in such stories as "An Experience of India", "A
Spiritual Call" and "How I Became a Holy Mother", the path
chosen by the narrator can lead her towards the complete
surrender of the individual personality, and the abandonment
of all objectivity in self-subjugation to the guru.

> Where I had advised psychiatry, Maji — the holy woman and
> friend — has advised pilgrimage. (p. 83)

There is double irony here, for the narrator may herself be
moving towards the disintegrated view of her own personality
that requires psychiatric help, and will herself (like Inder Lal's
wife, Ritu) seek remedy in pilgrimage. However, the novel stops
short before the narrator sets out on the next stage of her 'quest'
and although the reader may think of her as set upon a path
of almost inevitable self-destruction, he cannot doubt that her
career, in its end as in its course, is likely to be in the Rivers
family tradition of understated heroism.

Ruth Jhabvala leaves another approach open to the reader
on this question, however. In her sincerity and singlemindedness the narrator can be seen as an archetypal quest-
figure, a female Sir Percival seeking the Holy Grail. Like
Christian on his journey, she has had no lack of warning signals
along the way. Grandmother Tess and Great Aunt Beth
Crawford have warned her that Olivia has done 'dark and
terrible' things (p. 2), the missionary assures her that only
Christ Jesus can keep her out of the hell in which the derelicts
outside A.'s Hotel are so plainly burning (p. 4); Mrs Saunders
warns Olivia about Indian immorality, Major Minnies
thoughtfully cautions her against 'step(ping) over too far'
(p. 148); Dr Saunders pours contempt upon her interest in
Indian culture. The mental illness of Zahira, the Nawab's
beautiful and once loved wife, is repeated in Ritu, the wife of
Inder Lal, a parallel that casts an ironic light on the 'vision'
of both Olivia and the narrator: are they bound to end in
madness, too? Such features throw whole areas of the novel
into doubt, and cause the narrator to move and act in an aura
of imminent tragedy. But she is not necessarily doomed to end
in despair. She (like Olivia, and like Judy in *A Backward Place*)

has chosen to give herself to India as to a lover; her decision to stay on in India (like Olivia's to leave Douglas for the Nawab) is an act of surrender and an assertion of confidence in futurity that brings the narrator close to Judy in the earlier novel, and to Dev in the story "Like Birds, Like Fishes". They are, as it were, transformed into 'birds floating on the sky — drifting without thought or effort or fear, aerial and at ease'.

The narrator has, moreover, chosen a way that she has herself seen crowned with success in Maji's experience, and hopes herself to achieve one day the vigour Maji evinces on emerging from meditation. Maji tells her that 'it used to be very difficult for her to make the transition from *samadhi* back to ordinary life' (p. 162), and the narrator looks forward to a time when such a transition will be for her, as it now is for Maji, 'easy and effortless' (p. 163). The ambiguity on which the novel ends —

... my condition which will make it more and more difficult to get down again, even if I should want to ... (p. 181)

— combines an allusion to her pregnancy with a reference to an altered condition of mind. Despite the warning embodied in Chid's defeat, beyond the mists of the snow-covered mountains there still exists the possibility — remote to the cynical or the unbelieving, but real to the narrator, and a matter of everyday acceptance to millions of pilgrims in India — of perfect and endless joy. The fourth stage of human life — that of the *sanyasi* or religious recluse — is conceived of in Indian philosophy as a rarefied, purer state of existence, above the heat and dust of passion, a stage at which all things and all aspects of every question can be fully viewed and perfectly understood. No longer partisan, no longer involved in battle, the narrator's 'condition' could be regarded with justification as symbolic of her creator's hope regarding her own personal and artistic achievement in this novel.

Since conscientious and deliberate objectivity are essential to the narrator's purpose in undertaking the writing of her journal, the reader cannot expect overt satire or social criticism from her. The technique of cinematic flashback compensates for this by allowing the author to express implied criticism of certain matters without compromising the detachment of her narrator or disturbing the realistic surface of the novel by direct

verbal expression. Criticism of the moral and social
restrictiveness of British life in India in the 1920s is implied,
for instance, in the narrator's liberated approach to human
relationships: she gives sex as generously to Chid as she gives
him food and shelter, and her sexual relationship with Inder
Lal is warmly affectionate, an extension of genuine friendship.

One of the most striking examples in *Heat and Dust* of Ruth
Jhabvala's ability to give simultaneous expression to satiric,
ironic, thematic and analytic comment through the narrator's
sensibility without at any point altering the reader's impression
of 'Ms. Rivers' as a reliable and objective observer is to be found
in a scene set in the Knightsbridge flat of the Nawab's nephew,
Karim. The scene runs to a length of nearly six pages (pp. 96-
101), all of it packed with detail that is seemingly casually noted
by the narrator, but is — in the context of the picture presented
in the novel as a whole of a doomed and dying Royal India
—ambiguous and ironic. A sofa in the room recalls the
miniature paintings of Kangra and the Rajput states, in which
court ladies may be seen disporting themselves on jewelled
swings; taped sarod music to which nobody listens is an ironic
reminder that Karim's grandfather had been a poet, and a
patron in his time of music and poetry as living arts; the
paintings in Karim's 'den' depict the palace at Khatm as it had
glowed in the artist's imagination during the days of India's
greatness when everything had indeed been

> jewelled: the flowers in the garden, the drops of water in the
> fountain.

These carefully selected and disposed details that are beautiful
in themselves but have lost their vitality and meaning provide
an appropriate setting for the last of the Nawab's line: dressed
in the height of London boutique fashion, retaining the family
looks in an effeminate, affected way, the graceful and large-
eyed Karim is apparently planning to make his living by
becoming a contact-man (or pimp) for the further rape by the
West of his country and its wealth.

Karim tells the narrator a story of his ancestor, Amanullah
Khan (who had been the Nawab's hero), the narrator casually
mentions the Nawab himself, and the reader becomes aware
of a history of degeneration, in the course of which the vigour
of Amanullah Khan and the restricted but still 'hawk-like'

energy of the Nawab have dwindled to the attenuated shadow
of the past represented by Karim. The conversation of Karim
and Kitty's friends has nothing heroic about it, nothing
individual or creative despite their claims to the contrary (Kitty
is, her business partners assert, 'very creative'). It revolves
around the ways and means to be adopted of smuggling family
treasures out of the country in defiance of the Government of
India's tiresomely inquisitive customs officers. The narrator's
habitual courtesy and the polite detachment of her tone are
undisturbed by the smallest expression of direct criticism. Yet
the condition of these beautiful 'bright young people', ironically
presented through the careful selection of effective detail and
the use of echoes from the past to provide contrasts of different
kinds, is seen as being tragic and inevitable. Physically
delightful, they are spiritually dead and dying, representatives
of a tradition that was once forceful and inspirational, but has
now become little more than a sentimental memory of days of
style and 'charm' (p. 98).

Her skilful use of carefully selected detail for symbolic
purposes in the passage quoted above represents a development
of artistic devices that were first tried out in earlier writing.
The taped sarod music and the swing in Karim's flat are as
real as the hand-loomed rug that trips Pitu up in Get Ready
for Battle[11], but their use as symbols of a creative past
represents a significant advance on the simpler techniques of
the earlier novel, while still being of a piece with those parts
of Ruth Jhabvala's early fiction in which landscape and sky,
even when violated by ugliness and man's misuse, could hold
possibilities and hope of regeneration[12].

Although Heat and Dust contains satiric elements, it is not,
as we have seen, a satire nor even a satiric novel. Admittedly
the reader catches from time to time a flash of the old fire; Major
Minnies, the narrator informs us with calm detachment,

> had been in India for over twenty years and knew all there
> was to know about it; so did his wife. (p. 15)

There is here the habit of ironic undercutting within a sentence
that, frequent in such novels as The Householder, Amrita, The
Nature of Passion and Get Ready for Battle, brought Jane
Austen inevitably to mind. In Heat and Dust, however, Ruth
Jhabvala's satire is of the nature of Candide rather than of

Emma. Eastern swamis who prey upon the gullibility of
spiritual-minded Westerners attract her contempt and anger,
couched in the coolest, most courteous of tones:

> The young man told me that he and his girl friend had
> become very interested in the Hindu religion after attending
> a lecture by a visiting swami in London. It had been on
> Universal Love. The swami, in a soft caressing voice very
> suitable to the subject, told them that Universal Love was
> an ocean of sweetness that lapped around all humanity and
> enfolded them in tides of honey. He had melting eyes and
> a smile of joy. The atmosphere was also very beautiful, with
> jasmine, incense, and banana leaves; the swami's ... disciples
> ... were mostly Europeans and wore saffron robes and had
> very pure expressions on their faces as if cleansed of all sin
> and desire. Afterwards they had sung hymns in Hindi which
> were also about the flowing ocean of love. The young man
> and his girl had come away from this meeting with such
> exalted feelings that they could not speak for a long time;
> but when they could, they agreed that, in order to find the
> spiritual enrichment they desired, they must set off for India
> without delay. (p. 22)

A significant clue to one of the functions of the studied
detachment of style that contributes so much to the humour
of the passage above and has become characteristic over the
years of Ruth Jhabvala's narrative technique is provided quite
early in the novel, at the Nawab's dinner party:

> The Nawab, at the head of his table, also appeared to be
> listening to his guest with attention and respect. In fact, he
> was leaning forward in his eagerness not to miss a word.
> When Major Minnies' story turned amusing — he was telling
> them about a devilish clever Hindu moneylender in Patna
> who had attempted to outwit the Major many, many years
> ago when the latter was still green behind the ears — the
> Nawab, to mark his appreciation of the Major's humour,
> threw himself back in his chair and rapped the table; he only
> interrupted his laughter in order to invite his other guests
> to join in it. But Olivia felt he was putting it on: She was
> almost sure of it. (p. 17)

When Olivia knows the Nawab better, she finds that her

suspicions were well-founded. The Nawab's courtesy, invariably expressive of a respectful delicacy and affection when true friends are involved, conceals contempt and anger when the novel brings him into contact with three Englishmen in their official capacity: Major Minnies, the British political agent who has been appointed his advisor; Dr Saunders, who is in the habit of using his right arm to enforce his 'strong ideas about morality and how to uphold it' (p. 69); and Douglas Rivers, Assistant Collector of Revenue, who makes the mistake of attempting to separate Harry from the Nawab by arranging for a berth for him on an England-bound P&O liner. The Nawab's is an anger that can never be stilled while the British retain power in India and he must continue to rule by their decree. Describing his admired ancestor, the free-riding autocratic Amanullah Khan[13] to Olivia, the Nawab expresses his frustration:

> Olivia: I envy him. His name was feared by everyone ... Don't you think, Olivia, it is better to meet your enemies in this way than to have them secretly plotting against you and whispering slanders? ... Amanullah Khan was not the man to sit quiet when insulted. Not like me ... I have to, what can I do. I am helpless. (pp. 135-6)

Forced to live in an age in which royal rage such as his must hide itself from the light of day, the Nawab (unable to slay his opponent or slice off his arm — 'Wow!' says Karim, opening his beautiful eyes wide at the mere thought of his ancestor's exploits while recounting the tale to the narrator in London) has evolved an 'exaggerated courtesy' of manner with which to counter British bullying, conceal anger and express contempt.

It is from a comparable frustration and tension, it would seem, that Ruth Jhabvala has developed the satiric elements of her style. Her magnificent description of the Hochstadts' visit to the theatre in the last pages of *A Backward Place*, and of Durga's relations as they finally assume control of her house and her life in the story "The Widow" are early successes in the true satiric tradition; at once comic and deeply serious, they are expressive of contempt and angry concern that find a vent and source of temporary relief in laughter. Subjecting the many aspects of her life in India over twenty-five years there to repeated, remorseless analysis, she has developed a narrative tone that transcends, while still including, satire. In *Heat and Dust* the personal and psychological crises of her characters, Indian and European, are treated at greater length and in far greater detail than are the portraits of a pompous clown such as Dr Saunders or the comically confused seekers after Universal Love. The narrative tone remains as detached as before, but in her eighth novel coolness and objectivity lead to sympathy and better understanding.

Notes

1. R.P. Jhabvala, *Heat and Dust* (John Murray, London: 1975), p. 2. This novel was awarded the Booker Prize for Fiction in 1975. All references in this chapter and throughout this book are to the 1975 edition.
2. Meenakshi Mukherjee, op. cit., p. 5.
3. See pp. 6-7 of this book, for the relevant passage from "Myself in India".
4. R.P. Jhabvala, "Moonlight, jasmine and rickets", op. cit. The passage is quoted in note 5 to Chapter V.
5. 'And here, it seems to me, I come to the heart of my problem. To live in India and be at peace one must to a very considerably extent become Indian and adopt Indian attitudes, habits, beliefs, assume if possible an Indian personality. But how is this possible? And even if it were possible — without cheating oneself — would it be desirable? Should one want to try and become something other than what one is? I don't always say no to this question ... Other times it seems worthwhile to be defiant and European and — all right, be crushed by one's environment, but all the same have made some attempt to remain standing ... (pp. 19-20)
    ... Having once seen the sights in India, and the way it has been ordained that people must live out their lives, nowhere in the world can ever be all that good to be in again ... It is not possible to pretend otherwise. Or rather, one does pretend, but retribution follows ... People are not meant to shut themselves up in rooms and pretend there is nothing outside.' (p. 10) — R.P. Jhabvala, "Myself in India", op. cit.
6. There is perhaps a reflection here of Jane Austen's symbolic treatment of landscape in *Mansfield Park*, Vol. I, Chapter 10. Henry Crawford persuades Maria Bertram to let him help her to more 'at large':
    And for the world you would not get out without the key and without Mr Rushworth's authority and protection, or I think you might with little difficulty pass round the edge of the gate, here, with my assistance; I think it might be done, if you really wished to be more at large, and could allow yourself to think it not prohibited.
7. 'I wrote (*Heat and Dust*) rather differently from the others. I wrote great

blocks of present time and then great blocks of 1923. Then afterwards I cut them up and put them together to set each other off. So I have learnt a lot technically from film' — R.P. Jhabvala, quoted by A. Rutherford and K.H. Petersen, op. cit., p. 377; see also more recent remarks on the subject by the author, quoted in note no. 49 of the Notes to Chapter XI Writing for Film.

8. 'Sometimes ... writing fiction and screenplays go on simultaneously: I try themes out, for instance *Autobiography of a Princess* and *Heat and Dust* were written straight after each other and the same themes were in my mind' — R.P. Jhabvala, quoted by John Pym, op. cit., p. 18.

9. "Myself in India", op. cit., p. 8.

10. R.P. Jhabvala, "Moonlight, jasmine and rickets", op. cit.

11. See Chapter VI.

12. See Chapter VII.

13. See Chapters IV, VIII, for a discussion of R.P. Jhabvala's use of 'absent characters' in *Esmond in India* and *A New Dominion* respectively.

CHAPTER

X

The short stories

'A story is ... like a poem ... You can't cheat on a poem. It's one cry from the heart — just one — only that has to come out true and right.'[1]

Ruth Jhabvala's first volume of short stories, *Like Birds,Like Fishes*,[2] appeared in 1963, when she had already published five novels and was working on the cinematic version of one of them, *The Householder*. With one exception, the stories in the collection had been published earlier in American magazines[3] (incidentally confirming the impression conveyed by her novels to Western readers, of an author whose writing

shed a cool, clear light on post-Independence India). The
exception is the title story, which reveals Ruth Jhabvala's
awakening interest in the approach to life adopted by the
unfettered idealists she portrays sympathetically in her next
two novels — Sarla Devi and Gautam in *Get Ready for Battle*,
and Bal in *A Backward Place*. All the rest look back, chiefly
at what had gripped her attention since her arrival in India
in 1951: 'That's how I get to know a place, through writing'.[4]
The book contains satiric studies of Indian committee women,
social climbers and literary lions ("The Old Lady", "Lekha" and
"The Award"); sketches of helplessness and dispensability in
Indian lower middle-class life ("The Interview", "A Loss of Faith");
penetrating assessments of the way the Indian joint-family
functions to smother individualism, yet cushion disappointment
("The Widow", "Sixth Child"); a potted biography of a swami
in the making ("My First Marriage"); and two deeply felt essays
on loneliness and loss as experienced by individuals trapped
in an alien society ("The Aliens", "A Birthday in London").

A second collection, *An Experience of India*,[5] was published
three years later, and takes its prevailing mood and a new
direction from the essay that forms an introduction to the book,
"Myself in India". The studies of Indian life presented here
include a portrait of Chameli, a young woman of feeling and
simple affections whom circumstance and convention brand
as "A Bad Woman", and her own passions thrust unexpectedly
into complicated tragedy; explorations of the commercial film
world Ruth Jhabvala was getting to know during the making
of BOMBAY TALKIE and SHAKESPEAREWALLAH ("A Star and Two
Girls", "Suffering Women"); and two studies of Westernised
Indian women, in contrasting styles of compassionate irony
("Rose Petals") and high-spirited satirical comedy ("A Course
of English Studies"). The title story uses the cycle of response
to India described in the introduction[6] as the basis for a
fictional account of a Western woman's travels in India in search
of self-fulfilment. It was the first to be published among the
numerous studies of religious swamis and their deluded
Western devotees that stud Ruth Jhabvala's novels, stories and
screen-plays in the ten years between 1966 and 1976. The story
that seems to be the most deeply personal to the author,
however, is not "An Experience of India"[7], but 'The Housewife"
in which a most moving exploration of the theme of artistic

commitment is discreetly embedded in a domestic drama of middle-class marital infidelity.

A Stronger Climate (1968)[8] presents nine stories, six of which are about Westerners who come to India in search of a purpose in life ("A Young Man of Good Family") or of spiritual, intellectual and emotional enrichment ("A Spiritual Call", "The Biography", "Passion"), only to find themselves betrayed by India ("The Young Couple") or by their own capacity for self-deception ("In Love with a Beautiful Girl"). To these studies of 'Seekers', the author adds three studies of 'Sufferers', Westerners who have stayed too long in India, and for whom the rapture of their first encounter has turned into sour disillusionment, bewilderment, and the revulsion she describes as the third stage on her cycle of response to India ("Miss Sahib", "An Indian Citizen", "The Man with the Dog").

Her fourth collection, *How I Became a Holy Mother*,[9] followed eight years after *A Stronger Climate*, and bears out Ruth Jhabvala's statement that her interest lay from the 1960s onward no longer in India as a subject, but in "Myself in India".[10] Many of the stories are, despite their richness of observed detail and skilful characterisation, essays in self-analysis that turn over again and again themes deeply personal to their author. While the studies of Westerners in India are undertaken in a spirit of ironic amusement ("Two More Under the Indian Sun", "How I Became a Holy Mother"), the pictures of Indian life are in reality studies of different aspects of self-deception ("Bombay", "On Bail", "Prostitutes" and "Picnic with Moonlight and Mangoes"). Two stories are, in effect, analyses of passion and self-pity in women whom marriage has isolated from the world ("Desecration", "In a Great Man's House"), while two others study the sensibility of female individualists who desert their comfortable middle-class lives for solitude and freedom ("In the Mountains" and "The Englishwoman"[11]).

Reference has been made elsewhere in this book to instances in which some of the stories mentioned above take up aspects of the major themes that inspire Ruth Jhabvala's eight novels and the screenplays she has written for Merchant-Ivory films. The stories selected for discussion in this chapter, however, have been chosen not so much for their importance as links between the novels and the screenplays (although that aspect has not been overlooked), as for their technical interest. The singer in "The Housewife", who knows that success

> lay within her power, a little more effort and she would be
> there and then she could begin to set her sights on the next
> impossible step, (pp. 151-2)

is a recognisable projection of her creator, who has been
frequently compared to Chekhov and other masters of the short
story genre, but strives tirelessly in 'silence, exile and cunning'
towards a personal objective and a highly individual style.

Among many stories in all four collections which examine
critically or satirically the attitudes of 'modern' Indian women
of the upper and middle classes, "Lekha" is outstanding in the
range of its reference to the Indian social and cultural scene,
its insight into female psychology, and its evidence of an early
interest in technical experiment.[12] It is Ruth Jhabvala's first
attempt, and a highly successful one, at the indirect revelation
of character that we have seen in more finished and sophisticated forms in *Heat and Dust* and AUTOBIOGRAPHY OF A
PRINCESS. As in *Heat and Dust*, a female narrator relates the
story of another woman's scandalous love-affair, unconsciously
laying her own soul bare as she does so. There is a clear element
of social satire in this story, directed at 'Westernised' Indian
women and the civil service mentality (both of which are satiric
targets in the early novels, *Amrita* and *The Nature of Passion*).
The narrator, who is the wife of a senior civil servant, epitomises
one and reflects the other: in her opinion, eating with the fingers
from a round brass tray

> may be the traditional Indian way, but it is my opinion that
> it is not a nice way and that it would be better for India if
> everyone learned to eat in the way people do in the West.
> (p. 171)

The husband of her young friend Lekha is described in the
narrator's opening sentence as 'The head of our department
— my husband's department, that is' (p. 166), and it soon
becomes clear that a good deal of pushing and shoving goes
on among this 'happy group' (p. 166) of senior officers and their
wives to gain the favour of the head. Although the narrator
describes her own attitude to the youthful and inexperienced
Lekha as 'protective' and that of her arch-enemy, Mrs Nayyar,
as 'possessive', there is little to choose between the two ladies

in this matter.

Unlike 'Ms. Rivers' in *Heat and Dust*, the narrator of "Lekha" is not bent on self-analysis. On the contrary, she is perfectly satisfied with her way of life and her own personality, and the emptiness of both is only unconsciously revealed when Lekha's passionate love-affair with Govind, the narrator's bohemian brother-in-law, puts these complacent values at risk:

> I have been married now for ten years and I am fond of my husband and I have had three children by him, but we have always used restraint in our behaviour together. I pressed my face into my pillow and suddenly I began to cry ... very bitterly. (p. 178)

The story suggests that the narrator's unadmitted but none-the-less deeply felt sense of inadequacy and lack of fulfilment is closely linked with her deracination from that spirit of India which is found in her myths and age-old festivals, dance, song and folk ways. Govind, in his conventional sister-in-law's opinion an idler who spends his time in coffee-houses, is a skilled musician possessed moreover of the dark good looks associated with the god Krishna in his aspect of the lover. Awakened to the full potential of her body and spirit by her love for him, Lekha is transformed, for the duration of their love-affair, into an avatar of Radha, the milk-maid who symbolises in Indian mythology the concept of the human soul. Their likeness to the mythological couple strikes the narrator when she first sees them together (p. 176), and on subsequent occasions she describes them in terms that, while appropriate to the human reality of their very ardent feeling for each other, suggest the presence of superhuman power:

> Suddenly she kissed me on the neck; her lips and breath were very hot.
>
> When I got home, I lay down on the bed and shut my eyes. But I could not get rid of the picture of the two of them together ... Oh, it was nothing really that they did; it was only the understanding between them, and something else that I can't describe — something that had come rising out of them and filled the room. (p. 177)

The old crafts and rituals have yielded their place with the narrator and her circle to the merely 'pretty' and 'nice' and a

conventional style of living has been created by them which
is out of touch with the power of the myths in which these
rituals began. 'Christmas', thinks the narrator, 'is such a nice
festival; we always have a turkey dinner with plum pudding,
and so do all our friends' — while the custom of lighting lamps
on Diwali, although kept up 'because the children like it so
much ... is not in keeping with modern times' (p. 172). Similarly
we hear from the head of the 'department', whose wife is about
to dance to her lover's singing and drumming, that 'Government
is always telling us that we must preserve and foster our
cultural heritage' (p. 183).

This dilution that substitutes for the real thing is made
nonsense of when the real thing actually materialises in the
narrator's living-room:

> Govind sat on the floor by the *dholak* and began to beat it
> with his fingers and sing, while Lekha danced. He sang:
>
> > 'Bring, O bring, my beloved unto me!
> > O what ecstasy shall I knew with him always on the couch
> > strewn with flowers, in the white radiance of the moon.
> > O my friend, beautiful as a bird! I languish with love for
> > my lord.
> > What is this happening to me? Come, O friend!
> > Ask my lord to come to me, so that flower-adorned. I may
> > dance, sing and play with him. Why this delay?'
>
> And that was what Lekha danced ... 'I languish with love
> for my lord,' said her fingers. 'What is this happening to me?'
> said her eyes and her lips. The ankle-bells rang out as she
> stamped her feet. 'O what ecstasy shall I know with him
> always!' Govind flung back his head so that one could see
> the movement in his throat as he sang; his long brown
> fingers danced on the drum, his whole body swayed; he was
> smiling all the time so that his teeth and eyes flashed. 'Like
> a god,' she had said ... and now she was worshipping him
> with her dance. (pp. 183-4)

Lekha's dancing and Govind's singing at once express and
transcend their physical relationship. At that moment and for
the brief period of their love, the power in old myths seems
to reassert itself, giving the reader an opportunity to catch the
author's sense of what constitutes the true, unchanging India

and what — the scuffling for priority among the civil servants
and their wives, the cushions and table-runners, the 'nice', the
'pretty', the 'modern' and 'advanced', the official lip-service paid
to the classical arts — is merely transient, conventional and
worthless.

Although there are many portraits of Indian men of 'culture'
and politicians of consequence in Ruth Jhabvala's stories
(notably those of the Raja Sahib in "Desecration" and of the
Minister in "Rose Petals"), her character-study of a vain literary
personality in "The Award"[13] takes pride of place among them.
A young university lecturer preparing to write a Ph.D. thesis
on developments in Indian writing since Independence
interviews Dev Prakash, 'the Tagore of today', on the morning
of what later turns out to be the day he is awarded the Sahitya
Akademi prize for his poetry. There are many contrasts in the
story, some of them social: while the young lecturer supports
his family of four children, a mother and a widowed aunt on
Rs. 350 a month, the home of Dev Prakash's sister Usha in
which the interview takes place is opulently furnished. The
young man has not been able to afford new clothes for three
years, and he is working for his Ph.D. to qualify himself for
a position as senior lecturer in which he will earn a salary of
Rs. 650, rising to Rs. 900. Everything else — even literature,
to which he is genuinely responsive — must yield priority to
his need to better his prospects in order to survive. In contrast,
Usha's mind moves on clothes and party-giving. She ignores
her brother's visitor completely:

> There was nothing studied about the way she ignored the
> existence of the young man; his insignificance was too real
> for her to have to take up an attitude about it. (p. 48)

This is the background for Ruth Jhabvala's ironic study of
Dev Prakash, an amusing mixture of self-consequence and
self-deception. His self-image as described by him (and later
by his mistress, Aruna) to the young man is continuously
contrasted with his memories of the twenty-five years he has
spent in self-imposed 'exile' in London. Dev Prakash presents
himself as a patriotic, self-sacrificing, sensitive soul, but the
reality is that of a plump, self-indulgent poseur possessed of
a (very) minor talent, who has been quick to leap upon the
bandwagon of literary London's fads and fashions. The narrative

moves back and forth over a time-span of twenty-five years, and with each 'flash-back', the middle-aged poet's pretensions to greatness are gently pared away.

'Whatever I have written, whatever little I may have achieved, my inspiration has always been: India'. Who repaid him by ignoring him, wasting him, passing him over. For twenty-five years he had been what he called in exile and even now that he had come home, he felt more exiled than ever. (p. 45)

Asked to outline his position 'in regard to other Indian writers of today', Dev Prakash (who has evidently written nothing since Independence) makes a virtue of his sterility — 'Of course, I have always been something of an odd man out' (p. 46). He calls himself 'a poor scribbler', but has always enjoyed comfort and security. While in London,

the quaintly untidy rooms he had rented in Hampstead had not betrayed the handsome allowance that was sent to him every quarter from his share of the family business. (p. 47).

In contrast, the young man interviewing him in his sister's luxurious house is 'a poor scribbler'. Dev Prakash does not mention that his poem, "My Country is a Rose in my Heart" is derived from Yeats, as its title instantly informs the reader. Instead, he declares that throughout his years of exile 'there was this Ache' ... 'an unhealing wound in the heart' (pp. 48-9). His thoughts and memories, however, put this romantic sentimentality into proper perspective:

Plump and sensuous in the tight-fitting Indian clothes he wore, with his deep dark eyes in which one could read, if one wanted to, all the sufferings of the East, he was always a success with English women; and his patriotic sentiments, which he enunciated in a low, soft voice vibrating with feeling, woke a warm glow of indignation against oppression in all the right-thinking advanced circles in which he moved. (pp. 48-9)

His companion of those days, Isabel 'a handsome no-nonsense woman with an Oxford degree who wrote sensitive novels about personal relationships' had called the poem "gooey" (p. 49); amusingly, Dev Prakash feels that her opinion of it betrayed a 'lack of depth in her', a 'failure to feel passionately'. The poem

is considered 'beautiful' by the young man (in whose life there
is little beauty to provide a criterion) and 'moving' by Usha, who
has (like Prema in *Amrita*) a 'well of feeling in her to respond
to the profound and the poetic', not to mention the 'tear-
wringing emotion' that had moved her brother to write the poem
pp. 49-50).

His patriotism is similarly shown to have been little more than
mere self-indulgence:

> 'Sometimes people asked me,' Dev Prakash said, 'how can
> you, an Indian, bear to live in exile from your country? There
> was only one answer I could give.' His passionate eyes gazed
> impressively into the distance as he quoted this answer: 'It
> is better than to live as a slave in one's own land'. Though
> this was no longer an answer he could give after
> Independence. He had got so used to England and his cosy,
> shabby rooms in Hampstead, it had been difficult to leave.
> (p. 50)

After Independence he had discovered that his friends and
admirers 'no longer regarded him in the same light. There had
even seemed to be, though of course no one had ever spoken
it, an undermining undercurrent of why doesn't he go home?'
(p. 50). Gently, but mercilessly, Ruth Jhabvala strips away
pretension from both the man and from the quality of his mind
and inspiration. Dev Prakash is a counterfeit patriot, as he is
only a counterfeit poet. His heroic roles are amusingly undercut
by his affectionate Indian admirers:

> 'He has suffered in his life for his country and his art', said
> Aruna. 'Just think, for twenty-five years he lived in exile
> —twenty-five years, because he could not bear to be a slave!'
> 'The English winters are very cold', said Usha. 'Every year
> he suffered from chilblains'. (p. 53)

Dev Prakash is longing for the award, and his affectation of
unconcern is transparent. As they drink to his success, after
he has been officially informed that he has won it at last, he is

> vibrating with fulfilment ... (He had never felt in England)
> this oneness, this love, this union of spirit. (p. 59)

Yet all that has gone before proves that there is very little in
the room of all that he 'feels'. The young man, though he talks

conventionally of his pleasure at being present on such an auspicious occasion, has his sights fixed on the completion of his thesis and the obtaining of a higher salary (pp. 58-9). Usha is thinking of buying a new Banaras silk sari for Aruna's celebration garden party (p. 58), and Aruna's delight and pleasure at her hero's success is based on a mistaken view of his worth as a writer (p. 58) — his own view, which she has adopted, and now repeats:

> He is such a poet, such a fine soul, he sees everything different from ordinary people. (p. 58)

In contrast with "The Award", with its picture of wealth and upper-class ease and privilege, is "A Loss of Faith"[14], a tale of defeated principle and thwarted hope in a lower middle-class setting. The story concerns the efforts of a salesman to build an orderly, quiet and respectable life for himself and his family, only to be thwarted by forces over which he has no control: the tradition according to which, as head of a household, he must welcome and support aged relatives and an idle elder brother; the marriage arranged for him by his mother, in which he has no real knowledge of his wife's character to begin with and no control over it when he does; and his own quiet, submissive personality and habit of obedience to what is socially considered proper. He is reduced to a position that is almost unbearable:

> There was a new why in his life that he wanted to put to someone. He could not understand how things had come to this pass: he had always worked so hard; had wanted to keep everything decent and orderly and different from what it had been in his uncle's house. Yet, in spite of his efforts, the same disorder there had been in his uncle's house, the same sense of too much and too violent a humanity, had come to swallow his own life. He felt as if everything was closing in on him — the Muslim wives fighting upstairs, the crippled astrologer and, in his own room, the monstrous shapes of his mother, his wife, his grandmother, the shrill voices, the quarrels, dirt and poverty and moneylenders who had to be cajoled. He remembered how his uncle had clutched at his head and screamed: 'They are eating me up!' and that was how he was feeling himself, devoured and eaten. (p. 40)

Deprived of order at home, the shop in which he works begins
to seem 'like a deep source of orderliness and virtue, of
Goodness and Truth' (p. 39). Even the salary-scale 'was to him
like a law of God or Nature, incontrovertible' (p. 41). But even
this is rapidly taken from him. Used to accepting other people's
opinions, he begins to accept the view of life put forward by
Vijay, his derelict elder brother:

> 'The world sucks the juice out of us and then spits us out
> like an empty, shrivelled skin', said Vijay ... It was so, he
> knew now; he had always worked and hoped hard, but had
> got nothing. (p. 42)

He loses faith and joy in his work. When he asks the proprietor
of the shop in which he has worked for so long for a rise in
salary, he is refused. His one act of rebellion against the life
that has cheated him (and the proprietor, who is as remote
from him in the shop as God seems remote from him in his
life) is an unpremeditated act that surprises Ram Kumar
himself. He drops the wax doll that is the shop's model, which
he had hitherto loved to dress and adorn, in fragments on the
floor. He finds himself

> almost enjoying this little unexpected moment, though he
> would no doubt have enjoyed it more if he had not known
> that the cost of a new doll would be taken, month by month,
> out of his salary. (p. 44)

The shop, the proprietor and the doll have occupied in Ram
Kumar's life the respective positions of temple, God and image.
As the experience of Ram Kumar illustrates, man is driven by
instincts and deep compulsions he cannot explain to create the
conditions in which he lives, and often to destroy them: he is
the plaything, not of fate, but of tradition and his own
conditioned personality. Ruth Jhabvala has ironically named
her characters — 'Ram Kumar' (Prince Rama, the Indian hero-
King), 'Vijay' (victory) — in a story about subjection and spiritual
defeat.

In her story "The Widow"[15], Ruth Jhabvala uses satiric irony
to expose the social conventions of traditional India that can
often destroy the human personality, in ways permitted and
sanctified by time and religious custom. Durga has been
married as a very young girl to a man much older than herself,

and now a widow, has been trained by her late husband to
stand up to her relatives and live the independent life of a
property-owner. She has had no sexual fulfilment in marriage,
and her memories of her husband are of his kindness and
generosity to her, not of love —indeed, she recalls vividly

> his old-man smell, and his dried legs, when she had
> massaged them, with the useless rag of manhood flopping
> against his thigh. (p. 61)

Widowed, Durga lives as she pleases, growing 'plump and
smooth with it' (p. 62). She rules her elder relatives by the
power of her money and her independence, and appears to have
won the battle that took place after her husband's death as
to whether or not she was to be condemned to 'that perpetual
mourning, perpetual expiation, which was the proper lot of
widows' (p. 62). But Durga feels that 'somehow, somewhere,
she had been short-changed' (p. 63). She suffers from moods
of depression, and this weakness is used to advantage by an
old aunt, Bhuaji, who introduces her to the cult of Krishna
as a means of filling the gap in her life. The concept of Krishna
as lover appeals powerfully to the sexually deprived Durga, who
becomes 'dreamy and withdrawn' (p. 66) and far more tolerant
of her relatives than she had formerly been. When the tenants
in the upper part of Durga's house give notice and her relatives
plan to move in, however, they are disappointed. Durga is not
so dreamy that she is going to sacrifice a regular monthly
income: and Mr Puri, his wife, two daughters and a son move in.

Disappointed by Krishna's failure to come to her in any
satisfying way, Durga focuses her unfulfilled desires on the boy
upstairs whose name, Govind, recalls Krishna's incarnation as
a cowherd and lover of milk-maids. She rationalises her feelings,
and makes out that in Govind she sees the son her late
husband's impotence had robbed her of, but her response is
clearly to the young man's male virility:

> His teeth were large and white, his hair sprang from a point
> on his forehead. Everything about him was young and fresh
> and strong — even his smell, which was that of a young
> animal full of sap and sperm. (p. 74)

Durga begins to feed Govind and to give him money, always
telling herself she is acting like a mother to him (pp. 73-4).

Mrs Puri takes advantage of Durga's fondness for Govind to avoid paying the rent (p. 75). The relatives regard their patroness's growing friendship with the Puris as 'both ominous and unnatural' (p. 75). Bhuaji steps in to mend matters, and by a devious course of action that reveals her creator's close observation of life within the women's quarter of an Indian joint-family, succeeds in separating Durga from the Puris and in persuading her to get rid of them as tenants (pp. 76-82). Durga, for whom life's promise has ended, and whose personality is very near disintegration, spites the memory of her dead husband by giving away her silk saris, her jewellery and her cash-box to Bhuaji and her relatives, who now move in.

The last paragraph of this story provides a memorable example of Ruth Jhabvala's early satiric style. Durga has been driven into a state of mental breakdown by the circumstances of her life and the deliberate scheming of her relatives. This is now, through the operation of irony, 'rationalised' and sanctified as being in keeping with what is right and proper behaviour for Indian widows:

> The relatives were glad that Durga had at last come round and accepted her lot as a widow. They were glad for her sake. There was no other way for widows but to lead humble, bare lives; it was for their own good. For if they were allowed to feed themselves on the pleasures of the world, then they fed their own passions too, and that which should have died in them with the deaths of their husbands would fester and boil and overflow into sinful channels. Oh yes, said the relatives, wise and knowing, nodding their heads, our ancestors knew what they were doing when they laid down these rigid rules for widows; and though nowadays perhaps, in these modern times, one could be a little more lenient — for instance, no one insisted that Durga should shave her head — still, on the whole, the closer one followed the old traditions, the safer and the better it was. (p. 83)

The portrait of Durga in "The Widow" might usefully be compared with Bibhutibhusan Banerji's treatment of Indian widowhood in his novel *Pather Panchali*, where in the greater space afforded by the novel genre, the life of Indian women is viewed in three stages — girlhood, wifehood and widowhood — and both early marriage and the treatment of widows explicitly and movingly condemned. Ruth Jhabvala's more oblique presentation creates in Durga a picture of a warm human personality first deprived, then destroyed, by the unchangeable circumstances of Indian life.

In the story "Suffering Women"[16], which belongs to a later peiod than the four already considered in this chapter, plot is less tightly structured than before, and the author's interest appears to be focused on conveying the quality of her characters' feelings and experience rather than on shaping these things to a rigid pattern of cause and effect. The story satirises the unreal values and concepts purveyed by the Indian popular film industry through the experiences of two middle-aged actresses who are close friends:

> Anjana and Sultana ... had both played heroines in the same kind of second-grade films; both had been very popular among taxi-drivers, wrestlers and small boys queueing up for the four-anna seats on Saturday mornings. Sultana, with her tigress eyes and lithe figure, had played bold, manly parts and had been cheered out of thousands of throats as she galloped over the Khyber Pass, clutching in her arms the infant king whom she had rescued in the nick of time from his black-bearded murderers. Anjana, on the other hand, all soft bosom and melting eyes, had been made love to in trellissed bowers and danced ankledeep in meadows of white primroses. Offscreen, they were both equally romantic and had been remarkable for the number and intensity of their love affairs. (p. 172)

Anjana, now retired from her career as a movie idol, has an elderly lover, Thakkur Sahib, and a pretty teen-age daughter named Kiku. Her relationship with Thakkur Sahib is still most enjoyable, in contrast with the rather unsatisfactory one Kiku has with her somewhat effeminate boy-friend Rahul, and the very unsatisfactory ones Sultana has with a succession of young lovers. Ruth Jhabvala's comic portrait of Sultana (whose apartment is continually being redecorated by a lover who plans to become an interior decorator: 'He says he needs the practice', p. 168) is softened by compassion for the vulnerability of an ageing, yet passionate woman:

> 'Well, what can I do? He's so young, so lovely. Do you know

he doesn't have one single hair on his chest? Smooth,
smooth, like satin. Velvet,' she said in a voice like velvet.
(p. 184)

Sultana's unhappiness and the constant sight of a private
nursing home opposite her flat are permanent reminders to
Anjana of the 'terrible things (that) can happen' (p. 174).
Thakkur Sahib's description of his meeting with a formerly
well-known and popular star named Tara Bai who now 'looks
like an old beggar-woman' (p. 176) deepens her sense of
foreboding, and his casual admission, 'I was glad to get rid of
her' (p. 177) increases the sense of insecurity which, despite
occasional moments of 'bliss', Anjana will always feel. Personal
relationships — of a kind — provide her only refuge, and with
all their limitations, it is only Thakkur Sahib and Sultana who
give her some sense of 'safety' and of friendship.

The story "A Spiritual Call"[17] has close links with an
'ashram' sequence in the film BOMBAY TALKIE, in which Lucia
Lane briefly tries on the role of religious devotee before
submitting herself to 'fate' and her passion for Vikram. Daphne
is a Londoner who comes to India to seek a guru she has met
in Britain and 'undergo an intensive course of spiritual
regeneration' (p. 92). Her guide, whose name and personality
Ruth Jhabvala was later to build into the character of Swamiji
in her novel *A New Dominion*, is cheerful and serene,
immaculately dressed in cream-coloured silk, his beard and
shoulder-length hair shining 'in well-oiled waves'. He was not,
notes the narrator, a handsome man, 'yet there was an aura
of beauty about him ... due ... mostly of course to the radiance
of his personality' (p. 94). Ruth Jhabvala's narrative tone,
ostensibly straightforward, takes on ironic colouring when the
Swamiji of this story is described:

Swamiji had a very simple and beautiful message to the
world. It was only this: meditate; look into yourself and so,
by looking, cleanse yourself; harmony and happiness will
inevitably follow. This philosophy, simple as its end-product
appeared to be, he had forged after many, many solitary years
of thought and penance in some icy Himalayan retreat. Now
he had come down into the world of men to deliver his
message, planning to return to his mountain solitude as soon
as his task here was achieved. It might, however, take longer

than he had reckoned on, for men were stubborn and tended to be blind to Truth. (p. 96)

Daphne's adoration of her guru conquers all her scruples, her doubts regarding his previous career (pp. 87-8) and, amusingly, even her Oxford-trained revulsion at his poor written expression (p. 98). She becomes Swamiji's secretary, and is on the way to becoming as much his slave as Evie is the other Swamiji's slave in *A New Dominion*. Conflicts develop between Daphne and Helga, a German blonde in her thirties, who accuses Daphne of 'flirting' with their guru. But all is 'resolved' in the end. Daphne, wearing the sari Swamiji has given her and tripping over it sees Helga wearing just such another, and thinks *she* looks 'ridiculous' (p. 114). She has lost contact with reality — or else, is now on a 'higher' spiritual plane:

> She was completely happy to be going to California and anywhere else he might want her to accompany him. (p. 114)

"A Spiritual Call" belongs to that group of Ruth Jhabvala's stories in which 'her confident double-edged irony exposes with fine impartiality the neuroses of those who are seeking solace and the hypocrisy of those who are offering it'[18].

Dr. Meenakshi Mukherjee, whose perceptive analysis of Ruth Jhabvala's 'swami' stories I have just quoted, has also noted the existence in this author's *oeuvre* of 'numerous case studies of Europeans under the Indian sun'.[19] In "The Aliens"[20] Ruth Jhabvala presented the first of her Westerners to wilt in the heat of a Delhi summer. Peggy is the middle-class English wife of a young Indian car salesman, Dev. They live with his brother's family in a large house run, as in the days when Dev's and Suraj's father was still alive, by their mother. The story, one of Ruth Jhabvala's most vivid evocations of turbulent Indian family life, is told from Peggy's point of view: that of someone puzzled, irritated, and beginning to be seriously disturbed by the experience of living in India, but battling gamely on, clinging to principles and attitudes learned in another culture. Peggy is treated ironically, her inward comparisons sometimes sounding either absurdly complacent or somewhat unreasonable. For example, when she comes in to breakfast, neither her mother-in-law nor her sister-in-law

had had her bath yet, and consequently both looked

somewhat bedraggled, with their thick long hair coming down
and the crumpled saris in which they had slept all night.
Peggy, on the other hand, already looked crisp and smart
in her printed house-dress and with her sensible short hair
neatly brushed. (p. 84)

When she comments to Dev, 'Why do they always have to
quarrel and shout so loud?' Dev asks with surprise, 'Who?'
(p. 87). In contrast with the uninhibited display of passion by
Peggy's Indian relatives are her memories of home and England:

No one at home ever fought like that; sometimes, of course,
they had their little differences of opinion — especially on
washing-days, Mum did tend to get a bit out of temper then
— but they never forgot themselves and shouted the way
they shouted in this house. She was thankful that Mum and
Daddy couldn't hear them, they wouldn't know what to think.
Sometimes she herself didn't know what to think. (p. 87)

Dev's family and its endless noisy quarrels are presented in
a broadly comic manner, the noise exaggerated by the fact that
the reader is aware that it is falling upon Peggy's already
irritated ears.

It is interesting that Peggy and Dev have, despite their
different nationalities, been brought up on similar social
prejudices. She thinks shouting and losing one's temper betrays
low social origins his mother thinks that manual labour tells
the same story. The source of social 'disgrace' is different, but
the conviction that such 'disgrace' exists is amusingly shared.
Similarly, Peggy resents her mother-in-law's control over Dev's
will and his eating habits, but her dream of a future away from
this house merely substitutes her will for that of her mother-
in-law:

She thought wistfully again of a little place all to themselves.
She would make a lovely home. She would do all their own
cooking and have a servant only for the cleaning. She would
cook roast-meat and Yorkshire pudding and sausage and
mash and treacle pudding ... (p. 103)

Ruth Jhabvala shows little sympathy for Peggy's insularity, but
her predicament is treated with compassion. As she writes her
letter to 'Mum and Daddy', keeping her frustration and growing

depression bravely out of it, the intensity of her feelings and
the dogged way in which she is trying to keep them under
control are given full value:

> She wrote with her back very straight and her lips very tight
> and pressing her nib so hard that it made little holes in the
> paper.
>   She didn't know this, but she looked at that moment very
> much like her Mum had looked twenty years ago (during the
> war, with Daddy away in the army) queueing up for the
> rations or carrying in the coal on a rainy English winter
> morning. (p. 106)

Peggy's heroism, unvalued of course by everyone around her,
is provoked by the ceaseless domestic friction in the midst of
which she must live. Ruth Jhabvala's depiction on the Indian
extended family at home comes close to caricature in this story,
though the exaggeration is in some measure justified because
it is Peggy's sensibility that registers it. In the process there
develop exchanges rich in comedy and clues as to what is going
on in the minds of those involved:

> Sarla, leaning on the table with her elbow, her hair coming
> down over her face, never looked up except occasionally to
> throw dark glances at her husband; which he ignored with
> such insulting ease that soon she was throwing out more
> explicit hints: 'All morning my head has been hurting but
> who is there to ask are you well, are you ill, who is there
> to care what happens to me?'
>   The mother-in-law stroked Suraj's shoulder and said
> sweetly, 'Eat, son, eat in peace', though he hardly needed
> this encouragement. He leaned forward and helped himself
> to pickle. 'Poor boy, how hard he has been working all
> morning in the office'.
>   'Today we got our consignment of station wagons', he said.
> 'They have been delayed four months'.
>   'Four months!' echoed the mother with exaggerated
> sympathy. 'So much trouble — trouble and worry, that is
> how it is in business'.
>   'And that girl with the fat legs, she is also trouble and
> worry?' Sarla said.
>   'Children who don't eat are taken away at night by the

jackals', warned the Ayah. (pp. 97-8)

Later, after the family quarrel, there is silence from the bedroom occupied by Suraj and Sarla, and Peggy knows from experience the reason for this. Her own inhibitions emerge in her disapproving thoughts and prurient speculations:

> She knew it was wicked of her, but she often thought of them lying together on the bed. Sometimes, when they came out of their room, she could see in their faces what they had been doing in there; and Sarla often had marks on her. It made her feel quite sick to think of them. (p. 103)

When Sarla exhibits her sexual fulfilment to her mother-in-law, that lady's reaction is amusingly like Peggy's:

> 'Do up your blouse', she said crossly, 'have you no shame, with the servants walking about?' She sank down on the edge of the bed, slow and heavy like an old woman. Peggy had often noticed that, after Sarla had been with Suraj and looked the way she looked now, her mother-in-law turned herself into an old woman. She sat and sighed —'Such heat, it is too much for me to bear'. (p. 105)

This is an early instance of the Delhi heat being used by Ruth Jhabvala as a symbol of amorous passion: the mother-in-law, earlier scornful of Sarla's complaints about the heat (Sarla wants to get Suraj to accompany her on holiday in the hills, away from the lures of an overly attractive girl in his office), now — at the sight of Sarla's exposed bosom — cannot bear the heat either. Peggy's own irritations begin to seem unbearable as she gazes out of the window at 'the garden, the street beyond it, everything ... dead and still under the white-hot sun' (p. 87).

Peggy's pale skin is considered a drawback by her Indian relations, and her 'trimness' is a source of great amusement to the physically well-endowed women of the household. Her taste in clothes — 'coffee lace and taffeta skirt' ... 'pale greens and powder blues and ... dresses with Peter-Pan collars and little bows on them' (p. 93) — is too restrained to do herself or the family credit, and her frugal eating habits are considered a source of deprivation (of sex) to her husband and (of children) to his family (p. 94). There are connections between "The

Aliens" and another tale published in 1968, "The Young Couple", in which Naraian, like Dev, is very much under his mother's influences. Under increasing pressure, he gives up the flat he shares with his European wife Cathy, and they agree to move into the family mansion. In these stories, as in *The Nature of Passion*, the extended family is seen as octopus like, pulling people in from the periphery to the centre, there to swallow all that is divergent or individual in them, making them part of the one organism. Nonconformists are not encouraged, and in "The Aliens" it is clear that Peggy's differences in appearance and opinion are being tolerated only until she can be persuaded to abandon them.

A feature of great interest in this story is Ruth Jhabvala's study of the mother-in-law, who binds her sons to her by indulging their weaknesses, especially in the matter of food. There is a contrast here with Peggy's mother, who had been 'firm', and whose memory Peggy constantly invokes to gain strength to cope with her daily trials:

> ... good old Mum, who never complained, even when the waterpipes froze and she had to climb up in the loft and unfreeze them with hot-water bottles and her fingers all swollen with the chilblains. (p. 100)

Peggy's knowledge of England is very limited, and this limited view she applies amusingly to all that she sees, e.g., 'But he had been to England, he had had a nice education and ought to know better' (p. 101); or, 'He was a good boy — a nice steady type, with clean habits, as Mum and Doreen's mother and aunt Elsie and everyone had said; almost like one of our own boys, even if he was an Indian' (p. 102). Her family is as insular and limited in its outlook as Dev's, and the conflict between the two points of view is more comic than tragic because it is pitched at such a low level. However, the reader's sympathies are on the whole with Peggy rather than with her in-laws, partly because of her courage and determination, partly because it is only too obvious that defeat and not triumph awaits her in the future.

In "A Birthday in London"[21] a group of German Jews who have emigrated to Britain celebrate the birthday of Sonia Wolff, one of their number. The conversation revolves around the old days in Germany before the war and the Nazi regime, the

crudeness of British Jews, and the difficulty of passing on to
the children some sense of 'who they are'. They talk of travel,
but as is the case with every other subject, this has a bitter
undertone:

> Some people travel for pleasure ... for kicks ... and some
> travel because ... they are kicked. (p. 135)

They appear to be living a half-life, despite their brand-new
British citizenship: 'Yes, there we were all different people'
(p. 128). Eating *apfel strudel* and drinking coffee is part of the
celebratory ritual. Tragedy is passed over by common consent:
Sonia's late father had been, we are informed, 'a large, healthy,
handsome man who had loved good living and had died at
Auschwitz' (p. 127). Sonia breaks down when she reflects that
had fate willed otherwise, her son Werner might now have been
director of the family firm, and her daughter Lilo might have
enjoyed a delightful, indulged girlhood like her own instead of
knowing only the 'hard work in the Kibbutz' (p. 137). Werner's
joke about it being 'time to move on, Werner' upsets her since
it calls up a history of nomadic wandering. But the last word
is one of hope and determined cheerfulness:

> What have you achieved in your life? And then I answer
> myself I have survived, I am still alive, and this is already
> a success story. (p. 138)

"A Birthday in London" is the only published story in which
Ruth Jhabvala describes the life of expatriate German Jews in
the London she knew as a child. In later stories and novels
such as "The Man and His Dog", *A Backward Place* and "An
Indian Citizen", she depicts groups of expatriate Europeans in
India clinging together for comfort and mutual support. Her
own history of expatriation gives her studies of 'seekers' such
as the narrator in *Heat and Dust* and 'travellers' like Lee in
A New Dominion a special urgency and interest. It also
contributes, no doubt, to the sympathetic understanding
displayed by this author in stories such as "Miss Sahib", "The
Aliens", "The Young Couple" and "An Experience of India".

  The friends and acquaintances who celebrate Sonia Wolff's
birthday have been thrown together by the circumstances of
their departure from Germany and their arrival and shared
experiences in Britain. This, perforce, must substitute for the

Jewish family, the original members of which have been lost
to Auschwitz or Belsen, or are being scattered by the demands
of 'Israel' or of new professions and occupations. Beneath the
reminiscences that gloss over the horrors of loss, is the theme
of survival. The story explains the intense interest with which
Ruth Jhabvala draws the Punjabi survivors of Partition in
Amrita, her first novel, and expands on the subject in *The
Nature of Passion*, her second. It also sheds some additional
light on her compassion for the helpless individuals who are
moved hither and thither in her fiction by the whims of powerful
and influential men. Her exploration of the theme of unfettered
freedom in its Indian aspect of confidence in futurity, assurance
that God will provide, is informed by this personal involvement
and sympathy. She seeks there perhaps a solution to the
perennial problem of the individual caught up in circumstances
for which he is not responsible, and over which he has no
control.

Two amusing studies on the theme of self-deception are "A
Course of English Studies"[22] and "In Love with a Beautiful
Girl".[23] Nalini, the young heroine of the first story, comes from
an upper class family that is in the habit of skating gracefully
over Indian social realities:

> They were all great readers, and Nalini grew up on the
> classics. They were particularly fond of the English
> romantics, and of the great Russians. Sometimes they joked
> and said they were themselves like Chekhov characters. They
> ... lived gracious lives in a big house in Delhi, but were always
> longing for the great capitals of Europe, London, Paris, Rome
> — where culture flourished and people were advanced and
> sophisticated. (p. 107)

However it is not social inequality that concerns Ruth Jhabvala
in this story[24] but the personality of Nalini herself, and her
experiences in the British midlands university to which she goes
to study English literature:

> What she had (even if she didn't at the time know it) come
> to England for, what she expected from the place, what
> everything she had read had promised her, was love and a
> lover.
>   A girl in such a mood is rarely disappointed. (p. 110)

The dry ironic tone of the last sentence (so reminiscent of Jane Austen when writing of her sillier heroines) sets the mood for what will inevitably follow. Nalini's romance with one of her lecturers begins, despite the fact that she is a mediocre student and he is burdened with a wife and several unkempt children. Together they shop at supermarkets and picnic furtively in a disused shed off dry Marie biscuits, providing an ironic background to all of which are constant allusions to luxurious picnics in India and the vanished glories of the Augustan Age (which happens to be Dr Norman Greaves' special field). There is also the sobering experience of Mrs Crompton, Nalini's landlady, whose divorce from her husband stands as a warning of what might await Nalini and her lover in the future.

Nalini sees Mrs Crompton's feelings about her husband as 'living ... passion, it was the way a woman should be' (p. 125). Inspired by her landlady's story of an interview with the 'other woman', the romantic Nalini goes 'to call on Estelle Greaves' (p. 126), inviting her creator's ironic amusement at the formality, in the circumstances, of a social 'call'. Her resemblance to Shakuntala of *Esmond in India* emerges in a splendidly comic passage that follows, when she describes this visit to Norman:

> 'Why did you do it?' he said in a puzzled, tortured way. 'Whatever possessed you?'
> 'I wanted to clear the air', she said grandly; and added, even more grandly, 'I can't live with a lie'.
> He gave a shout of exasperation; then he asked 'Is that the sort of language you used with her?'
> 'Oh, with her'. Nalini shrugged and pouted. 'She's just impossible to talk to. Whenever you try and start on anything serious with her, she jumps up and says the shepherd's pie is burning. Oh Norman, Norman, how do you stand it? How can you live with her and in such an atmosphere?' (p. 127)

The affair ends, and Nalini writes to her loving mother in Delhi that people in England do not have 'hearts (that) are open to each other' (p. 135). She is back with the Romantics, she adds, but feels — accompanying the comment with three exclamation marks — that they must have been Indians in a previous birth.

For Norman Greaves, the exotic Nalini has seemed 'a vision and a glory'. For Richard, a young Englishman in Delhi in "In

Love with a Beautiful Girl", his beloved Ruchira embodies the passion of Indian music, art and sculpture. Nalini sees Norman as a cultivated Augustan, Ruchira sees Richard as her passport to a smart and interesting social life. The two youthful heroines, though by no means copies of one another, create romantic auras about themselves and their bemused English lovers. Limited themselves, they are also totally self-absorbed and do not for a moment consider their effect on the lives of the other people around them. There is comic disappointment all round: the reality is so very different from their romantic imaginings. A further comic point is made when Nalini in her annoyance forgets grand gestures for a typically middle-class Indian row:

'What did you want? Some great seething scene of passion and renunciation, such as Indians like to indulge in ?' (p. 129)

Norman asks this question, and a scene is exactly what he gets:

'Don't dare say anything bad against my country!'
'I'm not, for God's sake, saying anything bad against your country!'
'Yes, you are. And it's your wife who has taught you. I could see at one glance that she was anti-Indian'.
'Please don't let's talk about my wife any more'.
'Yes, we will talk about her. I'll talk about her as much as I like. What do you think, I'm some fallen woman that I'm not allowed to speak your wife's name? Give me my pins'. She plucked them from out of his hand and stabbed them angrily into her coil of hair. 'And I'll tell you something more. From now on everything is going to change. I'm tired of this hole and corner business. You must get a divorce'.
'A splendid idea. You're not forgetting that I have four children?'
'You can have ten for all I care. You must leave that woman! It is she or I. Choose'.
Norman got up and let himself out of the hut. At the door he turned and said in a quiet voice 'You know I'm no good at these grand scenes'. (p. 129)

Two stories in Ruth Jhabvala's fourth collection are extended analyses of the innermost feelings of two women about their own personalities and their right to privacy. "In the

Mountains"[25] concerns the way of life of an Indian woman
from a conventional middle-class family (they spend their time,
according to her, in 'Eating ... (and) making money', p. 27) who
has chosen to isolate herself in a small house in the mountains.
Her gentle, conventional mother is upset by her daughter's
individualism, but does not succeed in persuading her to
abandon her mountain eyrie. A link with *Heat and Dust* is
evident in the theme of self-chosen isolation, and also in the
way agility in mountain climbing is used as a symbol for
spiritual freedom.'Doctor Sahib', Pritam's rather disreputable
companion in her mountain life, is 'as nimble as herself' in
clambering up and down the mountains on which they live.
In contrast, Bobby (her associate of an earlier, romantic period
in her life) is 'in very poor condition' (p. 40).

"Desecration"[26] is perhaps the most powerful story in this
final collection, and centres upon the reaction of a sensitive
and passionate young woman to a triple invasion: of her body
and mind by her brutal and violent lover; of her heart by a love
that is like a disease which 'would get worse and pass through
many stages before it was finished with her' (p. 201); and of
her privacy by the gossips in the township neighbouring the
mansion in which she lives with her cultivated, elderly husband,
the Raja Sahib. At the end of the story, when Sofia is nearing
the point at which she can endure her emotional turmoil no
longer and will end it in suicide, her feelings are further agitated
by the realisation that the husband she has been deceiving is
living in his private hell of undisclosed sickness (p. 202) and
that

> there had never been anyone in the world who looked into
> her eyes the way he did, with such love but at the same time
> with a tender respect that would not reach farther into her
> than was permissible between two human beings. (p. 203)

And finally, "The Housewife", a story in which is reflected
the inevitable conflict that arises between a woman's artistry
and her domestic and personal life. Shakuntala, a loving faithful
wife, begins after twenty-five years of contented domesticity to
take singing lessons and finds that they become more important
to her than anything else in her world. Her affections have
hitherto been tranquilly shared among her husband, her
daughter Manju and her new young grandchild, and indeed

she loved all of them, but she could not deny to herself that her singing meant even more to her than her feelings as wife and mother and grandmother. She was unable to explain this, she tried not to think of it. But it was true that with her music she lived in a region where she felt most truly, most deeply herself. No, not herself, something more and higher than that. By contrast with her singing, the rest of her day, indeed her life, seemed insignificant. She felt this to be wrong but there was no point in trying to struggle against it. Without her hour's practice in the morning, she was as if deprived of food and water and air. (p. 138)

In the appearances and occasional failures to arrive of her singing teacher, and in his varied responses to Shakuntala's progress are reflected the ups and downs, the triumphs and disappointments of the creative experience. Yet this analysis (and perhaps, even, self-analysis) is carefully embedded in a story of ordinary middle-class life, featuring some very ordinary middle-class characters. An interfering aunt, a mercenary daughter, feminine squabbling and the duties of a housewife are all part of the story, but they are in the nature of props, necessary parts of the setting. So is the music-master's wife and the comic by-play of aunt Phuphiji's giving him tea, and make a scene about payments. The core of the story is in the artist's alternating joy and agony as inspiration greets and deserts her:

Shakuntala hardly noticed (Phuphiji and Manju). Her thoughts were day and night elsewhere, and she longed only to be sitting on the roof practising her singing while her teacher listened to her. But nowadays he seemed to be bored with her. He tended to stay for shorter periods, he yawned and became restless and left her before she had finished. When he left her like that, she ceased to sing but continued to sit on the roof by herself; she breathed heavily as if in pain, and indeed her sense of unfulfilment was like pain and stayed with her for the rest of the day. The worst was when he did not turn up at all. This was happening more and more frequently. Days passed and she didn't see him and didn't sing; then he came again — she would step up on the roof in the morning, almost without hope, and there he would be. He had no explanation to offer for his absence, nor did she ask for one. She began straightaway to sing, grateful and happy. (p. 156)

In this story, Ruth Jhabvala blends what is evidently a deeply felt personal testament on the subject of her art with a story of middle-class Indian domestic life. Writing is disguised as music, personal conflict externalised as domestic conflict involving other characters. The music master, despite his very unusual habit of materialising and disappearing is given a typical history (pp. 143-5), and partakes of afternoon tea. "The Housewife" transposes into a modern setting the legendary love of Radha, married milkmaid, for the god Krishna, musician and lover (an earlier version of this story, with younger lovers and a satiric, indirect exposition of a conventional narrator's character, may be seen in the short story, "Lekha"). With its assistance, and with that of her musical metaphor, Ruth Jhabvala explores the implications of an individual's commitment to art, especially the necessary abandonment of domestic concerns and considerations of personal safety or consequence by the woman who responds to the call of this special destiny:

> He entered her at the moment when, the structure of the raga having been expounded, the combination of notes was being played up and down, backwards and forwards, very fast. There was no going back from here, she knew. But who would want to go back, who would exchange this blessed state for any other? (p. 161)

Notes

1. R.P. Jhabvala, quoted by R. Agarwal, op. cit., p. 33.
2. R.P. Jhabvala, *Like Birds, Like Fishes* (John Murray, London: 1963). All references to stories in this collection in this chapter and throughout this book are to the 1963 edition.
3. *The New Yorker, Yale Review, Encounter* and *Kenyan Review.*
4. R.P. Jhabvala, quoted John Pym, op. cit., p. 18.
5. R.P. Jhabvala, *An Experience of India* (John Murray, London: 1966), 1968, 1971. All references to stories in this collection in this chapter and throughout this book are to the 1971 edition.
6. Quoted in Chapter 1 of this book.

7. The experiences of the narrator of "An Experience of India" with regard
    to travel around India appear to be based largely on information
    obtained from other Westerners in India, R. Agarwal reproduces the
    following exchange in his "Interview", op. cit. p. 35:

    R.A. You describe in detail the sexual habits of the Indians. What is
    your source of information in this regard?
    R.J. What a loaded question ... Mostly, the many foreign girls I meet
    who travel around India. They certainly have some very memorable
    experiences in that field here. I haven't yet met one who hasn't,
    in the course of her travels, learned quite a bit about the sexual
    habits of Indians. Often more than she wanted.

8. R.P. Jhabvala, *A Stronger Climate* (John Murray, London: 1968) 1976.
    All references to stories in this collection in this chapter and throughout
    this book are to the 1976 edition. *A Stronger Climate* bears the epigraph
    'They come no longer to conquer but to be conquered'.

9. R.P. Jhabvala, *How I Became a Holy Mother* (John Murray, London:
    1976). All references to stories in this collection in this chapter and
    throughout this book are, with one exception ('The Englishwoman")
    to the British edition. This story, which is not included in the British
    edition, was published by Harper and Row in the American edition
    of the book (also published in 1976), and references to it in ths book
    are therefore to the American edition.

10. "Myself in India", op. cit., p. 8.

11. See note 9 above, on "The Englishwoman".

12. See Chapter XI for further discussion of this story. "Lekha" appears
    in *Like Birds, Like Fishes*, pp. 166-188.

13. *Like Birds, Like Fishes*, pp. 45-59.

14. Ibid., pp. 23-44.

15. Ibid., pp. 60-83.

16. *An Experience of India*, pp. 162-87.

17. *A Stronger Climate*, pp. 90-114.

18. M. Mukherjee, op. cit., p. 5.

19. Ibid.

20. *Like Birds, Like Fishes*, pp. 84-106.

21. Ibid., pp. 132-9.

22. *An Experience of India*, pp. 106-36.

23. *A Stronger Climate*, pp. 11-32.

24. See A. Rutherford and K.H. Petersen, op. cit., p. 375.

    Q: Your novel, *Get Ready for Battle*, was your only attempt to deal
    with India's social problems. Can you explain why this is so?
    A: I don't know why I turned away from it. Maybe because it's just
    so hopeless.
    Q: Do you see any social role for the novelist in India?
    A: No, I don't think that is the role of the novelist. You'd write very
    poor novels if you tried to write social documents in India today.

25. *How I Became a Holy Mother*, pp. 26-47.

26. Ibid., pp. 176-203.

CHAPTER

XI

Writing for film
1960-1982

'I have learnt a lot technically from film'.[1]

Ruth Jhabvala's work in film began in 1960 when she wrote
the screenplay for the Merchant-Ivory cinematic version of her
own novel *The Householder*. Her creative association with
Merchant-Ivory still continues and has produced fourteen films
in the years between 1960 and 1988, seven of which are set
in India or have an Indian background, four in America.
Following are brief synopses:

1963 THE HOUSEHOLDER Prem (Shashi Kapoor), a young,

newly-married teacher, starts out with his inexperienced and homesick wife Indu (Leela Naidu) upon a stage in his life (that of head of a household) through which, according to Hindu tradition, a man passes after he has been a student and before he can consider devoting himself to spiritual concerns. Surrounded by other characters, both Indian and Western, who contrast with them or — still more comically — suggest themselves as models for imitation, Prem and Indu learn to care for each other and, ultimately, to love. The film had Satyajit Ray's assistance as editor, and gave Ruth Jhabvala her first experience as a screenplay writer.

1965 SHAKESPEAREWALLAH A small troupe of dedicated English actors tours India presenting Shakespeare plays in schools, colleges, convents and palaces, until they find their audiences taken from them by the Indian popular film. Like the Maharaja (Utpal Dutt) in whose palace they put on a private command performance, and the street entertainer whose trained monkeys dance for them, there seems to be no place in the new India for the Buckingham Players. The troubled love affair that develops between Lizzie (Felicity Kendal) and a young Indian playboy, Sanju (Shashi Kapoor) and its unsatisfactory conclusion mirror the last days of the British Raj in India. The film was based on the real-life experiences of the Kendal family. Music for it was composed by Satyajit Ray, and among many finely conceived and executed film portraits, Madhur Jaffrey deserves special mention for her interpretation of the role of a posturing, self-centred Indian film actress. The film was awarded the Silver Bear at the Berlin Film Festival of 1965, and the Prize of the Academie du Cinema for the Best Foreign Film of 1968.

1969 THE GURU James Ivory and Ruth Jhabvala collaborated in writing the script for this film about two youthful seekers after oriental wisdom: an English pop idol (Michael York) who comes to India to study the sitar, and a young spiritual seeker (Rita Tushingham) who is in search of the meaning of life. The musician they choose as their spiritual guide (Utpal Dutt) is a confused and temperamental artist who alternately exalts and disappoints them until they abandon their quest in favour of marriage to each other. Madhur Jaffrey and Aparna Sen are amusingly contrasted as the Ustad's hostile and jealous wives, and Subrata Mitra's colour photography captures the beauty of India's land and sea-scapes, with occasional witty explorations of domestic interiors. The music for THE GURU was composed and played by the Indian musician Ustad Vilayat Khan, and adds an extra dimension to a film of unusual loveliness.

1970 BOMBAY TALKIE A visually beautiful, witty satire on India's popular film industry. A Western authoress, Lucia Lane (Jennifer Kendal), whose novel *Consenting Adults* has been turned into a very successful movie, arrives in India in search of new ideas and sensations, which she looks to Vikram, a male film idol (Shashi Kapoor), and Hari Mehta, a poor screen-writer and idealistic poet (Zia Mohyeddin), to provide. She finds only a violent confirmation of the restless, unsatisfactory pattern into which her life has repeatedly fallen. The film's shock ending is at once true to the traditions of Bombay melodrama, and expressive of a disenchanted view of Indian society: the physical, finally fatal struggle of Vikram and Hari symbolizes a cultural and social dislocation that seems beyond repair.

1975 AUTOBIOGRAPHY OF PRINCESS The daughter of an Indian Maharaja (Madhur Jaffrey), living in self-imposed exile in a Kensington flat, runs off archive material, documentary footage and home movies for her own pleasure and that of her guest, Cyril Sahib (James Mason), an elderly Englishman who had been her late father's tutor and afterwards his secretary of state. Their 'tea-party' is an annual affair, a ritual celebration of the late ruler's birthday. It reveals the inner uncertainties of the two main characters, and provides through 'two delicately balanced portraits, a requiem for a life brilliant and decadent'[2]. David Robinson considered the film 'a valuable demonstration that a 60-minut~ chamber work, shot in six days, strict to the unities, moving outside the apartment no further than the stairway and doorstep, can open up much richer worlds than any epic spectacle'[3]. The suggestion of a homosexual attraction exerted by the Princess's father upon his devoted English secretary (subtly interpreted by Mason in what must surely be one of the finest performances of his long career) drew an unexpected reaction from the B.B.C., to which organization AUTOBIOGRAPHY (originally made for American television) was offered. The Head of Purchased Programmes (who as a Swede under-

standably may not share the peculiar and equivocal English
sentiment for royal and imperial India) replied to the
producer, Ismail Merchant: "I really was not very impressed
... I must also say that I thought the role in which you had
cast James Mason embarrassed me on his behalf. So sorry,
but I do not think this is for us. Kind regards".'4

1977 ROSELAND takes the Broadway landmark of Roseland, a
live-music dance hall and 'haven for serious dancers and
lonely hearts of all races and classes'5, as its subject and
setting. Three stories about Roseland habitues are narrated
by a tough-minded dance teacher (Helen Gallagher) and a
suave Master of Ceremonies (Don DeNatale). The first, "The
Waltz", concerns a widow (Teresa Wright) so obsessed with
her past that she and her audience see a vision of her
youthful self in every mirror she dances past; the second,
"The Hustle", presents a tale of rivalry between a wealthy
invalid (Joan Copeland) and an awkward innocent (Geraldine
Chaplin) for the attentions of a narcissistic gigolo
(Christopher Walken). In the final episode, "Peabody", an
elderly Central European immigrant and retired cook (Lilia
Skala) dreams of winning a dance prize before she dies.

1978 HULLABALOO OVER GEORGIE AND BONNIE'S PICTURES This
film, made for British television, is set in Jodhpur's splendid
Umaid Bhavan Palace (turned, according to the story, into
a hotel by its owner). Two art-collectors from the West are
drawn here by the wish to acquire, by fair means or foul,
the Maharaja's famous collection of miniature paintings
which few people have ever seen. Lady Gee (Dame Peggy
Ashcroft, in a beautifully thought-out and elegant
performance) represents a British museum of fine art, while
the rich young heir of an American canned food
manufacturer (Larry Pine) represents no interest but his own.
Among the film's many merits, Patrick Gibbs counted 'the
amiable character of the young Maharaja who is pleasure-
loving without any suggestion of the playboy, the character
of his sister, joint owner of the pictures ... or the pretty young
English blonde with Lady Gee who captivates the Maharaja
and recalls the palace ghost of a similar girl who danced her
way out of life'. Of Dame Peggy's playing, Gibbs commented:
'Her Lady Gee, living once, and now sometimes in her
memories, in Viceregal circles when she knew the Maharaja

as a child, is a truly memorable study with its subtle suggestion of a keen business sense being gradually overcome by the older artistic values around her'[6].

1979 THE EUROPEANS was Britain's official entry at the Cannes Film Festival of 1979. It was directed by Ivory from a screenplay by Ruth Jhabvala that reverently but unslavishly adapts Henry James's novel for the cinema. Set among the reds, golds and browns of a Massachusetts fall, and no doubt influenced by the debt both James and his adaptor owe to Jane Austen, the film moves with the delicacy of a North American *Mansfield Park*, as sophisticated and somewhat predatory cousins from Europe invade the rigidly conservative domesticities of a Boston family. 'By shifting the story from early summer to the Fall,' wrote Philip French of this film, 'the film-makers have given the picture an elegiac tone and enabled their British lighting cameraman, Larry Pizer, to provide a series of breathtakingly beautiful autumnal images. But Pizer also captures what Dr Leavis felt would be lost in a stage version — "the subtler and essential imagery by means of which the profounder preoccupations are engaged".' French found particularly striking the performances of Lisa Eichhorn as Gertrude Wentworth, and Wesley Addy as her father, who 'wonderfully embodies that lapidary description of him "he looks as if he were undergoing martyrdom, not by fire, but by freezing".'[7] Lee Remick plays Eugenia, and Tim Woodward her brother Felix, in a film that critics have found 'distinguished and memorable'[8], 'a film of practically faultless performance'[9], 'a beautiful, elegant, deceptively cool movie with a vibrant cast perfectly fulfilling the demands of a witty, perceptive script and intelligent direction'[10].

1980 JANE AUSTEN IN MANHATTAN The idea for this film originated in a play by the youthful Jane Austen (based on Samuel Richardson's novel, *Sir Charles Grandison*), as yet unpublished, which was auctioned in 1979 and bought by an American collector, presumed to be David Astor[11]. 'The idea,' said Ruth Jhabvala in an interview, 'is to have this very advanced theatre group in New York do the play, and see what they make of it. I think there always has to be a bizarre touch to everything we do, otherwise we don't feel quite at ease'.[12] Robert Powell and Anne Baxter are among

the players in a film that *Punch* succinctly described as
"elegant"[13], but which has drawn mixed reactions from the
critics, at least one of whom found 'the sequence of the
narrative ... botched, its acting a comical disgrace, its
dialogue wretched, its self-importance insufferable, its
treachery to the cause of literature unforgiveable, its
pretentiousness visible, its squandering of a priceless
opportunity profligate, its aesthetic imperceptions alarming,
its arrogance ludicrous'[14].

1981 QUARTET Screen version of Jean Rhys's tale of an
expatriate English girl in the Paris of the 1920s (played by
Isabelle Adjani, who won an award for her performance at
the Cannes Film Festival of 1981). While her Polish husband
is in jail, she is trapped in a love affair with a well-to-do
Englishman whose wife steers him into the entanglement.
Ruth Jhabvala's screenplay has been described by Dilys
Powell as 'a brilliant ... nervously strong rendering of a
painful human collision'[15].

Between 1960 and 1982, Ruth Jhabvala published five novels
and four collections of short stories. The chronological table
below, which indicates that she was working on fiction at the
same time that she was participating in the production of
Merchant-Ivory films, suggests a very close interaction during
this period between her efforts in the three different literary
forms of novel, short story and screenplay:

1960 *The Householder* published.
1961 James Ivory began shooting THE HOUSEHOLDER for
Merchant-Ivory films.
1962 A novel, *Get Ready for Battle*, published.
1963 A volume of stories, *Like Birds, Like Fishes* (dedicated
'For Jim and Ismail' — James Ivory and Ismail Merchant,
co-producers of Merchant-Ivory films) published. The film of
THE HOUSEHOLDER completed.
1964 Screenplay of SHAKESPEAREWALLAH written by Ruth
Jhabvala.
1965 A novel, *A Backward Place*, published. The film
SHAKESPEAREWALLAH completed.
1966 A volume of stories, *An Experience of India*, published;
dedicated 'For Jennifer and Shashi' (Jennifer Kendal and
Shashi Kapoor, stars of THE HOUSEHOLDER,

SHAKESPEAREWALLAH and BOMBAY TALKIE).

1967 The screenplay of THE GURU written by Ruth Jhabvala in collaboration with James Ivory.

1968 A volume of stories, *A Stronger Climate*, published. THE GURU was shot at Bikaner.

1969 THE GURU completed.

1970 The film BOMBAY TALKIE completed.

1972 A novel, *A New Dominion*, published.

1973 Ruth Jhabvala visited Jodhpur with James Ivory, Ismail Merchant and a small camera crew; at Jodhpur Palace the idea of AUTOBIOGRAPHY OF A PRINCESS was first discussed.

1975 A novel, *Heat and Dust*, published, winning the £5,000 Booker Prize for Fiction. The film AUTOBIOGRAPHY OF A PRINCESS completed.

1976 A volume of stories, *How I Became a Holy Mother*, published. The screenplay of THE EUROPEANS written. Ruth Jhabvala took up residence in New York. The award in April of a John Simon Guggenheim Memorial Fellowship gave her financial support for a year without the need to publish.

1977 The film ROSELAND completed.

1978 The film HULLABALOO OVER GEORGIE AND BONNIE'S PICTURES (made for television, set in India) completed.

1979 The film THE EUROPEANS completed. Nominated the official British entry at the 1979 Cannes Film Festival.

1980 The film JANE AUSTEN IN MANHATTAN completed.

1981 The film QUARTET completed.

Some of Ruth Jhabvala's screenplays have been published, *Shakespearewallah* by Plexus (London) and Grove Press (New York) in 1975, and *Autobiography of a Princess* by Harper and Row (New York) in 1975 and John Murray (London) in 1976. In these publications, detailed directions originally provided by the writer for camera shot and angle (if there had been any) are left out in order to present the general reader with a readable play uncluttered as far as possible by technical detail. But there is enough substantial material in the published scripts to render their comparison (and a comparison of the films that were made from them) with the fiction published in these years, a valuable and revealing exercise.

A screenplay generally provides — unless a writer hopes to direct his own films at some future date — only the basis upon

which many other technically skilled personnel build. No doubt
a professionally written screenplay can be, to all intents and
purposes, 'a pre-directed screenplay'[16], but it seems clear that
although Ruth Jhabvala has paid tribute to the director Satyajit
Ray, India's genius in the art of film[17], she has no aspirations
to film-direction herself. Her writing, in fiction as for the screen,
shows that she regards with controlled, but still very evident,
dislike the gigantic popular film industry that has robbed all
serious literature (including her own fiction) of its audience,
and caters in India to the crudest, most sentimental and
sensational public taste. Two of her films lodge an explicit
protest: SHAKESPEAREWALLAH presents a theatre audience that
would rather watch a posturing movie queen sign autograph
books than the murder of Desdemona by Othello on the stage;
and BOMBAY TALKIE delivers a neat satiric attack on a
commercial film industry that has left no place in India for
poetry, drama or human feeling.

In a bitter little scene at the start of BOMBAY TALKIE, the film
actor Vikram is reminded by the poet and script-writer Hari
that a popular Western film they are discussing was a book
before it was made into a film: 'People do write, you know
...*write*?' In a story based on Ruth Jhabvala's experience in film
studios, a film actor, Suraj, describes to two English girls the
role he plays in a film that is currently being made:

> They said it is my best role yet. I play a poor rickshaw-
> wallah and one day my sister is abducted by a rich man.
> The scene in which I realise what has happened is very
> emotional. There is no dialogue, only the expression on my
> face. It was a great strain playing this scene — ooph,
> afterwards I felt exhausted, terrible. You don't know what
> it is like for an actor: you see, we really *feel* what we are
> acting and it is, oh I can't explain, but a great burden here,
> on the heart.[18]

It is evident that Suraj himself is beginning to believe in the
ridiculous fantasies he must enact, and the two girls' deflating
comments help to place false sentiment such as this in a truer
perspective. Ruth Jhabvala subjects Kishan Kumar, a film actor
in her novel *A Backward Place*, to satiric treatment that exposes
a dislocated personality. He

had a lazy, drawling way of talking and sometimes, when
he remembered, he overlaid his St. Xavier's school accent
with an American one. (p. 103)

The charmingly boyish Kishan Kumar develops a monstrous
vanity[19], and Vikram degenerates as rapidly from being an
attractive, appealing young man into a dissolute 'maharaja',
the callous disregard for human feeling he ultimately displays
bringing about his death at the hands of the poet Hari. Ruth
Jhabvala was asked in 1974 if she had any explanation 'for
your cold reception in India?' She replied:

> I don't feel particularly neglected here. I think Indians don't
> read much anyway, so I don't really expect them to read my
> novels.[20]

This could be interpreted as a criticism of India's literary
establishment and her intelligentsia, and there is, possibly,
some such reflection included in it. But it is also an indictment,
delivered with characteristic restraint and supportive of the
exposures made in her films and in her fiction, of India's film-
crazy society.

Writing for the cinema allows Ruth Jhabvala to reach a far
larger audience than she could ever have envisaged for her
novels and stories before the award of the Booker Prize to *Heat
and Dust* in 1975. A concern to strip life of its illusions seems
to motivate her films and fiction alike during the period under
review, and it is evident that she often works out in her films
ideas that run as major themes through her fiction. The
transference of her attention from India as a subject to "Myself
in India" — a shift that has profoundly affected her fiction after
1965 — is reflected in several films made after THE
HOUSEHOLDER. They focus on Westerners who are involved in
trying to make creative 'sense' of India: the Buckingham Players
in SHAKESPEAREWALLAH through drama, Tom Pickle in THE GURU
through music, Lucia Lane in BOMBAY TALKIE through fiction,
Cyril Sahib in AUTOBIOGRAPHY OF A PRINCESS through biography,
Olivia Rivers and Anne Rivers in HEAT AND DUST through love
and spiritual self-seeking respectively. They are all, at one level,
externalisations of their creator's personal and artistic problems
of living (and 'surviving') in India. At another they are — or she
strives to make them — objective studies of a social and

psychological phenomenon that interests her deeply.

Asked in 1975 to say something about the influence of film on her work, Ruth Jhabvala referred to a 'personal influence':

> The films allowed me to travel a lot more and meet a great many people of all different types. You must have noticed that my early books were all set in Delhi but later on I do branch out and travel. That is entirely due to film.[21]

It is certainly true that the fiction written after 1960 ranges far more widely than before; geographically, as in *A New Dominion*, which takes its characters by stages (like Jenny, Tom and the Ustad in THE GURU) deeper into India, and socially more freely than ever up and down India's infinitely varied and graded social scale. The early novels were indeed all set in Delhi, and though they could be said to present India in microcosm, the later fiction travels not only through space but through time in ways that make Ruth Jhabvala's India begin to take on the aspects of a cosmic metaphor for life and universal experience. Prior to 1960 she wrote of Delhi as it changed around her, presenting what was essentially a picture of contemporary society in transition. The research into princely India's records undertaken with James Ivory in the making of the films seems to have permitted her to make contact in an immediate, visual way with India's recent past through photographs, documentary footage and such vivid accounts of palace life as Yvonne Fitzroy's *Courts and Camps in India* (1926). As a result, she ventures with increasing confidence out of present time and into that past (by means of devices such as Bulbul's songs and stories in *A New Dominion* and Jenny's 'vision' in THE GURU) until in *Heat and Dust* she succeeds in projecting a 1920s plot upon a 1970s situation, using a technique learned from her experience in the editing room that enables her to make the past appear to repeat and fulfil itself in the present.

The 'personal influence' upon Ruth Jhabvala of her work for the screen seems, however, to have been rather more profound than she suggests or can herself be expected to perceive (or at any rate discuss in an interview). By presenting possibilities for successive explorations from many different angles of certain major concerns personal to her, and for subjecting synopses and 'treatments' based on those concerns to assessment by others, screenplay writing seems to have allowed her

opportunity to express and gradually objectify her varying
approaches to India. The advance from *A Backward Place* to
Heat and Dust (as from SHAKESPEAREWALLAH to AUTOBIOGRAPHY
OF A PRINCESS) represents not merely a gain in technical
expertise, but a maturing point of view. The crisp humour of
the stories dealing with Westerners in India in *How I Became
a Holy Mother*, a collection of stories published in 1976 by an
author now resident in New York, shows that the theme of a
Westerner's struggle for survival in India, while still of interest
to her in 1976, is no longer at the troubled centre of her
creativity. After 1976 it becomes possible to see Ruth Jhabvala's
striving with India as an aspect of a larger struggle to come
to terms with life itself, the earlier (Indian) rounds of her battle
having ended — like Jacob's with the angel — in truce, despite
a temporarily disabling dislocation of her artistic point of view.
She too could have said of this strenuous experience: 'I have
seen God face to face, and yet my life is preserved'.[22]

Her work for the screen in my view not only reflects the major
theme of disillusionment with India that dominates her fiction
from 1963 to 1973, but by providing repeated opportunities for
its exploration turns her approach to the subject from mere
self-expression into objective analysis. Ruth Jhabvala is, by
habit and by inclination, a lonely writer, working in New York
as in New Delhi in complete isolation. Now, while a screenplay
may be written in solitude, turning it into a film needs the co-
operation of numerous other people and is preceded by a
process of assessment that makes the writer aware of the
existence of points of view other than his or her own.
Assessment of a synopsis — and even of a 'treatment' — may
go beyond the estimate of the film-editor as to whether or not
a particular effect called for by the writer would work as a
camera shot, and similar technical matters, to focus critically
upon the ideas on which the screenplay as a whole is based.
To turn over one's imaginative creations to comment, critical
assessment and interpretation by others, the training of some
of whom may be in artistic techniques that are non-literary or
only partly literary, could well be a chastening and self-
disciplining experience. Ruth Jhabvala's dedication of her
volumes of short stories to the co-producers of Merchant-Ivory
films and to an actor and an actress who starred in many of
the films she has scripted suggests that she has found her

necessary association with the film world both creative and rewarding.

'Like most novelists,' Ruth Jhabvala has written, 'I mix up a number of people I know (or have witnessed) in order to arrive at one character'.[23] It seems very likely that a good many of the personalities of her acquaintance that she splits up in this way are the actors and actresses with whom she has worked for so many years, and observed in their interpretation of her own creations and those of other screenwriters. The same actors reappear in a number of Merchant-Ivory films: Utpal Dutt appears as a maharaja in SHAKESPEAREWALLAH, as the Ustad in THE GURU, and as Bose, a director of pornographic films, in BOMBAY TALKIE. Madhur Jaffrey plays a film actress in SHAKESPEAREWALLAH, the Ustad's first wife in THE GURU, the Princess in AUTOBIOGRAPHY and the Begum of Khatm in HEAT AND DUST. The late Jennifer Kendal plays a European Woman at a Simla hotel in SHAKESPEAREWALLAH, the author Lucia Lane in BOMBAY TALKIE, and the neurotic Mrs Saunders in HEAT AND DUST. Aparna Sen plays the Ustad's second wife in THE GURU and Vikram's wife Mala in BOMBAY TALKIE. Shashi Kapoor plays Prem in THE HOUSEHOLDER, Suraj in SHAKESPEAREWALLAH, Vikram in BOMBAY TALKIE and the Nawab of Khatm in HEAT AND DUST. Nadira plays the courtesan in THE GURU and Anjana in BOMBAY TALKIE. It is likely that the cinematic personality of Shashi Kapoor 'reappears' in Ruth Jhabvala's fiction, not only in the story "A Star and Two Girls", but as Kishan Kumar in *A Backward Place*, as Gopi in *A New Dominion*, and even, perhaps, as the 'devastatingly handsome' Nawab of Khatm in *Heat and Dust*. Jennifer Kendal appears, similarly, to have experienced several fictional reincarnations, as Etta in *A Backward Place*, as the narrator in "An Experience of India", and possibly, too, as Olivia Rivers in *Heat and Dust*. Nadira can be glimpsed again and again in the fiction, most notably as Asha in *A New Dominion*, whose unpredictable, passionate personality glows through Ivory's description of the actress in his book on the films made by his company in India:

> She laughed a lot and flashed her eyes and told risque stories. We all tried ... to make her feel welcome, but I felt uneasy. There is always something a bit out of control about her; you never know what she will say or do next.[24]

Nadira may also be the starting-point for Ruth Jhabvala's characterisations of Anjana and Sultana in her story "Suffering Women", and for other characters in "Prostitutes", as well as for Renee in *Three Continents*.

James Ivory describes locations and incidents in India that appear, transformed into fiction, in Ruth Jhabvala's novels and stories, in particular *A New Dominion*.[25] Finally, not only does the structure of *Heat and Dust* base itself on techniques learned in the editing-room, but the central idea of that novel, in its linking of Olivia Rivers, Memsahib, with Ms. Rivers, self-seeker, has connections with James Ivory's comment on European women in India:

> These young women are still around today — no longer following Maharajas, but swamis. Whereas the followers of the Maharajas used to move from palace to palace in private trains with a trunkful of pretty dresses and evening slippers, the swamis' admirers travel from ashram to ashram in third-class cars on the Indian railway with a bedroll and a knapsack containing a cotton sari, an extra T-shirt, and some cheap plastic sandals from the bazaar.[26]

In tracing these and other connections between the films and Ruth Jhabvala's fiction (as in tracing the influence upon her fiction of English eighteenth century fiction and drama), what is of permanent interest is not the fact that the connections exist, but that her writing is enriched by their existence.

'A story,' the author told an interviewer in 1974, 'is ... like a poem ... You can't cheat on a poem. It's one cry from the heart — just one — only that has to come out true and right.'[27] In the volume of stories published in 1976 only two out of a total of nine focus on Westerners in India and in both of these, "How I became a Holy Mother" and "Two More Under the Indian Sun", there is discernible none of the anguish that moves earlier work in this period such as "Miss Sahib", "An Indian Citizen" or "An Experience of India". On the contrary, an amused irony marks them both as well as another on the same subject that appeared in the American edition of *How I Became a Holy Mother*, but was omitted from the British one. "The Englishwoman" describes a situation that closely resembles (in some things) the author's own in leaving India behind her in 1975 for a new life in the West, and expresses not anguish or self-searching but confidence and joy:

> When Sadie goes up to her own room, she is almost running
> in her excitement. She looks in the mirror and is surprised
> at the drained face that looks back at her. She doesn't feel
> like that at all — no, she feels the way she used to do, so
> that now she expects her bright eyes back again and her
> pink cheeks. She turns away from the mirror, laughing at
> her own foolishness; and she can hear her own laughter and
> it is just the way it used to be. She knows she won't sleep
> tonight. She doesn't want to sleep. She loves this feeling of
> excitement and youth.[28]

This story is written in the present tense, an unusual feature
suggesting that the whole has been constructed in the manner
of a 'treatment', the median stage in the evolution of a
screenplay from synopsis to shooting script. Ruth Jhabvala
builds into this story certain special effects, notably a 'dissolve'
from a moonlit Indian garden to a view of English downs, the
details of which are so noted as to suggest in practical, filmic
terms ways in which the emotions of the character experiencing
this vision can be conveyed.

> But as she goes on looking, the moonlit scene brightens until
> it is no longer that silver garden but English downs spreading
> as far as the eye can see, yellow on one side, green on
> another. The green side is being rained upon by mild soft
> rain coming down like a curtain, and the yellow side is being
> shone upon by a sun as mild and soft as the rain. On a raised
> knoll in the foreground there is an oak tree with leaves and
> acorns, and she is standing by this tree; and as she stands
> there, on the eminence overlooking the downs, strong winds
> blow right through her. They are as cold and fresh as the
> waters of a mountain torrent. They threaten to sweep her
> off her feet so that she has to plant herself down very firmly
> and put out her hand to support herself against the trunk
> of the tree (she can feel the rough texture of its bark). She
> raises her face, and her hair — not *her* hair but the shining
> hair of her youth — flies wild and free in that strong wind.[29]

While it is no doubt true that a successful fiction writer does
not necessarily possess the ability to write acceptable and
shootable screenplays, it is unlikely that a director or a

cameraman would fail to respond in terms of practical assent
to this story were it submitted to them as a treatment. "The
Englishwoman" suggests that Ruth Jhabvala has satisfied Lewis
Herman's dictum that "to write a complete shooting script, the
screenplay writer must not only be able to call the shots, but
he must, in addition, know all the angles."[30]

It is evident that writing for the cinema has developed the
talents Ruth Jhabvala possessed from the first as a writer of
fiction, of being able

> to express ... ideas in words that are amply descriptive and
> appropriate ... to recognize the subject material that is
> intrinsically dramatic ... to *see* characters, situations, and
> story developments as they can be related to a screenplay
> ... to relate outer, physical characteristics and actions to
> inner, emotional drives, and to integrate them naturally into
> a screenplay so that acceptance of psychological motivation
> will not be strained and, therefore, lost.[31]

One of the major artistic problems that faces a writer of fiction
who also writes screenplays, however, must be that of drawing
selectively for the purposes of her fiction from her acquired
'knowledge of the use of a vast tool chest of technical devices
without which a motion picture could not be made'.[32] A film
director would probably prefer, for example, to be made to see
an idea in terms of a picture rather than as a paragraph of
words which, however well written, verbally colourful or
mentally stimulating would appear from his point of view
'physically static'.[33] The necessity when writing for motion
pictures to keep elements continually in progressive motion,
to emphasise the visual at the expense of dialogue and to take
care when writing dialogue that only a specific overtone be given
to a particular line are among basic guidelines followed by
screenplay writers that would seriously limit the possibilities
open to a writer of fiction. If over-strictly followed they would
limit Ruth Jhabvala's scope almost intolerably, since it is her
inclination to 'load every rift with ore' in both narrative and
dialogue in order to achieve the ambiguity dear to the ironist
and the poet.

The early films she scripted for Merchant-Ivory reveal, to some
extent, the inevitable conflict that occurred between the novelist
in Ruth Jhabvala and the writer of screenplays. 'When one

writes about India as a European and in English (as I do),' she
wrote in 1975,

> problems of communication present themselves: how to
> translate the idiom of one language into another, how to
> present a scene to an audience unfamiliar with its most
> obvious ingredients (such as temples, bazaars, and motor
> cycle rickshaws).[34]

The problem announces itself in her early novels in an
abundance of descriptive detail; and although this detail is both
interesting and amusing, there is so much of it that a reviewer
of *The Nature of Passion* suggested that its author was 'too
preoccupied with the surface of her characters' lives to reveal
what lies beneath'.[35] This is a criticism that could justifiably
be extended to her earliest films as well. SHAKESPEAREWALLAH
impressed at least one Western film critic by 'its pure truth
in setting, presentation of character, conflict of cultures, and
by its tender humanity'; as a film about India in transition it
revealed what she called a 'Chekhovian evocativeness'.[36] This
is perfectly true. SHAKESPEAREWALLAH is a visually beautiful,
moving and satisfying film; but it is also true that there is a
good deal in it that could have been cut without loss. There
are amusing conversational 'bits' written in for the actor Shashi
Kapoor in the style of the passage quoted earlier in this chapter
from "A Star and Two Girls", with which Kapoor does very well.
But if one were to contrast SHAKESPEAREWALLAH with BOMBAY
TALKIE, in which the same actor plays the role of Vikram and
has similarly flamboyant things to do and to say, it becomes
evident that there has been a distinct improvement: not merely
in the actor, but in the script, every word, action and gesture
of Vikram in BOMBAY TALKIE illuminates character, keeps the
plot moving, and underlines themes. A comparison of
SHAKESPEAREWALLAH with AUTOBIOGRAPHY, another film about
India in transition, makes one aware of a sharp increase in
economy, and the existence of multiple layers of significance
in every word and action of the two stars, Madhur Jaffrey and
James Mason. Skilful adaptation of the techniques of the 'cut-
away', of indirection, and of the subjective camera to the
purposes of fiction is one of the means by which Ruth Jhabvala
gradually eliminates the detail presented through third-person
narrative in her early novels. Any one who reads *Heat and Dust*

immediately after *Amrita* or *The Nature of Passion* (or even
Esmond in India) will notice at once how description and
dialogue have been cut to a minimum, and what remain
concentrated and distilled. The frequently obtrusive narrator
of *Amrita* becomes less and less 'visible' with every novel
published after 1955, until in *A New Dominion* two of the
characters share in the narration. A comparison of *Amrita* with
Heat and Dust reveals an impressive economy in the later novel,
with no accompanying loss of interest or significance: the early
superfluity of descriptive detail has given way to a richness of
selective and symbolic detail. It would seem that in her writing
for the screen, Ruth Jhabvala gradually evolves ways of getting
more quickly to the heart of what she wants to do or say, until
in her later work both in film and in fiction every word is as
loaded as a word in a poem, the resources of the form itself
and of the various kinds of material built into that form being
exploited to the full.

From a technical point of view, part of the interest of BOMBAY
TALKIE arises from the fact that Ruth Jhabvala, whose finely
drawn literary effects have been as a general rule lost on a
reading public whose standards are shaped increasingly by the
commercial film, structures her criticism of the Bombay film
world on the pattern characteristically adopted by the
commercial film itself: the brash, raucous block-busters that
invite millions to a daily escape from reality and a daily
indulgence in sentiment and melodrama. In stories such as
"The Interview", and in her novel *A Backward Place*, she had
shown her awareness that popular Indian films provide escape
fantasies for people trapped in hardship and poverty; in *Amrita*
she had demonstrated, through the characters of Hari Sahni
and his sister Prema, how the standards disseminated by film
and radio as to what constitutes love and beauty have resulted
in cheapening the human relationships of real people, hindering
the development of a mature understanding of the self, and of
ordinay life. In BOMBAY TALKIE she examines the effects of
commercialism and of 'box-office success' on those involved in
the making of popular films — on actors, actresses, directors
and script-writers.

The design of BOMBAY TALKIE closely resembles that of certain
late eighteenth century English novels: Jane Austen's
Northanger Abbey almost certainly, and possibly also

T.L. Peacock's *Nightmare Abbey* and *Crotchet Castle*, which
make use of the character-types and stock situations of the
popular 'Gothic' and sentimental novels of that time to satirise
both contemporary attitudes and the popular forms themselves.
As John Gillett has noted, a satirical tone is set at the very
start of the film by 'the splendidly garish opening sequence'
— played in a Bombay studio with a Berkeley-like production
number involving girls dancing on the keys of a giant
typewriter.[37] But even before this, the film has made its point:
the credits are fashioned to resemble the giant film posters and
hoardings that dominate the streets and crowded squares of
Bombay. The film's characters are anti-types of the stock
character-types of the popular film — handsome hero, beautiful
exotic heroine, gross villain, virtuous and devoted wife, religious
swami. They act and interact in the stock film settings of
ostentatious interiors, mirrored and opulently carpeted, hung
with chandeliers and satin drapes; smart flats; hotel rooms;
dimly lit night-clubs. The action features (and satirises) the
stock incidents of the popular film: song-and-dance routines,
wrestling matches, comic songs, clowning, violence culminating
in murder, romantic lovesongs, the villain's attempt to rape the
hero's pure wife, the intervention of fate in the direction of
human affairs, scenes shot in famous beauty-spots and places
of historical interest, and a religious message to sweeten the
formula.

The delicate, precisely placed yet compassionate, ironies
well-known to Ruth Jhabvala's readers, and Ivory's intuitive
understanding of them, emerge in filmic understatement as the
shadowed sculptures in the caves at Elephanta look down upon
Vikram and Lucia playing at being 'Consenting Adults' in
between takes of Vikram's current film. The clowning in
BOMBAY TALKIE (unlike that in the average Hindi movie, where
it is generally extraneous to the plot) takes the form of an
imitation of Vikram's acting style by an aspiring younger actor
who is, as their mutual 'friend', the retired actress Anjana Devi,
says, 'Exactly as you were at his age' — a remark that neatly
sums up her own sexual relationship with each of the two
young men, while reminding Vikram that he is beginning to
lose his spectacular good looks and might soon become
dispensable.

Jane Austen and Peacock create fictional worlds in which

novel-struck heroines and heroes find real life more complex
and interesting than the contrived extravagances of Ann Radcliff
and Charlotte Smith. The 'real' world of Catherine Morland in
Northanger Abbey admits evil only in the conquerable forms
of General Tilney's mercenariness and John Thorpe's self-
importance; Jane Austen renders these characters harmless,
and wastes little time in bringing a suitably happy ending into
view in the best traditions of the sentimental novel. But the
violent knifing of Vikram by Hari that ends BOMBAY TALKIE can
lead to no such optimistic conclusion. It is not only Vikram
(symbol of materialism and spiritual shallowness, whose charm
we have seen gradually obscured by moral darkness) who dies,
but Hari (poet, idealist, sensitive and generous lover) who dies
with him. In these last scenes, the two parts of what Hari has
earlier called India's spirit — soul and body, art and
commercialism, feeling and materialism — wrestle in a
deathgrip, dragging each other down to an end in which neither
can be said to be the victor. It is a pessimistic end, reflecting
(very neatly) the melodrama that is a feature of the form upon
which the film is based, but also expressing Ruth Jhabvala's
disillusioned view of more in India than its film industry. The
voice of good sense and idealism, strong in Jane Austen's Henry
Tilney, who acts independently of his mercenary father, is weak
in Hari: for although Hari is aware of the flaws in Lucia's
character, and intensely critical of the values of the Bombay
film world, he is forced to serve the whims of both. Jane
Austen's world had not yet become the fractured society that
the Victorian novelists perceived and drew in their novels; the
areas of disillusionment penetrated by them are not areas in
which she had any need, or impulse, to venture. But they are
areas of contemporary life (and not only in India) in which an
optimistic happy ending would not be true to the facts. Ruth
Jhabvala's refusal to take refuge in optimism or sentimentality
in imitation of the form she is satirising distinguishes BOMBAY
TALKIE'S uncompromising attitute and tightness of structure
from the milder, more resigned comedy of THE GURU, and
indicates the originality and honesty with which she approaches
her subject. As in her writing of fiction, she uses a literary model
as a starting-point for BOMBAY TALKIE, but the final work is
shaped by principles drawn as much from experience as from art.

    BOMBAY TALKIE is very closely related to the novel Ruth

Jhabvala published two years after its release, *A New Dominion*.
The film, like the novel, falls structurally into three sections,
the ashram sequence of the film matching 'The Holy City'
interlude of *A New Dominion*: in both, the characters try on
other roles and attempt other possibilities before abandoning
themselves to fate and the dictates of their own temperaments.
Lucia's experiences in the ashram (treated comically in the film)
develop, via such among Ruth Jhabvala's stories as "A Spiritual
Call" and "An Experience of India", into the sinister, yet moving
ambiguities of Lee's experiences at Swamiji's "Universal Society
for Spiritual Regeneration in the Modern World" in *A New
Dominion*.[38] Hari's role of sensitive, distressed observer is
repeated in the novel's character Raymond: both are involved,
through their idealism, in developments which, though
superficially amusing, are fundamentally tragic: the
degeneration of Vikram and Gopi, the self-deceptions of Lucia
and Asha. Anjana Devi, the ageing film-actress and sybil of
BOMBAY TALKIE who surrounds herself with young men hopeful
for a career in films, is a preliminary sketch for Ruth Jhabvala's
searching and compassionate portrait in *A New Dominion* of
the decadent princess Asha, who feeds on the youthful Gopi
in the same way. The gradual deterioration of Vikram from film
hero to dissolute 'maharaja' under the fatal influence of the
sensual Lucia and the corrupt Bose has close connections with
Gopi's degeneration in *A New Dominion* from selfish immaturity
to a cunning, exploitative 'experience' during his months of
tutelage by Asha and Raymond.

The three novels published by Ruth Jhabvala during the years
she worked with Merchant-Ivory while living in India,
1960-1975, present an area in which the techniques she derived
from screenplay writing can be observed in detail as they affect
her writing of fiction. She has referred to a 'technical' influence
upon her fiction:

> I went a lot into the editing room so I know how you cut
> a film. It's shot in a certain order and you bring all that into
> the editing room and shuffle it about to bring out the stronger
> scenes, to offset them, to use counterpoint ... I have learnt
> a lot technically from film.[39]

In *A Backward Place* may be seen what are perhaps the earliest
examples of her adaptation of the technique of using 'cut-aways'

to relieve tension; immediately after Etta insults Bal at the
Hochstadts' picnic, there is a complete and abrupt switch
(pp. 188-9) to two other characters —Jaykar and Sudhir — in
an indoor setting (at the Cultural Dais). Again, after Etta tries
to kill herself and is rescued by the Hochstadts, there is a
similar switch (p. 245), this time to Sudhir in a train leaving
Delhi. Here the 'cut-away', while still helping to relieve tension
achieves rather more: Etta's 'failure' in coming to terms with
India is by this means juxtaposed with Sudhir's 'success', and
it is in this section of the novel that the glory of the real India
asserts itself in his imagination (p. 247) to make its claim upon
the soul of the individual 'who accepted it and rejoiced in it
and gave himself over to it, the way a lover might' (p. 248). This
technique is used to even better effect in *A New Dominion*, when
immediately after Swamiji's noctural violation of Lee leaves her
whimpering 'in rage and disgust' (p. 170), there is a transition
from the ashram to Bulbul's ascendancy over Asha at Banubai's
house that simultaneously relieves tension and connects Lee's
helplessness with Asha's, thus economically bridging over some
narrative or dialogue that would otherwise have been needed
to explain why Lee moves in with Asha in the next scene
(p. 172). This 'cut-away' is combined very effectively with the
screenplay writer's technique of indirection which, while
economising on dialogue, simultaneously flatters the 'audience'
— here the novel's readers — by permitting them to reach
certain intended conclusions independently. As in a film, the
shock value of indirection is intellectually stimulating: the
weakness of Lee and Asha in the hands of their 'evil angels',
Swamiji and Bulbul, is effectively brought out by means of this
transition, and the reader responds once again to the moral
point Ruth Jhabvala makes by providing her characters with
'spiritual guides' on their journey whose instructions are often
ambiguous and prove destructive or misleading.

In *Heat and Dust* the technique is seen at what is, perhaps,
its best in Ruth Jhabvala's fiction, when Olivia breaks down
in the graveyard because Douglas has unconsciously echoed
the Nawab's words on learning of her pregnancy. There follows
an immediate switch to the 1970s story and to the narrator's
discussion, in her characteristically matter-of-fact tone, of
Rivers family history. The cut-away is effected smoothly through
a fleeting reference to Olivia's baby —'Douglas did have a son',

writes the narrator — but its immediate purpose (to relieve
tension) once achieved, other matters relevant to character and
theme are brought in that connect, rather than separate, the
two 'scenes'. Douglas's dreams of a son who will carry on the
heroic Indian tradition of the Rivers family are, by means of
the transition, quickly shown to have been denied in the short-
term (since the narrator's father went into the antique business
instead of into the I.C.S.). Yet, his dreams are fulfilled in the
long-term, since the narrator is (though Douglas would hardly
approve) fulfilling them even as she writes her journal (p. 155).
The narrator's casual remark in connection with Child, that
'his own family never had any connection with India' (p. 156),
is a literary equivalent for filmic indirection that lets the reader
glimpse for the first time in the novel the subjective passion
and growing emotional turmoil behind the narrator's stance
of careful objectivity. The 'cut-away' as Ruth Jhabvala uses it
here, while seeming to tactfully lead the reader away from
Olivia's distress and Douglas's concern for her, actually makes
a connection between the narrator and Olivia that includes the
similarity of their experiences up to this point as well as the
deep feeling that links their otherwise dissimilar temperaments;
it also links the narrator with Douglas, emphasising through
understatement a common pride in family traditions and
inherited values. A good deal of the satisfaction the reader
derives from *Heat and Dust* is created by means of the filmic
technique of indirection as adapted to Ruth Jhabvala's ironic
purposes.

Some mention has been made (in Chapter VIII) of the
unconventional division of *A New Dominion* into 'scenes' rather
than chapters. These move and shift with an attention to
principles regarding variation of mood and maintenance of
significance in contriving each such shift, that reflects
experience gained in the editing room. The organisation of these
scenes into three main movements, titled respectively 'Delhi',
'The Holy City', and 'Maupur' closely imitates the design of THE
GURU, in which film the characters move similarly from Bombay
through Banaras to 'Bajapur' in their search for truth and
enlightenment. Particularly interesting in this connection is
Ruth Jhabvala's adaptation of what film-makers call the
subjective camera technique for Lee's inner monologues in this
novel. The narrative of *A New Dominion*, which is presented

in the third person throughout the novel,' moves at times
—always effectively and significantly — into the first person.
This is done legitimately in letters written by characters to one
another or in letters written by Raymond to his mother, which
advance the action while simultaneously illuminating character
and temperament; but most spectacularly and daringly in the
inward thoughts and impressions of Lee. The subjective camera
technique achieves an illusion by which a cinema audience
views the action through the eyes of one of the characters in
a film; in *A New Dominion*, the switch from third person to first
has the impact of a change not only in visual angle, but in
personal and moral point of view.

In her use of the subjective camera technique for inner
monologue, Ruth Jhabvala obeys the screenplay writer's rule
that it is a method to be used sparingly and judiciously. She
employs it only for Lee's meditations. By its means the reader
becomes gradually and disturbingly aware that Lee has
mistaken her own passionate experience of first love for spiritual
devotion:

> ... it really seems to me there is something like a column
> of light over the hutment where he is. And all I have to do
> is to concentrate on that and then I feel everything is all right
> — no not all right but marvellous, marvellous! as long as
> he is there, I don't have a thing to worry about. (p. 166)

The best example of this technique as adapted to fiction is
perhaps the section titled 'Lee' (pp. 152-4) in which a visit paid
by Miss Charlotte and Raymond to Swamiji's ashram is
presented through Lee's eyes and from (apparently) her point
of view;[40] it is, however, not her own, but Swamiji's. Later in
the novel, the same technique is used to show her — now under
Miss Charlotte's influence — inclined to see Swamiji as the
source of death and evil (p. 208). Such a handling of Lee allows
Ruth Jhabvala to introduce into a novel the variety and interest
the technique commands (when properly used) in a film. It also
helps her to subtly indicate Lee's obtuseness to the significance
of what goes on around her, her extreme suggestibility, and
her capacity for self-deception.

Visual detail can sometimes claim, through a sudden spiritual
manifestation it makes possible, the title of a filmic epiphany.
Such details have been described as

the rare touches of genius that ... are the result of experience,
knowledge, and a conditioned intuition that make for the
difference between a hack screenplay writer and one who,
like the Elizabethan dramatists, is to be considered a poet.

For these bits of filmic epiphany can be considered as pure
poetry. They are lyrical interpolations that soar with
unalloyed beauty.[41]

We glimpse such a revelation for a brief moment when the
Princess prepares to see her guest off in AUTOBIOGRAPHY:

PRINCESS :   Well, that's the way it is. We just have to
                    learn to manage. (*She gathers up more food
                    for him: a whole cake.*)
CYRIL SAHIB :   Princess! Please!
PRINCESS :   It will do for tomorrow's lunch as well ...
                    (p. 159)

The cake in question (upon which the camera dwells lovingly
for a long moment) is a Fuller's walnut, as sold by Fortnum
and Mason of Piccadilly. The Princess is indeed, as she says,
'managing', but this detail underlines the nostalgic excitement
with which she has prepared to celebrate this special occasion,
doing so in the lavish style to which the Maharaja had been
accustomed. A touch that lays even more effective claim to the
title of a filmic epiphany is Ruth Jhabvala's use of a particular
sequence from the documentary footage shot in Jodhpur, to
end this film:

PRINCESS :   She is better than ever. You'll see ... Of
                    course like all the old court musicians she
                    is living in very straitened circumstances now
                    ... At first I felt so sad to find her living in
                    that place. I think it was part of the palace
                    stables, or perhaps even the sweepers'
                    quarters ... It's no more than a hole in the
                    wall ... She is all alone and suffers terribly
                    with gall stones. But gay! Like a bird. She
                    seems happy about everything. As if all the
                    good things that happened in the past are
                    still there and even better ones to come ...

Footage of eighty-year-old woman singer of Jaisalmer. She

sings love songs in her old voice, with coquettish looks. She
is gay and like a bird. After a time, and with the singer still
singing, we see the PRINCESS *escorting* CYRIL SAHIB *down the*
stairs. She helps him on with his hat and coat and hands
him his umbrella and the parcel of food she has tied up for
him. She is very careful and protective about him. They go
down together to the street and say goodbye. She watches
him walk down the darkening London street. THE PRINCESS
shivers and draws her thin silk sari around her and goes in,
closing the door. (pp. 160-61)

The Princess's concern for the singer's circumstances matches
her protectiveness of Cyril Sahib: like the singer, he has been
a family retainer, and it is her duty and her pleasure to care
for such people. But her description of the singer as living 'in
a hole in the wall' is, albeit unconscious, a poetic illumination
of the conditions of her own life and that of her guest. They
are, all of them, living 'in straitened circumstances'. The
euphemism glosses over the daily humiliations she and Cyril
Sahib have to encounter and ignore, she from such people as
the youth who delivered the film-projector at the beginning of
the afternoon, he in the train during the rush-hour. 'You have
to learn to push, that's the only way. I do it' (p. 159). This
remark recalls the mixture of bravado and bewilderment,
betrayed by the dispossessed maharajas in the interviews
shown a little earlier in the film, and makes Ruth Jhabvala's
screen princess part of India's history.

The actions of the characters in the final sequences of
BOMBAY TALKIE carry through most effectively a detailed network
of inverted 'wedding' symbolism that culminates in a vision of
Lucia dressed in 'bridal' white reclining regally on Mala's bed
in Mala's wedding sari as Hari sprinkles 'confetti' (his torn-up
poems) over her; this is reinforced by the later development
in Lucia's flat when she steals Vikram's shoe in a desperate,
mock-playful attempt to keep him with her, an unconscious
travesty of a traditional Indian marriage custom. This technique
— of exploiting carefully selected detail for symbolic significance
— is used very effectively in AUTOBIOGRAPHY, in which 'a large
and imposing portrait of a Maharaja in the uniform of a British
Army regiment dominates the room' and is used throughout
the film in a manner comparable with Ibsen's use of General

Gabler's portrait throughout his play *Hedda Gabler*. The Princess garlands the portrait, and at various moments in the course of her interview with Cyril Sahib, looks up towards it in gratitude or in self-justification. The portrait symbolises the occasion, which is a celebration of the late Maharaja's birthday. As will become clear, its youthfulness and impressiveness are deceptive. The Maharaja did not always remain so; but his daughter's garlanding of the handsome portrait is symbolic of her wish to perpetuate the idea — half myth, half memory — of the original's virtue. She is turning her whole life into an attempt to immortalise her father in his heroic aspect; and if she cannot persuade Cyril Sahib to do this in his book, she will achieve it by appropriately editing her memories of him. The portrait is also the focus, at the beginning of the film, of Cyril Sahib's interest: he cannot, as the Princess notes amusedly, 'tear himself away'. It is the portrait, reminiscent of a once happy relationship with the original, that brings Cyril Sahib back year after year to what is no doubt always a fairly painful interview with the Princess.

Both *A New Dominion* and *Heat and Dust* reveal, in their richness of selected symbolic detail, the lessons Ruth Jhabvala has learned in writing for cinema. The roly-poly pudding in the 'scene' titled 'Swamiji Eats Lunch' is a perfect example of the 'epiphany' as James Joyce first used the term in *Stephen Hero*; more than anything else or any other conversation in *A New Dominion*, this passage lights up the egotism of the novel's evil genius:

The bearer came up with the next course but Swamiji ignored him for he was taken up with what he was saying: he leaned towards Raymond and his eyes did not look shrewd or laughing now but they glittered in a strange, passionate way: 'I want her to be mine. She must be mine completely in heart and soul and — yes, Raymond,' he said, easily able to read his companion's thought, 'in body also, if I think it necessary. That is quite by the way. Ah,' he said, turning at last to the bearer who had been patiently even reverently waiting, and helping himself from the tray, 'I think this is called roly-poly pudding, isn't it? A great favourite with me.'

And he smiled — first at the pudding, and then, his eyes beginning to rove and dart again, at the American lady at

the next table who had been greedily awaiting this smile;
and then his eyes roved further, all round the dining room,
at all the foreign guests eating their lunch, and he regarded
them in a sort of easy, speculative manner as if one day
perhaps, if he wanted to, if he cared to, they would all be
his. (p. 123)

If the cake in AUTOBIOGRAPHY is a symbol of good living and
luxury, the roly-poly pudding embodies the greed of Swamiji
and his fellow-diners for more even than the food that is in
front of them, carrying in its very name associations with
Swamiji's plumpness and joviality. It simultaneously sums up
what has gone before and foreshadows what is to come in 'a
sudden spiritual manifestation, whether in the vulgarity of
speech or of gesture, of a memorable phase of the mind
itself'[42]. A similarly effective use of symbolic detail can be seen
in the narrator's description of Karim's Knightsbridge flat in
Heat and Dust, to which reference has been made earlier (see
Chapter IX). The miniature paintings on the walls, the sofa
fashioned from a palace swing, the physical grace of Karim
himself and of his wife Kitty are all (like the Maharaja's portrait
in AUTOBIOGRAPHY) survivals from a past that has lost its
beauty, its vigour and its meaning.

A fuller appreciation of Ruth Jhabvala's achievement in Heat
and Dust emerges from an awareness of the skill and daring
with which she adapts cinematic technology to her special
purposes in writing fiction. Reference has already been made
(see Chapter IX) to her use of the device of 'flashback' in
designing the structure of the novel. The placing of her cut-
aways here appear to have been guided principally by thematic
concerns particular to its composition. An examination of the
way in which transitions are managed from present to past and
back again yields more evidence of the amount she has 'learnt
... technically from film'. The flowers the narrator receives at
the shrine at Khatm leave her palm 'sticky and with a lingering
smell of sweetness and decay that is still there as I write' (p. 14).
Since the next section begins with the words: 'Olivia first met
the Nawab at a dinner party he gave in his palace at Khatm',
one can imagine an easy transition from the flowers, evocative
of nostalgia for the past, by means of a filmic 'match-dissolve'
perhaps to a formal arrangement of flowers on the palace table,

or to the flowers in Olivia's corsage as she drives, filled with pleasurable anticipation, to Khatm. A similarly easy transition is achieved when, Maji having recommended a pilgrimage to the snow-covered shrine for Ritu's mental illness, a flashback to 1923 begins with the information that Mrs Crawford and Mrs Minnies had left for Simla: the transition implies that taking to the hills is a universal way of coping with emotional 'disturbances' such, for instance, as the passion Olivia is beginning to feel for the Nawab. Section 14 switches from the dead beggar-woman Leelavati to the sick Harry; section 15 from the *hijras* dancing for Olivia and the Nawab to the gulmohar tree, 'spreading its branches like a dancer' (p. 124); Olivia's plans for an abortion in section 20 switch to a midwife in the 1970s who greets the narrator, and thence to Maji, who ensures that the narrator's baby will not be lost, a thematic reflection on the fact that the withdrawal of Empire promises a more hopeful future for inter-racial relationships than existed in the past. In short, Ruth Jhabvala's interweaving of present with past in *Heat and Dust* reveals the concerns that move and find expression in her writing of fiction.

An examination of the structure of the screenplay of AUTOBIOGRAPHY OF A PRINCESS, the film that preceded the publication of *Heat and Dust*, illuminates Ruth Jhabvala's craftsmanship in both the genres of novel and film-script. The film is basically one long scene, during which the Princess entertains Cyril Sahib to afternoon tea, and into this fictional sequence are interpolated, at six different points in the script, four kinds of photographic material: archive material retrieved by James Ivory from the store-rooms of Indian palaces, which are in essence photographic records of state occasions and royal junketings of the 1920s; interviews specially recorded for Merchant-Ivory with dispossessed maharajas and maharanis, ex-royals now accommodating themselves with some difficulty to life without its privileges; documentary footage shot on location by the Merchant-Ivory crew, of musicians, dancing girls, religious ceremonies, animal sacrifices and hunting expeditions; and a fictional sequence in the style of the silent films. The Princess starts off the afternoon's 'entertainment' with films of sporting events that culminate in pig-sticking and a leopard hunt. Ruth Jhabvala's screenplay makes her intensions clear:

CYRIL SAHIB *looks a bit uneasy by the end of this story; they have been watching a leopard tear a tethered kid to pieces; the* PRINCESS *is excited, a bit out of breath ... She tells these old stories as if she were telling them for the first time and as if it were all new to* CYRIL SAHIB.

The documentary footage has thus been used to establish a crucial difference in the point of view of the two observes. The callousness explicit in the film (and implicit in the Princess's accompanying story of the death of her father's shikari Purush Chand) disturbs Cyril Sahib but it 'excites' the Princess. Next the Princess shows her guest some excerpts from the interviews with maharajas, having first established her own attitude to them with the emotional admission: 'I cried and cried' (p. 145). However, the films shown have been edited in the screenplay to stress royal India's parasitic side.[43] The selection of the excerpts and their juxtaposition convey an impression of the inordinate luxury of the maharajas' style of living, especially when compared with that of the more ordinary and humble Indians who occasionally appear alongside. We are made to feel — along with some sympathy — a little scorn for these helpless butterflies who are finding life when shorn of its luxuries so difficult to get used to. An unsympathetic view is established by judicious editing of the interviews to stress such features as the Rajmata of Jaipur's wish that she could spend her leisure as she did in happier days — six weeks of skiing, six weeks by the sea — Jodhpur's description of his entry into politics and his bitterness about the public change in attitude toward princes — 'We are Public Enemy No. 1' — and Prince Jagat's indecision regarding the choice of a career. By juxtaposing with this view the Princess's extremely subjective and sympathetic one, Ruth Jhabvala creates a filmic equivalent for her characteristically ironic narrative tone: the viewer is made to 'experience' both sympathy and scorn, and arrives by this path at a balanced view of princely India, its great days and its decline.

A third sequence of films run off by the Princess presents footage 'of shabby processions and confused events', in the course of which Cyril Sahib's inability to distinguish one event from another serves to indicate that his memory, like the Princess's, is not to be trusted: he might be seeing India through

Prem (Shashi Kapoor) and Indu (Leela Naidu), the newly-weds in THE HOUSEHOLDER (1963)

Lizzie (Felicity Kendal) in SHAKESPEAREWALLAH (1965) Photo: Subrata Mitra

Sanju (Shashi Kapoor) in SHAKESPEAREWALLAH (1965) Photo: Subrata Mitra

The Ustad (Utpal Dutt) and his disciple Jenny (Rita Tushingham) in THE GURU (1969) Photo: Subrata Mitra

Jenny (Rita Tushingham) in THE GURU (1969) Photo: Subrata Mitra

Rita Tushingham and Michael Yorke as two young Western visitors who approach India through her music, from THE GURU (1969) Photo: Subrata Mitra

Pop-star Tom Pickle (Michael Yorke) and Jenny (Rita Tushingham) attend a Bombay party in THE GURU (1969) Photo: Subrata Mitra

Pincho Kapoor as the Maharaja and Nadira as the courtesan in a dream sequence from THE GURU (1969) Photo: Subrata Mitra

Madhur Jaffrey as the Princess, pours tea for Cyril Sahib (James Mason in AUTOBIOGRAPHY OF A PRINCESS) (1975) Photo: Walter Lassally

Lucia Lane (Jennifer Kendal) and Hari Mehta (Zia Mohyeddin) in BOMBAY TALKIE (1970) Photo: Subrata Mitra

Lisa Eichhorn as Gertrude Wentworth in THE EUROPEANS (1979) Photo: Larry Pizer

Robin Ellis and Kristin Griffith as Robert and Lizzie Acton in a scene from THE EUROPEANS (1979) Photo: Larry Pizer

Robin Ellis, Kristin Griffith and Lee Remick in the ball-sequence from THE EUROPEANS (1979) Photo: Larry Pizer

the mist of his own disillusionment. While watching a film of Jodhpur's female entertainers, he contributes his own anecdote about the Maharaja:

> ... And the girls too, in their tawdry dresses. What happens to the singing and dancing girls when they get old? When I asked His Highness, he said, 'They die of pox in the bazaar.' He laughed when he said it, so I suppose he was joking ... (pp. 149-50)

His story reinforces an impression established earlier by the Princess's account of the death of Purush Chand. Although the Princess praises Papa's 'generosity', the two stories leave us uneasily pondering the possibility that the Maharaja was in reality a callous ruler, insensitive to the needs of his dependents.

The fourth and fifth sequences are not actual films run off and viewed by the two characters, but are presented as memory or visionary flashbacks. The fourth sequence belongs, as it were, to Cyril Sahib: it represents his memories of India, and exemplifies his way of looking at it. The scenes shown include shots of idols in religious ceremonies, 'the squirming, squealing rats' of the Rat Temple, and a gory animal sacrifice at Jodhpur in which, as the screenplay puts it, 'The swords come down, the heads are struck off with one blow, the cannons fire from the ramparts, and the little boys touch their foreheads with fingers dipped in blood' (p. 157). The sequence builds up the sense of acute physical revulsion that is, in Ruth Jhabvala's view,[44] an inevitable part of the Westerner's experience of India, and James Mason's ravaged face as it turns to the camera gives this aspect of her picture of India formidable support. This part of AUTOBIOGRAPHY places Cyril Sahib among Ruth Jhabvala's fictional studies of Westerners on the cycle of Indian experience, comparable with such characters as Esmond in *Esmond in India*, Etta in *A Backward Place*, Raymond in *A New Dominion* and Harry and Chid in *Heat and Dust*.

The fifth sequence belongs to the Princess. It consists of a flashback

> *to a suite in a luxurious London hotel, like the Savoy, circa 1945. A blowsy Englishwoman is urging the Maharaja to come to bed. She is no longer in her first youth; her hair is bleached;*

he is wearing a satin nightgown. The Maharaja, in his
dissolute aspect, is drawn down onto the bed by the
Englishwoman. They lie full-length for a moment. Suddenly
the door bursts open and a man jumps into the room. He is
a photographer. He starts taking pictures with a flash camera.
Another man comes into the room, short, wearing a rain-coat
and carrying an umbrella. The Maharaja leaps out of bed,
starts around it towards a bureau opposite. The short man
starts belabouring him with the umbrella. The Maharaja
manages to get his pistol out of the bureau drawer. He aims
it and fires. After the shot, there is a silence. This whole scene
— silent and melodramatic — is as dated as a silent film;
as dated as the hotel suite itself. (pp. 157-8)

Ruth Jhabvala appears to have intended to present the incident
(on account of which the Maharaja lost his throne) as the
Princess visualises it. She describes the Maharaja and his
mistress in terms that accord with the Princess's inability to
imagine any beauty or grace in their relationship: she has to
be 'blowsy', he has to be 'dissolute', it is not love that she sees
enacted on the bed but the sordidness of mutual exploitation.
The melodrama of the scene, its staginess and the jerky
movements of the actors, are indications of the Princess's
inability to imagine the scene as taking place between real
people possessed of real emotions and human affections.

In the actual film, the scene emerges somewhat differently.
The silent film aspect, with its wooden acting, is preserved, but
the two principals are differently seen. The Englishwoman is
not unattractive in the way that the word 'blowsy' suggests,
and the Maharaja is a tall, rather vague figure in a dressing-
gown. He is not grotesque or in any way 'dissolute'; not even
plump. It would appear that in the course of its translation
into film one side of Ruth Jhabvala's authorial intention has
been modified, perhaps in accordance with the appearance and
personalities of the actors available. What does remain is an
impression that the Princess sees her father's disgrace and the
events that led to it as unreal, shadowy as a silent movie; and
this is very much in keeping with her wish to forget all about it.

Finally Ruth Jhabvala interpolates the sixth sequence, footage
of the aged singer of Jaisalmer already described in this chapter
and in Chapter IX, a perfect and appropriate end to what John

Gillett has called her 'elegy for a past age'. It is a small point, but worth noting in this connection, that a character is introduced into *Heat and Dust* — Maji, the elderly widow and 'holy woman' of Satipur — who connects India's past and present while representing its indomitable spirit and its traditional skills, as does Bari Moti Bai, the singer in AUTOBIOGRAPHY OF A PRINCESS.

Spoken dialogue in the novels written after 1960 is set out with an increased effectiveness that is in part the result of the economy practised in screenplay writing in which

> it can be stated dogmatically that there is almost no place ... for long speeches ... unless, of course, the character of a person talking is one who is being portrayed as verbose.[45]

But whereas in writing a screenplay, a writer of dialogue must take care that only a specific overtone is given to a particular line of dialogue for the guidance of the actor, the elimination of such a specifying direction by a novelist would increase the possible significances, even ambiguities, of a given line and increase the reader's participation. A comparison of Ruth Jhabvala's writing of dialogue in her films and in her fiction makes this very clear. In BOMBAY TALKIE, for example, the critical attitudes adopted by Hari towards the film world and its representatives, Vikram and Bose, have to be (and are) explicitly stated. The acerbity of his remarks takes away somewhat from the sensitivity of this character, and makes him a fractious, even irritating personality. 'Oh, Hari, don't be such a bloody bore!' says Lucia pettishly on one such occasion, and even though her remark reveals her own insensitivity, it is not unjustified. Ruth Jhabvala uses a flexible narrative style to express the ironically critical attitudes of similar characters in *Amrita* and *A Backward Place*. The explicitness demanded by the film medium prevents a similarly restrained handling of Hari. The reader of *A New Dominion*, however, is made continually aware of multiple significance, not only in narrative, but in exchanges of apparently casual dialogue. When Raymond points out places of interest to Asha and Gopi during their boatride at Banaras, we are aware not only of the surface meaning of his words, but of the embarrassment and pain of mind that those words are intended by him to discipline and conceal. Words in Ruth Jhabvala's later novels do not only pick up possible variations of meaning, but seem to echo through time: for instance, in *Heat and Dust*, when the Nawab talks to Olivia of Paradise:

> There are certain people who if they are absent life becomes hard to bear. Once I asked a faqir from Ajmer (a very holy person): 'Why *these* people? Why they and not others?' He gave me the following reply which I like very much: 'These are the people who once sat close to you in Paradise.' (p. 132)

To the Nawab, as to the narrator (who found that entering the grove was 'like being received into Paradise', p. 124), this grove and its spring bring similar thoughts, and create a setting for love that seems a 'miracle' amidst the dust and heat of ordinary life and painful social relationships.

Equally interesting is the manner in which Ruth Jhabvala handles situations in which communication between characters has become impossible or non-existent. In BOMBAY TALKIE, a desperate Lucia makes a long distance telephone call to her young daughter in Switzerland, manages to get through, but fails to communicate: an effect created by means of a telephonic filter, which permits the voice of the person at the other end of the wire to be heard by the audience. In *A New Dominion*, language and point of view create the barrier through which Raymond talks to Bulbul on the telephone, receiving only a jumbled and disturbing message (pp. 55-56). In *Heat and Dust*, the evidence of a failing marriage is registered indirectly, and by implication:

> ... But he never did arrive before her; somehow he seemed to be kept at the office later and later, and when he came home he was so tired that he went to sleep very soon. Olivia stayed up much later, sitting by the window to catch some cool air. She was usually still asleep when he left in the morning; he always left very early so as to be able to ride out on inspection before the sun got too hot. (pp. 115-16)

Music, like dialogue, if often used effectively in Ruth Jhabvala's early work, especially to make a satiric point or illuminate character. In *Amrita*, their liking for popular radio songs indicates the sentimentality of Hari Sahni and his sister Prema, while the Indianised Western dance music played by a band in *The Nature of Passion* (see p. 69) reflects the imitated

artificialities Nimmi and Ved take for elegance and
sophistication. In writing for film, Ruth Jhabvala seems to
become aware of the possibilities of other, much more complex
and interesting, ways of using sound. In THE GURU, the sitar
music that sounds across the ruinous landscape in the film's
last scenes symbolises the India that Tom Pickle and Jenny
realise at last is beyond their reach. In BOMBAY TALKIE
'background music' that has been played in different moods
and at different speeds throughout the film resolves itself at
the end of it into a tawdry, 'night-club' lyric that ends on the
words ... 'and so goodnight', which makes an authorial point
about the shallow (though outwardly 'glamorous' and exciting)
relationships we have been observing. In AUTOBIOGRAPHY, the
lyricism of an ancient court singer — 'Gay! Like a bird'
—symbolises the true spirit of India.

In early short stories, Ruth Jhabvala had occasionally
experimented with musical effects as a means of conveying
thematic concerns. In "Lekha" as Lekha dances to Govind's
singing, the conventional sitting-room falls away, and the reader
is temporarily transported into a world given meaning and
illuminated by Radha and Krishna's art and their passion for
each other. The undoubted effectiveness of this treatment of
music is increased several fold in another story (written after
Ruth Jhabvala had participated in the making of two films),
"The Housewife"; here the description of a musical theme
simultaneously bodies forth the consummation of physical love,
the social dilemma faced by the principal character, and a
statement of artistic commitment:

> The tune he was singing began in her mind too and she
> smiled to it and let it unfold itself in all its glory ...
>
> He was about the same age as her husband but lean, hard,
> and eager; as he came on top of her, she saw his drugged
> eyes so full of bliss and he was still smiling at the tune he
> was playing to himself. And this tune continued to play in
> her too. He entered her at the moment when, the structure
> of the raga having been expounded, the combination of notes
> was being played up and down, backwards and forwards,
> very fast. There was no going back from here, she knew. But
> who would want to go back, who would exchange this blessed
> state for any other?[46]

Music is employed repeatedly and in varied ways to illuminate character and theme in *A New Dominion*. Raymond, we learn

> had grown very fond of Indian music. It had become for him like a distillation of everything he loved in Gopi and everything he loved in India. These two were now inextricable. (pp. 35-6)

This is a revelation that becomes even more touching when we see that Gopi himself can appreciate nothing above the musical level of 'The Donkey Serenade', and respond to nothing more demanding in literature than the 'squashy' sentimentalities of Urdu lyrics. Banubai, whose 'prophetic' declarations are reminiscent of Western Bible-bashing, has an unexpectedly sweet voice: she sings devotional songs with joy, her voice 'as pure as the waters of a mountain stream' (p. 142). Bulbul, on the other hand, has a voice that was 'hoarse and grating and rather wicked; with relish she sang of the awaited lover, describing his round strong arms and his thighs which were also round and strong' (p. 171). The contrast in musical texture and choice of song subtly emphasises the roles of Banubai and Bulbul as Asha's 'good' and 'evil' angel respectively. In the scene titled 'Music at Rao Sahib's', the raucous hymn-singing led by a vigorous lady minister competes with the artistry of two classical musicians:

> The raga had now reached the stage where the maestro was showing his skill at ornamentation. He strung and restrung his notes like pearls and each pearl had been rounded by generations of artistry. Such music demanded a quality of the ear as refined and a sensibility as delicate as the music itself. Raymond desired to give these but could not help being distracted by what was happening in the lit-up part of the garden. (pp. 86-7)

When they finish, there is only Raymond left to applaud them. These musical contrasts create a scene that is both ironic and unforgettably comic, limning with remarkable economy the philistine values that rule 'the new dominion' of social and political India.

The hymn-singing at Swamiji's ashram is the feature that, above all else, draws the mixed lot of devotees there

to such a pitch of excitement and frenzy that it became
almost unbearable for them, the joy of it exhausted them
and who knows what would have happened every morning
and evening if he hadn't known the exact point at which to
stop them. (p. 67)

The submerged impetus to sexual orgy — always arrested at
the right moment and prevented from surfacing — keeps the
inmates of the ashram at emotional simmering-point, and
leaves Lee, who is one of the most impressionable among them,
always 'feeling exalted and purified' (p. 81). A New Dominion
is rich in its use of musical reference and association, but
perhaps an even more effective use of music — because more
subtle — can be seen in Heat and Dust. At Karim's
Knightsbridge flat,

> they had a tape playing of sarod music — no one was
> listening but it made a good background to their talk which
> was carried on in high-pitched, rather bird-like voices.
> (pp. 96-7)

The quiet comment that 'no one was listening but it made a
good background' sums up the cultural and spiritual decline
that the beautiful objets d'art in the flat individually body forth.
Anything more would have been superfluous. Ruth Jhabvala's
use of musical reference in her fiction, like her handling of
dialogue and narrative, seems to owe its impressive gain in
economy and multiple significance to her experience in using
sound effects and devising dialogue in writing for the cinema.

It is no accident that the reviews accorded to AUTOBIOGRAPHY
OF A PRINCESS could, with little or no alteration, be applied to
Heat and Dust. To the comments quoted at the beginning of
this chapter should be added Derek Malcolm's praise: 'Tactful
but resonant, full of irony yet without a hint of malice'[47]. The
novel, like the film, achieves its subtlety by focussing on
characters who are engaged in deliberate editing of historical
fact so as to present a finished fiction they can adopt as
historical truth. The Princess in AUTOBIOGRAPHY shuts her mind
to what she considers distasteful. We have an early instance
of this at the beginning of the film, when she erases from her
consciousness all memory of the loutish, unhelpful youth who
set up the projector:

PRINCESS (*rather grandly*) : That will do.
YOUNG MAN (*with heavy sarcasm*) : Oh, thanks very much.
PRINCESS :   No, thank you. You've done very well. You may
                    call for it in the morning. But please *not* before
                    eleven o'clock.
YOUNG MAN : We'll have to see about that. It depends on
                    my day.

*This is his last attempt to salvage some vestige of British
independence. Of course she doesn't hear it. He retires with
a rather routed air. She calls after him, as a gracious afterthought:*

PRINCESS : Thank you. You have been very kind.
She forgets — dismisses — him at once ... (p. 138)

A few minutes later, when her guest has arrived, it is to another
young man that the Princess refers, not this one whom she
has evidently blotted out of her memory or made over into
someone else:

PRINCESS :   Everything is ready, you see, for our annual
                    birthday treat. And I have the tapes for the
                    interviews as well. Such a nice young man
                    brought them over from the BBC. He said I
                    could keep them as long as I liked. A charming
                    boy. We became friends ... (p. 140)

Her behaviour in this trivial matter prepares us for what she
will do when more serious issues are involved:

CYRIL SAHIB *is still turning the pages of the album — in self-
defence, to hide the expression on his face. Suddenly she puts
her hand on the page he has come to.*

PRINCESS : Don't look at that.
CYRIL SAHIB : Your wedding pictures.
PRINCESS :   I hate them. It's the one thing I can't forgive him
                    for ... I don't mean that. Of course he was
                    thinking — as always — only of my good ...
                    (*Looking briefly at Bunny's picture, in bridegroom
                    attire*) He wasn't bad looking. (*Flicking over the
                    page*) But of course nothing — nothing
                    —compared to him. (p. 153)

The Princess's recollections of her father and of her own life are not only blurred by sentimental affection and nostalgia (a point sensitively picked up by direction and photography that cause James Mason to study Madhur Jaffrey's face attentively while she looks at the photographs and speaks enthusiastically about them), but she is even now in the act of editing them.

A moment later, when Cyril Sahib draws out of the album the photograph of the ageing Maharaja, the Princess 'snatches it from him and throws it on the fire' (p. 157). She has edited out of their future celebrations the evidence that her handsome hero degenerated into 'a gross, dissolute, middle-aged man' (p. 151). Next year, it is implied, she might edit out of her album (and her memory) the unpleasant evidence of her own unhappy marriage. We are watching the creation of a fictional autobiography, even while the Princess believes herself to be engaged in a true and accurate recreation of her father's life and career.

AUTOBIOGRAPHY OF A PRINCESS appears to have clear connections with "The Biography", a story Ruth Jhabvala wrote some five years before working on the film, in which the middle-aged niece of an Indian political leader who has (like the Princess) been educated in Europe and made a hero of the dead man, achieves a sense of personal fulfilment through helping an American scholar write his biography:

> ... she broke out: 'Look at me, I'm emancipated, I'm educated —' Quite unexpectedly, her eyes filled with tears. She turned aside her face to wipe them away; as she did so, she smiled ruefully and said, 'Why don't you write *my* biography?' and for a moment Jonathan wished he could.[48]

Cyril Sahib is involved in what seems at first sight to be more legitimate editing; he is researching the life of Denis Lever, an Englishman whose work for and among the people of India he believes to have placed Lever very far above the majority of his contemporaries, British or Indian. It is soon apparent, however, that in writing Lever's biography Cyril Sahib is striving to compensate for the time and talent he had himself wasted in India as 'His Highness's parasite'.

Heat and Dust takes up these ideas, but carries them much further. Its narrator, like the Princess and like Anita in "The Biography", is examining and re-creating the experience of someone she considers 'special', extraordinary. But while they are most immediately concerned with the past and the present, and with the future only in a vague way, the narrator of *Heat and Dust* fastens on Olivia Rivers as a model for her own future existence. Cyril Sahib's journey to India is over; or rather, it is being continued at a safe distance from reality in his mind and memory where, as he says, things seem often to run together and become blurred. Ms. Rivers is just beginning her real quest as the novel ends. As she stands poised above the heat and dust of the material world below her mountain top, she asserts a clarity of vision and a range of understanding that the reader can only hope is really hers.

Ruth Jhabvala has from the first, it seems, seen fiction with a dramatist's eye. She supplies such early novels as *Amrita* and *The Nature of Passion* with the tight structure of stage plays, and even with casts of characters. The process by which the comparative simplicities of satiric drama yield to the complexity of ironic fiction has been hastened, it would appear, through her experience of working repeatedly within the extremely narrow limits of a screenplay. In *Heat and Dust* the narrator of the novel is herself one of its two central characters, and the interpreter of the other's life and letters. It would be difficult to envisage sparer or more richly concentrated versions of this novel and of AUTOBIOGRAPHY OF A PRINCESS, the film with which it is most closely linked from a technical and thematic point of view.

Despite the fact that Ruth Jhabvala's increasing technical skill as a writer of screenplays has helped her to devise ways and means to make the cinema screen yield workable equivalents for her established fictional techniques, it is not as a screenwriter that she sees herself, but as a novelist. 'The film director knows nothing,' she wrote in 1971,

> of the exquisite, lonely enjoyment that the placing of a semicolon can bring to a writer — no, *his* semicolons have to be wrested out of the combined efforts of actors, cameramen, set designers, lighting electricians, sound recordists and their army of assistants.[49]

Ruth Jhabvala claims no special credit for the many films directed by James Ivory to which she has contributed by writing screenplays, and for the considerable international acclaim many of them (especially SHAKESPEAREWALLAH, AUTOBIOGRAPHY OF A PRINCESS, THE EUROPEANS, HEAT AND DUST, THE BOSTONIANS and A ROOM WITH A VIEW) have attracted:

> The novels, of course, are just mine, but the films are Jim's.[50]

AUTOBIOGRAPHY broke many established general rules of script-writing by confining its characters to a single area, limiting their physical actions, and assigning them long, uninterrupted monologues, yet brought off an undoubtedly successful work of cinematic art. Ruth Jhabvala's novel *Heat and Dust*, however, does not only gather together and employ skills gained in writing screenplays and other fiction, but is the artistically controlled examination in two separate but cunningly connected movements of a personal dilemma that informs all her writing from *A Backward Place* on. Its complexity interestingly, eluded the camera. 'I want to move on, go higher up', writes the narrator of HEAT AND DUST:

> Unable to see, I imagine mountain peaks higher than any I've ever dreamed of, the snow on them is also whiter than all other snow — so white it is luminous and shines against a sky which is of a deeper blue than any yet known to me. (p. 180)

The impulses to personal and artistic expression that have united in shaping Ruth Jhabvala's work to a strong, continuous development towards increased understanding and skill reverberate through these words in a way that might only too easily be lost, when filmed, in period detail or local colour.

HEAT AND DUST, was directed by James Ivory and released in 1982. Although she had said before undertaking the task that she would 'rather do something new'[51], Ruth Jhabvala's screenplay has won several awards in its own right, and provided the basis for one of Merchant Ivory's most successful and popular films. It does not attempt to grasp the subtleties of characterisation that distinguish the 1970s sections of the novel, choosing to emphasize instead the colour and pageantry of the British Raj. Perhaps Ruth Jhabvala could envisage no closer binding together of the techniques of film and fiction than she has already achieved in writing her novel; and it is to the world of the novel, as she declared in 1971, that she 'belongs':

Everyone has heard about how films corrupt writers. I have always taken this corruption to mean the reducing of one's talent for the sake of money and easy living. Now I realise that the temptation is different and that it lies in the *escape* that films offer. The escape is from a prison imposed by one's own temperament. 'The world of silence, exile and cunning' is bleak and demanding. One seems to be always alone and usually in the dark. But films fling open doors to arenas where there is noise and lights and where clowns are tumbling about. It is fun to tumble about with them for a while. Only, afterwards to go back where one belongs ... that's not always so easy.[52]

Notes

1. Quoted by A. Rutherford and K.H. Petersen, op. cit., p. 377.
2. Dilys Powell, review in *The Sunday Times* (London) 7 March 1976.
3. David Robinson, "Shrine for the Raj", review in *The Times* (London) 5 March 1976.
4. Ibid.
5. 'F.R.', "Slow dancing", review in *Times*, 17 October 1977.
6. Patrick Gibbs, "Ivory excels in comedy of manners", *Daily Telegraph* (London) 28 June 1979.
7. Philip French, "Ivory elegy", *The Observer* (London) Sunday 1 July 1979.
8. P.P. McGuinness, "Memorable vignette", review in *The National Times* (Australia) 3-9 February 1980.
9. Colin Bennett, *The Age* (Melbourne), quoted in pamphlet distributed on behalf of David Stratton's Showcase Theatre, 387 New South Head Road, Double Bay, Sydney, 1980.
10. Geraldine Pascall, review in *The Weekend Australian*, 26 January 1980.
11. See John Pym, op. cit., p. 17.
12. Ibid.
13. *Punch* "Film Guide" of 6 August 1980.
14. Benny Green, "Plain Jane", review in *Punch*, 16 July 1980, p. 113.
15. "Pure Ivory", review in *Punch*, 22 July 1981, p. 152.
16. Lewis Herman, *A Practical Manual of Screen Playwriting* (Forum Books, Cleveland and New York: 1963) 1969 ed., p. 173.
17. The only Indian cinema for me, as for practically everybody else, is Satyajit Ray, such a giant and so truly Indian. When I see his films, I know that I couldn't make the right film in India, because mine would only be a European view'. R.P. Jhabvala, quoted by John Pym, op. cit., p. 17. It should be noted that Ray helped edit THE HOUSEHOLDER and wrote the music for it, cf. Barbara Grizzuti Harrison, "India, Inc.",

in *Harper's* March 1982, p. 67.

18. R.P. Jhabvala, "A Star and Two Girls", in *An Experience of India* (John Murray, London: 1966) 1971 ed., p. 50.

19. See Chapter VII for a discussion of Ruth Jhabvala's characterisation of Kishan Kumar.

20. Quoted by R. Agarwal, op. cit., p. 35.

21. Quoted by A. Rutherford and K.H. Petersen, op. cit., p. 377.

22. *Genesis* 32:30.

23. Personal communication, 1978.

24. James Ivory, *Autobiography of a Princess: Also Being The Adventures of an American Film Director in the Land of the Maharajas* (Harper and Row, New York: 1975), pp. 125-6. All references made in this chapter and throughout this book to the screenplay of the film AUTOBIOGRAPHY OF A PRINCESS relate to pp. 131-61 of Ivory's book, where it is published in entirety.

25. See Chapter VIII.

26. Ivory, op. cit., p. 36.

27. R. Agarwal, op. cit., p. 33.

28. R.P. Jhabvala, "The Englishwoman", op. cit., p. 37.

29. Ibid., p. 38.

30. Lewis Herman, op. cit., p. 119.

31. Ibid., pp. 5-6.

32. Ibid., p. 7.

33. Ibid., p. 6.

34. R.P. Jhabvala, "Moonlight, jasmine and rickets", op. cit.

35. *Times Literary Supplement* review, 14 December 1956.

36. *Toronto Globe and Mail* review, 9 October 1967.

37. John Gillett, *Monthly Film Bulletin* (August 1971) p. 160.

38. See pp. 192-194.

39. Quoted by A. Rutherford and K.H. Petersen, op. cit., p. 377.

40. See pp. 188-9.

41. Lewis Herman, op. cit., p. 261.

42. Ibid., p. 260.

43. The interviews are printed in full in James Ivory, op. cit.

44. See Chapter I.

45. Lewis Herman, op. cit., p. 211.

46. R.P. Jhabvala, "The Housewife", in *An Experience of India*, p. 161.

47. Review by Derek Malcolm, *The Guardian* (London) 4 March 1976.

48. R.P. Jhabvala, "The Biography", in *A Stronger Climate* (John Murray, London: 1968) p. 48.

49. R.P. Jhabvala, "Writing for films", The Illustrated Weekly of India, 21 March 1971, p. 25; See also R.P. Jhabvala, "Writers and Cinema", *TLS* 18 November, 1983, p. 1287: '(In the editing room) I have learned a whole new method of narration by watching scenes being moved to and fro in various juxtapositions, and time-schemes manipulated through flashbacks and flash-forwards. It has been a two-way traffic for me —What I have learned in films I have put back into my books, and what I have learned about characterisation, relationships, happenings and everything else that goes into writing fiction I've put

to use in writing films. I can't think what it would have been like for
me to have had one and not the other. I've needed both to keep me
going — I mean imaginatively as well as financially.

50. R.P. Jhabvala, quoted John Pym, op. cit., p. 18.
51. Ibid., p. 17.
52. R.P. Jhabvala, "Writing for films", op. cit., p. 27.

CHAPTER

XII

'Immersion into America':
In search of love and
beauty (1983) and three
continents (1987)

Q. *Is there one thing you might just like to do which you have not done before?*

A. Something I would like to do is combine my three backgrounds: my European background because it was Continental; and then I had an English education. Then I had a 25-year immersion into India and now I am beginning an immersion into America. So if I can bring all these elements together, well, that's just fine by me.[1]

In Search of Love and Beauty appeared eight years after *Heat and Dust*. During this period the author had made important changes in her life. She had left India to take up residence in New York (and eventually to take up American citizenship), and had become increasingly involved in writing screenplays that translate the work of a personally admired master of the English novel, Henry James, to the cinema screen.

Her work on James's THE EUROPEANS and THE BOSTONIANS appears to have assisted the process by which she was, during this period, getting to know America by means of writing about its people and places. There is also to be considered her work on the screenplay for the Merchant-Ivory film HULLABALOO OVER GEORGIE AND BONNIE'S PICTURES (1978), in which a young American art-collector and the representative of a British museum of fine art struggle for the possession of a Maharaja's famous collection of Indian miniature paintings. In the *oeuvre* of Ruth Jhabvala *In Search of Love and Beauty* occupies, therefore, the position of a masterpiece for which a number of minor works in various genres have provided experience and trial-runs. (It is a position comparable to those occupied in the case of her 'Indian' fiction by her novels *A New Dominion* and *Heat and Dust*, the publication of the first of which was preceded by several stories involving Indian holy men and Western spiritual self-seekers,[2] and the second by the technically innovative screenplay for the film AUTOBIOGRAPHY OF A PRINCESS.[3])

In two short stories published in 1978 in *The New Yorker*, Ruth Jhabvala published interesting studies of predators and American victims: "Parasites" is set in an old Manhattan brownstone mansion, "A Summer By The Sea" focuses on a particularly grim holiday spent at a beach house by an American family. In the latter story a young American woman speculates about the origins of Hamid, an Indian visitor to the United States:

> ...I guess Hamid had a stronger personality than the rest of us, including Boy. Or maybe it was because he is a foreigner, an Oriental — someone different in an exotic way — and we kept looking at him in a fascinated way to see what he would do next.
> At first we thought that he must be some kind of prince,

on account of his looks, but he was too poor for that, really.
He never had any money at all. Not that it bothered him,
because there were plenty of people eager to pay for anything
he needed. Boy said that maybe he came from one of those
very ancient royal lines that were extinct now, except maybe
for a few last descendants working as coolies in Calcutta.
Or maybe, Boy said — he has plenty of imagination and also
quite a bit of Oriental background, thanks to his study of
art history — Hamid was a descendant of a line of famous
saints, dating back to the thirteenth century and handing
down their sainthood from generation to generation.[4]

The satire directed here at a handsome Indian tramp who lives
like a parasite on the goodwill and generosity of his naive
American friends blends, almost imperceptibly, with the tone
of innocent wonder natural to Susie, the story's perplexed young
American narrator. Susie, who is clear-sighted enough to realize
that it is not sainthood but eroticism that dwells in Hamid's
beautiful eyes, is one of his victims. Another is her husband
Boy, whose elaborate theories spring not only from a lively
imagination and a smattering of 'Oriental background', but from
willing self-deception: Boy, a homosexual, is infatuated with
Hamid. A third victim is Susie's mother. Hamid calls her 'Golden
Oldie' behind her back, but he is not above flirting outrageously
with her in order to amuse himself and distress Boy.

The emphasis in "A Summer By The Sea" is not so much
on Hamid and his mysterious 'Indian' background, as on the
Americans whose psychological weaknesses he exposes and
pitilessly exploits. Boy's romantic speculations regarding
Hamid's 'sainthood' link Hamid with Swamiji, the religious rogue
of Jhabvala's *A New Dominon*, while his youth, spectacular good
looks and callous heart link him with Gopi in the same novel,
and look forward to the character of Crishi in *Three Continents*,
the novel that followed *In Search of Love and Beauty* in 1987.
Boy, Susie and Susie's mother find their lives laid waste by
Hamid in much the same way that Raymond, Lee and Asha
are reduced to despair by Swamiji and Gopi in *A New Dominion*
and they too are willing victims, who joyfully open their hearts
and homes to the predator as Lindsay, Michael and Harriet
Wishwell gladly donate their family home 'Propinquity' to the
Fourth World Movement represented by Crishi.

That the predators in this short story and in *Three Continents*
happen to be Indian is entirely by the way. Their origins are,
as a matter of fact, shrouded in mystery, and India's
contribution to their genesis is partial, not total. 'It was ...
difficult to make out his nationality,' remembers Harriet, years
after her betrayal by Crishi:

> His way of speech was a strange mixture — sometimes there
> was a slight Oriental lilt, and he used the usual International
> Americanisms; but his most basic accent was the sort of
> Cockney that was fashionable at the time ... His appearance
> too was ambiguous: At first sight, he might have been an
> Italian or a Spaniard, but then there were his slightly slanted
> eyes, his double-jointed fingers, his very slim ankles, and
> (narrow) feet ... [5]

This 'ambiguity' of origin indicates that exploitation would have
come from one source or another, so obvious and inviting to
the predator are the weaknesses displayed in all three works.
    During this period Ruth Jhabvala was also keeping fictionally
'in touch' with India, and in "Farid and Farida" (a story about
the making of an Indian/international 'holy mother' that
appeared in 1984 in *The New Yorker*) some familiar notes recur:

> "She's wasted up here", (Sunil) said.
> Farid sat up. "What's on your mind?" he said.
> "It's ridiculous", Sunil grumbled. "Instead of sitting under
> that tree of hers, she could be making a fortune in London.
> Not to speak of New York".
> "You must be crazy", Farid said in a shaky voice.
> "You're crazy", Sunil said. "You and she both. But it's
> always the same story with you two. You have absolutely
> no business sense".
> "Business!" Farid shouted. "What's she got to do with
> business! She's beyond all that now".
> "All right, call it something else, then. Call it whatever you
> like. But I'm telling you, she'll go over big. They've never seen
> anything like her before. There's money in what she does
> — *money*", he repeated, irritably rubbing his thumb and
> middle finger together to make his meaning clear.[6]

Despite the fact that Ruth Jhabvala achieves in it, with
conspicuous success, her stated intention to combine her 'three

backgrounds' if she can, reactions to *In Search Of Love And
Beauty* were mixed and in many cases perplexing to the author,
who had been receiving (especially after *A New Dominion* and
Heat and Dust) a hostile press in India, but who had been
recognized by most Western critics as a novelist of major
importance. 'I have never before been so misunderstood, on *both*
sides of the Atlantic'.[7]

In Search of Love and Beauty is a novel in which the image
of India seems at first sight to be unimportant and peripheral.
Instead, it is the 'Continental' background Ruth Jhabvala
wished to explore in her American fiction that seems best
represented in the private lives and secret longings of the
Sonnenblick family and their circle, German-Jewish refugees
who are building new lives for themselves in the United States.

The novel focuses in particular on Bruno and Louise
Sonnenblick, their daughter Marietta, her son Mark and
adopted daughter Natasha, and Louise's childhood friend Regi;
also on Leo Kellermann, a charismatic 'genius' with whom both
Louise and Regi are deeply and inescapably in love. As these
European refugees recreate their pre-war lives amidst New
York's 'unending vista of towering buildings' with the help of
their own imported furniture, cosy reunions in restaurants like
the Old Vienna, and pastries from Blauberg's, readers of earlier
Jhabvala novels would recall her sympathetic studies in *To
Whom She Will* and *The Nature of Passion* of Punjabi refugees
striving to keep their shattered community lives whole in the
Delhi of the 1950s. But there is an important difference between
the early fiction and this recent novel, for in the latter Ruth
Jhabvala makes direct contact for the first time in her published
fiction with the obliterated world of her German childhood.
Louise, she notes, 'had grown up in the suburb of D — in
Germany' (p. 30). Whether or not D — stands for Dresden
(which, like Cologne, the novelist's birthplace) was bombed out
of existence during the Second World War, we read for the first
time in any of her novels and stories of a schoolgirl who lived
in 'a villa with a garden in which grew apple and plum trees',
and travelled by tram every day to school.

India 'officially' enters this European-American world only on
page 22 when the restless Marietta, prototype of the Western
self-seekers in Ruth Jhabvala's later fiction, discovers at a
dance recital in New York an Indian sarod player named Ahmed

'and with him India and the particular brand of fulfilment to be discovered there'. Unlike the European expatriates in their West Side and Central Park apartments, Ahmed has no intention of settling down in the United States. He 'linked life in the West', and takes happily to Scotch, cigarettes, late-night TV and Marietta, but his life and his music cannot be uprooted from the Indian soil. When Marietta follows him to India, Ruth Jhabvala summarizes through Marietta's responses to India an aspect of her own relationship with the land in which she lived for twenty-five years.

Marietta's initial enthusiasm for all things Indian places her at first in Stage One of the cycle of Indian experience that Ruth Jhabvala has described in her essay "Myself in India"[8] and memorably explored in her characterisations of Lee and Raymond in *A New Dominion* and of the narrator in *Heat and Dust*:

> How she exclaimed! And at what he considered such common, everyday things, one was almost ashamed of them. She adored, simply adored, the bazaars and the merchants ... copper pans, otr silver ornaments, textiles fluttering in the wind, gaudy sweetmeats — such colours, she had never seen, never dreamed such colours! She liked the smells, too, of incense and clarified butter, and even the denser ones of rotting vegetables and even more sinister rotting things —even those didn't bother her, for she regarded them as part of everything: as the beggars were part of it all, and the corpses on the pyres, and the diseased people healing themselves in the sacred river, and the very fat priests ... She wondered and wondered at everything and exclaimed and shone with joy so that there was absolutely no language barrier — feeling streamed out of her.[9]

Despite this early enthusiasm, however, Marietta does not surrender her Western sensibility: 'She wanted to see everything but as herself' (p. 25). She is saved, therefore, from the disillusionment and revulsion Ruth Jhabvala associates with later stages of her cycle, and while heavy German furniture and upholstery darken her mother's West Side apartment, the Indian influence lights up Marietta's flat in Central Park West. Her oriental rugs 'bloom' with delicate floral motifs', while raw silk furnishings, 'a shining gold Buddha', and exquisite Indian miniatures in golden frames illuminate her stylish, if unsettled, way of life (p. 27).

While Marietta represents in the novel what is essentially a sensitive Westerner's enthusiasm for India, a hint of deeper, more serious concerns is conveyed through Ahmed. He, unlike Marietta, is 'restful', 'impassive', 'imperturbable' (p. 23). He is a disciplined musician who experiences his moments of most intense joy when he is either making or listening to music. He makes no personal or moral judgements about the astonishing people and experiences he encounters in the West, but his personality and his outlook on life and art combine to make an implicit statement that is not lost on those about him who have eyes to see and wit to understand it:

> When Leo asked Ahmed about his music: "Is it of the senses or of the spirit?" then Ahmed understood him less than ever. He had no conception of any division between the two, and if he had thought about it, he would have said, surely the one is there to express the other? That was what his music was for — he knew this so deeply that he had absolutely no thought or words for it. (p. 88)

Ahmed's inability to understand a question that adopts as a first principle the concept of a culture in which the spirit and the senses are on opposite sides of an artistic fence reminds the reader of A New Dominion of the musicians in that novel whose art still survives in an India divided between the forces of spirituality and materialism.[10] Like them, Ahmed is part of an ancient tradition with which the West appears to have lost touch. In view of the chasm that exists between Ahmed's unspoken philosophy of life and art and the worldliness and sensuality of voluble, 'pot-bellied and short-breathed' Leo Kellermann, it is ironic that 'Ahmed's music opened up Leo's Tantric period' (p. 89), providing inspiration and starting-point for a new variation on the pseudo-philosophical theories Kellermann expounds to the impressionable members of his trendy Academy of Potential Development.

Kellermann's question indicates the nature of the division at the theoretical heart of his 'philosophy', a code which implicitly separates the spiritual and physical aspects of human experience. The 'Tantric period' is one of a variety of stages through which that philosophy passes before reaching its

culmination in what Kellermann calls 'The Point' at which,
hopefully, man's highest spiritual and physical experiences
intersect. It is on his journey towards 'The Point' that we have
our last glimpse of Kellermann driving blindly into snow and
a mist that is partly real, partly a symbol of his own confusion
of mind and spirit (p. 226).

In her characterization of Leo Kellermann, Ruth Jhabvala
achieves her aim of inclusiveness, combining her 'three
backgrounds' at a very ambitious level that takes *In Search of
Love and Beauty* far beyond the comparatively easy satiric
strokes of HULLABALOO and "A Summer by the Sea". Until he
encounters Ahmed in New York, there seems to be nothing
'Indian' in either Kellermann's genesis or his personality. On
the contrary, he is very 'European' indeed, has arrived in New
York from Europe in the 1930s as a penniless refugee, and
makes his first appearance on page one of the novel among
a group of German and Austrian woman expatriates whom he
manages from the very start to fascinate with his charm and
impress with his ideas.

But as things turn out, Kellermann's impact on American
life as depicted in the novel is not human in any narrowly
national sense but superhuman. He enters the story on a note
of divinity: "An Apollo! — A god," cries Regi to Louise, describing
this new and superb phenomenon, and as his extraordinary
influence spreads together with his fame, Kellermann becomes
a cult figure, the 'reigning deity of the Old Vienna' (p. 37) and
the 'beneficent deity' of the massive Victorian Gothic house in
the Hudson Valley that enshrines his Academy of Potential
Development (p. 12). Described at various points in the novel
as a 'pagan god' (p. 102) possessed of a 'great Olympian laugh'
(p. 3), and admirers who are at once his 'followers' and
'disciples' (p. 8), Kellermann has in common with that other
'*phenomenal*' personality Swamiji in *A New Dominion* the

> wonderful gift of making each (woman) feel that he was in
> intimate contact with her, on the deepest and most thrilling
> level; and moreover, that he had absolutely no difficulty in
> understanding as well as condoning whatever secret, or
> secret longing, she might be harbouring. (p. 2)

To Louise Sonnenblick, whose lover he becomes, Kellermann
is nothing less than 'a *tornado*' (p. 38), and even in the most

unlikely situations retains his divine aspect: for example, while
taking a bath and demanding that his back be scrubbed, he
holds out a loofah as if it were a trident (p. 102). The lives of
Regi and Louise are changed by his theories (p. 39). Religious
symbolism thickens about Kellermann, whose very hair
resembles a 'burning bush' (p. 16) and 'a prophet's halo' (p. 87),
whose garments include a 'robe like a monk's' (p. 11), and who
cultivates in later life 'an air of benign blessing' (p. 67).

But such associations are counteracted, if not entirely given
the lie, by symbolism of a very different, indeed sinister kind.
Suggestions of the bestial and of a rank, mysterious underworld
combine in the very name of this European adventurer who,
like Hamid in "A Summer by the Sea", 'never really had any
difficulty in getting people to look after him' (p. 1); and cluster
about the 'den', the 'lair', the 'escape hatch' to which
Kellermann flees from time to time in order to avoid his disciples
and be himself. His classes in physical expression culminate
in a 'Day of Wrath' in the description of which animal references
proliferate: 'roaring as of lions, such bellowings of bulls,
chatterings of monkeys, shrieks of hyenas' (p. 40). To Regi, forty
years after he first enchanted her, he becomes — still larger
than life — an 'old monster' (p. 48). Mark sees him as a
'stranded whale' (p. 8), and as 'some superannuated circus
animal' (p. 85).

These divine and bestial images are brought together skilfully
in the 'Dionysian figure' of a tramp whose appearance wins from
little Natasha (the character who, above all others, seems to
be her creator's persona in this novel) tears of 'overwhelmed
pity for all the hungers of humanity':

> Natasha led (her grandmother) to the corner: the awful
> vision was still there. He sat enthroned on the dustbin, like
> a god wafted up from its depths. He was enormous and red
> in the face and wore a hat without a crown on his wild hair;
> a pair of stiff black trousers encased one massive leg but
> was ripped open on the other, exposing a surprisingly soft,
> lily-white expanse of thigh. His trident, or escutcheon, was
> an empty bottle held aloft in one hand, and he was
> alternately shouting and singing to passers-by. (p. 14)

It is Natasha, perceptive beyond her years, who draws her
disgusted grandmother's attention to the fact that the derelict

tramp resembles Leo Kellermann. The scene, which ends with
Louise thrusting coins and reproaches simultaneously on the
tramp, permits the reader an oblique insight into the mixture
of sensual and spiritual elements in Kellermann's character,
and foreshadows the novel's penultimate scene in which the
founder of the Academy of Potential Development, crazed with
the despair of an ordinary unrequited love, drives (evidently to
his death) with Natasha beside him, 'glad to be there with him:
not that she could do anything as, blinded with tears, he drove
them further into snow and mist, but at least so he wasn't
alone' (p. 226).

The blending of spiritual and bestial associations in Ruth
Jhabvala's characterization of Kellermann builds on the
methods she had used in building up the personality of that
other seeming charlatan Swamiji in *A New Dominion*.
Particularly striking in the earlier characterization were Lee's
recollection of her sexual encounter with her *guru* in bestial
terms,[11] and the scene in which Swamiji runs 'a broad, pale
tongue swiftly round his lips' as he tells Raymond of his (overtly
spiritual) desire that Lee should return to him.[12] The
similarities do not end there. Swamiji's ashram parallels
Kellermann's Academy, and the conversation of both men
ambiguously combine spiritual and sexual elements: for
example, Swamiji's statement that 'the old Lee must be broken
before the new Lee can be formed, and we are now only at the
first stage of our task'[13] has a parallel in Kellermann's pursuit
of Marietta:

> Leo ... issued many invitations to her — which she ignored
> as she did her best to ignore everything to do with him. But
> Leo had never given up. He loved it when people resisted him,
> nothing pleased him more. 'It's like fishing', he said — 'It's
> no fun unless the fish resists; unless it struggles — flaps
> and fights and wriggles for its life until — yupp! you've got
> it: up in the air where you want it, dangling there, with all
> your hook, line and sinker inside it'. He tended to use this
> image for both his sexual and his spiritual conquests. (p. 21)

But in Kellermann's ability to communicate intimately and
secretly with each of the women who make up the adoring circle
that surrounds him, there is not only a reflection of Swamiji's
easy fascination of a roomful of admiring Western tourists,[14]

but an intimation of a divine power (possessed by the god Krishna, and celebrated in countless expressions of Indian art, music and poetry) to speak directly and individually to the innermost hearts of a group of men and, especially, of women.[15]

Here, then, so cunningly woven into the stuff of her novel as to be unobtrusive and almost invisible, and yet undoubtedly at the very centre of it, is Ruth Jhabvala's image of India, larger than life, containing within it intimations of divine joy and intense disgust, of god and beast, of Heaven and Hell.[16] The ironic presentation of Swamiji's character had made it possible for two contradictory, yet perfectly consistent, interpretations of his personality to run through A New Dominion: spirituality on the one hand, opportunism on the other. Although there is no soft-hearted Natasha to weep for him, it is not possible for the careful reader to dismiss Swamiji as a mere sensualist and charlatan.

And so it is with Leo Kellermann. As the founder of a grandiose 'Academy of Potential Development' Kellermann is a fit subject for his creator's satire; and in Ruth Jhabvala's earlier fiction would certainly not have escaped the last. But this novel expresses, through Natasha, a compassion that transcends satire, impelling her to what is presumably her final, fatal, act of 'self-immolation' (p. 30). The reader is able to see Kellermann with the eyes of his creator as more pitiable in his final, dreadful and banal despair than any of his helpless victims.

The novel is rich in half-ironic, half sad detail that tells all about its characters and the lives they lead. 'Don't have any more of that', says Mark to his loutish and half-drunken homosexual lover. 'It's not nice for you to be drinking in the middle of the afternoon. Drink milk, or a Tab or something. But milk is best, a growing boy like you —' (p. 58), words that reflect his own confusions and through which we can hear the maternal tones of his Jewish mother and grandmother. Or the little scene at the Old Vienna, during which Mark, discussing business with a middle-aged American from Oregon while his thoughts are busy with his lover's presence at a table a few feet away, amiably places his hand on the knee of his prospective client's wife 'under the table and smiled at her over it ... He felt a bond with her ... Only Mr Cross — successful male, husband, father, Elk — was out of it'. (p. 133)

As a whole, *In Search Of Love and Beauty* presents a society whose members, despite the wealth and comfort in which they live, find little to delight them except very briefly and very superficially. They are all continually on the move, travelling in search of some perfect experience which is always out of reach. What makes this novel especially haunting is that the author deceives her readers into believing they can find sources of happiness where the characters forgot or scorned to look: in Natasha's love of her restless foster-brother, for instance, and in personal relationships the potential of which is destroyed time and again by the partners' selfishness or self-deception.

The sheer length (384 pages) of *Three Continents* is surprising and even a trifle discomforting to readers who come to this most recent of Ruth Jhabvala's novels in the knowledge that her development over the last thirty years has been consistently towards concentration and economy, both of material and expression. Most reviewers seem, in the face of this perplexity, and in the absence in the novel of the author's characteristic irony, to have confined their critical efforts to the task of relating the novel's plot for the benefit of their readers. 'Ruth Jhabvala's new novel is a replay of her short story "How I Became a Holy Mother"', states one fairly typical review:

> The story is short, funny, and sad. The novel is long, exciting, and sour.

Both are warnings to dumb Anglo-Saxon girls not to fall in with phoney Eastern sects. In the story the sect was of a comparatively harmless hippy type and operated on a begging bowl. The glossy Fourth World Movement operates on computers, teleprinters and cocktail parties; there are overtones of EST and the Moonies.

Harriet Wishwell (significant name) and her homosexual twin Michael are 19. They have plenty of old money and stand to inherit two substantial New England properties on their 21st birthday — the day towards which the novel moves, and on which it ends. Orphans of divorce, they have grown up symbiotically close, withdrawn, puritanical, idealistic and far from bright.

Steeping themselves in mystic literature, they plod away at 'transcending their own egos': easy meat for the Fourth World gang whose message is global but vague. Michael is converted first and invites the leaders to stay. They descend like royalty, and their brainwashed, efficient entourage establishes the movement's headquarters on the Wishwell estates.

The charismatic trio of leaders consists of the Rawul, an old Harrovian Indian princeling with an infinite capacity for making meaningless speeches; his gorgeous wife, the Rani; and Crishi, their adopted son. Crishi is irresistible to both sexes and soon in bed with both twins. His past is murky: the son of an Assamese prostitute, he has served several sentences and driven his teenage English wife to suicide.

Besides, he's not the couple's adopted son. They are not even married. The Rani (actually plain Renee) is a bent Eurasian dealer in Indian art. Crishi is her accomplice, lover, and the father of her child — whose official father is a wimpish Old Etonian art dealer in St James's.

These outlandish relationships unfold quite intelligibly as Mrs Jhabvala skilfully spins two simultaneous yarns: one a detective story revealing twist by twist the Asian's sinister, fraudulent past; the other a shocker shunting the twins towards their gruesome fate.

Early on Crishi makes sure of a stake in their fortune by marrying Harriet. She not only has to take turns with Michael, but also to share her husband with Renee in the same bed. Totally besotted, she accepts this along with Crishi's unkindness and neglect, persuading herself with idiot logic that he has noble motives for everything he does, including smuggling and mugging.

Mrs Jhabvala is having another bash at three favourite themes: charismatic movements; India; and sexual thraldom. About the first she has little new to say; Indians she doesn't seem to like much any more; but very few recent writers have brought off sexual thraldom as well as she did in *Heat and Dust* and again here. Crishi is as vivid, tempting and tactile as Cheri, and has a larger repertoire of seductive behaviour.

But the novel depends on the ironic disjunction between Harriet's dopey first-person narrative and our understanding of what is really going on. Unfortunately Mrs Jhabvala despises her anti-heroine to the point where irony turns into sarcasm. In the long run — 384 pages long — this has a lowering effect.[17]

Ruth Jhabvala's first published novel, *To Whom She Will*, was very lengthy one indeed, and reading it in the light of her later work, especially that miracle of compression *Heat and Dust*, we become aware that a good deal of that length went into descriptions which 'explained' the Indian scene to the (Western) reader.

Three Continents, a novel that begins in America, moves to Britain, and ends in a tiny Indian princely state named Dhoka, could have acquired its length because of the range and variety of its settings, but in fact does so because the naivety of its narrator requires that everything that happens is spelled out in terms that she can understand. Since Harriet is innocent to the point of stupidity and is by no means capable of the subtle ironies that Ruth Jhabvala has perfected through novel after novel, the experiment produces not revelation but — for the first time in Jhabvala's fiction — tedium. And this is the more disappointing because there is a great deal in the novel which could, differently told, have succeeded.

Naive by nature, blinded still further by love, Harriet cannot or will not perceive that she is being exploited and humiliated by the Fourth World Movement to which she is ready to dedicate her life and her fortune. 'Although matters are clearly being handled by experts all around her, Harriet lives in a little girl's world which transforms everything into fairytale'.[18] She is, in fact, very close in spirit and mental capacity to Lee of *A New Dominion*, and a good deal less intelligent than even Katie of the story "How I Became A Holy Mother" or Susie of "A Summer By The Sea". It is worth noting that Ruth Jhabvala was wisely sparing in her use of Lee as a narrator or originator of interior monologue in *A New Dominion*, interspersing with Lee's invariably obtuse or confused impressions of the Indian life around her the acute observations of Raymond. Giving *A New Dominion* over entirely to Lee would have produced a very different book — it would have produced, in fact, a book very like *Three Continents*, which resembles *A New Dominion* in its 3-part structure, its themes of religious, cultural and sexual exploitation, and even in many of its characterisations. In the two short stories mentioned above, the brevity of the form ensures that the reader does not weary of an obtuse narrator.

In choosing such a narrator as Harriet for this novel, it is quite as if, in an effort to test herself, a supreme duellist had decided to fight with one hand tied behind her back. In one of the best of her early stories, "Lekha", Ruth Jhabvala used the narrative voice of an extremely conservative and conventional Indian woman: but not of a stupid one. Her choice of Harriet as narrator places almost unbearable restrictions on skills which have in previous work achieved their most subtle effects through ironic ambiguity. The good things in the novel — notably the character of Harriet's husband (and principal exploiter) Crishi, who shares by virtue of his name as well as of his personality the attractive, yet sinister Krishna-like attributes of Swamiji and Leo Kellermann — are swamped by Harriet, whose naivety survives everything, even the murder of her beloved twin, Michael.

'Having assimilated all this Indian experience I don't want to forget it or cast it off; what I want to do is to take it out again as a Westerner, enriched by what I have learned there'.[19]

Where *Three Continents* fails by attempting the impossible, *In Search of Love and Beauty*, which confronts 'life's disenchantments with alert and humorous resilience'[20], unobtrusively achieves this personal authorial aim through a plot that brings together characters convincingly representative of its author's 'three backgrounds' to work out a universal theme. It does this most triumphantly through the chief of those characters, the novel's anti-hero Leo Kellermann — Apollo, Krishna, and Superman.

Notes

1. Ruth Prawer Jhabvala, interviewed by Patricia W. Mooney: 'Another Dimension of Living', in *Newsweek* 31 October 1977.
2. See, for example, the characters of Hans Loeuwe in *The Householder* (1960); Lee in *A New Dominion* (1972); the narrator in *Heat and Dust* (1975); also the short stories "A Spiritual Call" and "How I Became A Holy Mother".
3. See Chapter XI.
4. Ruth Jhabvala, "A Summer by the Sea", in *The New Yorker* 7 August 1978, pp. 26-34.
5. Ruth Prawer Jhabvala, *Three Continents* (John Murray, London:

1987), pp. 23-4. All references in this chapter and throughout this book are to the 1987 British edition.

6. "Farid and Farida", in *The New Yorker*, 15 October 1984, p. 46.
7. Personal communication to the author.
8 Quoted in Chapter I.
9 Ruth Prawer Jhabvala, *In Search of Love and Beauty* (John Murray, London: 1983), pp. 24-5. All references in this chapter and throughout this book are to the 1983 edition.
10. See Chapter XI for a discussion of Ruth Jhabvala's use of an elderly female musician in the film AUTOBIOGRAPHY OF A PRINCESS to symbolize India's indomitable spirit and traditional skills.
11. Cf. *A New Dominion*, p. 169
12. *A New Dominion*, p. 179.
13. *A New Dominion*, p. 121
14. *A New Dominion*, p. 123
15. Cf. the discussion of Swamiji in Chapter VIII.
16. Cf. R.P. Jhabvala, 'Moonlight, jasmine and rickets' (1975), op. cit.
17. Gabriele Annan, 'Old money and new Sects', review of *Three Continents*, in the *Sunday Telegraph* 18 October 1987,
18. Anita Brookner, 'Stupidity is in the head of the beholder', review of *Three Continents*, in *Spectator* 24 October 1987.
19. R.P. Jhabvala, quoted A. Rutherford and K.H. Petersen, '*Heat and Dust*: Ruth Prawer Jhabvala's experience of India' (1976). p. 377.
20. Peter Kemp, 'The great pursuit', review of *In Search of Love and Beauty*, in the *Observer* 10 April 1983, p. 33.

Bibliography

A. Ruth Prawer Jhabvala's Works

A Backward Place (John Murray, London: 1965). A novel.

Amrita (W.W. Norton & Company, Inc., New York: 1956). U.S. edition of *To Whom She Will* (1955). Dedicated 'For My Mother'. A novel.

A New Dominion (John Murray, London: 1972). Reprinted 1974. U.S. edition (Harper and Row, New York: 1973) under title *Travelers*. A novel.

An Experience of India (John Murray, London: 1966). "Reprinted 1968, 1971. Dedicated "For Jennifer and Shashi: 'Bombay Talkie' ". A collection of short stories, with the essay "Myself in India" (see below) as Introduction.

A Stronger Climate (John Murray, London: 1968). Reprinted 1976. Epigraph: 'They come no longer to conquer but to be conquered'. A collection of short stories.

"A summer by the sea", in *The New Yorker*, 7 August 1978, pp. 26-34. A short story.

Autobiography of a Princess, screenplay of film of the same title, published on pp. 131-161 of James Ivory, *Autobiography of a Princess* (see below).

"Disinheritance". Text of public lecture delivered on the occasion of the award to the author of the Neil Gunn International Fellowship in Edinburg in 1979. Published in *Blackwoods Magazine*, July 1979.

Esmond in India (George Allen & Unwin Ltd., London: 1958). Dedicated 'For C.S.H. Jhabvala'. A novel.

"Farid and Farida". Short story, *The New Yorker*, 15 October 1984, pp. 40-50.

"Foreign wives", in *The London Magazine*, January 1968, pp. 12-22. A short story.

Get Ready For Battle (John Murray, London: 1962). Dedicated 'For C.S.H.J. again'. Bears the epigraph: 'Treating alike pleasure and pain, gain and loss, victory and defeat, then get ready for battle'. A novel.

Heat and Dust (John Murray, London: 1975). A novel. Awarded the Booker Prize for Fiction in 1975.

How I Became A Holy Mother and Other Stories (John Murray, London: 1976). U.S. edition published by Harper and Row, New York (1976) contains a story omitted from the British edition, "The Englishwoman" (see below).

"India overpowered me". Letter to the *Sunday Times*, in which the author protests at the simplification effected and the erroneous impression given of her relationship with India by an interviewer in the *Sunday Times Magazine* of 13 July 1980. Published in the *Sunday Times*, 3 August 1980.

In Search of Love and Beauty, (John Murray, London, and William Morrow, New York: 1983). In press. A novel. The American edition contains a drawing by C.S.H. Jhabvala of the New York skyline as seen from the window of the novelist's apartment.

Like Birds, Like Fishes and Other Stories (John Murray, London: 1963). Dedicated 'For Jim and Ismail'.

"Living in India", in *The London Magazine*, September 1970, pp. 41-51, reprinted from *An Experience of India* (1966) see above.

"Moonlight, jasmine and rickets", *The New York Times*, 22 April 1975.

"Myself in India", *The Illustrated Weekly of India*, 27 February 1972, pp. 31-35, reprinted from *An Experience of India* (1966) see above.

"Of love and sorrow", in *The Writers' Workshop Miscellany*: 10, January-April 1962, pp. 31-35. A short story.

"Open city: Letter from Delhi", in *Encounter*, May 1964, pp. 40-44.

Out of India. (William Morrow, New York: 1986) A collection of 15 previously published Jhabvala stories. Includes the well-known piece 'Myself in India' (first published in 1966, see above), 'Two More under the Indian Sun', 'On Bail', 'Passion', and the early (1963) story 'The Widow'.

"Parasites", in *The New Yorker*, 13 March 1978, pp. 34-43. A short story.

"Ruth Prawer Jhabvala's testament", excerpts from Ruth Prawer Jhabvala's commemorative lecture on the Scottish novelist Neil Gunn in *The Hindustan Times Magazine*, 27 July 1980, p. 10.

Shakespearewallah. Screen play for film of the same title, in *Savages. Shakespearewallah: Two Films by James Ivory.* (Plexus, London: 1973)

"The Englishwoman", in *How I Became a Holy Mother and Other Stories* (Harper and Row, New York: 1976), pp. 22-38, see above.

The Householder (John Murray, London: 1960). Dedicated 'For Renana, Ava and Firoza-Bibi'. A novel.

The Nature of Passion (George Allen & Unwin, Ltd., London: 1956). Dedicated 'To M.A. and P.A.'. A novel.

Three Continents. (John Murray, London and William Morrow, New York: 1987). A novel. Dedicated 'For James Ivory and Ismail Merchant', with the additional note: 'My thanks and deep appreciation to the John D. and Catherine T. Mac Arthur Foundation for their most liberal and liberating —support'.

To Whom She Will (George Allen & Unwin, Ltd., London: 1955). Reprinted 1956. Dedicated 'For My Mother'. Bears epigraph:

> For if she bides a maiden still
> She gives herself to whom she will;
> Then marry her in tender age
> So warns the heaven-begotten sage.
>
> > (*The Panchatantra*, trans. Arthur W. Ryder)

Published in the U.S. under title *Amrita* (see above), in 1956. A novel.

Travelers (Harper and Row, New York: 1973). U.S. edition of *A New Dominion* (1972) see above. A novel.

"Writers and the Cinema". Contribution to a symposium on the subject, in *Times Literary Supplement* 18 November 1983, p. 1287.

"Writing for films", in *The Illustrated Weekly of India*, 21 March 1971, pp. 24-27.

B. Selected Literary Criticism and Books of General Reference

Agarwal, Ramlal. "An interview with Ruth Prawer Jhabvala", *Quest* 91 (September-October 1974), pp. 33-36.

_____ "Forster, Jhabvala and readers", *The Journal of Indian Writing in English*, 3:2 (July 1975), pp. 25-27.

_____ "Jhabvala doesn't merely scoff", *The Times of India*, 19 October 1975.

_____ "Outsider with unusual insight", *The Times of India*, 25 March 1973.

_____ "Two approaches to Jhabvala", *The Journal of Indian Writing in English*, 5:1 (January 1977), pp. 24-27.

Annan, Gabriele. "Old Money and New Sects". Review of *Three Continents*. In *Sunday Telegraph*, 18 October 1987.

Asnani, Shyam M. "Jhabvala's novels: A thematic study", *The Journal of Indian Writing in English*, 2:1 (January 1974), pp. 38-47.

Bailey, Elizabeth. "In the Realm of the Past". Review of the film *Heat and Dust* in Newsweek, 21 February 1983.

Beliappa, Meena. "A study of Jhabvala's fiction", *The Banasthali Patrika*, No. 12 (Special Issue on Indo-English Literature, January 1969), quoted by S.M. Asnani (see above), p. 43.

Blackwell, Fritz. "Perception of the guru in the fiction of Ruth Prawer Jhabvala", "A European Emigre in India". In "Asiaweek Literary Review", *Asiaweek* 15 February 1985. Includes a short interview with the novelist. *The Journal of Indian Writing in English*, 5:2 (July 1977), pp. 6-13.

Borthwick, Meredith. "Autobiography of a princess", L.I.P. (double issue), Nos. 2 and 3 (1977), pp. 127-128.

Bradbury, Nicola. "Filming James", *Essays in Criticism* 29: 4 (October 1979) pp. 293-301.

Brookner, Amita. 'Stupidity is in the head of the beholder'. Review of *Three Continents*. In Spectator, 24 October 1987. This review, by a fellow novelist and Booker Prize-winner, considers *In Search of Love and Beauty* to be Ruth Jhabvala's 'best novel', and *Three Continents* itself 'an intelligent but unsatisfactory' work. Camber Porter, Melinda. "Scriptwriter for Ivory". In 'The Arts', *The Times* 13 July 1978, p. 12. An interview with the novelist and scriptwriter.

Coleman, John. Review of AUTOBIOGRAPHY OF A PRINCESS in

The New Statesman, quoted in a pamphlet prepared and distributed by Ronin Films Pty Ltd., 136 Blamey Crescent, Campbell, A.C.T. 2601, Australia.

Colvin, Clare. "Double Vision". In *The Times* (London) 31 January 1983. Article on the Merchant-Ivory film-making partnership.

Contemporary Literary Criticism: Excerpts from the Criticism of the Works of Today's Novelists, Poets, Playwrights and other Creative Writers. Gale Research Co., (Detroit: 1975) Vol. 4, ed. Carolyn Riley. Contains extracts from criticism of D. Rabinowitz, B.G. Harrison, F. Levy, R. Winegarten, and L.S. Fallis (see below) on pp. 256-259.

Current Biography, Vol. 38: No. 3 (March 1977), "Ruth Prawer Jhabvala", pp. 27-30.

Daily Telegraph review of *Jane Austen in Manhattan*, in *Daily Telegraph* 25 July 1980.

David Stratton Showcase Theatre Pamphlet for THE EUROPEANS, Sydney 1980.

Davies, Russell. "Tea and memories", review of AUTOBIOGRAPHY OF A PRINCESS, in *The Observer* (London), 7 March 1976.

Dell'Oso, Anna-Maria. 'Another winner on India'. Review of the film *Heat and Dust* in *Sydney Morning Herald* (Australia) 13 August 1983.

De Souza, Eunice. "The blinds drawn and the airconditioner on: The novels of Ruth Prawer Jhabvala", *World Literature Written in English*, 17:1 (April 1978), pp. 219-224.

————— "The expatriate writer", a paper presented at the 4th Triennial ACLALS Conference, New Delhi, January 1977, 9 pp.

Dunkley, Chris. "Mystery and Mystification". Review of *Jane Austen in Manhattan* in the *Financial Times* 9 July 1980.

Ezekiel, Nissim. "Cross cultural encounter in literature", *The Indian P.E.N.*, 43:11 and 12 (1977), pp. 4-8. Includes comment on *Heat and Dust.*

Fallis, Laurence S. Review of *Travelers*, in *Books Abroad*, 48:2 (Spring 1974), p. 419; reprinted in *Contemporary Literary Criticism* (see above).

Financial Times review of *Jane Austen in Manhattan*. In *Financial Times* 25 July 1980.

'F.R.', "Slow dancing", review of ROSELAND in *Time*, 17 October 1977.

French, Philip. "Ivory elegy", review of THE EUROPEANS in *The Observer* (London) Sunday 1 July 1979.

French, Philip. "Ivory elegy", review of THE EUROPEANS in *The Observer* (London) Sunday 1 July 1979.

_____ "Journey to India". Review of the film *Heat and Dust*. In *The Observer* 6 February 1983.

Gemmill, Janet Powers. Review of *How I Became a Holy Mother*, in *World Literature Written in English*, 16:2 (November 1977), pp. 380-381.

Gibbs, Patrick. "A Jewel from the East". Review of the film *Heat and Dust*. In the *Daily Telegraph* 4 February 1983.

_____ "Sydney film festival: Ivory excels in comedy of manners", review of HULLABLOO OVER GEORGIE AND BONNE'S PICTURE, in *The Daily Telegraph* (London), 28 June 1979.

_____ "When East was East ...", review of AUTOBIOGRAPHY OF A PRINCESS, in *The Daily Telegraph* (London), 5 March 1976.

Gilbert, Martin. *Final Jouney: The Fate of the Jews in Nazi Europe* (Allen and Unwin, London: 1979)

Gillett, John. Review of BOMBAY TALKIE in *The Monthly Film Bulletin* (London), August 1971, p. 160.

_____ "Merchant-Ivory", *Sight and Sound*, London (Spring 1973), pp. 95-97.

Goodman, Walter. Review of *Three Continents* in *International Herald Tribune*, 18 August 1987.

Gooneratne, Yasmine. "Apollo, Krishna, Superman: The Image of India in Ruth Prawer Jhabvala's *In Search of Love and Beauty*". *In Ariel* 15, 2 (April 1984). The University of Calgary Press; pp. 110-117; reprinted in S.N.A. Rizvi (ed) *Essays on Poetry and Fiction* (Vasant A. Shahane Commemorative Volume) Doaba House, Delhi 1988.

_____ "Contemporary India in the writing of Ruth Prawer Jhabvala", in *Westerly* 4 (December 1983). The University of Western Australia pp. 73-80.

_____ "Film into fiction: The influence upon Ruth Prawer Jhabvala's fiction of her work for the cinema, 1960-1976", *World Literature Written in English*, 18:2 (November 1979), pp. 368-386.

_____ "Irony as an instrument of social and self-analysis in Ruth Prawer Jhabvala's *Heat and Dust*", *New Literature Review*, 4 (1978), pp. 41-50.

_____ "Ruth Jhabvala: Generating heat and light", review of

Heat and Dust and *How I Became a Holy Mother*, in *Kunapipi*, 1 (1978), pp. 115-129.

―――――― "Ruth Prawer Jhabvala". In H. Bock and A. Werttheim (eds) *Essays on Contemporary Post-Colonial Fiction*. Max Hueber Verlag, Munich 1986; pp. 205-223.

―――――― "Satirical semicolon; Ruth Prawer Jhabvala's screenplay for BOMBAY TALKIE", in *The Journal of Indian Writing in English*, guest ed. Kirpal Singh, 8: 1-2 (January-July 1980) pp. 177-181.

―――――― "The making of an American superman: Ruth Prawer Jhabvala's *In Search of Love and Beauty*". In *CRNLE Reviews Journal* 2 (December 1983) pp. 11-13.

―――――― " 'The proper accoutrements of style and sensibility': Eighteenth century influences on the fiction of Ruth Prawer Jhabvala". In S. Nandan (ed) *Language and Literature in Multi-Cultural Contexts*, pp. 141-168. Association for Commonwealth Literature and Language Studies. University of the South Pacific, Suva, Fiji 1983.

―――――― " 'Traditional' elements in the fiction of Kamala Markandaya, R.K. Narayan and Ruth Prawer Jhabvala", *World Literature Written in English*, 15:1 (April 1976), pp. 121-134.

Gray, Paul. 'Tributes of Empathy and Grace'. Review of *Out of India*. In *Time* 12 May 1986.

Green, Benny. "Plain Jane", television review of JANE AUSTEN IN MANHATTAN, in *Punch*, 16 July 1980, p. 113.

Grimes, Paul. "A passage to U.S. for writer of India", in *The New York Times*, 15 May 1976.

Hamilton, Alex. "The book of Ruth", an interview with Ruth Prawer Jhabvala (following the award of the Booker Prize to *Heat and Dust*), *The Guardian*, 30 November 1975.

Harrison, Barbara Grizzuti. "India, Inc.: Hullabaloo over Merchant-Ivory Pictures", *Harper's*, March 1982, pp. 65-70.

―――――― "We're off to see the Guru", review of *Travelers* in Ms (December 1973) pp. 28, 31, reprinted in *Contemporary Literary Criticism* (see above).

Herman, Lewis. *A Practical Manual of Screen Playwriting* (Forum Books, Cleveland and New York, The World Publishing Co.: 1963, 1969).

Hughes, David. "A Shadow called India". Review of the film *Heat and Dust* in *Sunday Times* (London) 6 February 1983.

Humphreys, A.R. "Fielding and Smollett", in Boris Ford, ed. *The Pelican Guide to English Literature IV: From Dryden to Johnson* (Penguin Books, Harmondsworth: 1970).

Isar, R.f. "Is India just heat and dust?" In *Hindustan Times* 9 November 1980; an article that challenges Ruth Jhabvala's theory about Europeans in India (see "Myself in India", above).

Ivory, James (compiler). *Autobiography of a Princess: Also Being the Adventures of an American Film Director in the Land of the Maharajas* (Harper and Row, New York: 1975). British edition published by John Swope and others, and screenplay written by R.P. Jhabvala on pp. 131-161.

Jobson, Sandra. "Heroines in love with India", review of *Heat and Dust*, in *Sydney Morning Herald*, 10 January 1976.

Jussawalla, A. (ed). *New Writing in India* (Penguin Books, Harmondsworth: 1974, 1977).

Kael, Pauline. "The Current Cinema: The Woman Question". Review of *The Bostonians*, which takes an opposite view to that presented by Vincent Canby in the *New York Times* (see above, and Chapter XI Writing for Film). In *The New Yorker* 6 August 1984, pp. 68-72.

Karnani, Chetan. "Ruth Jhabvala's backward place", a paper presented at the 5th Triennial ACLALS Conference, Suva, 1980. 14 pp.

———— "Satirical Indian novel", reveiw of *A Backward Place*, in *The Journal of Commonwealth Literature*, 3 (1968), pp. 132-133.

Kemp, Peter. "The Great Pursuit". Review of *In Search of Love and Beauty* in *The Observer* 10 April 1983, p. 33.

Kumar, S.N. Review of *Heat and Dust* in *The Literary Criterion*, 12:2-3 (1976), pp. 226-228.

Levy, Francis. "A passage to nowhere", *The New Leader*, 18 February 1974, p. 19; reprinted in Contemporary Literary Criticism (see above).

Majumdar, R.C. (ed.) *The History and Culture of the Indian Peope*. Volume I. George Allen & Unwin, London: (1951) 1957.

Malcolm, Derek. Review of AUTOBIOGRAPHY OF A PRINCESS in *The Guardian*, 4 March 1976.

Maslin, Janet. "The Screen: Redgrave in James's 'Bostonians'". Review of *The Bostonians*, in *New York Times* 2 August 1984.

McGuinness, P.P. "Memorable vignette", review of THE

EUROPEANS in *The National Times*, 3-9 February 1980.

McLeod, Mark. "Devastating, compassionate", review of *How I Became a Holy Mother in the Sydney Morning Herald*, 15 January 1977.

Mellors, John. "Merging with India", *The London Magazine*, 16:3 (August-September 1976), pp. 92-97.

Millar, Gavin. "Mixed Up Together". Review of the film *Heat and Dust*. In *Sight & Sound* 52, 1 (Winter 1982).

Mukherjee, Meenakshi. "Inside the outsider", a paper presented at the 4th Triennial ACLALS Conference, New Delhi, January 1977.

_____ "Journey's end for Jhabvala", in *Explorations in Modern Indo-English Fiction*, ed. R.K. Dhawan (Bahri Publications Pvt. Ltd. New Delhi: 1982), pp. 208-213.

_____ *The Twice-Born Fiction: Themes and Techniques of the Indian Novel in English* Heinemann Educational Books, London and New Delhi: 1971).

Narayan, Shyamala A. Introduction to a bibliography of Indian writing in English in 1975, in *The Journal of Commonwealth Literature*, 11:2 (December 1976), pp. 82-84. Includes comment on *Heat and Dust*.

New York Times, 13 July 1973. "A novelist of India reflects two worlds", author unnamed. Reprinted in *The National Times*, 7-12 January 1974, p. 18, with the new title: "Rot and a deep sense of melacholy: a major writer dissects modern, middleclass India".

Observer Profile: 'A heritage of lonely wandering'. In *The Observer*, 10 April 1983.

Owen, Lyn. "A passage from India to America", *The Observer Review* (London), 9 April 1978, p. 30.

Pascall, Geraldine. Review of THE EUROPEANS in *Weekend Australian Magazine*, 26 January 1980.

Pocock, Tom. "Thoroughly Modern Memsahib". Review of *Heat and Dust* in *The Standard* 3 February 1983.

Powell, Dilys. Review of AUTOBIOGRAPHY OF A PRINCESS in *The Sunday Times* (London), 7 March 1976.

_____ "Pure Ivory", review of QUARTET in *Punch*, 22 July 1981, p. 152.

_____ "Tale From the Raj". Review of the film *Heat and Dust*. In *unch* 9 February 1983, p. 45.

Pulleine, Tim. "A palpable heat". Review of the film *Heat and*

Dust, in *The Guardian* 13 February 1983.

Pym, John. *The Wandering Company. 21 years of Merchant Ivory Films*. B.F.I. Publishing, 1983.

———— " 'Where could I meet other screenwriters?': A conversation with Ruth Prawer Jhabvala", *Sight and Sound*, London (Winter 1978), pp. 15-18.

Rabinowitz, D. Review of *Travelers* in *The New York Times Book Reveiw* 8 July 1973, pp. 6-7; reprinted in *Contemporary Literary Criticism* (see above).

Raghavan, G.N.S. *Understanding India* (Indian Council for Cultural Relations, Delhi: 1976).

Ramanujan, Molly. "Passages of India". In *Maroon*, University of Chicago, 12 May 1984. Reviews a dramatic presentation by Arnold Aprill of two Jhabvala stories ("How I Became A Holy Mother" and "Desecration") sponsored by the City Lit Theater Company and presented at the Victory Gardens Studio, Chicago, in 1984.

Raphael, Isabel. "Big Apple". Review of *In Search of Love and Beauty*. In *Time* 14 April 1983.

Reed, John. Review of *An Experience of India* in *The Christian Science Monitor*, quoted by S.M. Asnani (see above).

Riddell, Elizabeth. "Writer's skill and wit move West". Review of *In Search of Love and Beauty, in The Bulletin* (Australia) 30 August 1983.

Robinson, David. "Shrine for the Raj", review of AUTOBIOGRAPHY OF A PRINCESS in *The London Times*, 5 March 1976.

Rutherford, Anna. "Ruth Prawer Jhabvala's window on India", *ACLALS Bulletin*, 4th Series: No. 3 (1975), pp. 27-29.

———— and K.H. Petersen, "*Heat and Dust*: Ruth Prawer Jhabvala's experience of India", *World Literature Written in English*, 15:2 (November 1976), pp. 373-378. Includes extracts from an interview with Ruth Jhabvala immediately after the award to her of the Booker Prize for *Heat and Dust* in 1975.

Sethi, Sunil. "Familiar Ghosts". Review of the film *Heat and Dust* in *India Today* 30 November 1983.

Seymour-Smith, Martin. "Sad Guru". Review of *In Search of Love and Beauty*. In *Financial Times* 9 April 1983.

Shahane, Vasant A. "An artist's experience of India: Ruth Prawer Jhabvala's fiction', *The Literary Criterion*, 12:2-3 (1976), pp. 47-62.

_____ *Ruth Prawer Jhabvala* (Arnold-Heinemann, New Delhi: 1976).

_____ "Ruth Prawer Jhabvala's *A New Dominion*", *The Journal of Commonwealth Literature*, 12:1 (August 1977), pp. 45-55.

Singh, Jacqueline. "Dear Mrs Jhabvala", *The Illustrated Weekly of India*, 3 September 1972, pp. 22-23.

Stevens, A. Wilber. "Concept and form in contemporary Indian fiction", *Actes du VIe Cpmgres de l'Association Internationale de Litterature Comparee* (August 1970), pp. 711-715.

Stiles, Peter. "India and the western sensibility in the fiction of Ruth Prawer Jhabvala", unpublished M.A. dissertation, Macquarie University, 1979.

The Films of James Ivory. An illustrated brochure published by Contemporary Films Ltd., 55 Greek Street, London WIV 6DB. (undated).

Times of India interview with Ismail Merchant: "How now, Mr Europeanwallah?" In 'The Arts: Films' *Times of India* 22 February 1981.

_____ Review of a Merchant-Ivory retrospective of nine films shown in Delhi in 1983. Focuses particularly on *Heat and Dust*. In *Times of India*, 16 October 1983.

Tuohy, Frank. "Metropolitan Margins". Review of *In Search of Love and Beauty*. In *Times Literary Supplement* 15 April 1983.

Verghese, C.P. 'A note on *Esmond in India*', *The Journal of Indian Writing in English*, 4:2 (July 1976), pp. 33-37.

_____ *Problems of the Indian Creative Writer in English* (Somaiya Publications, Bombay: 1971).

Walsh, William. "Nataraja and the packet of saffron", *Encounter*, 23:4 (October 1964), pp. 78-83. Includes the following comment on Ruth Jhabvala: 'Her characters are a trifle routine, her prose is pedestrian, but she is an expert analyst of domestic friction'.

Wapshott, Nicholas. "And Jane Austen Makes Four". Review of *Jane Austen in Manhattan* in *Times* (London) July 1980.

Weinraub, Bernard. "Ruth Prawer Jhabvala: Writer known for her India novels changes focus". In *International Herald Tribune*, 1-2 October 1983. An interview with the novelist, following the publication of *In Search of Love and Beauty*.

Williams, Haydn Moore. "English writing in free India 1947-1967', *Twentieth Century Literature*, 16:1 (January 1970), pp. 3-15.

_____ "R.K. Narayan and R. Prawer Jhabvala: Two interpreters of modern India", *Literature East and West*, 16:4 (April 1975 for December 1972), pp. 1136-1153.

_____ "Strangers in a backward place: Modern India in the fiction of Ruth Prawer Jhabvala", *The Journal of Commonwealth Literature*, 6:1 (1971), pp. 53-64.

_____ *The Fiction of Ruth Prawer Jhabvala* (Writers' Workshop, Calcutta: 1973).

_____ "The Yogi and the Babbitt: Themes and characters of the new India in the novels of R. Prawer Jhabvala", *Twentieth Century Literature*, 15:2 (July 1969), pp. 81-90.

Winegarten, Renee. 'Ruth Prawer Jhabvala: A Jewish passage to India', *Midstream*, (March 1974), pp. 72-79, extracts of which are reprinted in *Contemporary Literary Criticism* (see above).

Wordsworth, Christopher. "Ripples from an old Indian scandal", review of *Heat and Dust*, in *Weekend Australian Magazine*, 10 January 1976.

C. Unpublished Sources

"Hullabaloo over Georgie and Bonnie's Pictures". Dialogue Continuity.

"Jane Austen in Manhattan". Dialogue List.

"Roseland". An Original Screen Play by Ruth Prawer Jhabvala.

"The Europeans". Post-Production Script.

"The Guru". Original Screen Play by Ruth Prawer Jhabvala and James Ivory.

(All the property of Merchant Ivory Productions, 17 West 60th Street, New York, NY 10023.)

Index

A Doll's House, See under Ibsen, Henrik
A Passage to India, See under Forster, E.M.
Académie du Cinema, 279
Addy, Wesley, 282
Adjani, Isabelle, 283
Agarwal, Ramlal, 11-12, 31, 32, 122, 148, 165, 223, 276, 277
Anand, Mulk Raj 71-72
  Works of:
  The Coolie, 72
Ashcroft, Dame Peggy, 281
Asramas (stages of Aryan life), 123
Astor, David, 282
Austen, Jane, 15, 17, 18, 19, 23, 27, 36, 38, 47, 59, 60, 84, 87, 93, 103, 104, 105, 121, 245, 246, 248, 272, 282, 294-95, 296
  Works of:
  Emma, 23, 38, 59, 103, 104, 246
  Mansfield Park, 19, 20, 60, 84, 87, 248, 282
  Northanger Abbey, 19, 20, 23, 47, 294-95, 296
  Persuasion, 23
  Pride and Prejudice, 18, 19, 20, 21, 23, 36, 105, 121
  Sense and Sensibility, 19, 20, 21, 87, 93
Avatar, 11

B.B.C, 280-281
Banerjee, Bibhutibhusan, 262
  Works of:
  Pather Panchali, 262
Baxter, Anne, 282
Berlin Film Festival, 279
Bhagavad Gita, 78, 119, 152
Boccaccio, 23
Booker Prize for Fiction, 10, 284, 286
British Film Institute, 12

Buddhist Literature, See Dhammapada
Bunyan, John, 28
  Works of:
  The Pilgrim's Progress, 28
Burney, Fanny, 19, 21, 23, 87, 93
  Works of:
  Evelina, 21, 23, 87, 93

Candide, See under Voltaire
Cannes Film Festival, 282, 283
Chaplin, Geraldine, 281
Chekov, Anton, 18, 23, 293
Chaucer, 23
Coolie, The, See under Anand, Mulk Raj
Coomaraswamy, Ananda, K, 169
Copeland, Joan, 281
Courts and Camps in India, See under Fitzroy, Yvonne
Crotchet Castle, See under Peacock, T.I.

de Souza, Eunice, 72, 75
De Maupassant, 23
De Natale, Don, 281
Dhammapada, 211, 223
Dutt, Utpal, 279, 289

Eichorn, Lisa, 282
Emma, See under Austen, Jane
Evelina, See under Burney, Fanny

Fielding, Henry, 92
Fitzroy, Yvonne, 287
  Works of:
  Courts and Camps in India, 287
Food, Social importance of, 3-4
Forster, E.M. 5, 16, 86, 169, 196
  Works of:
  A Passage to India, 5, 16, 196
  A Room with a View, 81, 317
  Maurice, 8
French, Philip, 282

Gallagher, Helen, 281
Gibbs, Patrick, 281
Gillet, John, 295, 308-9
Gita Govinda, 135-36
Goldsmith, Oliver, 55

Harding, D.W., 27
Hedda Gabler, See under Ibsen,
  Henrik
Herman, Lewis 301
Hogarth, William 93
Humphreys, A.R. 92-93

Ibsen, Henrik, 24
  Works of:
  A Doll's House, 24, 182
  Hedda Gabler
Illustrated Weekly of India 319
Ivory, James, 8, 223, 234, 279,
  282, 283, 284, 289, 290, 295,
  316-17
Iyengar, K.R.S., 165

Jaffrey, Madhur, 279, 280, 289,
  293, 319
Jaipur, royal family of, 306
James, Henry, 282, 322
  Works of:
  The Bostonians, 282, 322
  The Europeans, 282, 322
Jataka Tales, 23
Jhabvala, Cyrus S.H., 3
Jhabvala, Ruth Prawer,
  awards, 9, 12, 279, 284, 286
  background, 1-2, 21, 321, 325,
  328, 335
  being Jewish, 21, 170
  Comments on her own work,
  2-3, 7, 8, 9, 11, 12, 17-18, 21,
  25-26, 27, 29-30, 35, 83, 106,
  150, 153, 194, 217-18, 223,
  250-52, 269, 290, 321
  Critical assessments of, 10, 17,
  18, 21, 36-7, 74-75, 80, 92,
  265, 278-80, 289, 316, 317,
  319
  fiction and film, connections
  between, 2, 8-9, 161, 185-87,
  194, 201-202, 204-205, 234,
  252, 264-65, 278, 286, 288,

290-309, 315, 317-18
  irony, use of, 2, 18-19, 26-27,
  36, 53-55, 59-60, 63, 77,
  86-87, 90-92, 99-100, 106,
  118-20, 128-29, 145-46, 159,
  164, 172-73, 207, 242, 244,
  245, 265, 295, 331, 333, 334,
  335
  life and literary career of, 1-31,
  321, 335
  settings of her fiction, 12,
  18-19, 22, 35, 68-70, 174-75,
  193-94, 196-97, 231-32,
  244-45, 321-22, 324, 325-26,
  334, 335
  symbolism, use of, 24-26, 29,
  50, 68, 77, 112, 121, 138,
  193-94, 196-97, 288
  westerners in India described,
  2, 4, 5, 7, 8, 9, 10, 16, 95-98,
  113, 142-44, 150, 192-93,
  197-98, 199, 200, 225-27,
  251-52, 265-68, 286-87, 307
  Collections of Short Stories: *An
  Experience of India* (1966) 251,
  283, (contains) "A Bad Woman"
  251; "A Course of English
  Studies" 5, 16, 251, 271-73; "A
  Star and Two Girls", 10, 251,
  289, 293; "A Experience of
  India", 8, 9, 10, 251, 270, 289,
  290, 297; "Myself in India", 8,
  11, 16, 29-30, 32, 33, 106,
  107-108, 121, 165, 194, 223,
  248, 251; "Rose Petals" 251,
  256; "Suffering Women", 17,
  251, 263, 290; "The Housewife",
  231, 251, 253, 274-75, 276.
  A Stronger Climate (1968) 252,
  284 (contains) "A Spiritual
  Call", 9, 242, 252, 264-65, 297;
  "A Young Man of Good Family",
  252; "An Indian Citizen" 7, 67,
  252, 270, 290; "In Love with a
  Beautiful Girl" 252, 272-73;
  "Miss Sahib" 7, 252, 270, 290;
  "Passion", 252; "The Biography"
  16, 252, 315; "The Man with
  the Dog", 67, 252, 270; "The

Young Couple" 252, 269
*How I Became a Holy Mother
and Other Short Stories* (1976)
10, 32, 284, 288, 290,
(contains) "Bombay" 10, 252;
"Desecration" 252, 256, 274;
"How I Became a Holy Mother,
238, 242, 290, 332, 334; "In a
Great Man's House" 252; "In
the Mountains" 252, 273-74;
"On Bail" 252; "Picnic with
Moonlight and Mangoes" 252;
"Prostitutes" 252, 290; "The
Englishwoman" 7, 10, 252,
290-91; "Two More under the
Indian Sun" 252, 290
*Like Birds Like Fishes and
Other Stories* (1963) 2, 6,
250-51, 283 (contains) "A
Birthday in London" 2, 12, 181,
250, 269-70; "A Loss of Faith"
14, 171, 251, 259-60; "Lekha"
251, 253-56, 335; "Like Birds
Like Fishes", 243, 251-52; "My
First Marriage" 14, 251; "Sixth
Child" 251; "The Aliens", 4, 7,
67, 171, 251, 269; "The Award"
14, 17, 251, 256, 259-60; "The
Interview", 171, 187, 251, 294;
"The Old Lady" 251; "The
Widow" 247, 251, 260-63
Essays of:
Moonlight, Jasmine
and Rickets" 32, 33, 164, 165,
223, 249;
"The Short Story in England
1700-1750" 2
Novels of:
A Backward Place (1965), 4, 5,
7, 14, 15, 16, 17, 23, 24, 25,
26, 30, 50, 60, 90, 100, 107,
115, 164, 166-94, 202, 205,
229, 230, 237, 242, 247, 251,
270, 283, 285, 288, 289, 294,
297, 307, 309
A New Dominion (or *Travelers*)
(1972-73), 4, 5, 7, 8, 9, 13, 16,
19, 22, 23, 24, 28, 29, 30, 106,
107, 113, 145, 159, 167, 187,
195, 223, 227, 238, 264, 265,
270, 284, 287, 289, 290, 297-8,
299, 300, 307, 309, 312, 313,
322, 325, 326, 327, 328, 330,
331, 334
Amrita (or *To Whom She Will*)
(1955-56), 3, 4, 5, 7, 12, 13,
14, 16, 19, 20, 21, 23, 28,
34-74, 77, 79, 85, 86, 90, 92,
95, 106, 115, 145, 160, 168,
173, 180, 187, 189, 202, 221,
245, 258, 271, 294, 309, 325,
334
Esmond in India (1957) 2, 3, 4,
5, 7, 8, 14, 15, 16, 23, 24, 56,
67, 94-121, 145, 153, 162, 168,
172, 193, 205, 229, 272, 309
Get Ready for Battle (1962) 9,
15, 16, 18, 48, 60, 107,
150-64, 175, 184, 202, 245,
251, 283
Heat and Dust (1975) 8, 9 10,
12, 13, 16, 19, 22, 23, 26, 27,
28, 30, 107, 113, 159, 161,
170, 193, 204, 224-48, 253,
270, 284, 286, 287, 288-90,
293, 298-99, 310, 313, 315-17,
322, 325, 326
In Search of Love and Beauty
(1983) 11, 16, 23, 107, 321-22,
325-32, 335
The Householder (1960) 3, 4, 5,
7, 28, 43, 48, 74, 106, 123-47,
162, 187, 245, 283
The Nature of Passion (1956) 3,
5, 7, 15, 16, 19, 20, 21, 28,
48, 49, 67, 76-93, 95, 102,
106, 107, 116, 125, 127, 144,
145, 162, 164, 189, 192, 212,
245, 271, 293, 294, 310, 316,
325
Three Continents (1987) 11, 12,
107, 324, 332-35
To Whom She Will (or *Amrita*),
See under Amrita (or *To Whom
She Will*)
Travelers (or *A New Dominion*),
See under A New Dominion (or
Travelers)

Films based on her Novels:
HEAT AND DUST, 8, 317
THE HOUSEHOLDER 8, 278-79
Screenplays of: 9, 252
Autobiography of a Princess,
284, 305-309, 322;
Shakespearewallah, 185, 220,
279, 283, 284-85, 293; The
Europeans 282; The
Householder 278-79;
Films based on Screenplays:
A ROOM WITH A VIEW, 8, 317
AUTOBIOGRAPHY OF A PRINCESS,
8, 30, 161, 192, 204, 234, 235,
253, 284, 288, 293, 301-305,
310, 313-15, 317
BOMBAY TALKIE 8, 14, 17, 107,
121, 187, 251, 264, 280, 284,
285, 286, 293, 294-97, 309-310
HULLABALLOO OVER GEORGE AND
BONNIES PICTURES, 8, 281, 284,
322, 328
JANE AUSTEN IN MANHATTAN, 8,
282, 284
MAURICE, 8
QUARTET, 8, 283, 284
ROSELAND, 2, 8, 281
SHAKESPEAREWALLAH, 8, 251,
283, 286, 288, 317
THE BOSTONIANS, 8, 317
THE EUROPEANS, 2, 8, 282, 284,
317
THE GURU, 8, 9, 279, 284, 286,
287
THE HOUSEHOLDER, 8, 238, 250,
283
Stories in Magazines:
"Farid and Farida", 324;
"Parasites", 322; "A Summer by
the Sea", 322-24, 328, 329, 334
Jodhpur, 284
maharaja of 306

Kapoor, Shashi, 278, 279, 280,
283, 289, 293
Kautilya, 123, 140
Kendal, Felicity, 279
Kendal, Jennifer, 280, 283, 289
Kipling, Rudyard, 86

MacArthur Foundation Fellowship,
12
Mahabharata, 29
Malcolm, Derek, 313
Malgudi, 13, 14, Also see
Narayan, R.K.,
Mansfield Park, See under Austen
Jane
Manu, 123, 140
Mason, James, 280, 281, 293,
319
Merchant, Ismail, 8, 281, 283,
284
Merchant Ivory Productions, 185,
220, 252, 278-92, 322
Merchant Ivory Jhabvala, 12
Book on films of,
Mitra, Subrata, 279
Mohyeddin, Zia, 280
Molière, 23
Works of:
Candide 245
Mr. Sampath, See under
Narayan R.K.
Mukherjee, Meenakshi, 10, 265,
277
Museum of Modern Art, New
York, 12

Nadira, 289, 290
Naidu, Leela, 261
Naipaul, V.S., 11, 13, 23, 33
Narayan, R.K., 13, 14, 31, 165,
185
Works of:
Mr Sampath, 185
The Reluctant Guide, 185
Nazi Germany, 1-2, 170-71, 325
Neil Gunn International
Fellowship, 12
New Yorker, The, 322-24
Nightmare Abbey, See under
Peacock, T.I.
Northanger Abbey, See under
Austen, Jane

Panchatantra, The, 74-5
Pather Panchali, 262; also see,
Banerjee, Bibhutibhusan and

Ray, Satyajit
Peacock, T.I., 295, 296
  Works of:
  Crotchet Castle, 295-96
  Nightmare Abbey, 295-96
Persuasion, See under Austen,
  Jane
Pine, Larry, 281
Pizer, Larry, 282
Pope, Alexander, 23
Powell, Dilys, 280, 318
Powell, Robert, 282
Prawer, Leonora Cohn, 1
Prawer, Marcus, 1
Pride and Prejudice, See under
  Austen, Jane
Punch, 283

Radhakrishnan, S., 78
Rajasa (the nature of passion),
  78
Rau, Santha Rama, 34-35, 74
  Works of:
  Remember the House, 34-35, 74
Ray, Satyajit, 279, 318
Remick, Lee, 282
Rhys, Jean, 283
Richardson, Samuel, 282
  Works of:
  Sir Charles Grandison, 282
Robinson, David 280

Sen, Aparna, 279, 289
Sense and Sensibility, See under
  Austen, Jane
Shakespeare, William, 23, 99
  Works of:
  As You Like It, 99

Sheridan, R.B., 55
Sir Charles Grandism, See under
  Richardson, Samuel
Skala, Lilia, 281
Smollet, Tobias, 93
Swift, Jonathan, 23

The Book of Job, 23
The Bostonians, See under
  James, Henry
The Europeans, See under James,
  Henry
The Pilgrim's Progress, See under
  Bunyan, John
The Reluctant Guide, See under
  Narayan, R.K.
Tushingham, Rita, 279

Upanishads, 123
University of London, 2, 12
Ustad Vilayat Khan, 280

Vanaprastha, 12
Vedas, 78
Vivekananda, 169
Voltaire, 23, 245
  Works of:
  Candide, 245
Vyom, 112-13

Walken, Christopher, 281
Williams, Haydn Moore, 18, 36,
  75, 93, 165
Woodward, Tim, 282
Wright, Teresa, 281

Yeats, W.B., 16, 257
Yorke, Michael, 279